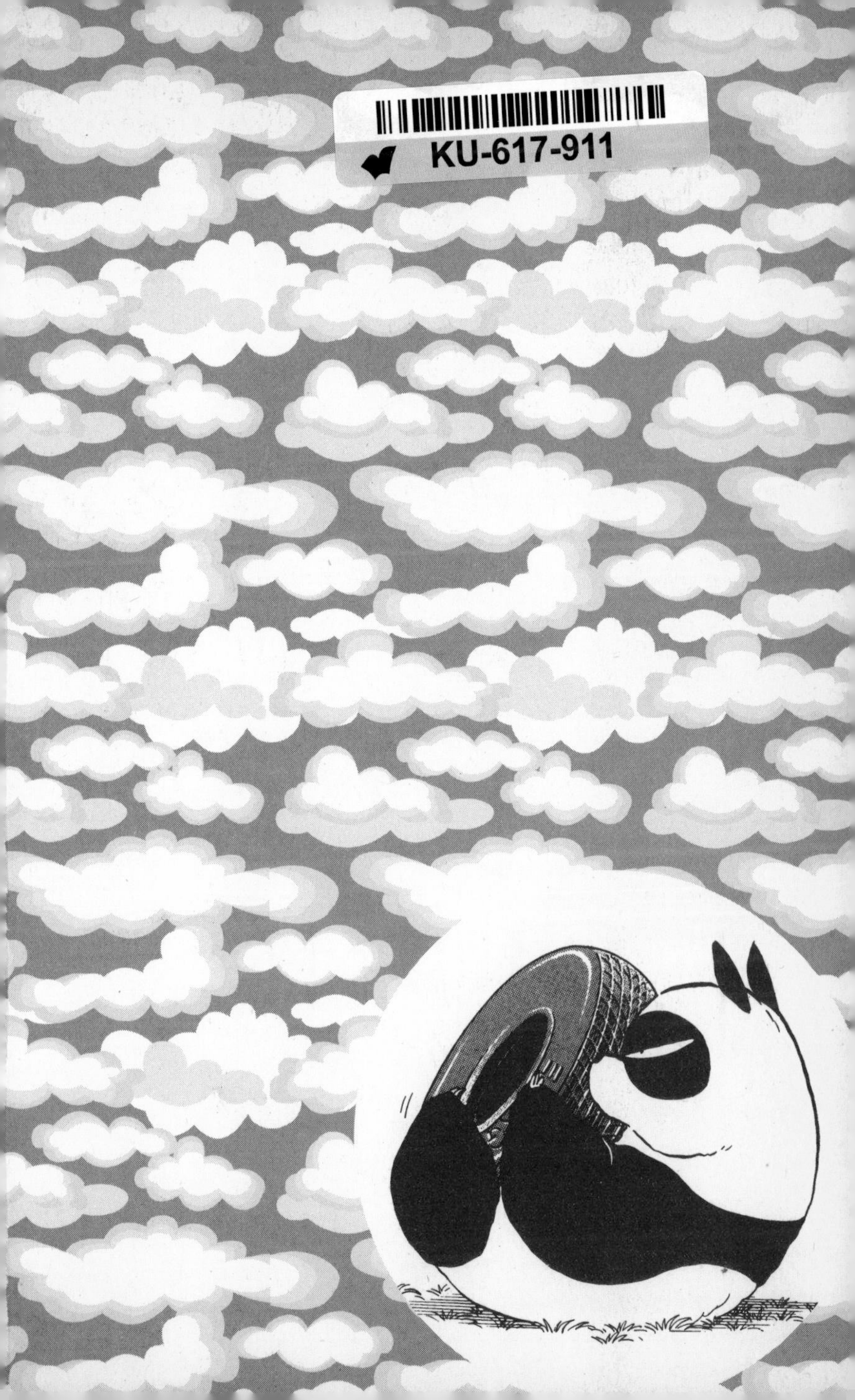

RANMA 1/2

VOL. 10
Action Edition (2nd Edition)

Story and Art by
RUMIKO TAKAHASHI

English Adaptation/Gerard Jones and Toshifumi Yoshida
Touch-Up Art & Lettering/Wayne Truman
Cover and Interior Design & Graphics/Yuki Ameda
Editor (1st Edition)/Trish Ledoux
Editor (Action Edition)/Avery Gotoh
Supervising Editor (Action Edition)/Michelle Pangilinan

Managing Editor/Annette Roman
Editorial Director/Alvin Lu
Director of Production/Noboru Watanabe
Sr. Dir. of Licensing & Acquisitions/Rika Inouye
VP of Sales & Marketing/Liza Coppola
Executive V.P./Hyoe Narita
Publisher/Seiji Horibuchi

RANMA 1/2 is rated "T+" for Older Teens. It may contain violence, language, alcohol or tobacco use, or suggestive situations.

Printed in Canada.

Published by VIZ, LLC
P.O. Box 77010
San Francisco, CA 94107

1st Edition Published 1997
Action Edition
10 9 8 7 6 5 4 3 2
First Printing, APRIL 2004
Second Printing, November 2004

www.viz.com

store.viz.com

Ranma 1/2

VOL. 10   Action Edition

STORY & ART BY
RUMIKO TAKAHASHI

STORY THUS FAR

The Tendos are an average, run-of-the-mill Japanese family—on the surface, that is. Soun Tendo is the owner and proprietor of the Tendo Dojo, where "Anything-Goes Martial Arts" is practiced. Like the name says, anything goes, and usually does.

When Soun's old friend Genma Saotome comes to visit, Soun's three lovely young daughters—Akane, Nabiki, and Kasumi—are told that it's time for one of them to become the fiancée of Genma's teenaged son, as per an agreement made between the two fathers years ago. Youngest daughter Akane—who says she hates boys—is quickly nominated for bridal duty by her sisters.

Unfortunately, Ranma and his father have suffered a strange accident. While training in China, both plunged into one of many "cursed" springs at the legendary martial arts training ground of Jusenkyo. These springs transform the unlucky dunkee into whoever—or whatever—drowned there hundreds of years ago.

From now on, a splash of cold water turns Ranma's father into a giant panda, and Ranma becomes a beautiful, busty young woman. Hot water reverses the effect...but only until next time. As it turns out, Ranma and Genma aren't the only ones who have taken the Jusenkyo plunge—and it isn't long before they meet several other members of the Jusenkyo "cursed."

Although their parents are still determined to see Ranma and Akane marry and carry on the training hall, Ranma seems to have a strange talent for accumulating surplus fiancées...and Akane has a few stubbornly determined suitors of her own. Will the two ever work out their differences, get rid of all these "extra" people, or will they just call the whole thing off? What's a half-boy, half-girl (not to mention all-girl, *angry* girl) to do...?

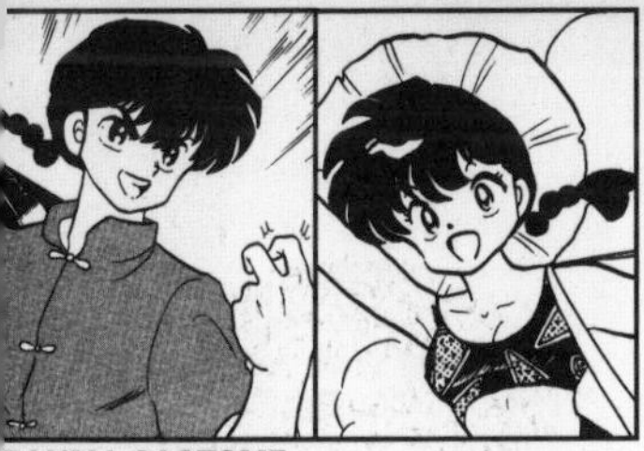

RYOGA HIBIKI
Melancholy martial artist with no sense of direction, a hopeless crush on Akane, and a stubborn grudge against Ranma. Changes into a small, black pig Akane's named "P-chan."

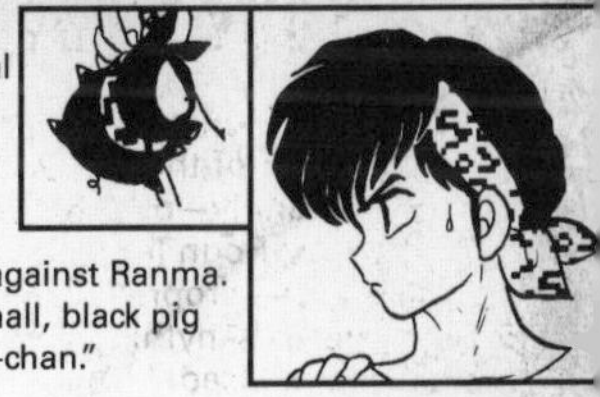

RANMA SAOTOME
Martial artist with far too many fiancées, and an ego that won't let him take defeat. Changes into a girl when splashed with cold water.

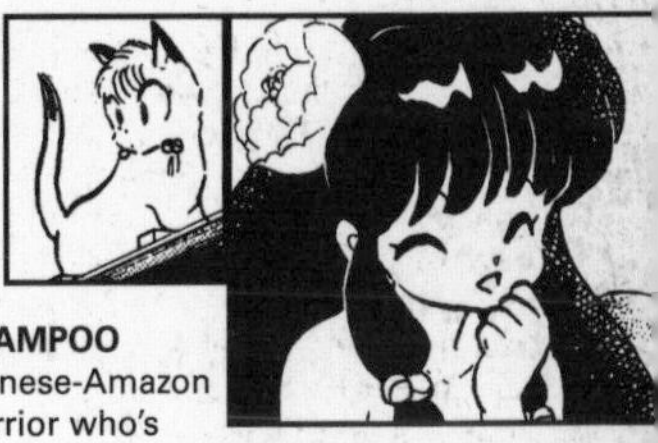

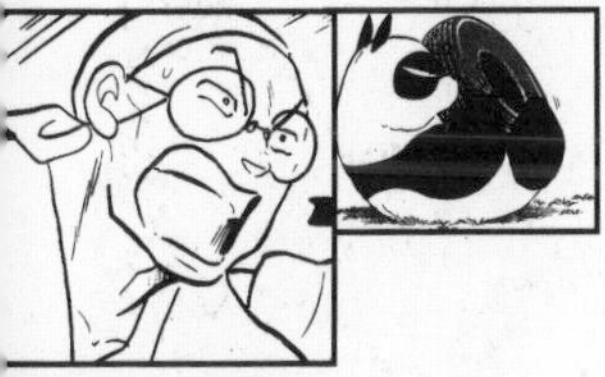

SHAMPOO
Chinese-Amazon warrior who's gone from wanting to kill Ranma to wanting to marry him.

GENMA SAOTOME
Ranma's lazy father, who left his wife and home years ago with his young son (Ranma) to train in the martial arts. Changes into a panda.

COLOGNE
Shampoo's great-grandmother, a martial artist, and matchmaker.

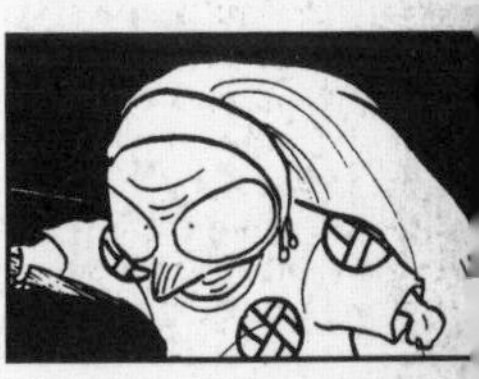

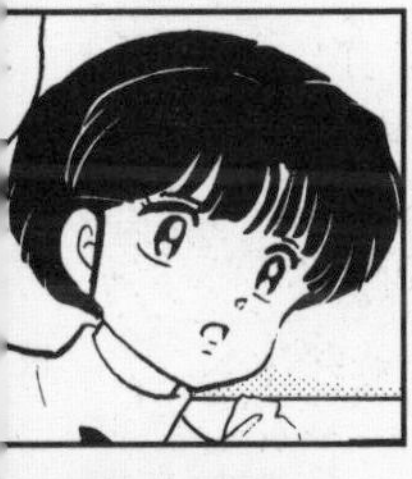

AKANE TENDO
Martial artist, tomboy, and Ranma's reluctant fiancée. Has no clue how much Ryoga likes her, or what relation he might have to her pet black pig, P-chan.

HAPPOSAI
Martial arts master who trained both Genma and Soun. Also a world-class pervert.

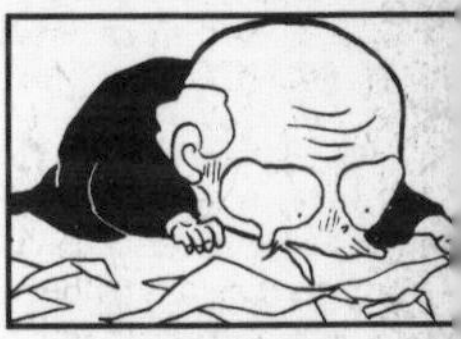

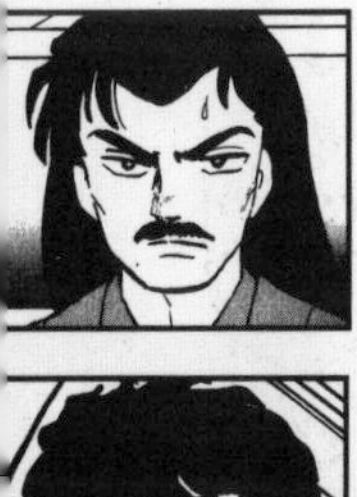

SOUN TENDO
Head of the Tendo household and owner of the Tendo Dojo.

UKYO KUONJI
Ranma's childhood friend. Has a flair for cooking and a dislike of Akane. Also weilds a mean spatula.

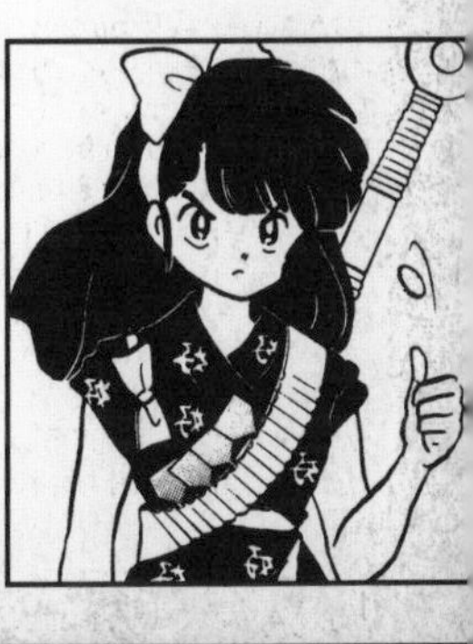

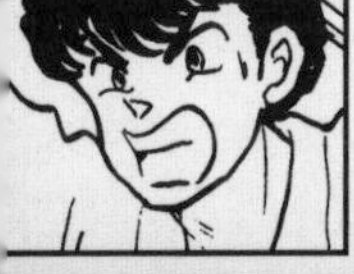

TATEWAKI KUNO
Blustering upperclassman with a love of the ancient Japanese arts, Akane Tendo, and the mysterious "pig-tailed girl," who he has no idea is really girl-type Ranma.

CONTENTS

Part 1

EMBRACEABLE YOU

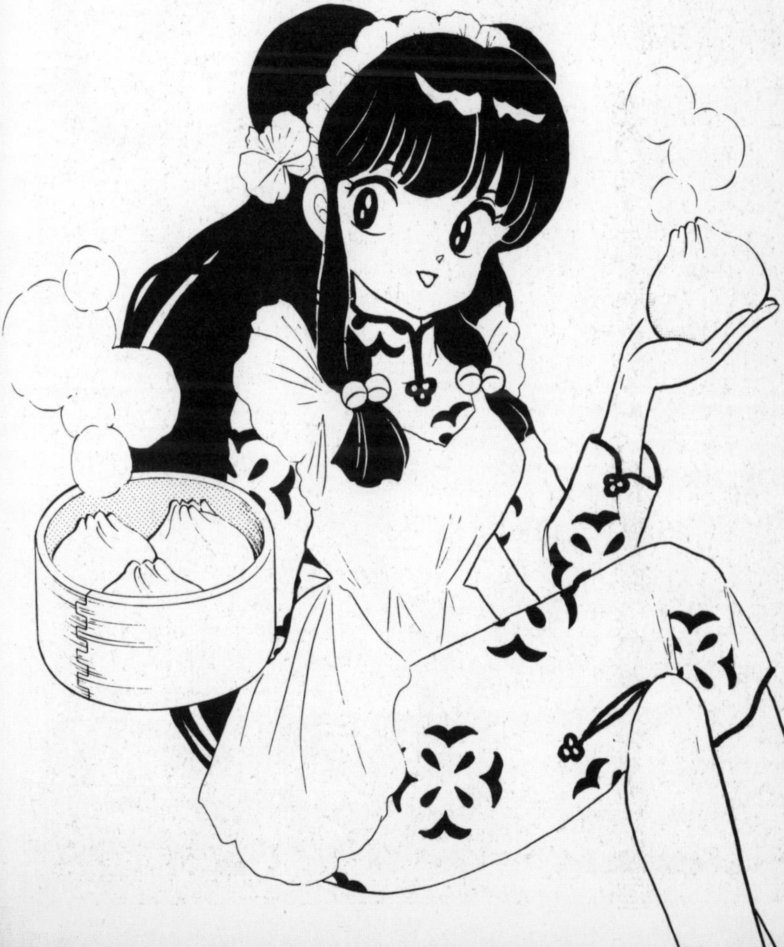

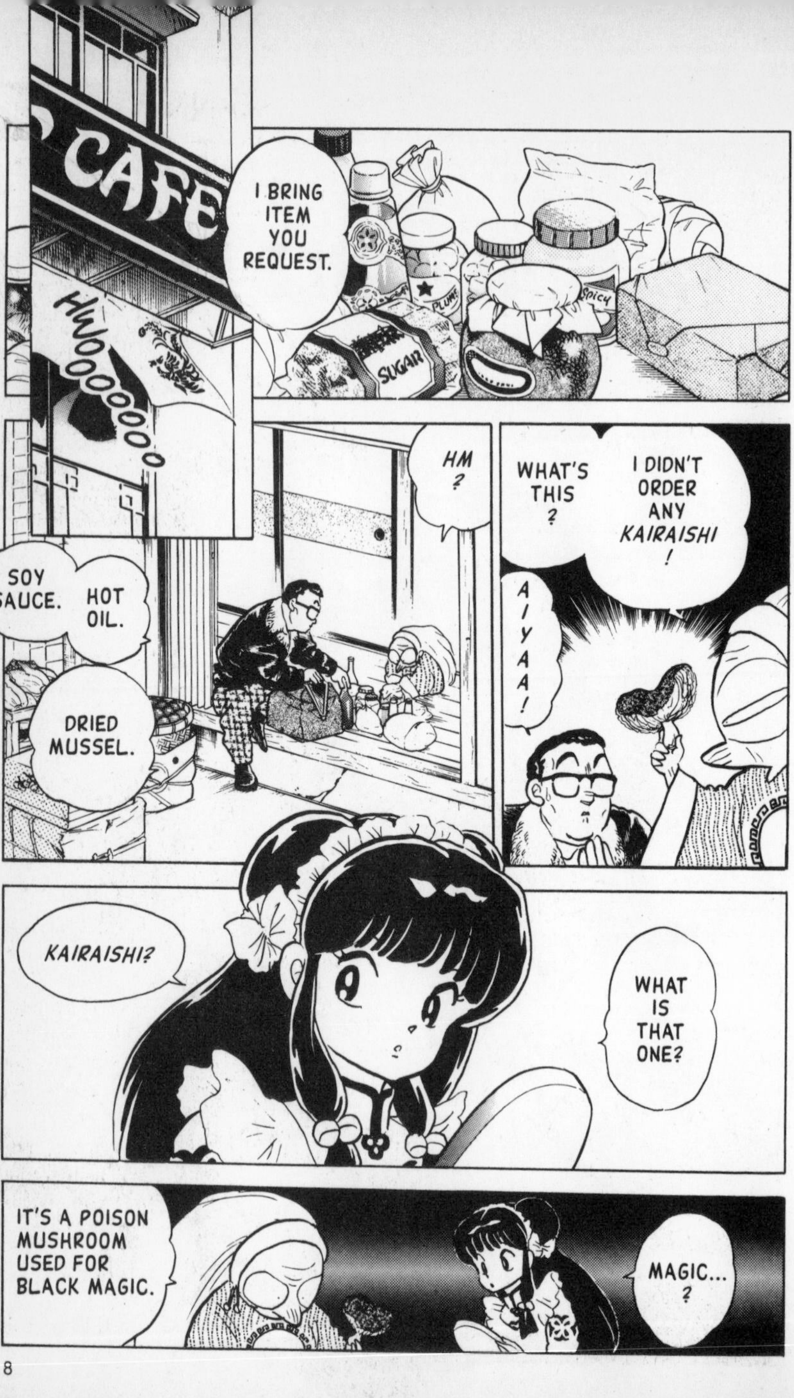
CAFE
HWOOOOOOOO
I BRING ITEM YOU REQUEST.
PLUM
SPICY
SUGAR
HM?
SOY SAUCE.
HOT OIL.
DRIED MUSSEL.
WHAT'S THIS?
I DIDN'T ORDER ANY KAIRAISHI!
AIYAAA!
KAIRAISHI?
WHAT IS THAT ONE?
IT'S A POISON MUSHROOM USED FOR BLACK MAGIC.
MAGIC...?

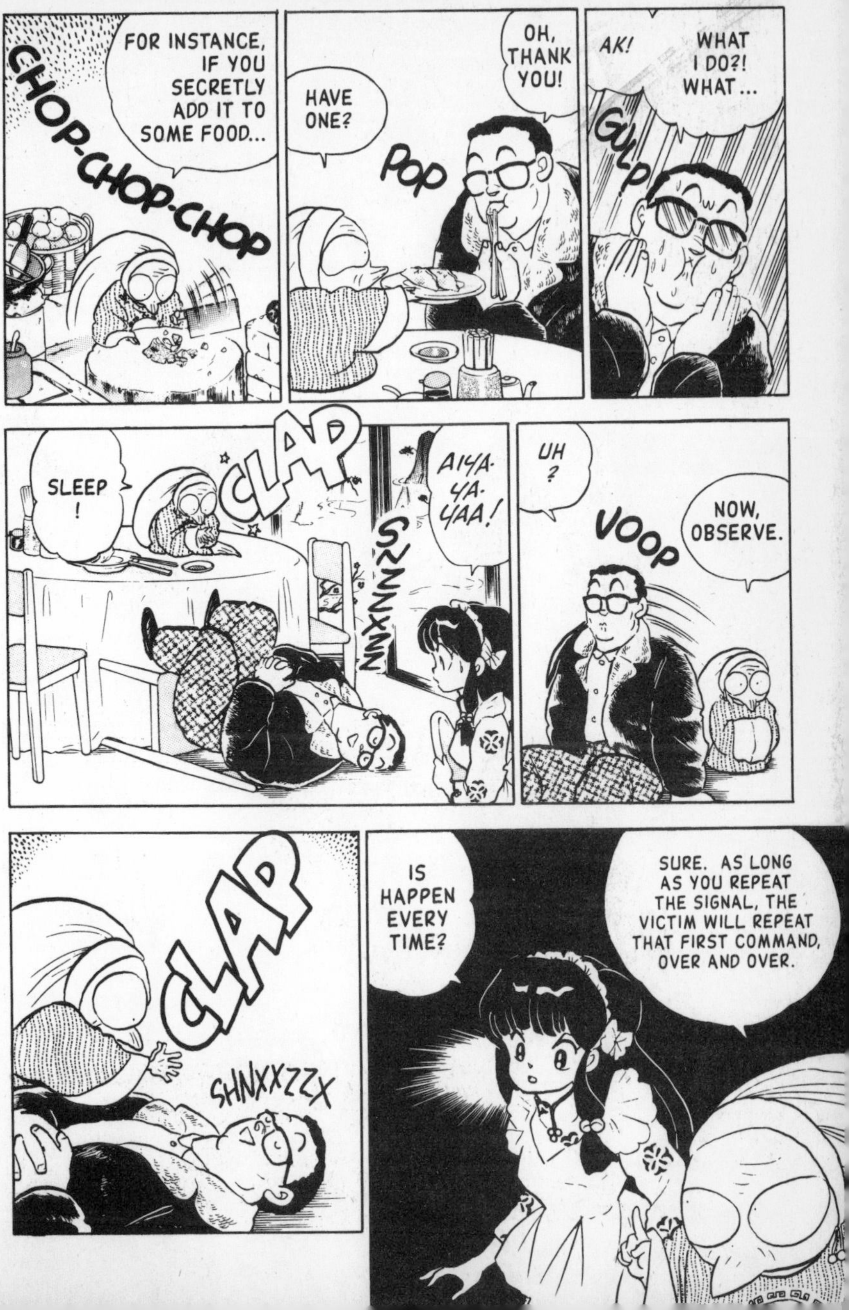
CHOP-CHOP-CHOP-CHOP
FOR INSTANCE, IF YOU SECRETLY ADD IT TO SOME FOOD...
HAVE ONE?
POP
OH, THANK YOU!
AK!
WHAT I DO?! WHAT...
GULP
SLEEP!
CLAP
AIYA-YA-YAA!
SNZZZXXN
UH?
VOOP
NOW, OBSERVE.
CLAP
SHNXXZZX
IS HAPPEN EVERY TIME?
SURE. AS LONG AS YOU REPEAT THE SIGNAL, THE VICTIM WILL REPEAT THAT FIRST COMMAND, OVER AND OVER.

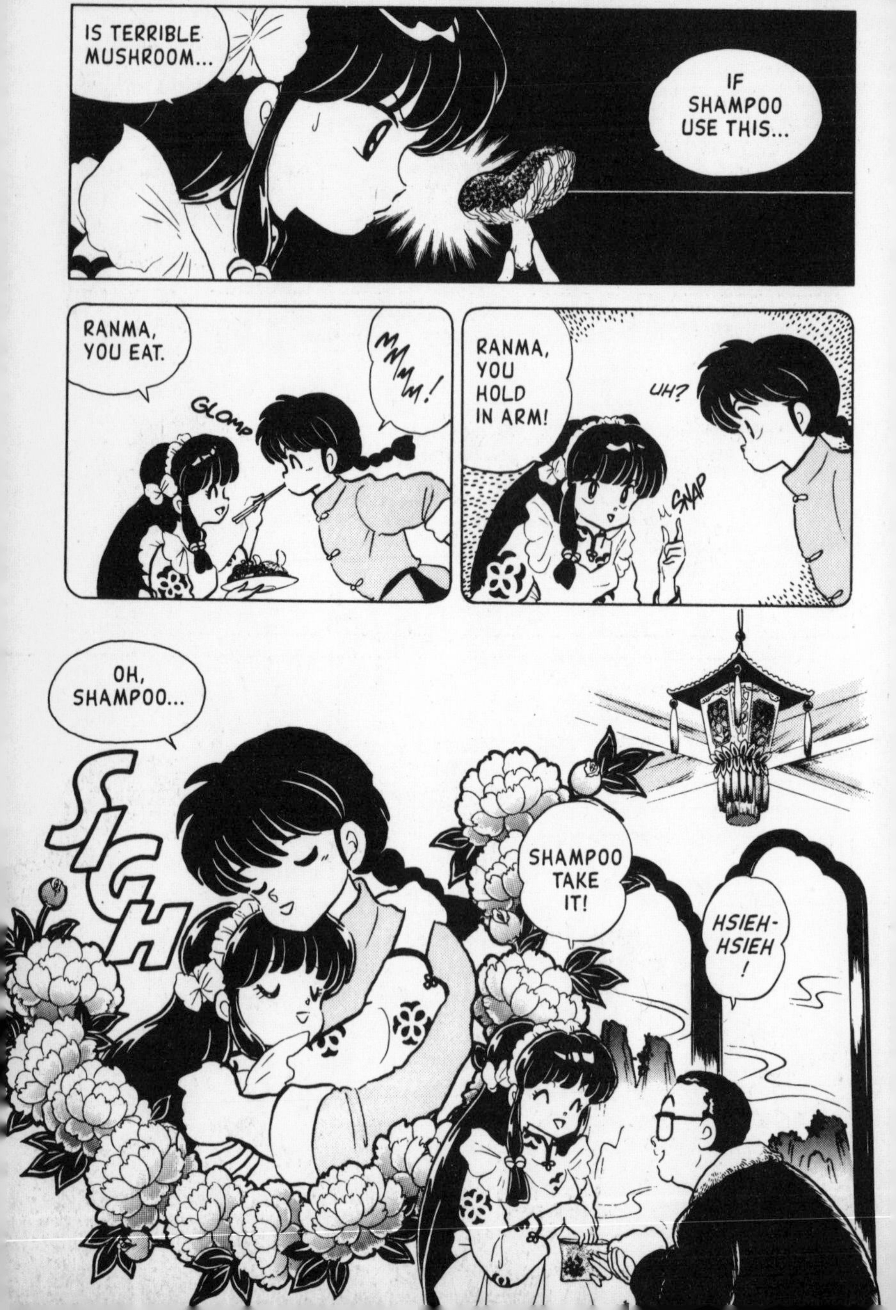
IS TERRIBLE MUSHROOM...
IF SHAMPOO USE THIS...
RANMA, YOU EAT.
GLOMP
MMMM!
RANMA, YOU HOLD IN ARM!
UH?
SNAP
OH, SHAMPOO...
SIGH
SHAMPOO TAKE IT!
HSIEH-HSIEH!

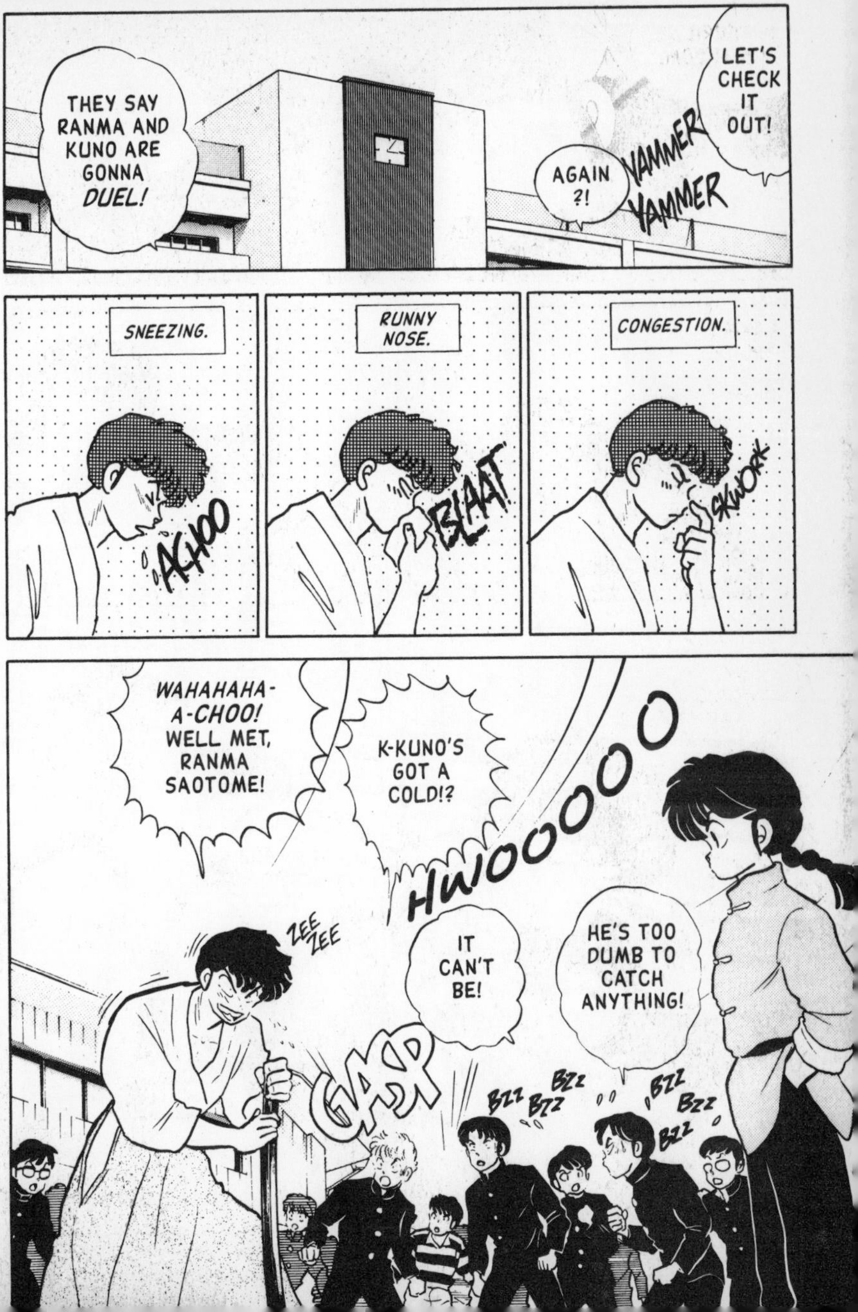
THEY SAY RANMA AND KUNO ARE GONNA DUEL!
AGAIN ?!
YAMMER YAMMER
LET'S CHECK IT OUT!
SNEEZING.
ACHOO
RUNNY NOSE.
BLAAT
CONGESTION.
SKWORK
WAHAHAHA-A-CHOO! WELL MET, RANMA SAOTOME!
K-KUNO'S GOT A COLD!?
HWOOOOOO
ZEE ZEE
IT CAN'T BE!
HE'S TOO DUMB TO CATCH ANYTHING!
GASP
BZZ BZZ BZZ BZZ BZZ BZZ

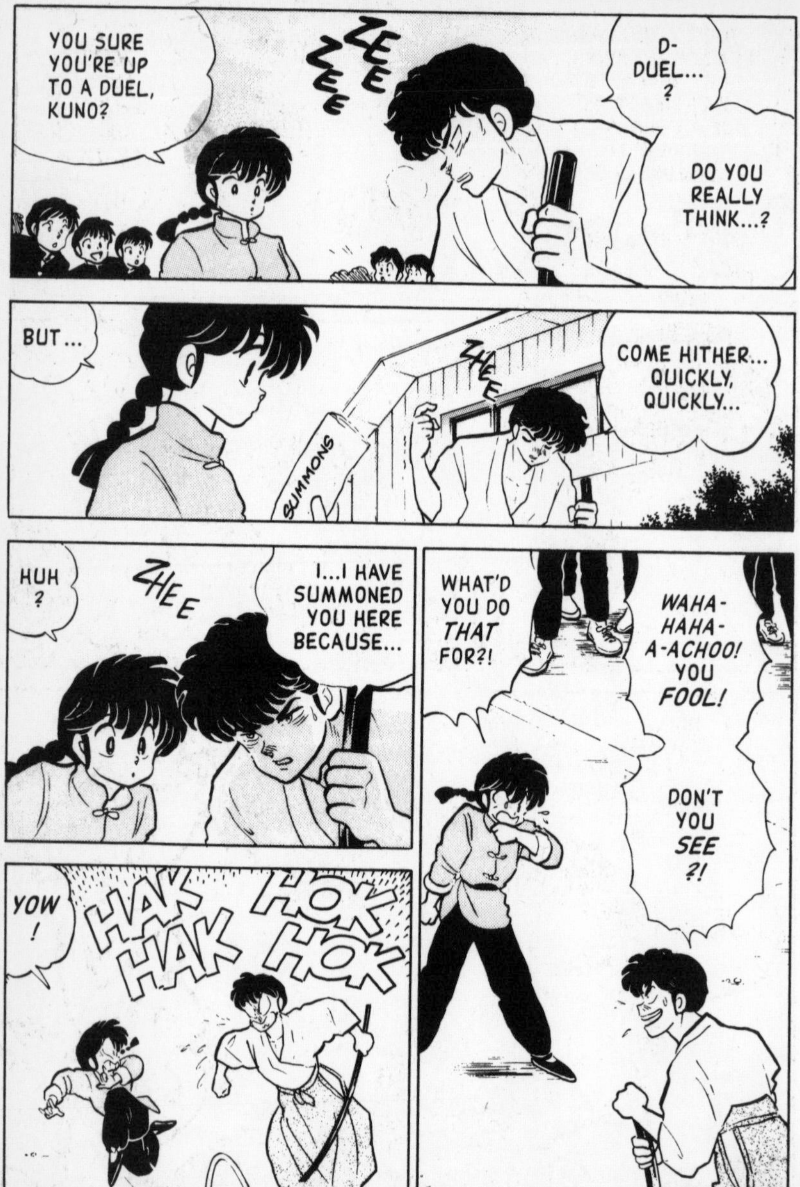

YOU SURE YOU'RE UP TO A DUEL, KUNO?
ZEE ZEE ZEE
D- DUEL...?
DO YOU REALLY THINK...?
BUT...
SUMMONS
ZHEE
COME HITHER... QUICKLY, QUICKLY...
HUH?
ZHEE
I...I HAVE SUMMONED YOU HERE BECAUSE...
YOW!
HAK HOK HAK HOK
WHAT'D YOU DO *THAT* FOR?!
WAHA-HAHA-A-ACHOO! YOU *FOOL!*
DON'T YOU *SEE*?!

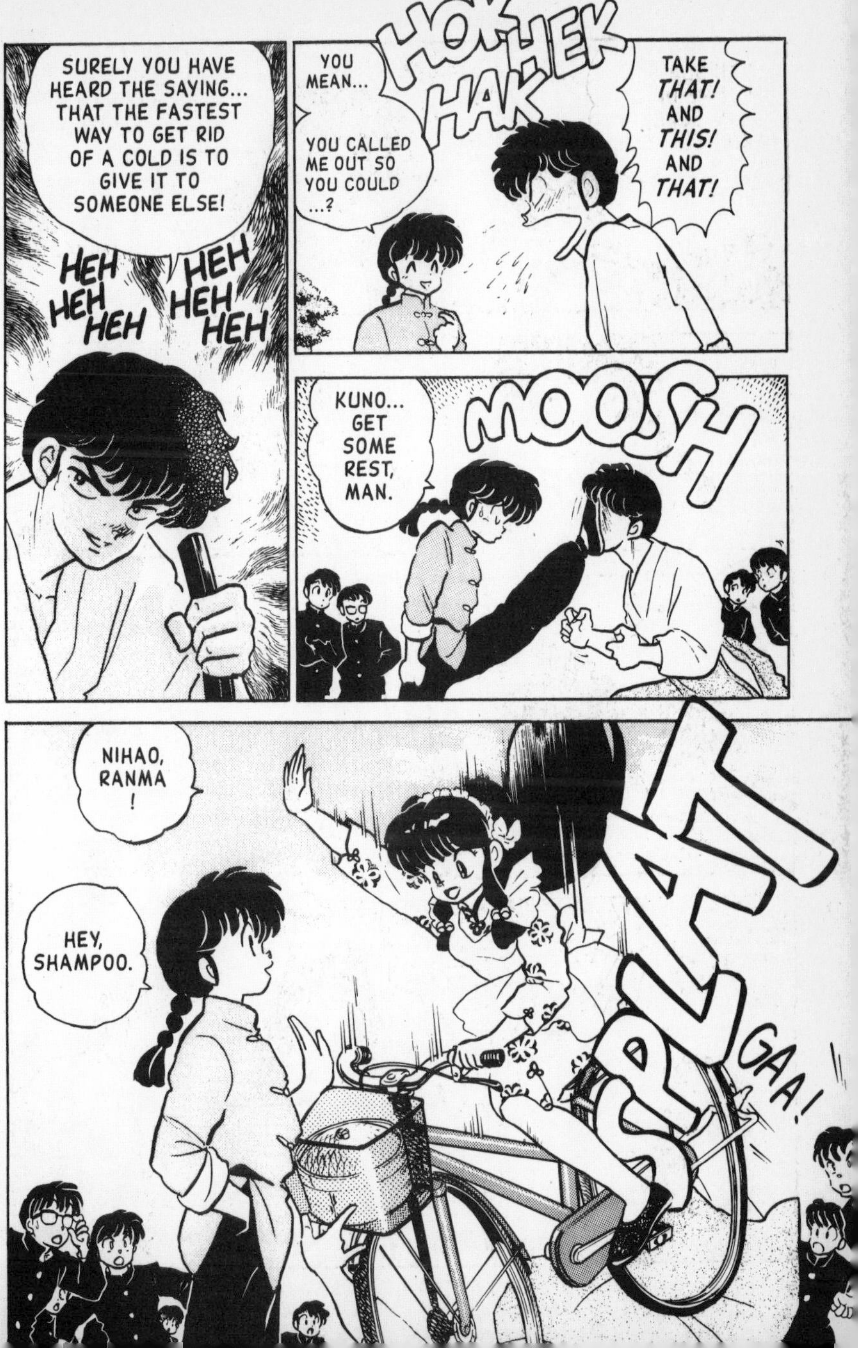
SURELY YOU HAVE HEARD THE SAYING... THAT THE FASTEST WAY TO GET RID OF A COLD IS TO GIVE IT TO SOMEONE ELSE!
HEH HEH HEH
HEH HEH HEH
YOU MEAN...
YOU CALLED ME OUT SO YOU COULD ...?
HOK HEK HAK
TAKE THAT! AND THIS! AND THAT!
KUNO... GET SOME REST, MAN.
MOOSH
NIHAO, RANMA!
HEY, SHAMPOO.
SPLAT
GAA!

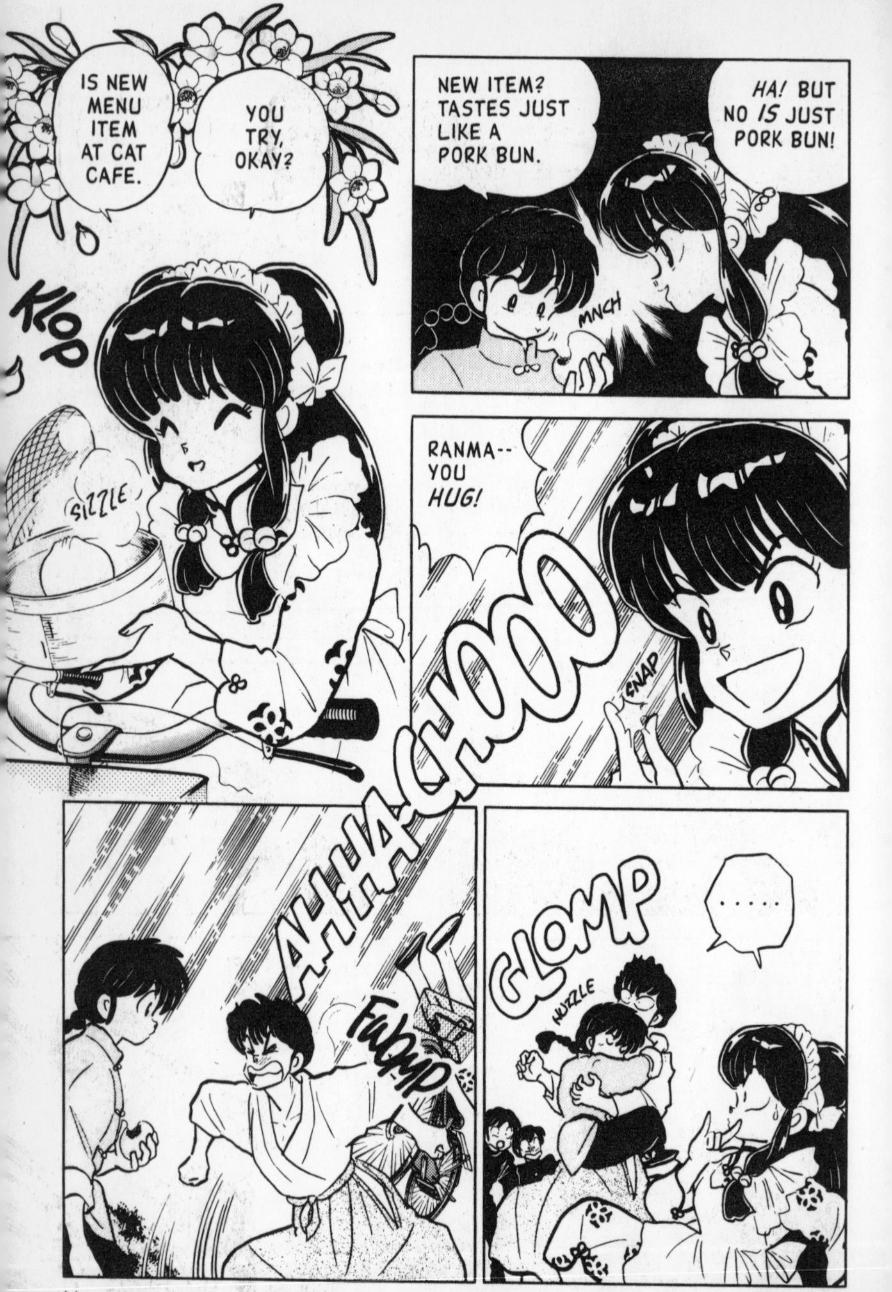

IS NEW MENU ITEM AT CAT CAFE.
YOU TRY, OKAY?
KLOP
SIZZLE
NEW ITEM? TASTES JUST LIKE A PORK BUN.
HA! BUT NO *IS* JUST PORK BUN!
MNCH
RANMA-- YOU *HUG!*
SNAP
AHHACHOOO
FWOMP
GLOMP
NUZZLE
. . . . .

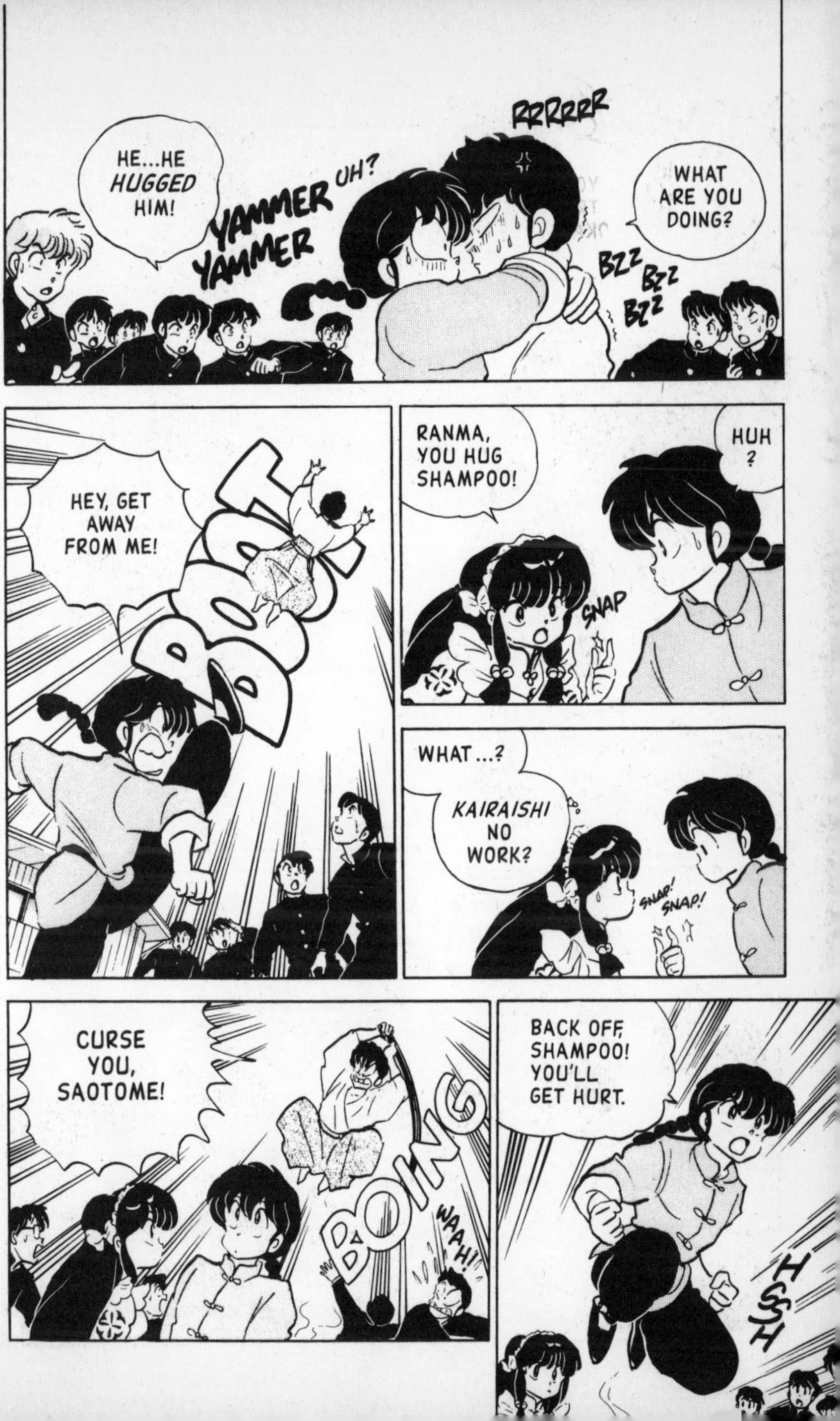
HE...HE HUGGED HIM!
YAMMER YAMMER
UH?
RRRRRR
WHAT ARE YOU DOING?
BZZ BZZ BZZ
HEY, GET AWAY FROM ME!
BOOT
RANMA, YOU HUG SHAMPOO!
HUH ?
SNAP
WHAT ...?
KAIRAISHI NO WORK?
SNAP! SNAP!
CURSE YOU, SAOTOME!
BOING
WAAH!
BACK OFF, SHAMPOO! YOU'LL GET HURT.
HSSH

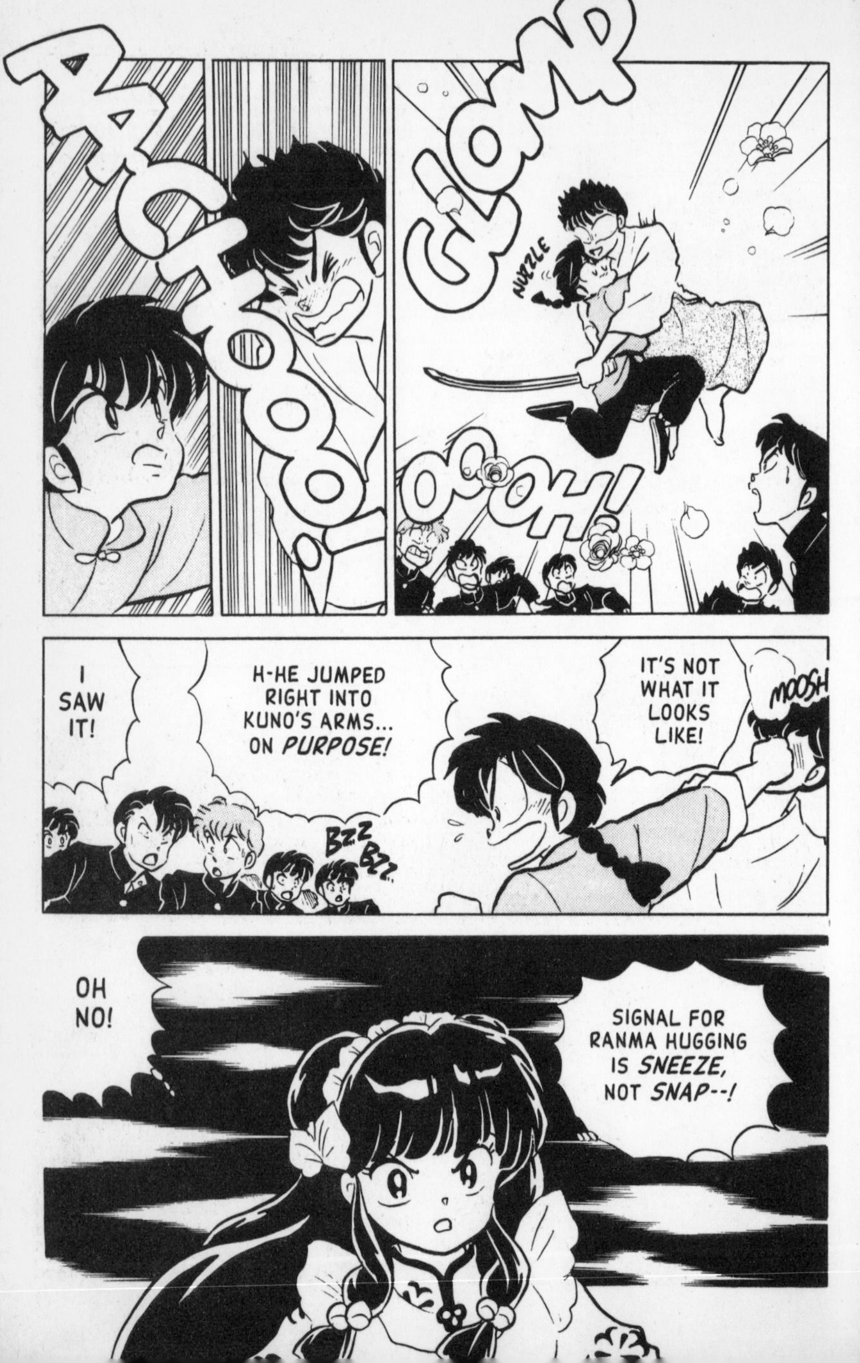

ACHOO!
GLOMP
NUZZLE
OOOH!
I SAW IT!
H-HE JUMPED RIGHT INTO KUNO'S ARMS... ON *PURPOSE!*
BZZ BZZ
IT'S NOT WHAT IT LOOKS LIKE!
MOOSH
OH NO!
SIGNAL FOR RANMA HUGGING IS *SNEEZE,* NOT *SNAP*--!

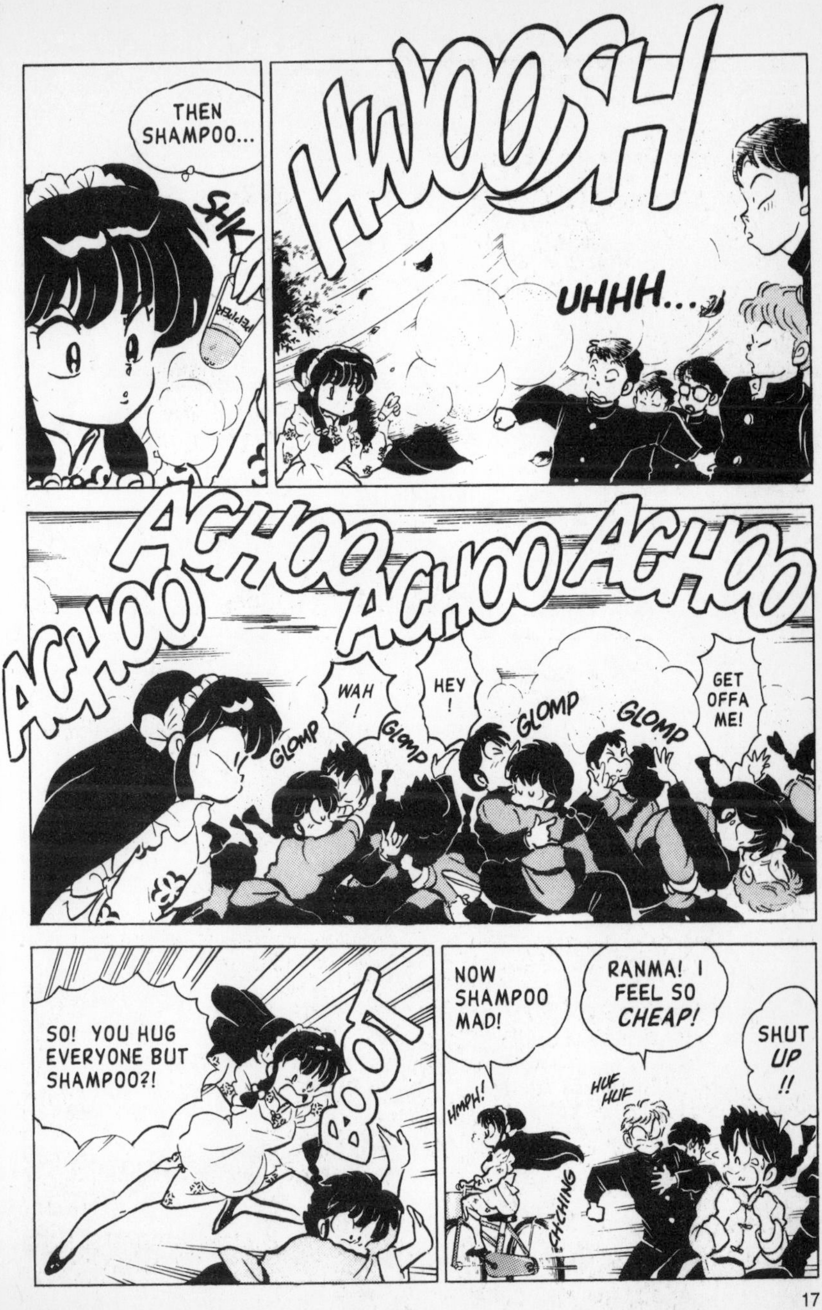

THEN SHAMPOO...
SHIK
HWOOSH
UHHH...
ACHOO
ACHOO
ACHOO
ACHOO
GLOMP
WAH!
GLOMP
HEY!
GLOMP
GLOMP
GET OFFA ME!
SO! YOU HUG EVERYONE BUT SHAMPOO?!
BOOT
NOW SHAMPOO MAD!
RANMA! I FEEL SO *CHEAP!*
SHUT *UP* !!
HMPH!
HUF HUF
CHCHING

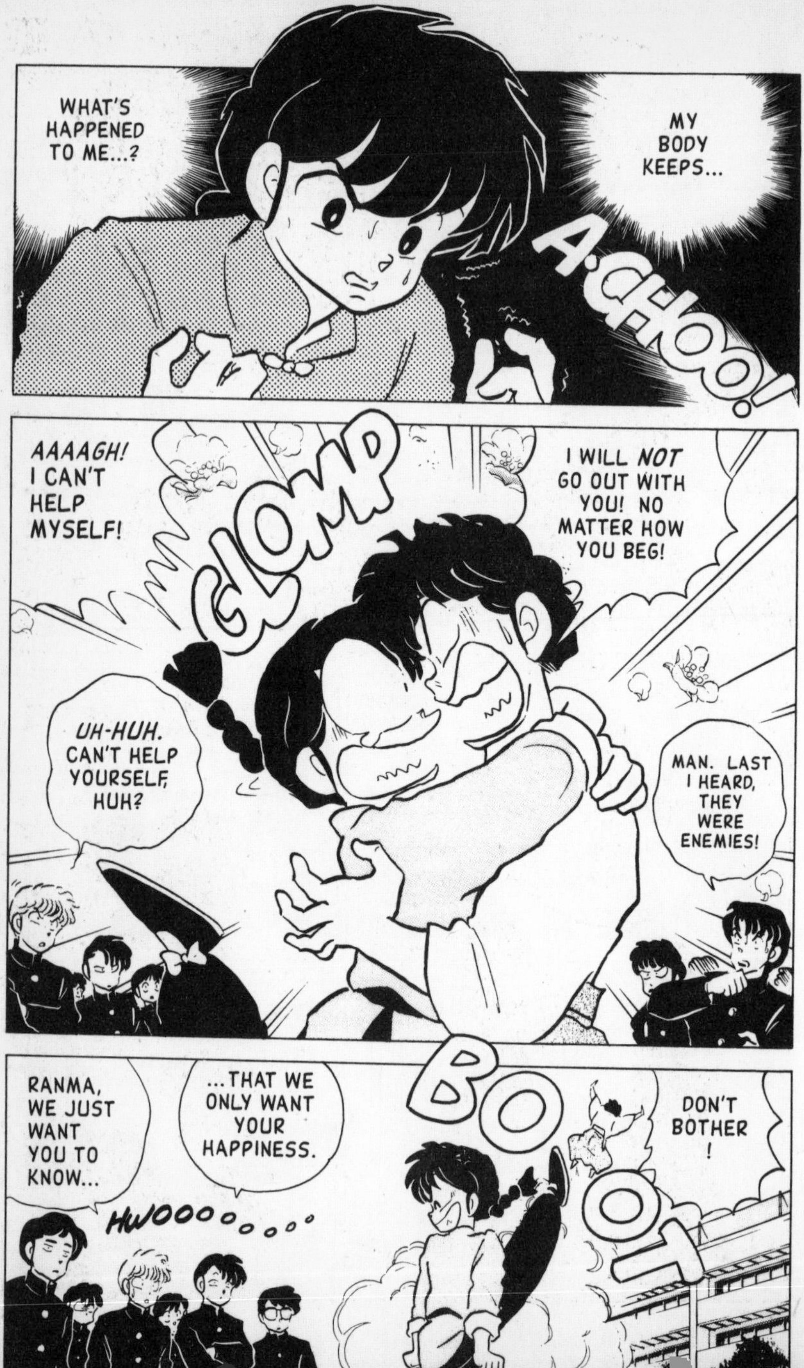
WHAT'S HAPPENED TO ME...?
MY BODY KEEPS...
A-CHOO!
AAAAGH! I CAN'T HELP MYSELF!
GLOMP
I WILL *NOT* GO OUT WITH YOU! NO MATTER HOW YOU BEG!
UH-HUH. CAN'T HELP YOURSELF, HUH?
MAN. LAST I HEARD, THEY WERE ENEMIES!
BOOOT
RANMA, WE JUST WANT YOU TO KNOW...
...THAT WE ONLY WANT YOUR HAPPINESS.
DON'T BOTHER!
HWOOOOoooo

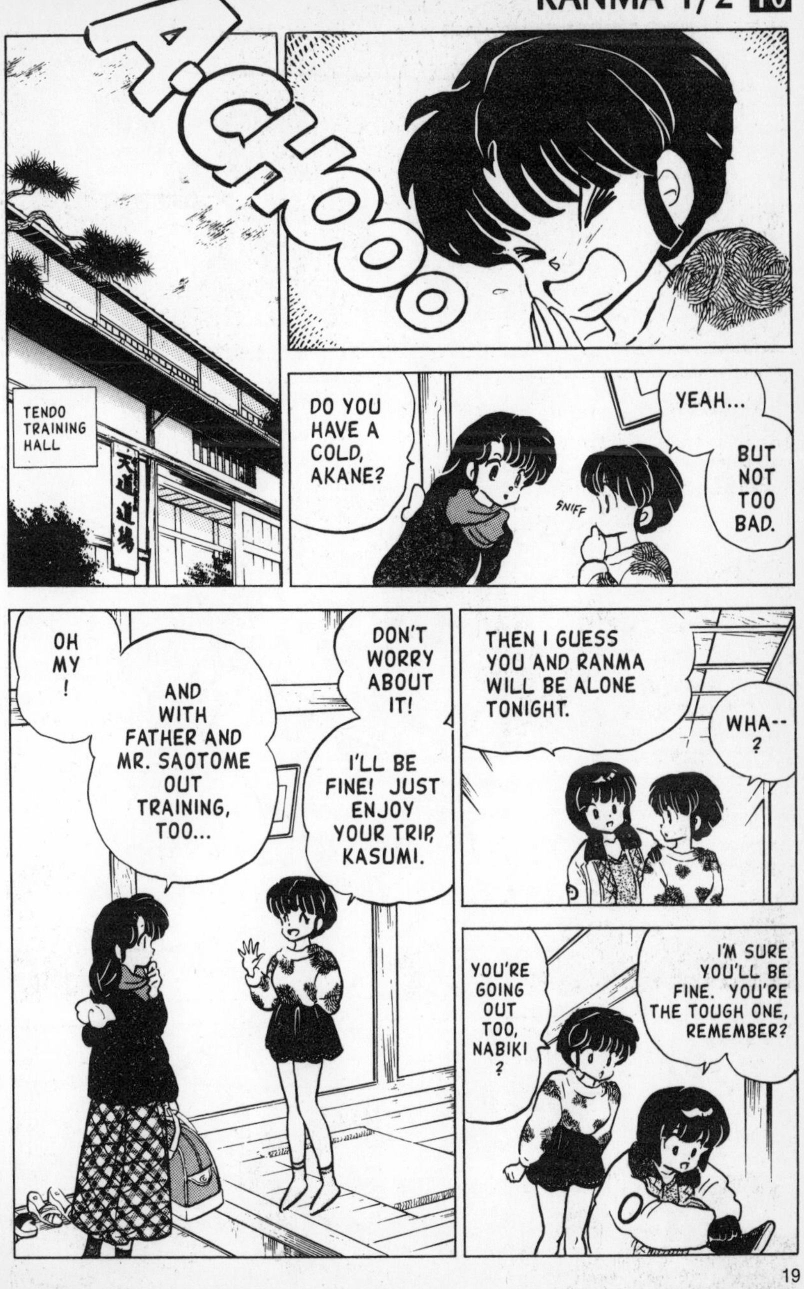
TENDO TRAINING HALL
天道道場
A-CHOOO
DO YOU HAVE A COLD, AKANE?
SNIFF
YEAH...
BUT NOT TOO BAD.
OH MY!
AND WITH FATHER AND MR. SAOTOME OUT TRAINING, TOO...
DON'T WORRY ABOUT IT!
I'LL BE FINE! JUST ENJOY YOUR TRIP, KASUMI.
THEN I GUESS YOU AND RANMA WILL BE ALONE TONIGHT.
WHA--?
YOU'RE GOING OUT TOO, NABIKI?
I'M SURE YOU'LL BE FINE. YOU'RE THE TOUGH ONE, REMEMBER?

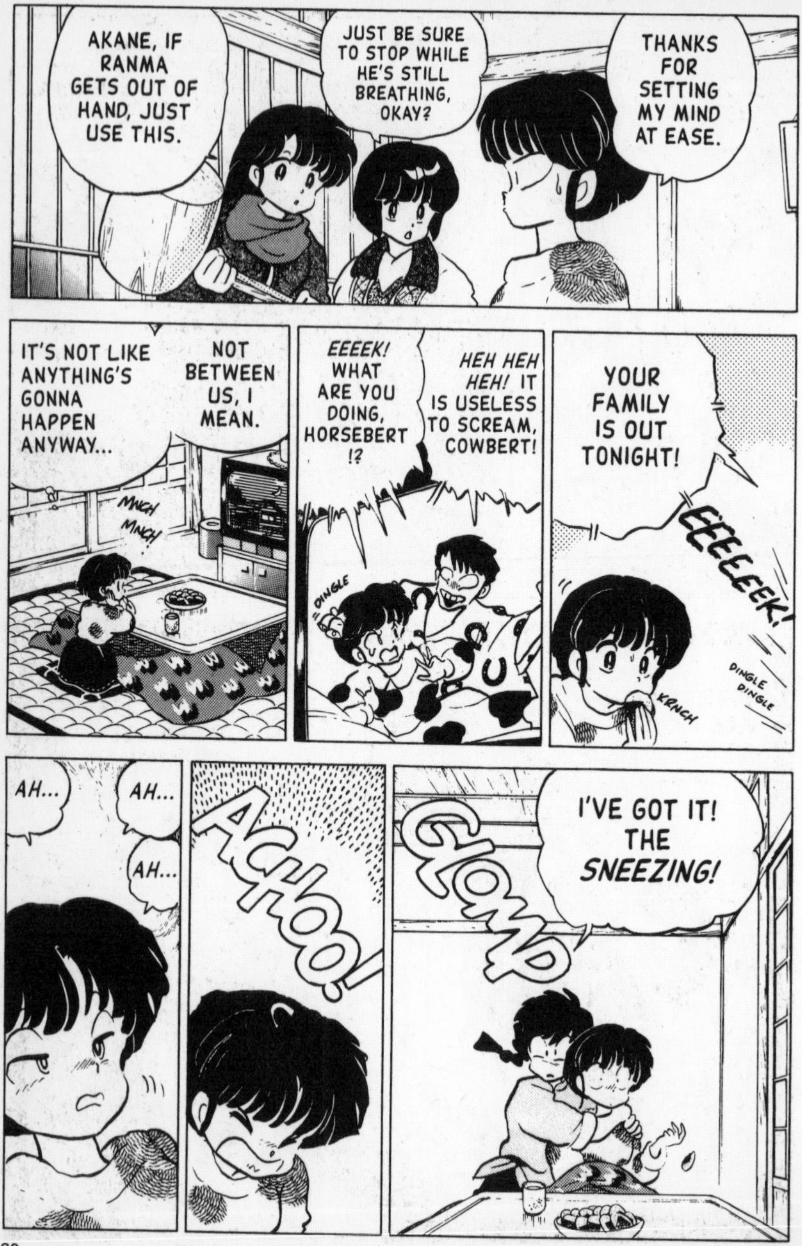
AKANE, IF RANMA GETS OUT OF HAND, JUST USE THIS.
JUST BE SURE TO STOP WHILE HE'S STILL BREATHING, OKAY?
THANKS FOR SETTING MY MIND AT EASE.
IT'S NOT LIKE ANYTHING'S GONNA HAPPEN ANYWAY...
NOT BETWEEN US, I MEAN.
MNCH MNCH
EEEEK! WHAT ARE YOU DOING, HORSEBERT!?
HEH HEH HEH! IT IS USELESS TO SCREAM, COWBERT!
DINGLE
YOUR FAMILY IS OUT TONIGHT!
EEEEEEK!
DINGLE DINGLE
KRNCH
AH...
AH...
AH...
ACHOO!
CHOMP
I'VE GOT IT! THE SNEEZING!

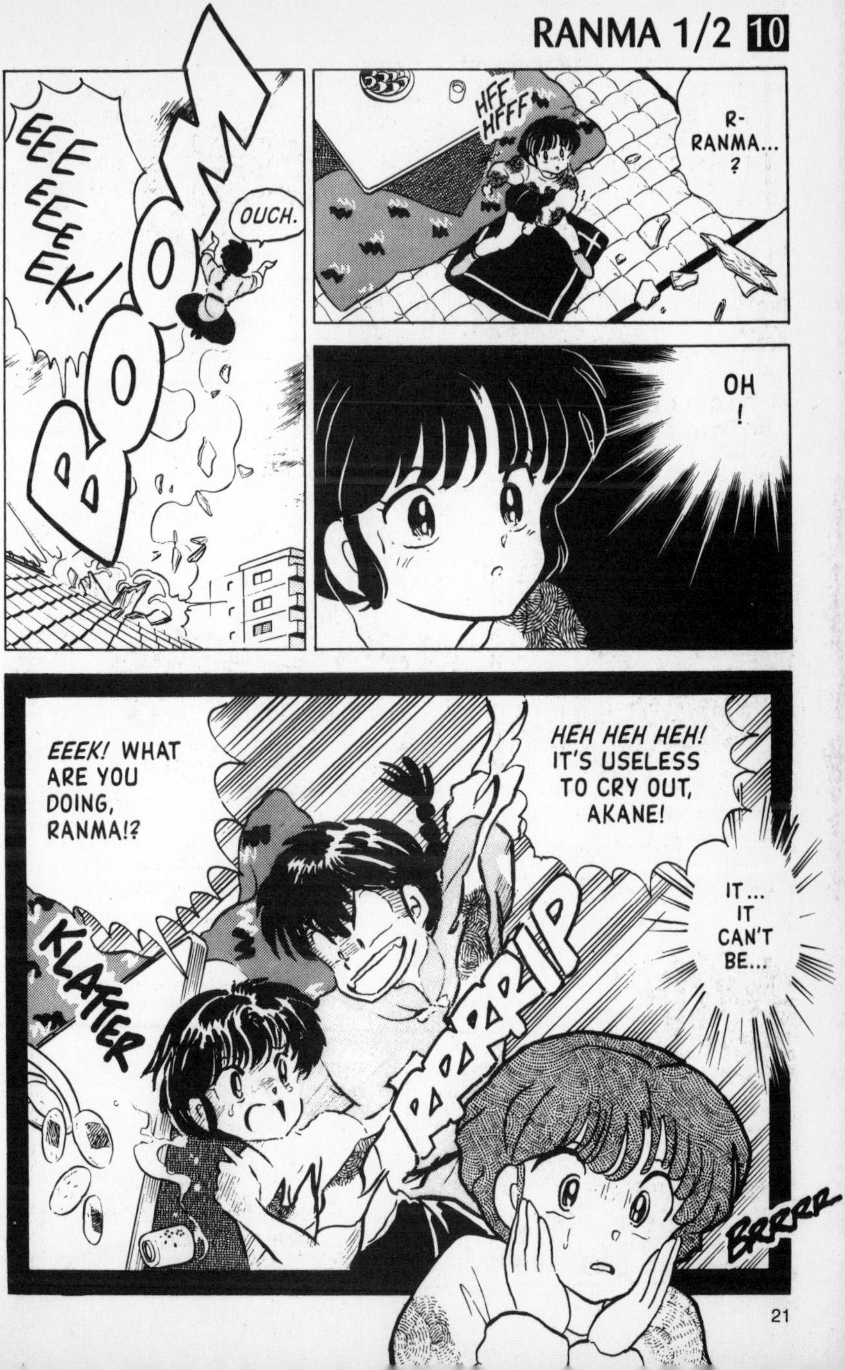
EEEEEEEEK!
BOOM
OUCH.
HFF HFFF
R-RANMA...?
OH!
EEEK! WHAT ARE YOU DOING, RANMA!?
HEH HEH HEH! IT'S USELESS TO CRY OUT, AKANE!
KLATTER
RRRRRIP
IT... IT CAN'T BE...
BRRRR

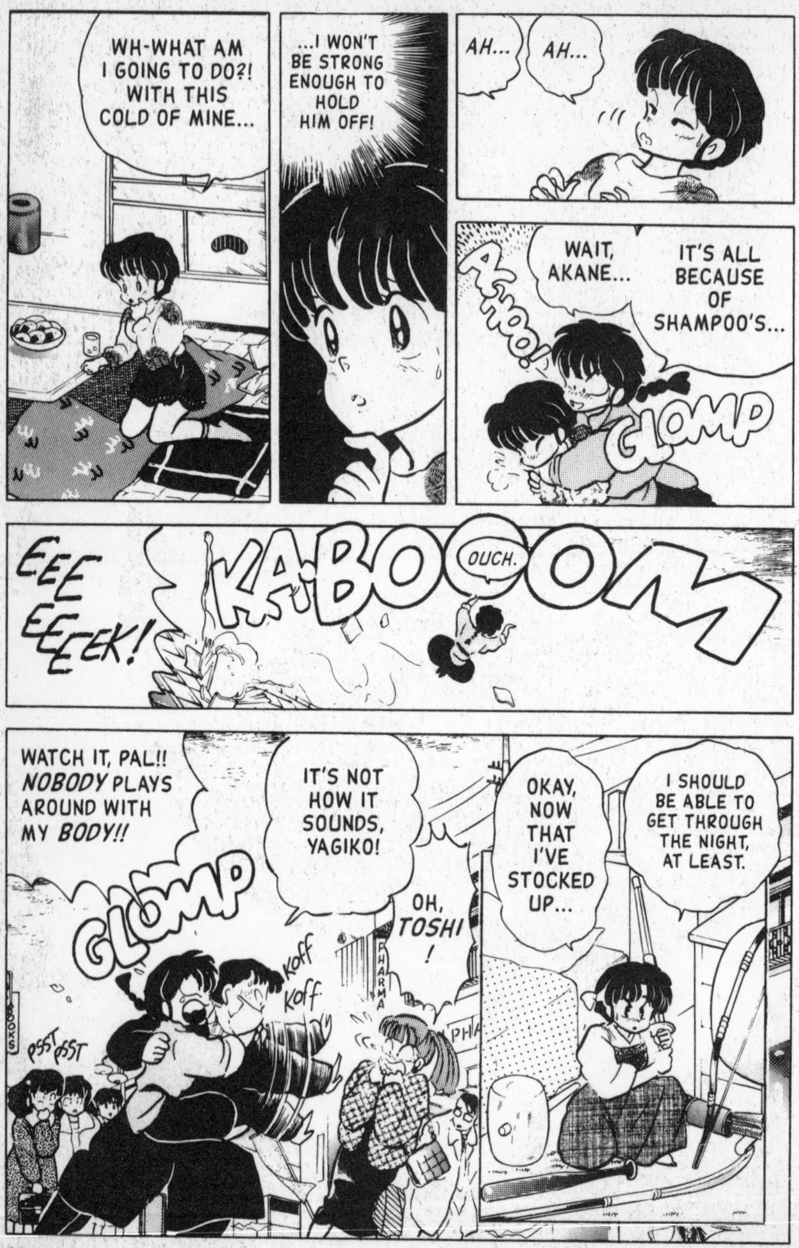
WH-WHAT AM I GOING TO DO?! WITH THIS COLD OF MINE...
...I WON'T BE STRONG ENOUGH TO HOLD HIM OFF!
AH...
AH...
WAIT, AKANE...
IT'S ALL BECAUSE OF SHAMPOO'S...
ACHOO!
GLOMP
EEE EEEEEEK!
KA-BOOOM
OUCH.
WATCH IT, PAL!! NOBODY PLAYS AROUND WITH MY BODY!!
GLOMP
IT'S NOT HOW IT SOUNDS, YAGIKO!
KOFF KOFF
PSST PSST
OH, TOSHI!
OKAY, NOW THAT I'VE STOCKED UP...
I SHOULD BE ABLE TO GET THROUGH THE NIGHT, AT LEAST.

Part 2

HOLD ME CLOSE

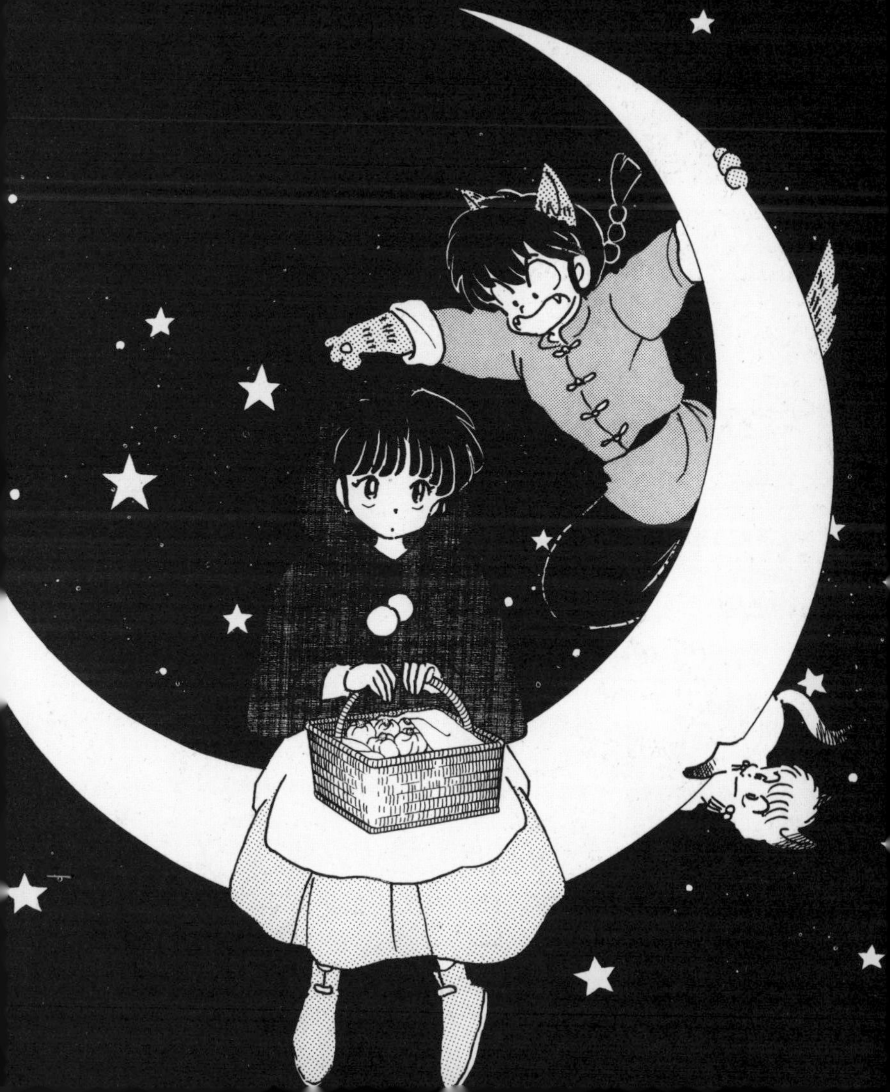

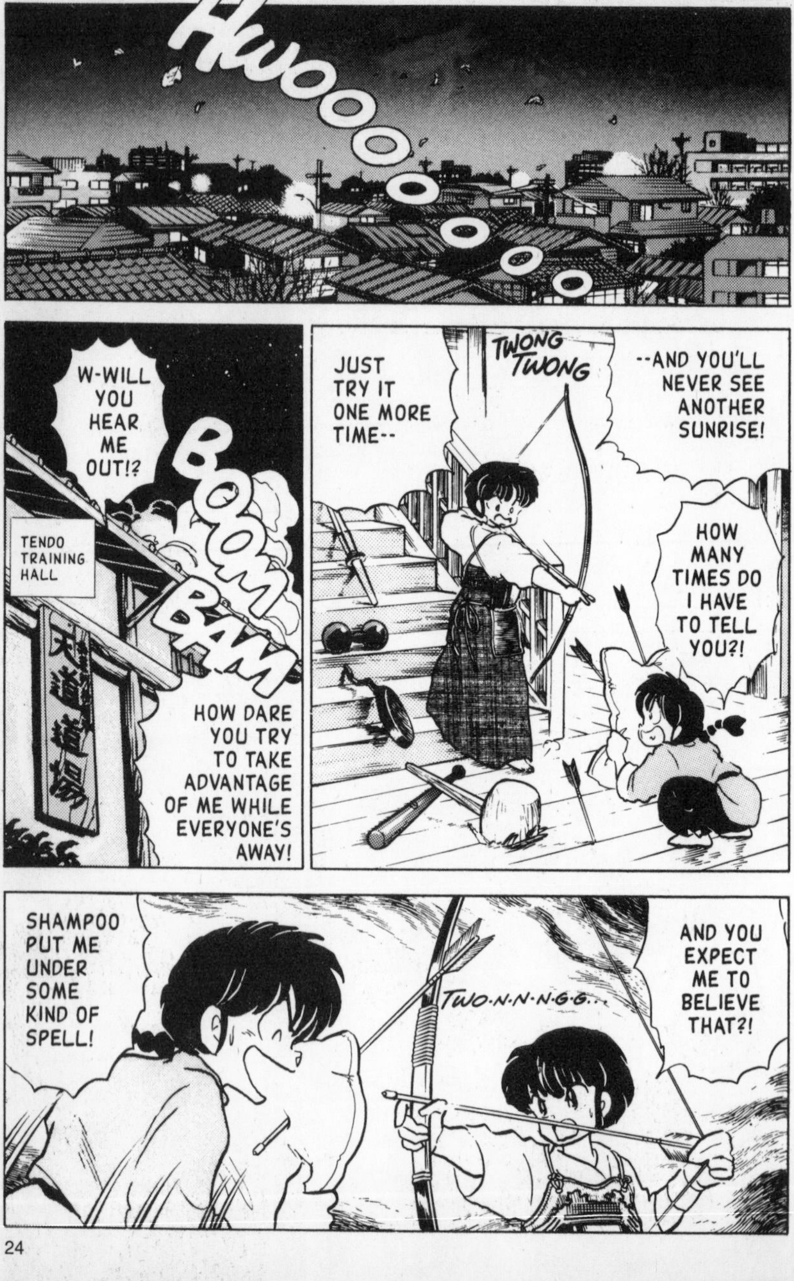
HWOOOOOOO
W-WILL YOU HEAR ME OUT!?
TENDO TRAINING HALL
天道道場
BOOM BOOM BAM
HOW DARE YOU TRY TO TAKE ADVANTAGE OF ME WHILE EVERYONE'S AWAY!
JUST TRY IT ONE MORE TIME--
TWONG TWONG
--AND YOU'LL NEVER SEE ANOTHER SUNRISE!
HOW MANY TIMES DO I HAVE TO TELL YOU?!
SHAMPOO PUT ME UNDER SOME KIND OF SPELL!
TWO-N-N-N-G-G...
AND YOU EXPECT ME TO BELIEVE THAT?!

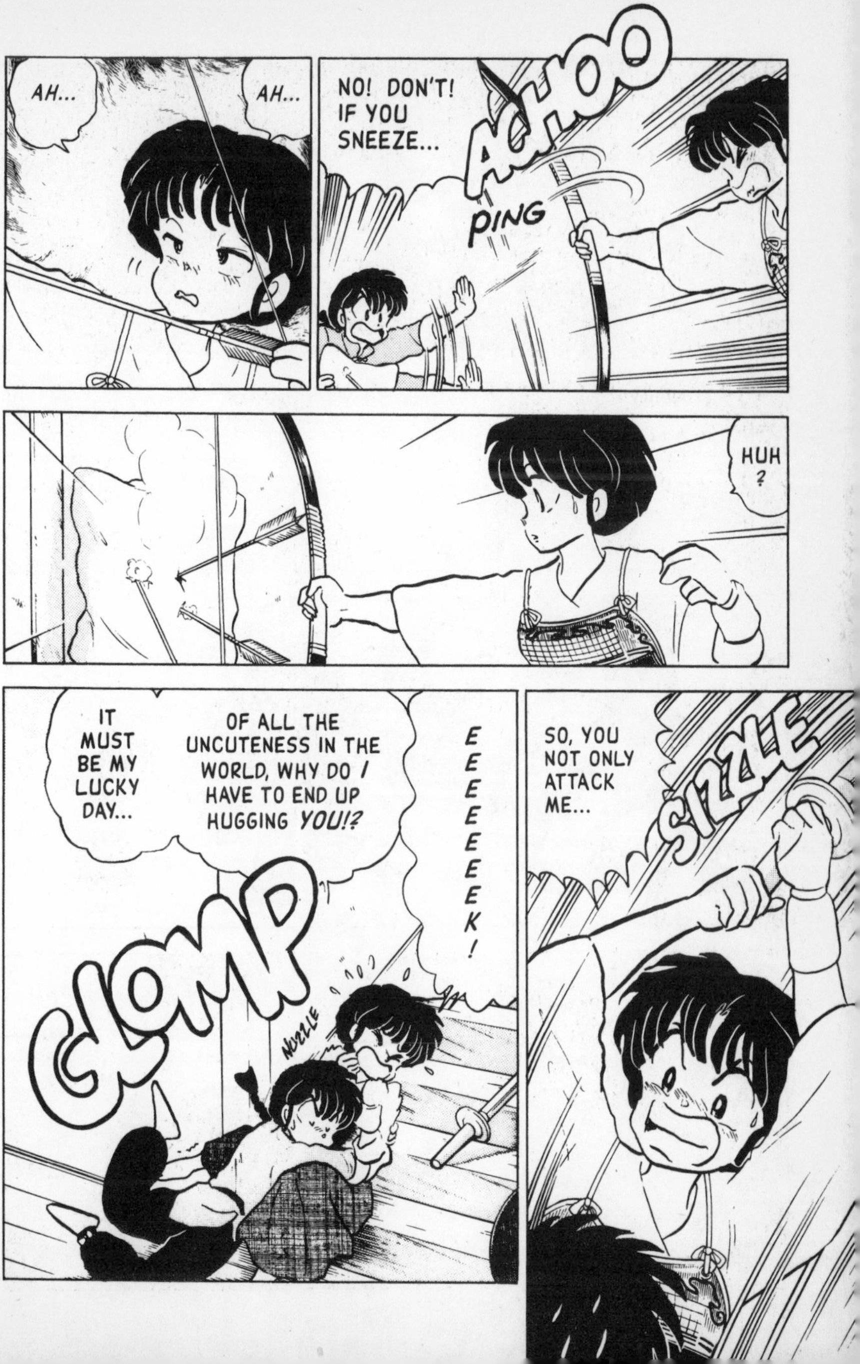
AH...
AH...
NO! DON'T! IF YOU SNEEZE...
ACHOO
PING
HUH ?
IT MUST BE MY LUCKY DAY...
OF ALL THE UNCUTENESS IN THE WORLD, WHY DO I HAVE TO END UP HUGGING YOU!?
EEEEEEEK!
CLOMP
NUZZLE
SO, YOU NOT ONLY ATTACK ME...
SIZZLE

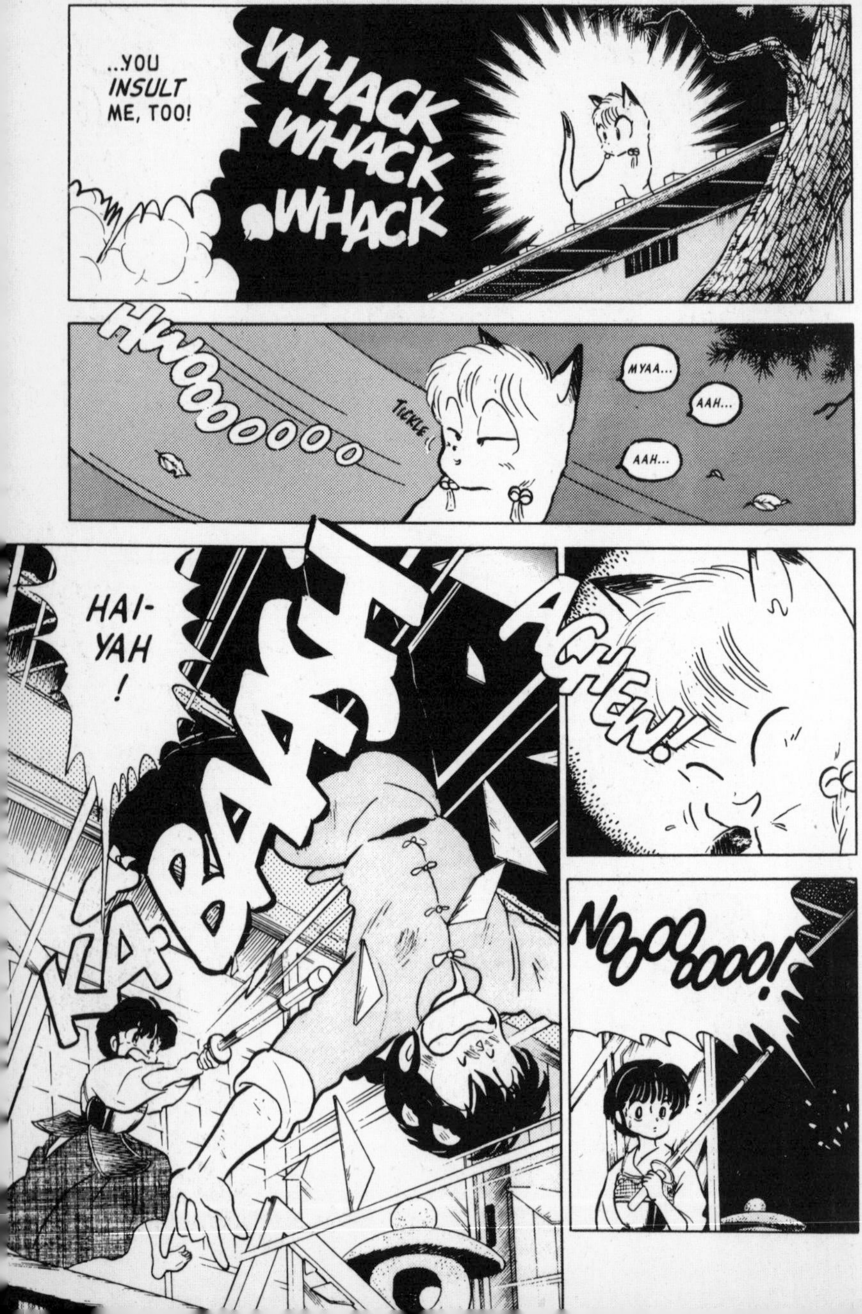
...YOU INSULT ME, TOO!
WHACK WHACK WHACK
HWOOOOOOOO
TICKLE
MYAA...
AAH...
AAH...
HAI-YAH!
KABASH
ACHEW!
NOOOOOOOO!

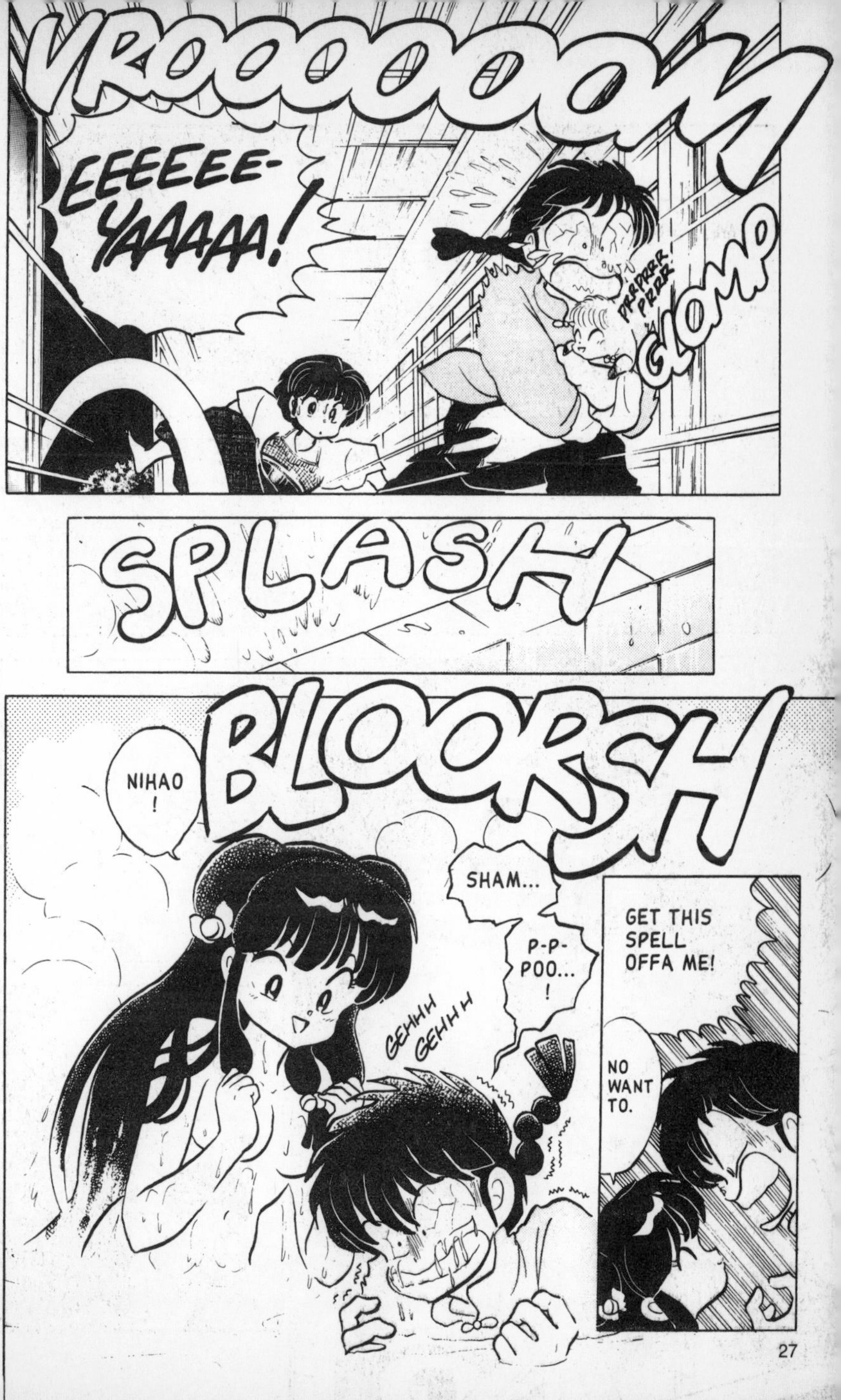
VROOOOOOM
EEEEEE-
YAAAAA!
PRRPRRR PRRR
GLOMP
SPLASH
NIHAO
!
BLOORSH
SHAM...
P-P-
POO...
!
GEHHH GEHHH
GET THIS
SPELL
OFFA ME!
NO
WANT
TO.

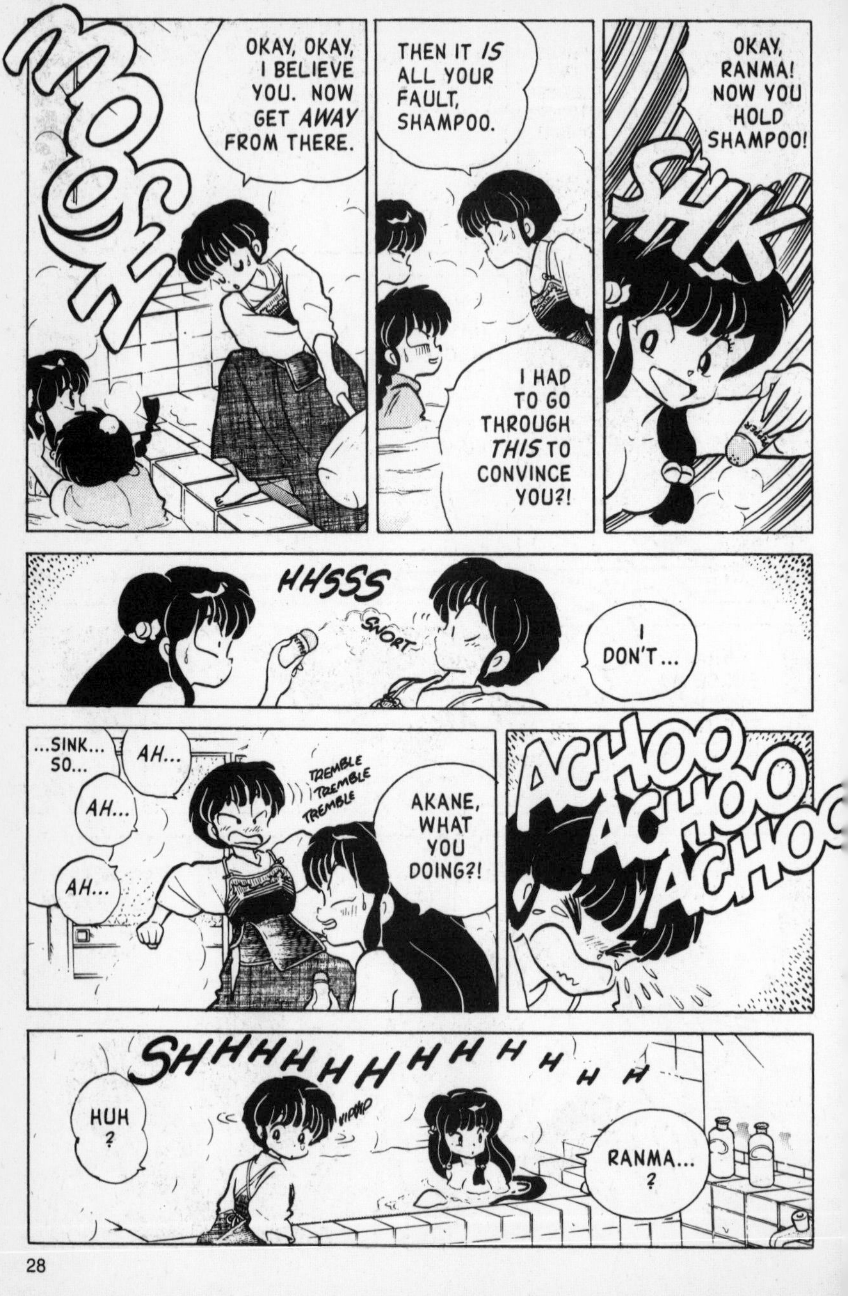
MOOSH
OKAY, OKAY, I BELIEVE YOU. NOW GET AWAY FROM THERE.
THEN IT IS ALL YOUR FAULT, SHAMPOO.
I HAD TO GO THROUGH THIS TO CONVINCE YOU?!
OKAY, RANMA! NOW YOU HOLD SHAMPOO!
SHIK
HHSSS
SNORT
I DON'T...
...SINK... SO...
AH...
AH...
AH...
TREMBLE TREMBLE TREMBLE
AKANE, WHAT YOU DOING?!
ACHOO ACHOO ACHOO
SHHHHHHHHHHHHHH
HUH ?
RANMA... ?

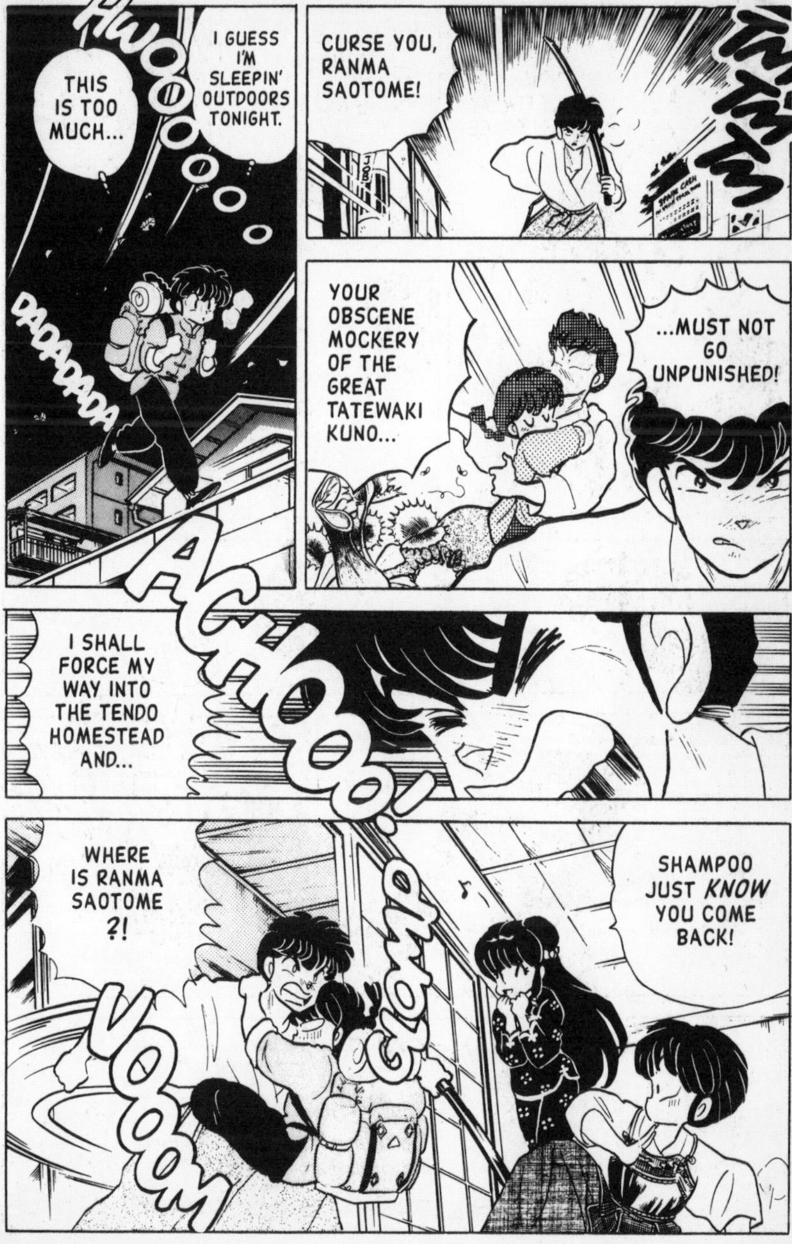
HWOOOOOOOO
THIS IS TOO MUCH...
I GUESS I'M SLEEPIN' OUTDOORS TONIGHT.
DADADADADA
CURSE YOU, RANMA SAOTOME!
TIM TIM TIM
YOUR OBSCENE MOCKERY OF THE GREAT TATEWAKI KUNO...
...MUST NOT GO UNPUNISHED!
ACHOOO!
I SHALL FORCE MY WAY INTO THE TENDO HOMESTEAD AND...
WHERE IS RANMA SAOTOME ?!
SHAMPOO JUST *KNOW* YOU COME BACK!
CLOMP
VOOOOM

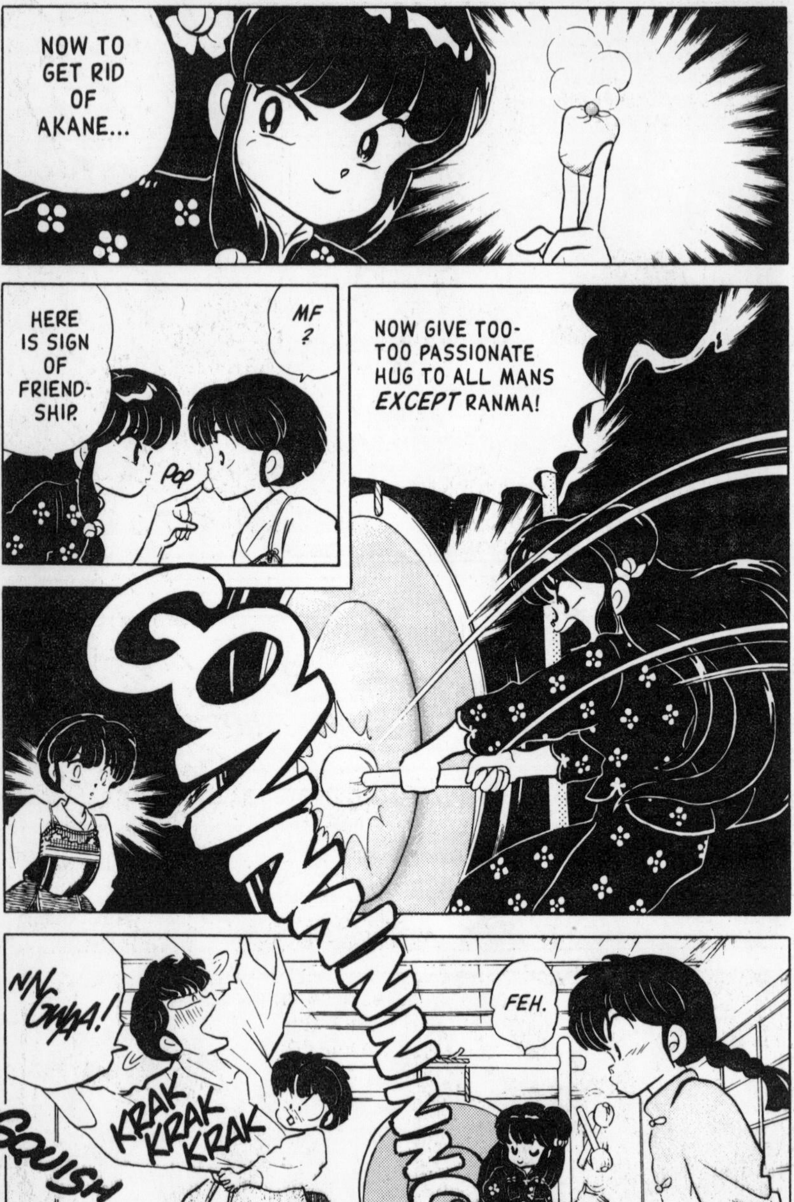
NOW TO GET RID OF AKANE...
HERE IS SIGN OF FRIEND-SHIP.
MF?
POP
NOW GIVE TOO-TOO PASSIONATE HUG TO ALL MANS *EXCEPT* RANMA!
GONNNNNNNNNG
NNGWAA!
SQUISH
KRAK KRAK KRAK
FEH.

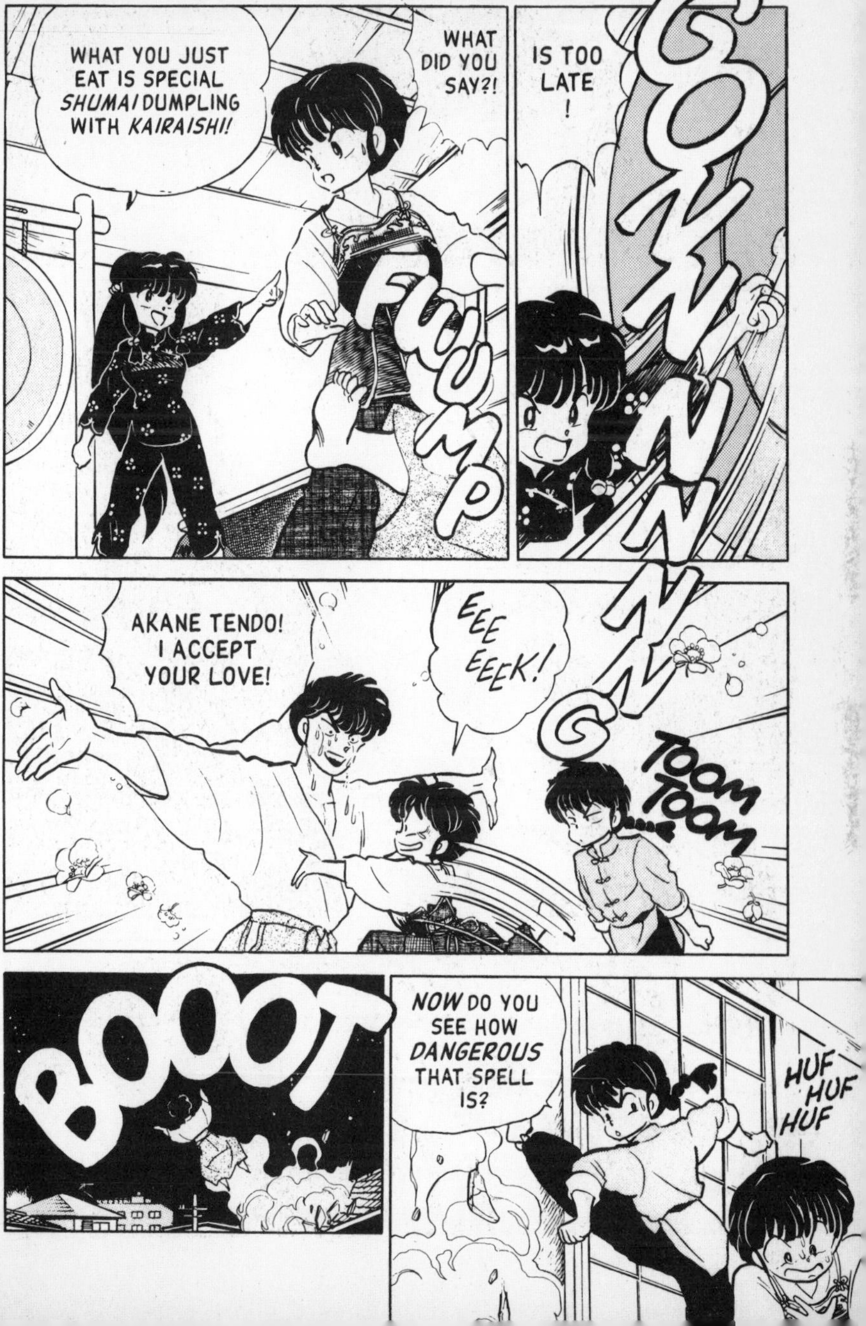
WHAT YOU JUST EAT IS SPECIAL *SHUMAI* DUMPLING WITH *KAIRAISHI*!
WHAT DID YOU SAY?!
FUUUMP
IS TOO LATE!
GONNNNNG
AKANE TENDO! I ACCEPT YOUR LOVE!
EEEEEEK!
TOOM TOOM
BOOOT
NOW DO YOU SEE HOW *DANGEROUS* THAT SPELL IS?
HUF HUF HUF

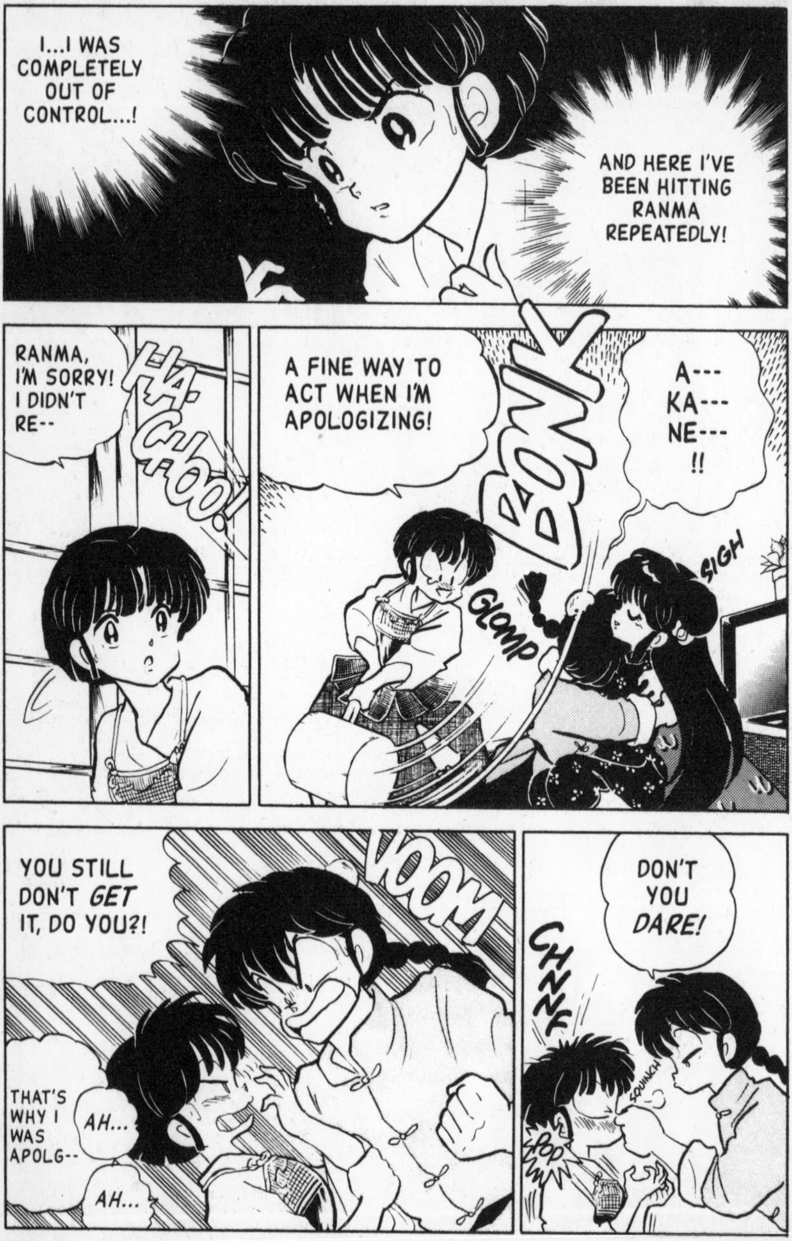
I...I WAS COMPLETELY OUT OF CONTROL...!
AND HERE I'VE BEEN HITTING RANMA REPEATEDLY!
RANMA, I'M SORRY! I DIDN'T RE--
HA-CHOO!
A FINE WAY TO ACT WHEN I'M APOLOGIZING!
BONK
A--- KA--- NE--- !!
GLOMP
SIGH
YOU STILL DON'T *GET* IT, DO YOU?!
VOOM
THAT'S WHY I WAS APOLG--
AH...
AH...
DON'T YOU *DARE!*
CHNNK
SQUINCH
POP

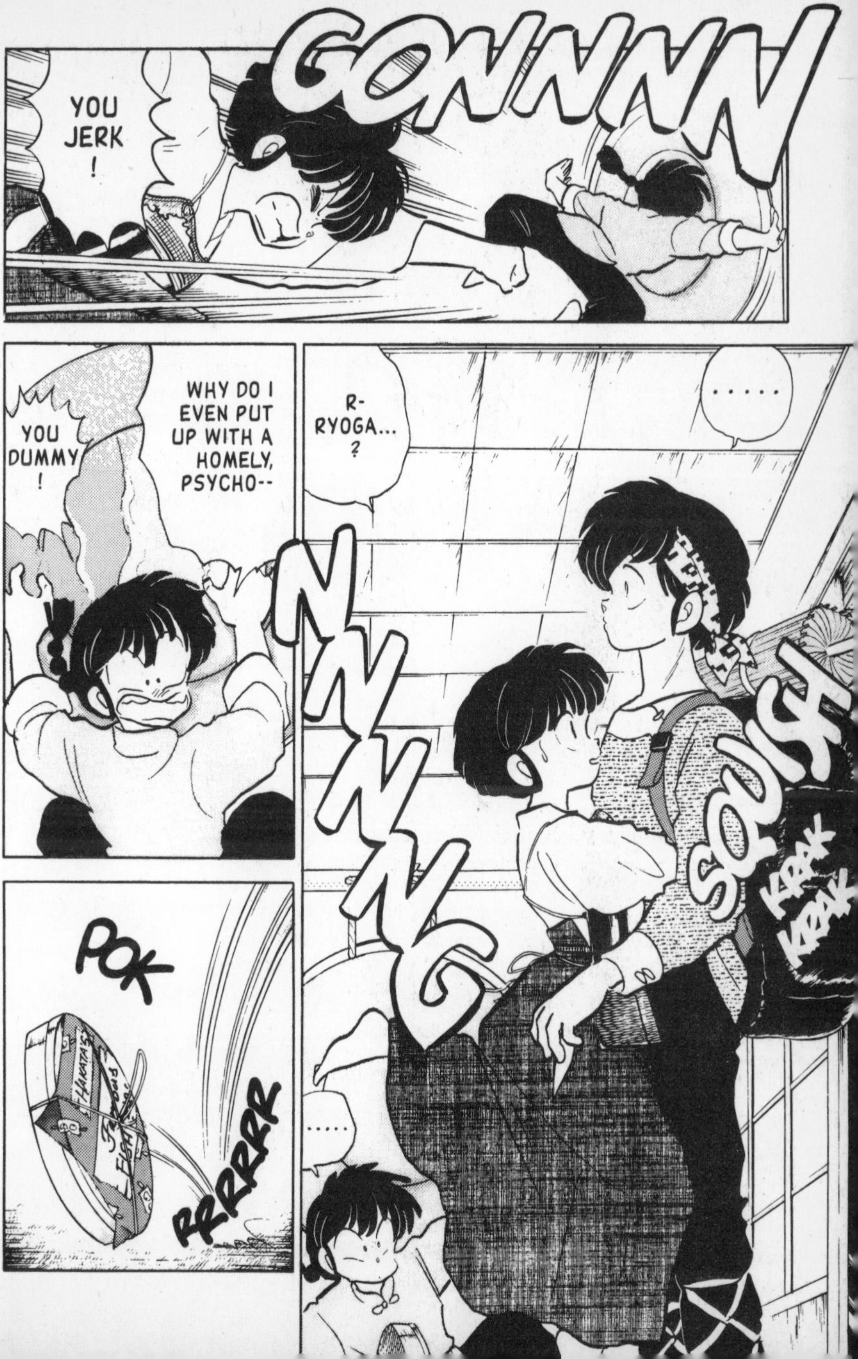
YOU JERK!
GONNNN
YOU DUMMY!
WHY DO I EVEN PUT UP WITH A HOMELY, PSYCHO--
POK
RRRRRR
R-RYOGA...?
......
NNNNNG
SQUISH
KRAK
KRAK
.....

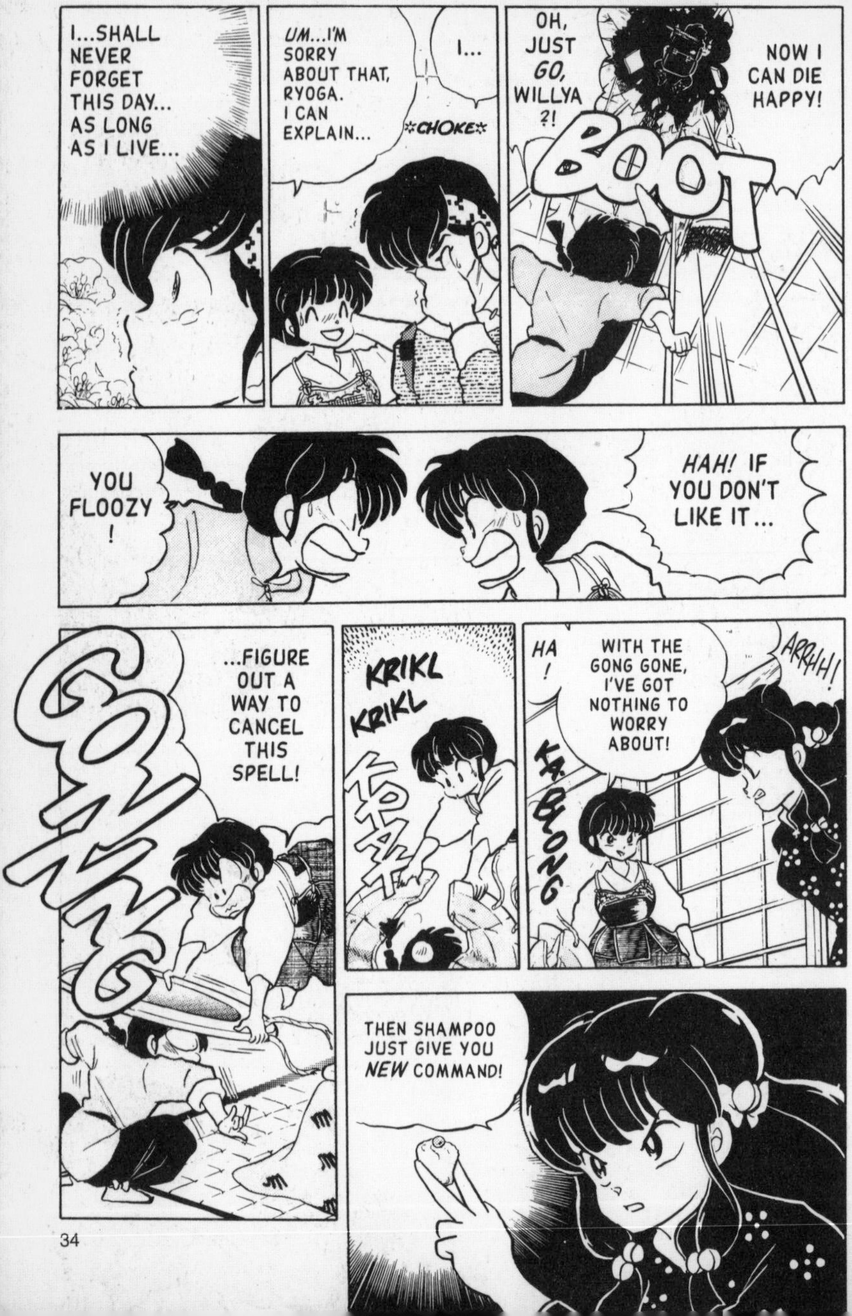
I...SHALL NEVER FORGET THIS DAY... AS LONG AS I LIVE...
UM...I'M SORRY ABOUT THAT, RYOGA. I CAN EXPLAIN...
I...
CHOKE
OH, JUST GO, WILLYA ?!
NOW I CAN DIE HAPPY!
BOOT
YOU FLOOZY !
HAH! IF YOU DON'T LIKE IT...
...FIGURE OUT A WAY TO CANCEL THIS SPELL!
GONNNG
KRIKL KRIKL
KRAKK
HA !
WITH THE GONG GONE, I'VE GOT NOTHING TO WORRY ABOUT!
KA-BLONG
ARRHH!
THEN SHAMPOO JUST GIVE YOU NEW COMMAND!

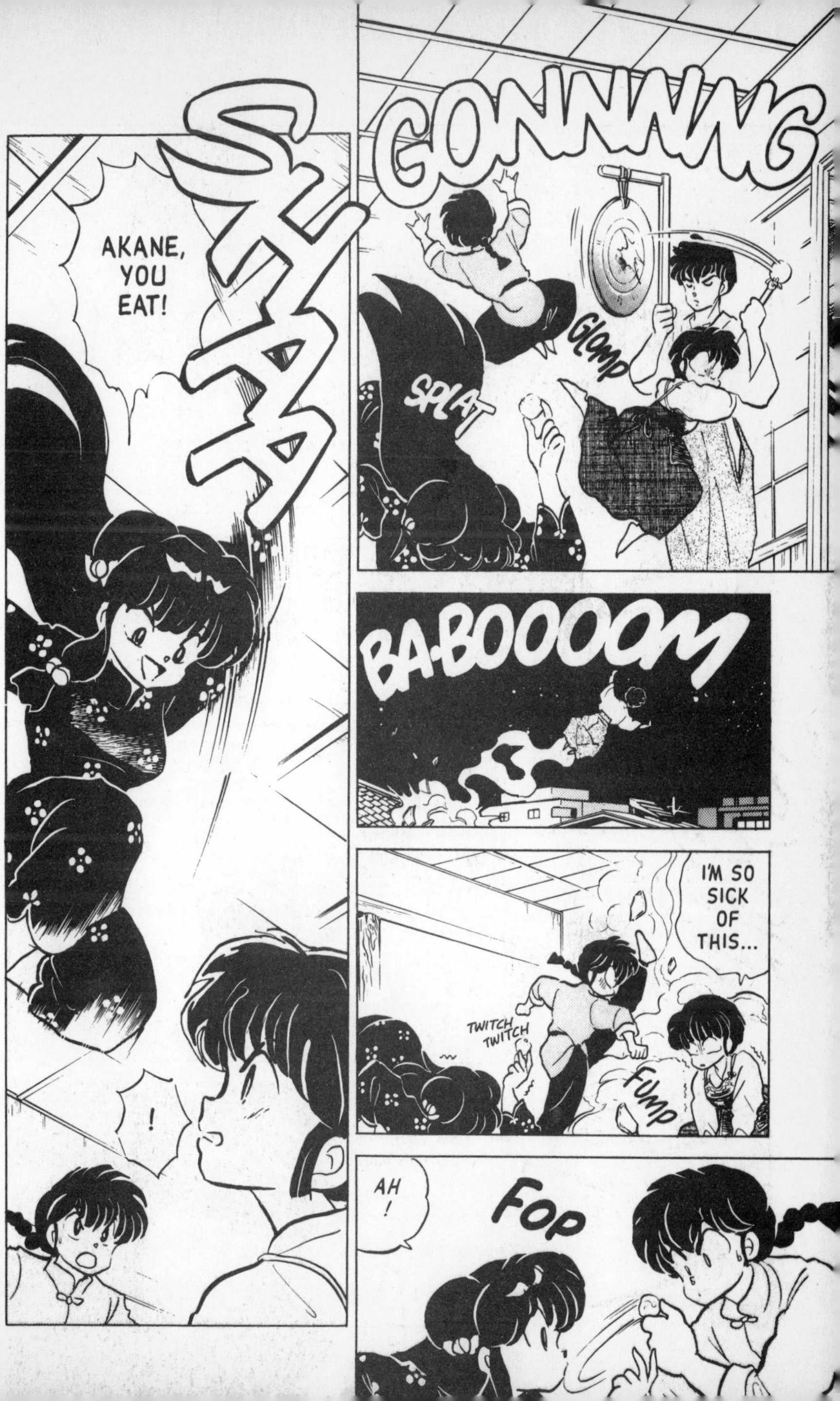
SHA
AKANE, YOU EAT!
!
GONNNNG
GLOMP
SPLAT
BA-BOOOOM
I'M SO SICK OF THIS...
TWITCH TWITCH
FUMP
AH!
FOP

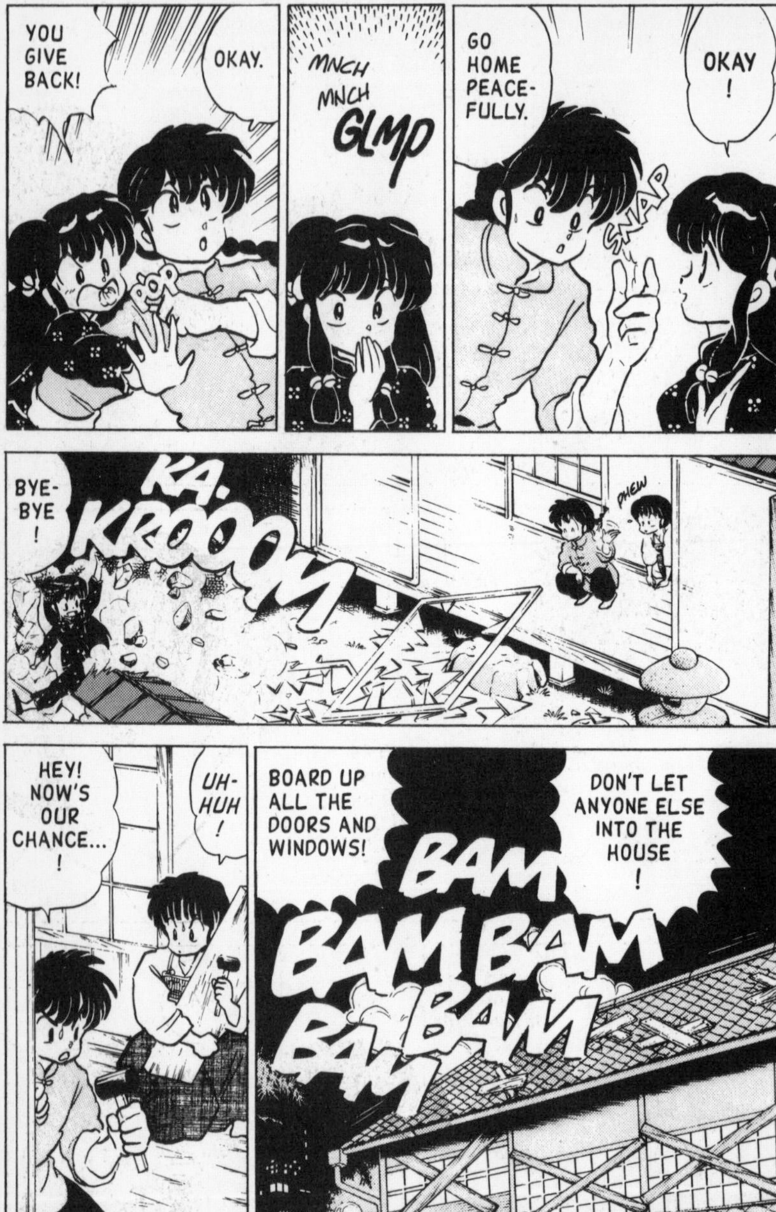
YOU GIVE BACK!
OKAY.
POP
MNCH MNCH GLMP
GO HOME PEACE-FULLY.
OKAY!
SNAP
BYE-BYE!
KA-KROOOM
PHEW
HEY! NOW'S OUR CHANCE...!
UH-HUH!
BOARD UP ALL THE DOORS AND WINDOWS!
DON'T LET ANYONE ELSE INTO THE HOUSE!
BAM BAM BAM BAM BAM BAM

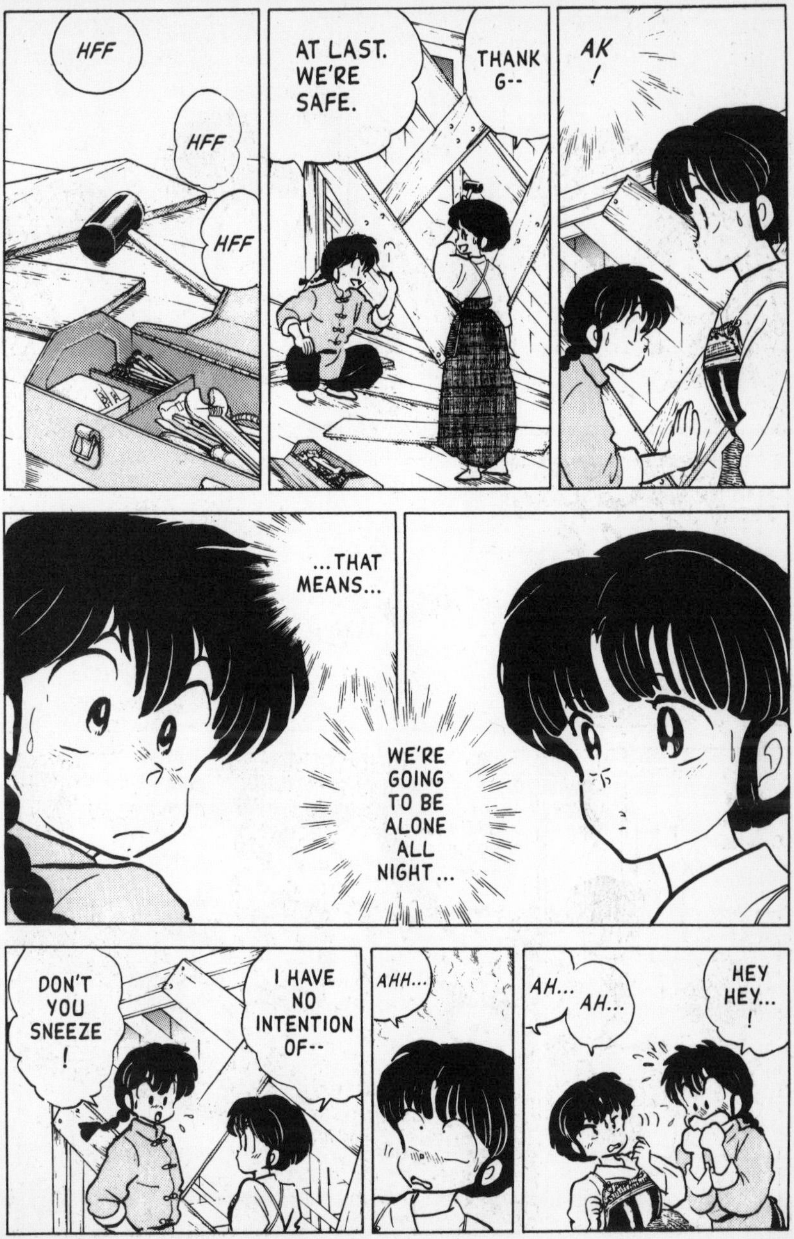
HFF
HFF
HFF
AT LAST. WE'RE SAFE.
THANK G--
AK !
...THAT MEANS...
WE'RE GOING TO BE ALONE ALL NIGHT...
DON'T YOU SNEEZE !
I HAVE NO INTENTION OF--
AHH...
AH...
AH...
HEY HEY... !

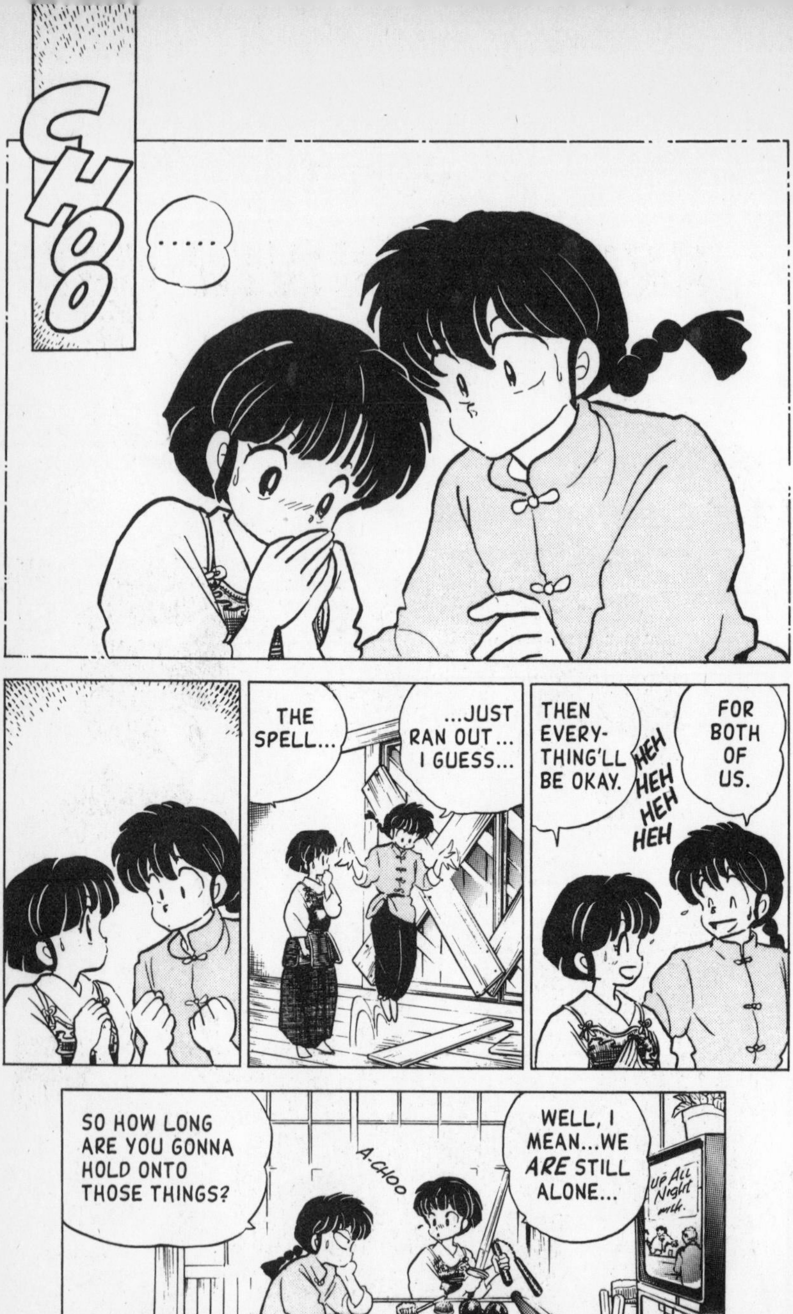
CHOO
......
THE SPELL...
...JUST RAN OUT... I GUESS...
THEN EVERY-THING'LL BE OKAY.
HEH HEH HEH HEH
FOR BOTH OF US.
SO HOW LONG ARE YOU GONNA HOLD ONTO THOSE THINGS?
A-CHOO
WELL, I MEAN...WE *ARE* STILL ALONE...
UP ALL Night

Part 3

AKANE'S POWER-UP!

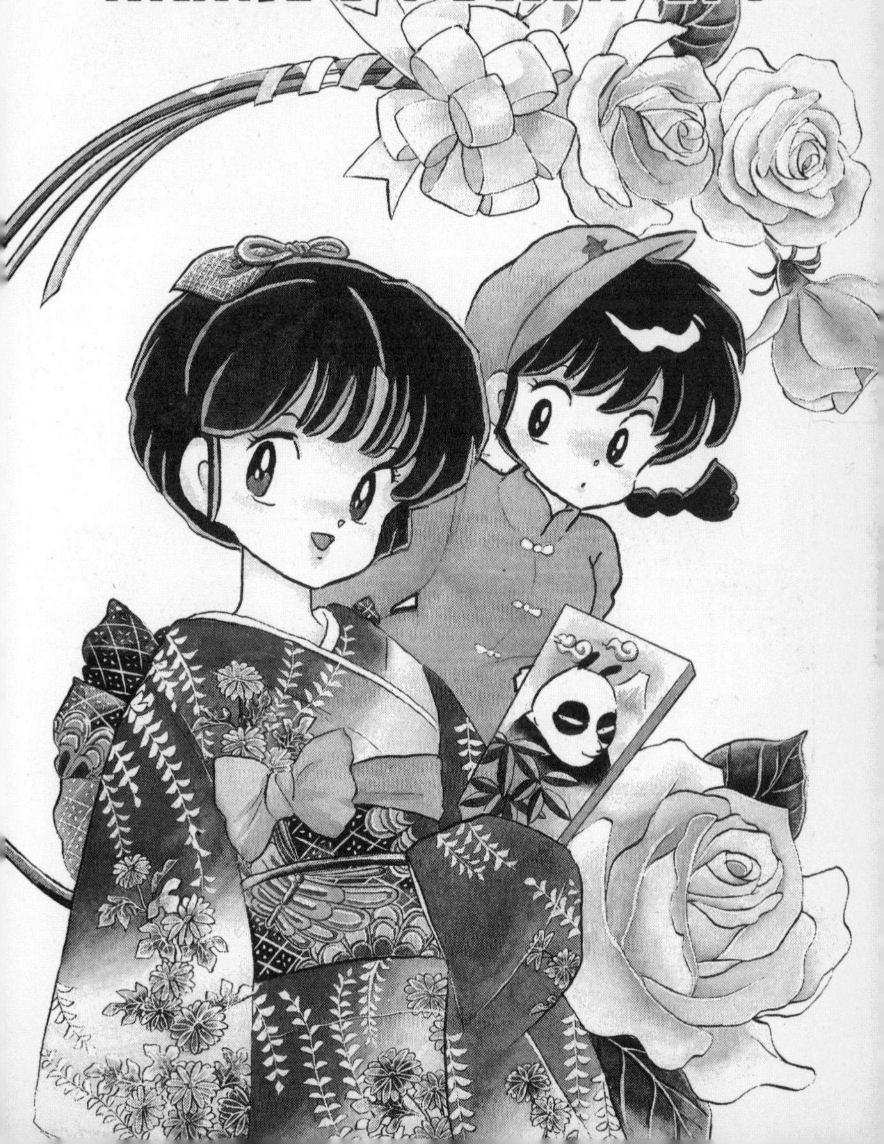

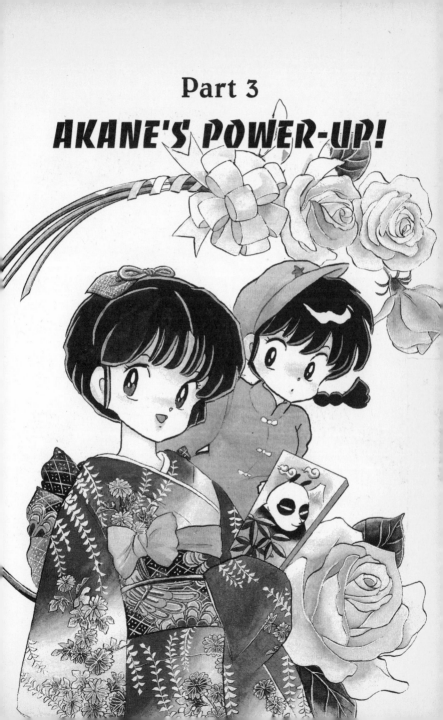

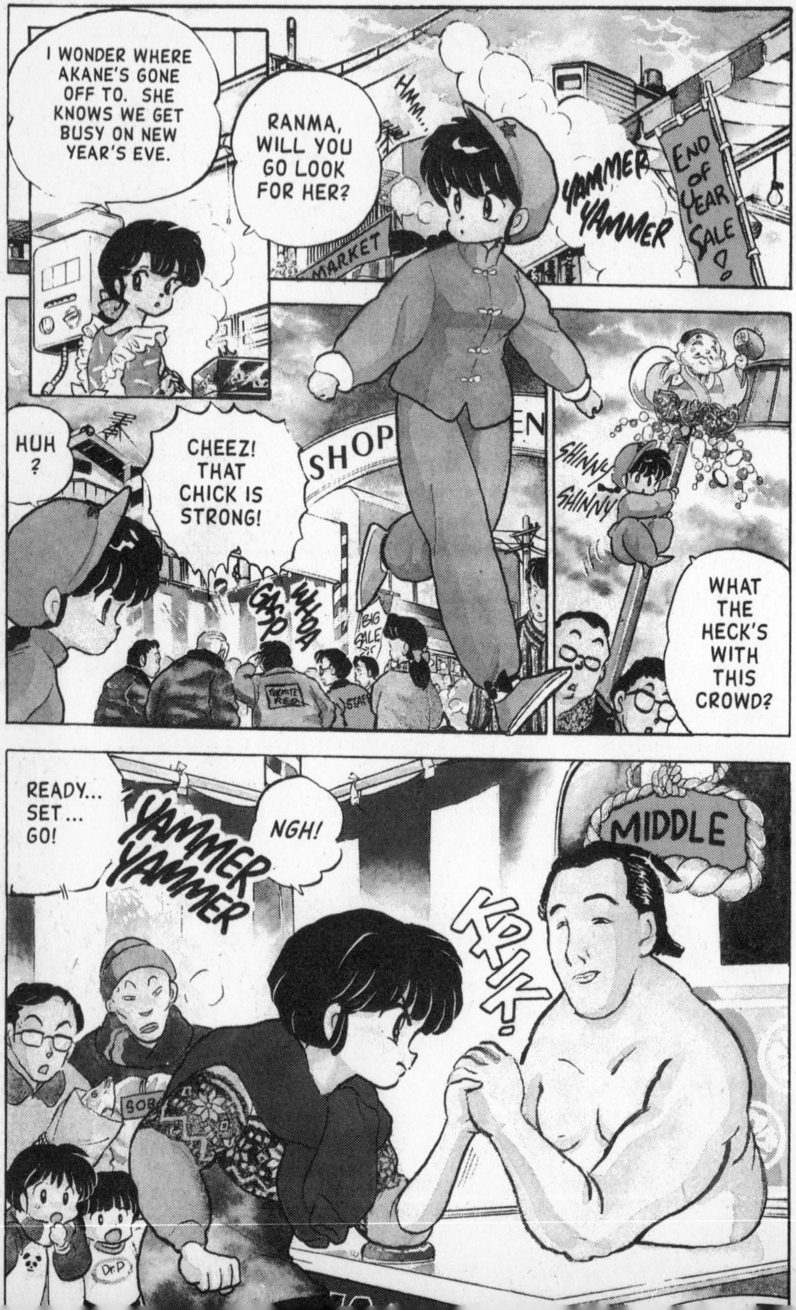
I WONDER WHERE AKANE'S GONE OFF TO. SHE KNOWS WE GET BUSY ON NEW YEAR'S EVE.
MARKET
RANMA, WILL YOU GO LOOK FOR HER?
HMM...
YAMMER YAMMER
END OF YEAR SALE!
HUH?
CHEEZ! THAT CHICK IS STRONG!
SHOP
GASP
WHOA
BIG SALE
SHINNY SHINNY
WHAT THE HECK'S WITH THIS CROWD?
READY... SET... GO!
YAMMER YAMMER
NGH!
MIDDLE
KRIK!
Dr.P

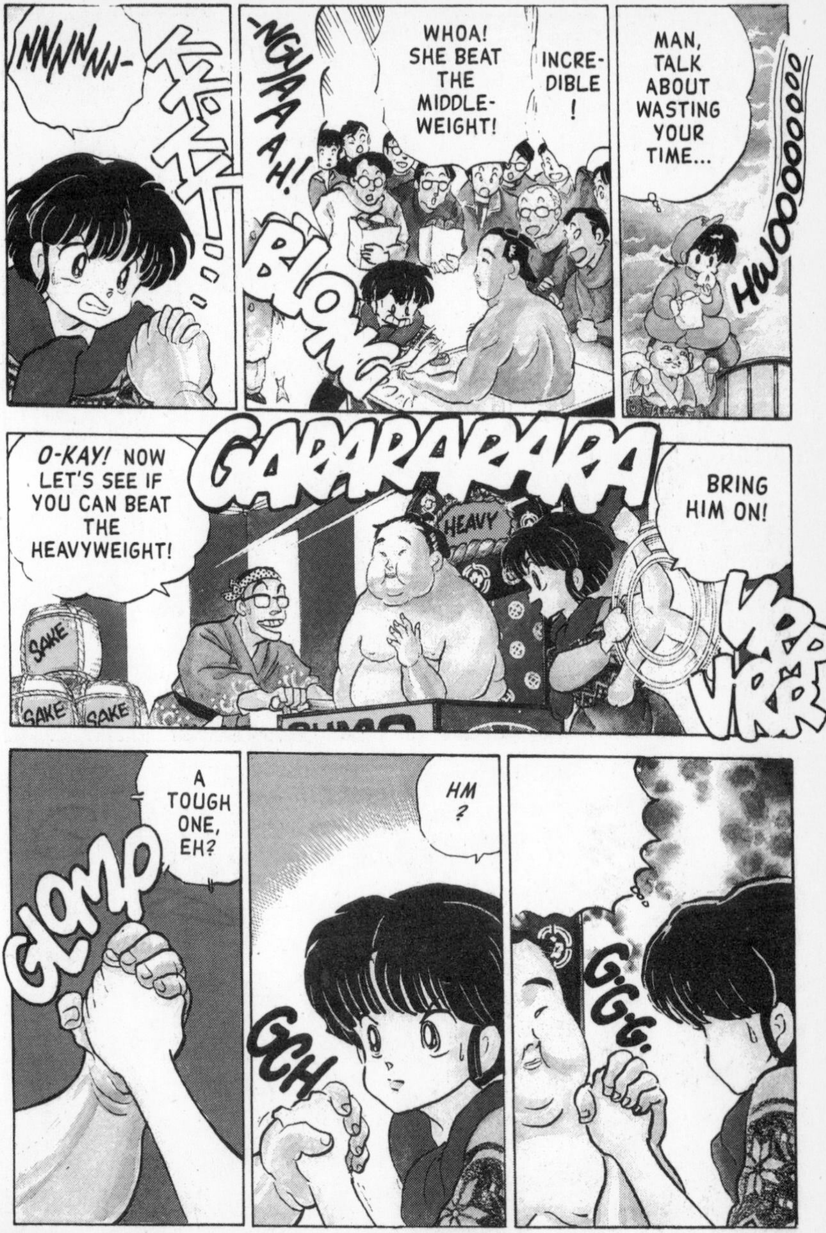
NNNNNN-
-NGHAAAAH!
WHOA! SHE BEAT THE MIDDLE-WEIGHT!
INCRE-DIBLE!
BLONK
MAN, TALK ABOUT WASTING YOUR TIME...
HWOOOOOOOOO
GARARARARA
O-KAY! NOW LET'S SEE IF YOU CAN BEAT THE HEAVYWEIGHT!
HEAVY
SAKE
SAKE
SAKE
BRING HIM ON!
VRRR
VRRR
A TOUGH ONE, EH?
GLOMP
HM?
GCH
G-G-G.

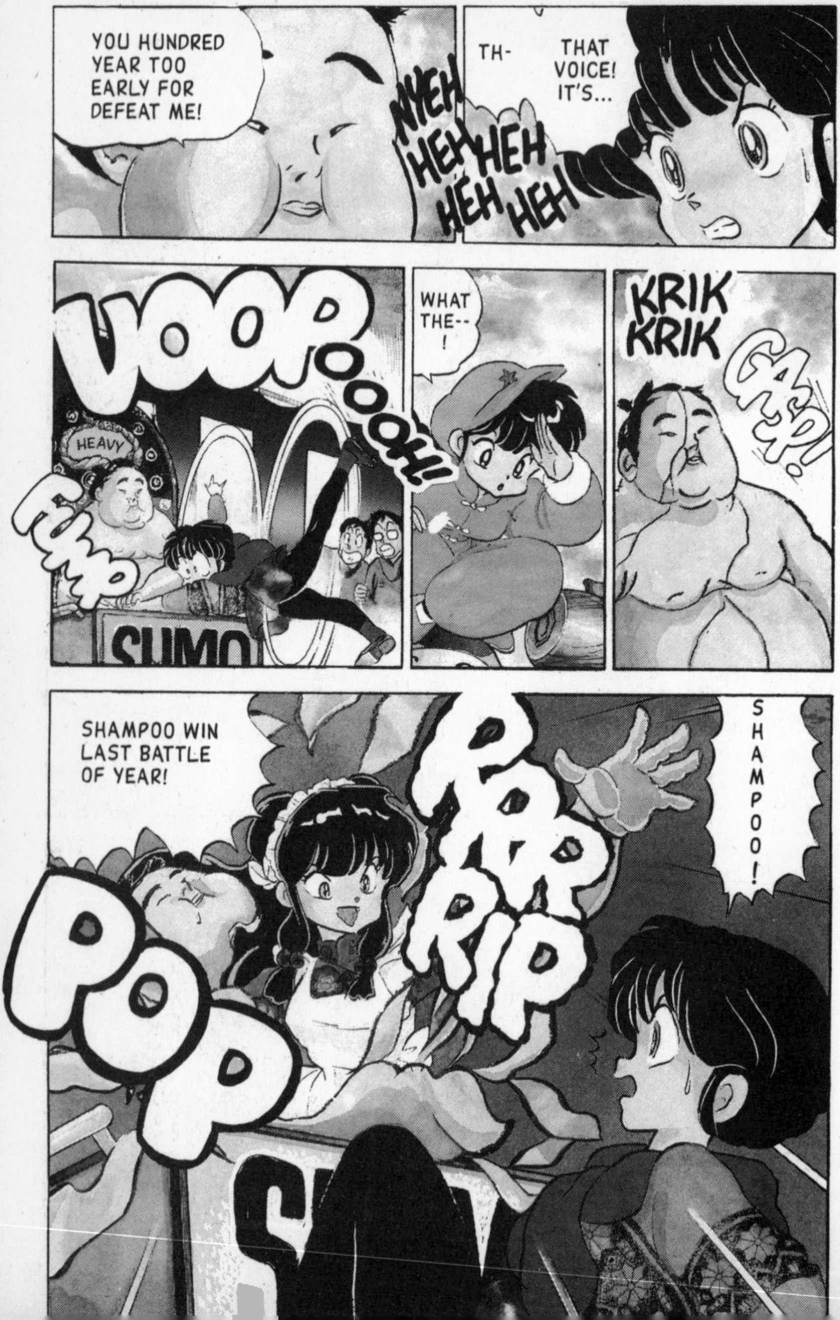

YOU HUNDRED YEAR TOO EARLY FOR DEFEAT ME!
NYEH HEH HEH HEH HEH HEH
TH-
THAT VOICE! IT'S...
VOOPOOOOH!
HEAVY
FUMP
SUMO
WHAT THE--!
KRIK KRIK
GASP!
SHAMPOO WIN LAST BATTLE OF YEAR!
RRR RIP
POP
SHAMPOO!

WHOA--!!

AN EVEN **STRONGER** CHICK! INSIDE IT!!

SO!!

POO!

AKANE WEAK AS ALWAYS BEEN!

YAMMER YAMMER

SUMO MACHINE

ONE MORE TIME!

AIYAA!

SHAMPOO NO HAVE TIME FOR THIS!

PAP

SHAMPOO IN MIDDLE OF DELIVERY.

BA-BONK

HEAVY

SUMO MACHINE

SHAMPOO WASTE TIME FOR STUPID CONTEST.

VSHHH

1st Prize 2nd Prize Prize

IF WE FIGHT FOR RANMA, SHAMPOO FIGHT YOU ANYTIME!

BYE NOW!

CHI-RING

ARRR...

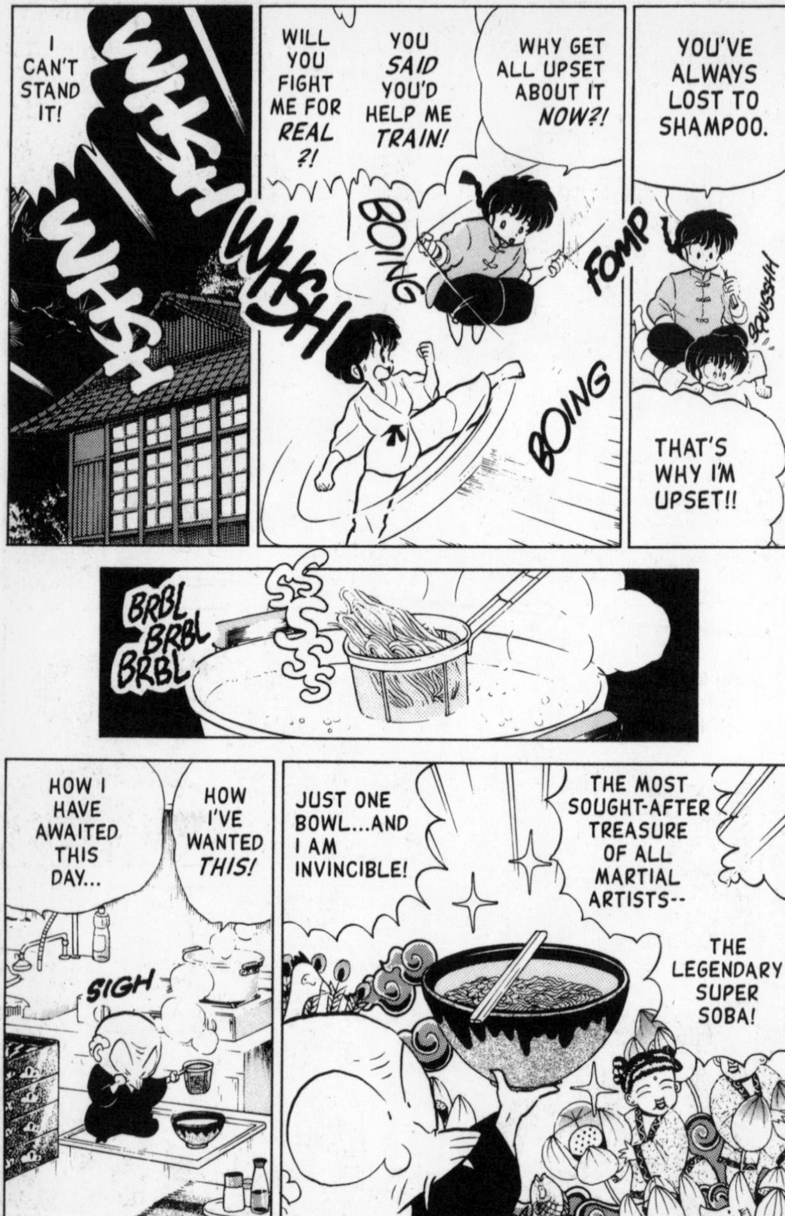
I CAN'T STAND IT!
WHSH WHSH
WILL YOU FIGHT ME FOR REAL ?!
YOU SAID YOU'D HELP ME TRAIN!
WHY GET ALL UPSET ABOUT IT NOW?!
BOING
WHSH
FOMP
BOING
YOU'VE ALWAYS LOST TO SHAMPOO.
SQUISSHH
THAT'S WHY I'M UPSET!!
BRBL BRBL BRBL
HOW I HAVE AWAITED THIS DAY...
HOW I'VE WANTED THIS!
SIGH
JUST ONE BOWL...AND I AM INVINCIBLE!
THE MOST SOUGHT-AFTER TREASURE OF ALL MARTIAL ARTISTS--
THE LEGENDARY SUPER SOBA!

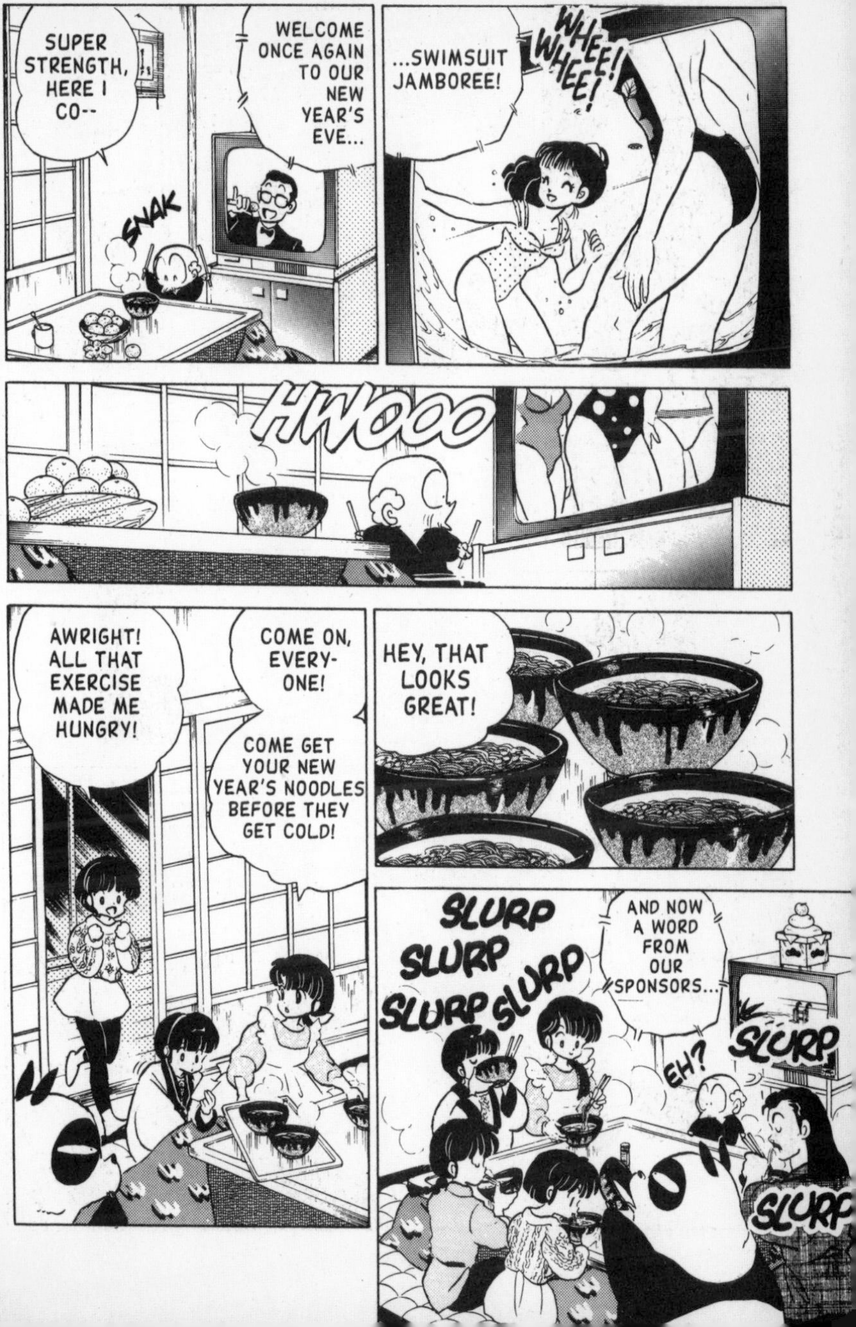
SUPER STRENGTH, HERE I CO--
SNAK
WELCOME ONCE AGAIN TO OUR NEW YEAR'S EVE...
...SWIMSUIT JAMBOREE!
WHEE! WHEE!
HWOOO
AWRIGHT! ALL THAT EXERCISE MADE ME HUNGRY!
COME ON, EVERY-ONE!
COME GET YOUR NEW YEAR'S NOODLES BEFORE THEY GET COLD!
HEY, THAT LOOKS GREAT!
SLURP
SLURP
SLURP SLURP
AND NOW A WORD FROM OUR SPONSORS...
EH?
SLURP
SLURP

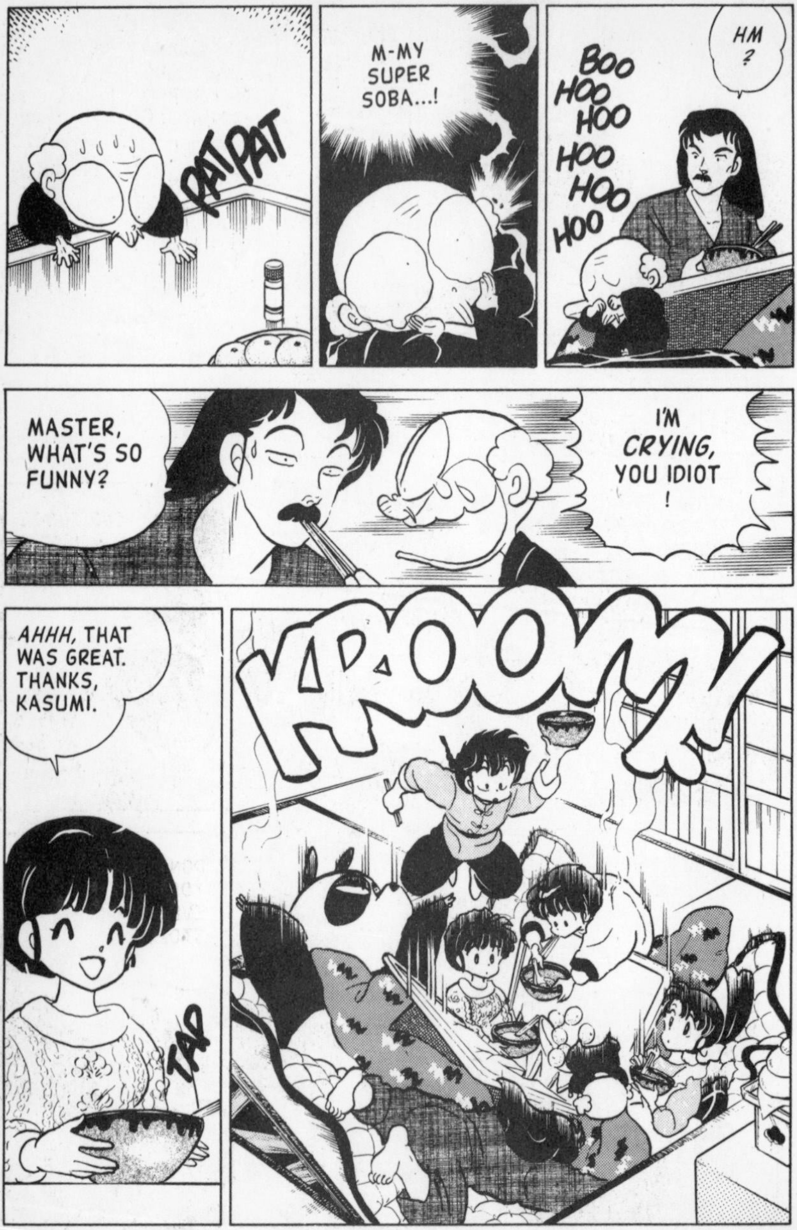
PAT PAT
M-MY SUPER SOBA...!
BOO HOO HOO HOO HOO HOO
HM ?
MASTER, WHAT'S SO FUNNY?
I'M *CRYING*, YOU IDIOT !
AHHH, THAT WAS GREAT. THANKS, KASUMI.
TAP
KROOM

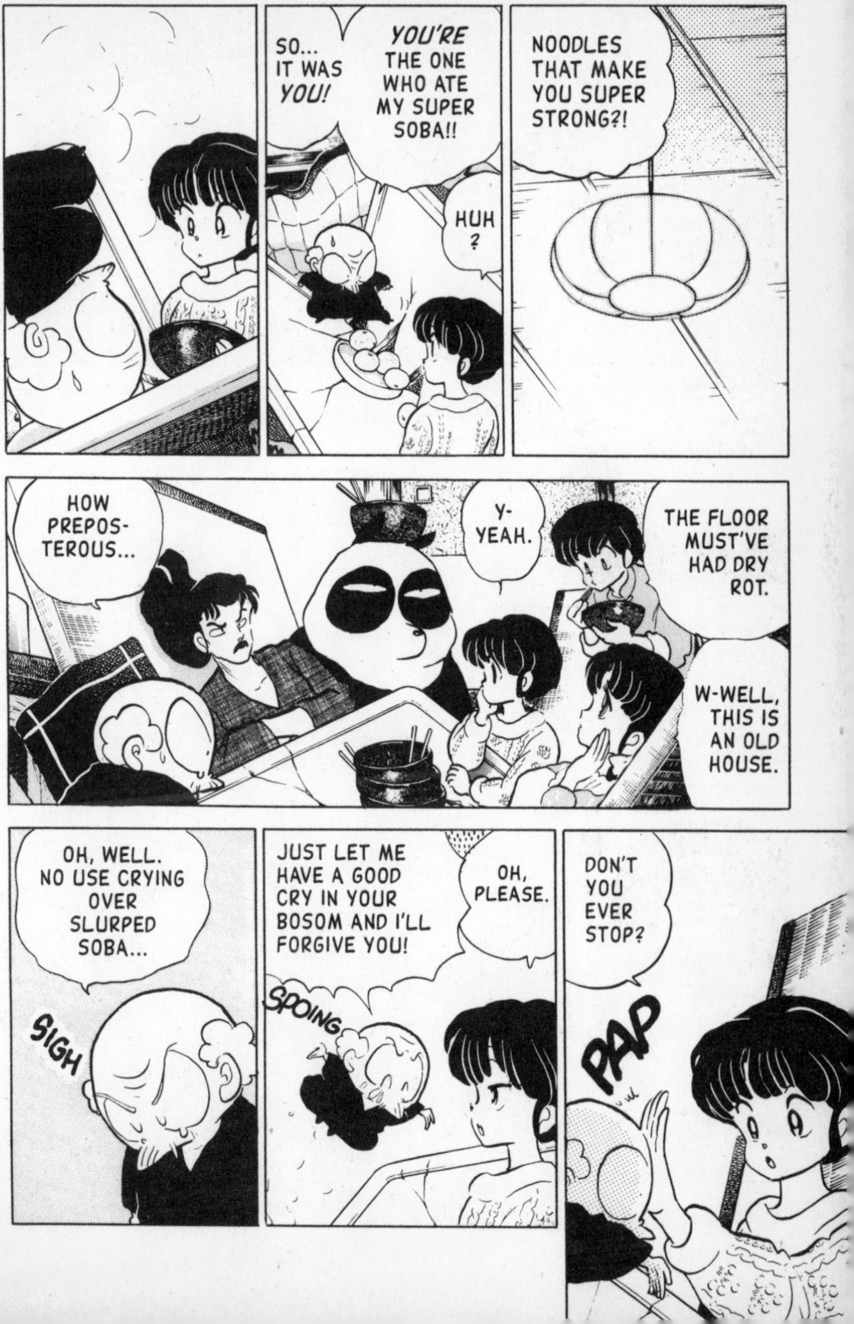
SO... IT WAS YOU!
YOU'RE THE ONE WHO ATE MY SUPER SOBA!!
HUH?
NOODLES THAT MAKE YOU SUPER STRONG?!
HOW PREPOS- TEROUS...
Y- YEAH.
THE FLOOR MUST'VE HAD DRY ROT.
W-WELL, THIS IS AN OLD HOUSE.
OH, WELL. NO USE CRYING OVER SLURPED SOBA...
SIGH
JUST LET ME HAVE A GOOD CRY IN YOUR BOSOM AND I'LL FORGIVE YOU!
OH, PLEASE.
SPOING
DON'T YOU EVER STOP?
PAP

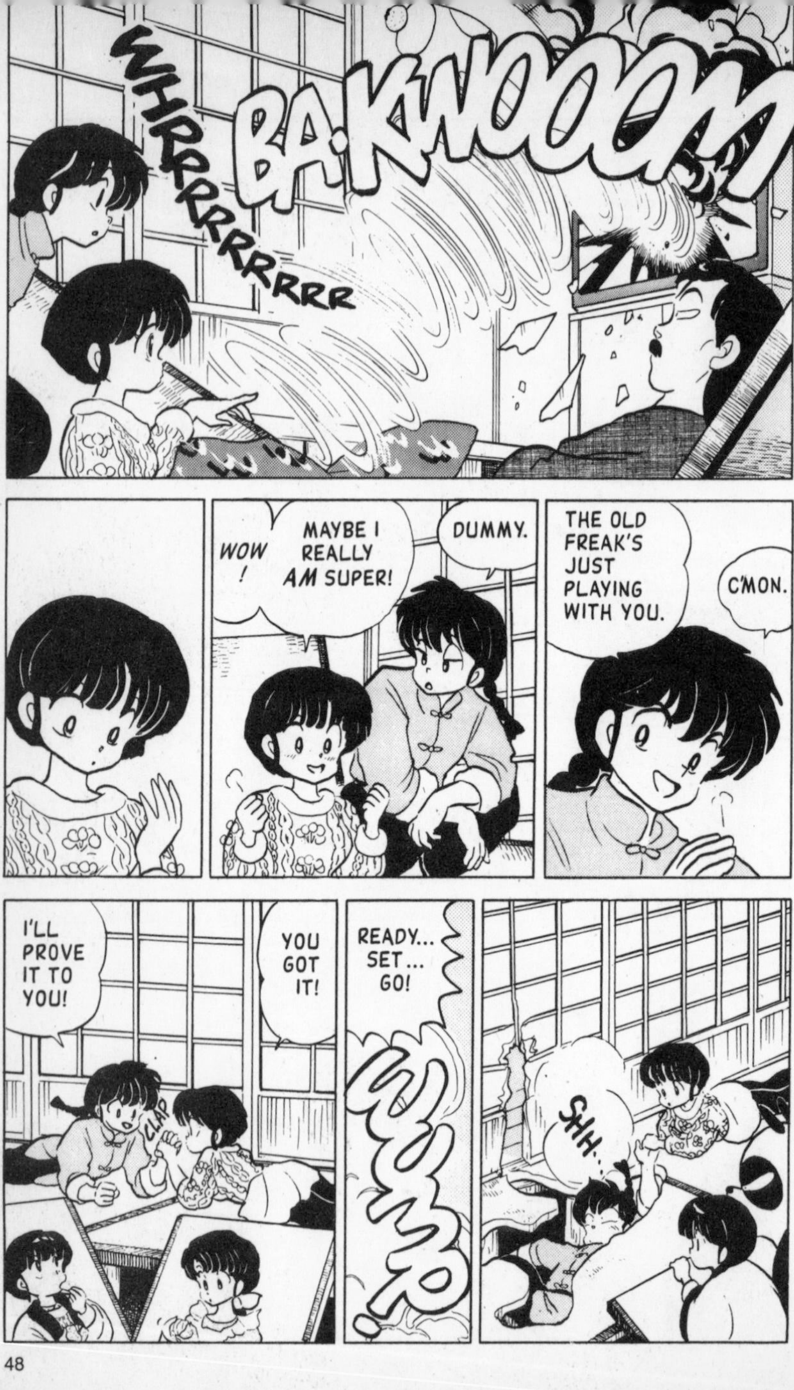
WHIRRRRRRRRRR
BA-KWOOOM
WOW!
MAYBE I REALLY AM SUPER!
DUMMY.
THE OLD FREAK'S JUST PLAYING WITH YOU.
C'MON.
I'LL PROVE IT TO YOU!
CLAP
YOU GOT IT!
READY... SET... GO!
WUMP!
SHH...

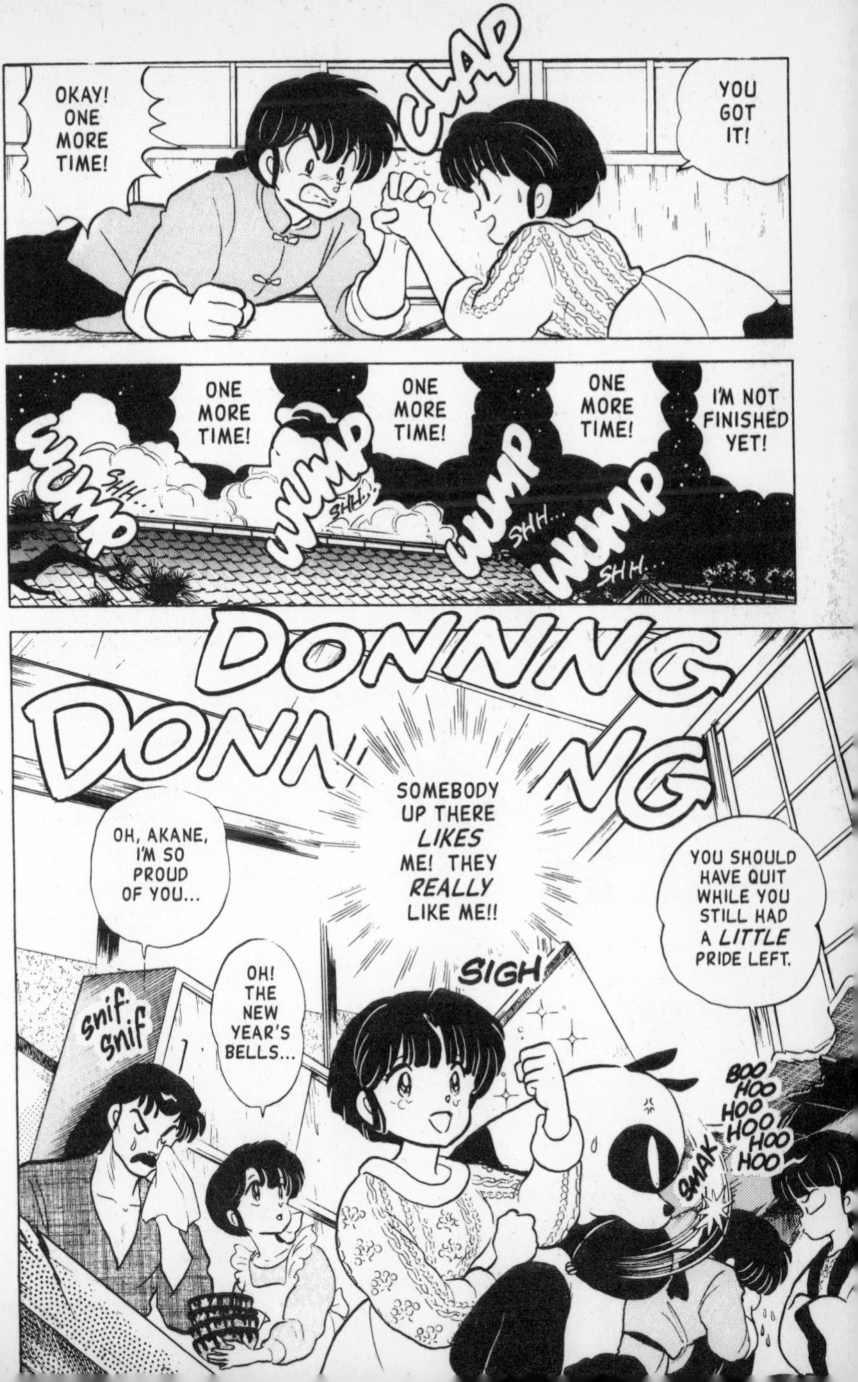
OKAY! ONE MORE TIME!
CLAP
YOU GOT IT!
WUMP
SHH...
ONE MORE TIME!
WUMP
SHH...
ONE MORE TIME!
WUMP
SHH...
ONE MORE TIME!
WUMP
SHH...
I'M NOT FINISHED YET!
DONNNG
DONNNG
OH, AKANE, I'M SO PROUD OF YOU...
SOMEBODY UP THERE *LIKES* ME! THEY *REALLY* LIKE ME!!
YOU SHOULD HAVE QUIT WHILE YOU STILL HAD A *LITTLE* PRIDE LEFT.
snif snif
OH! THE NEW YEAR'S BELLS...
SIGH
SMAK
BOO HOO HOO HOO HOO HOO HOO

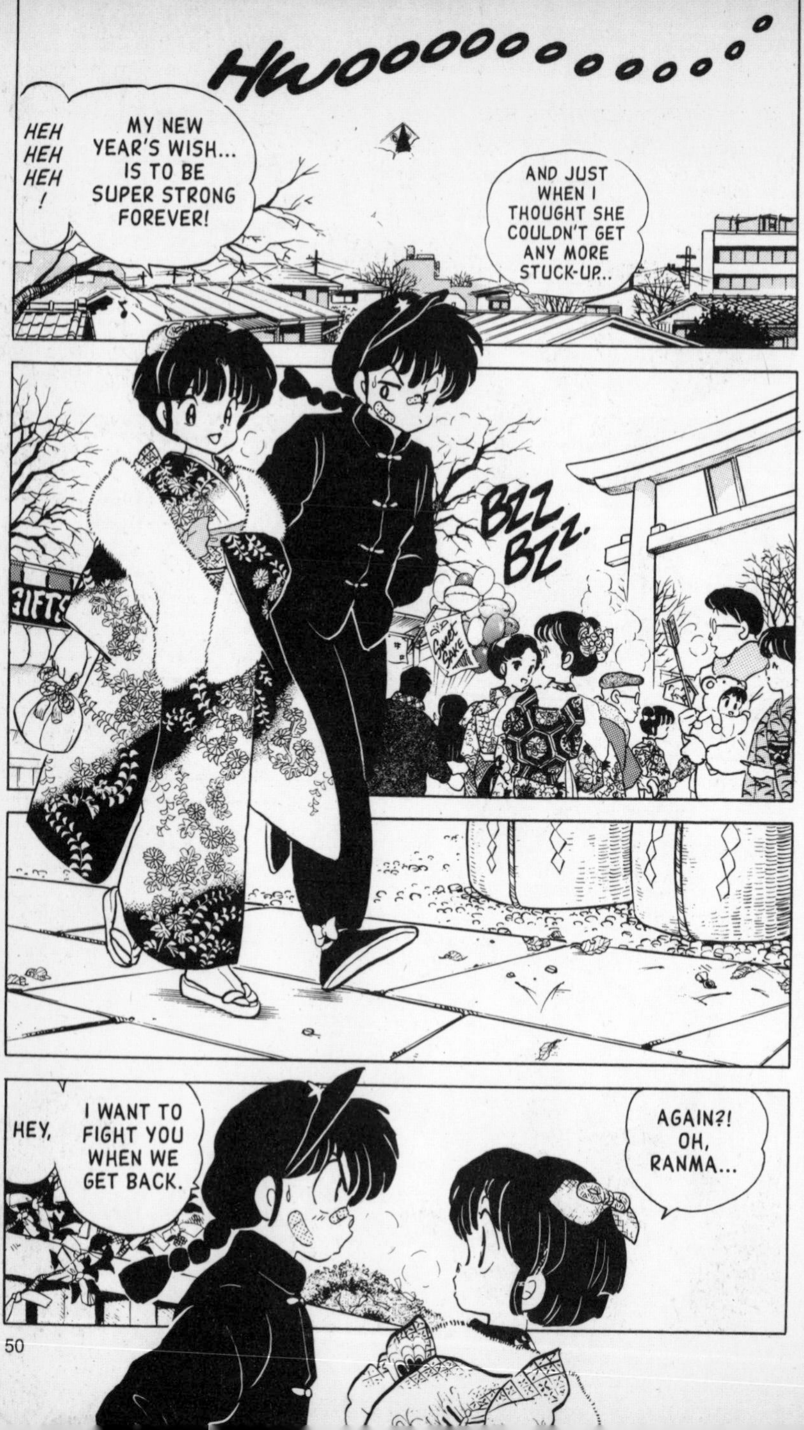
HWOOOOOOOOOOOOOO
HEH HEH HEH!
MY NEW YEAR'S WISH... IS TO BE SUPER STRONG FOREVER!
AND JUST WHEN I THOUGHT SHE COULDN'T GET ANY MORE STUCK-UP..
GIFTS
Sweet SAKE
BZZ BZZ.
HEY,
I WANT TO FIGHT YOU WHEN WE GET BACK.
AGAIN?! OH, RANMA...

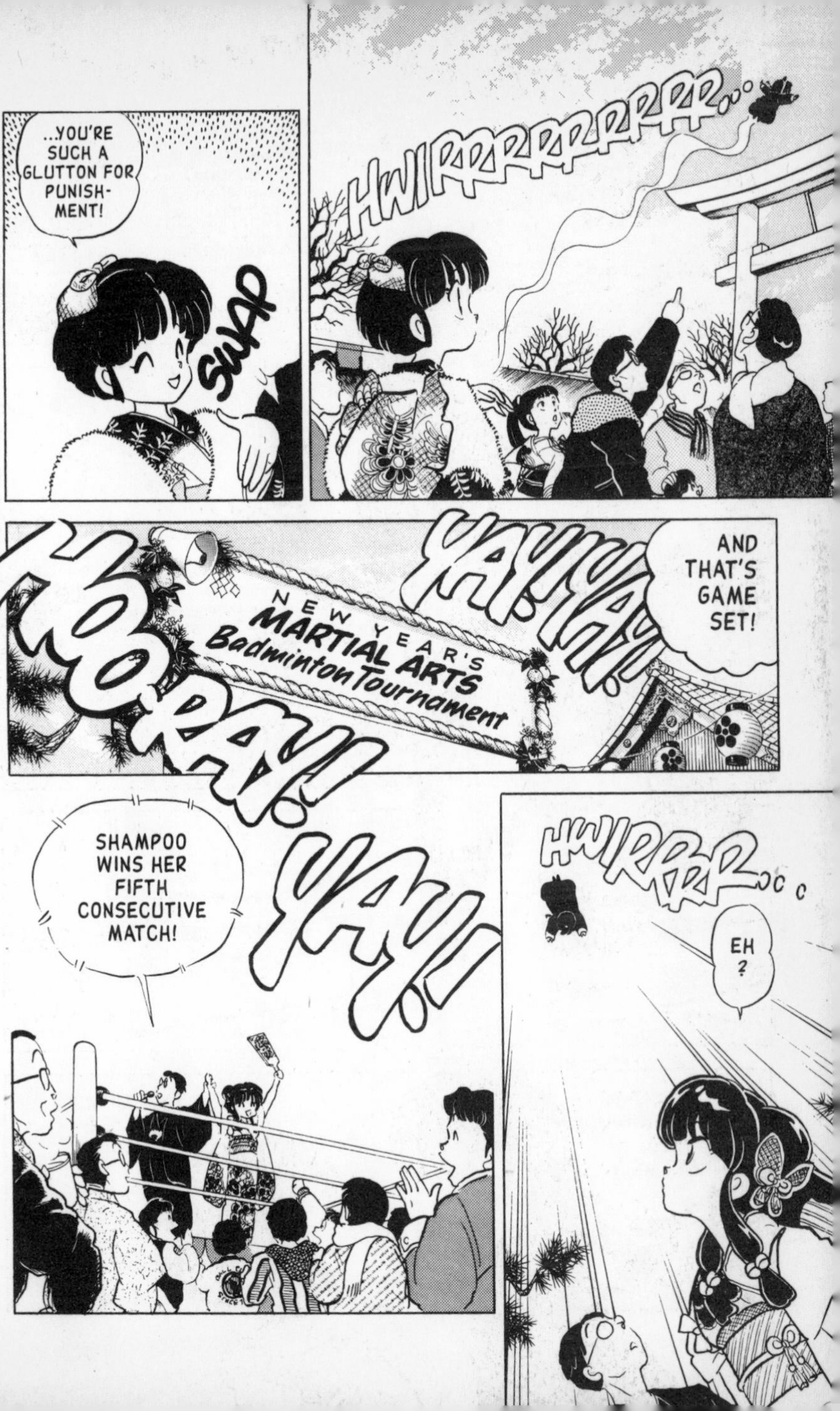
...YOU'RE SUCH A GLUTTON FOR PUNISH-MENT!
SWAP
HWIRRRRRRRRRR...
YAY! YAY!
HOORAY!
NEW YEAR'S MARTIAL ARTS Badminton Tournament
AND THAT'S GAME SET!
SHAMPOO WINS HER FIFTH CONSECUTIVE MATCH!
YAY!
HWIRRRR...
EH?

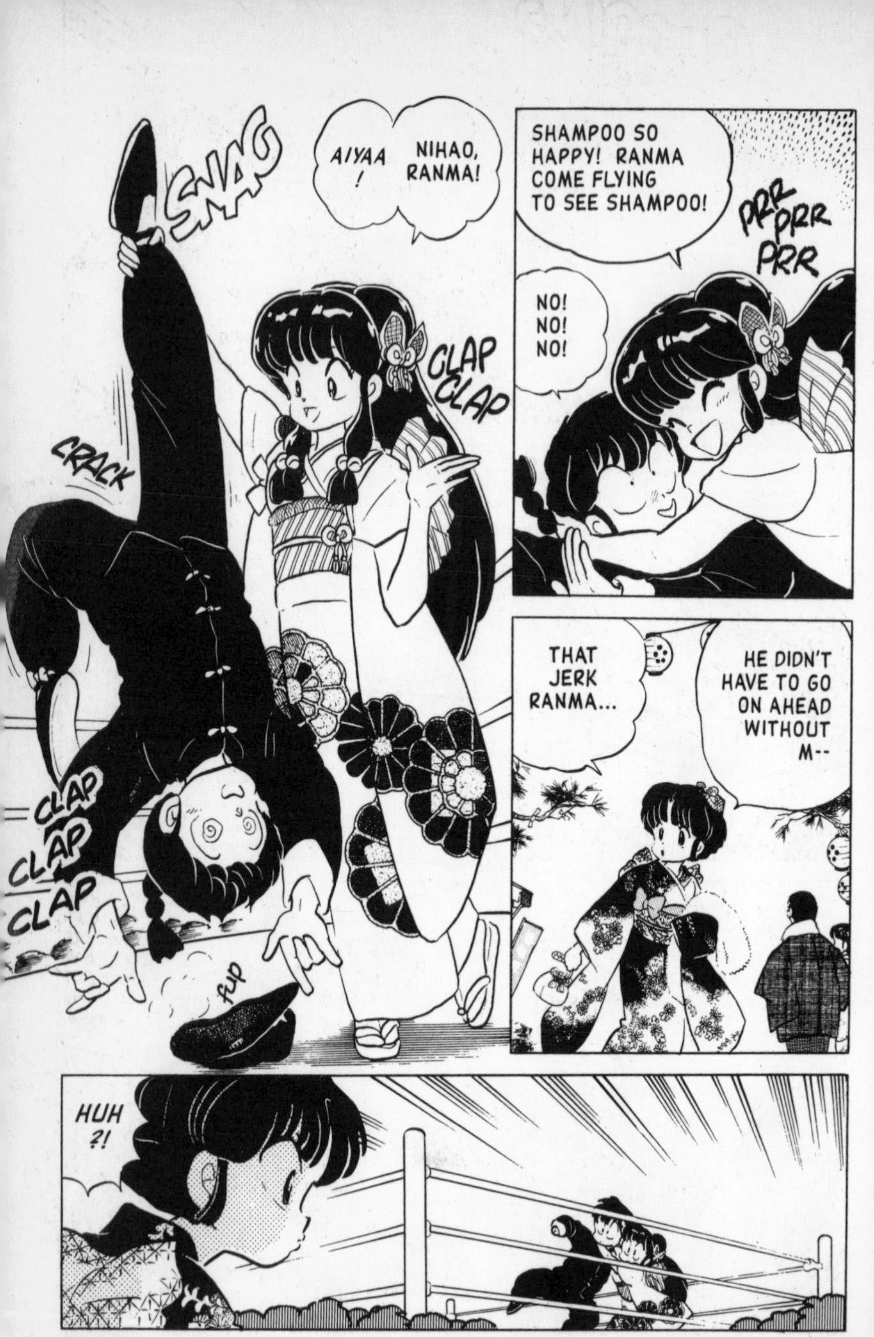
SNAG
AIYAA!
NIHAO, RANMA!
CLAP CLAP
CRACK
CLAP CLAP CLAP
FUP
SHAMPOO SO HAPPY! RANMA COME FLYING TO SEE SHAMPOO!
PRR PRR PRR
NO! NO! NO!
THAT JERK RANMA...
HE DIDN'T HAVE TO GO ON AHEAD WITHOUT M--
HUH ?!

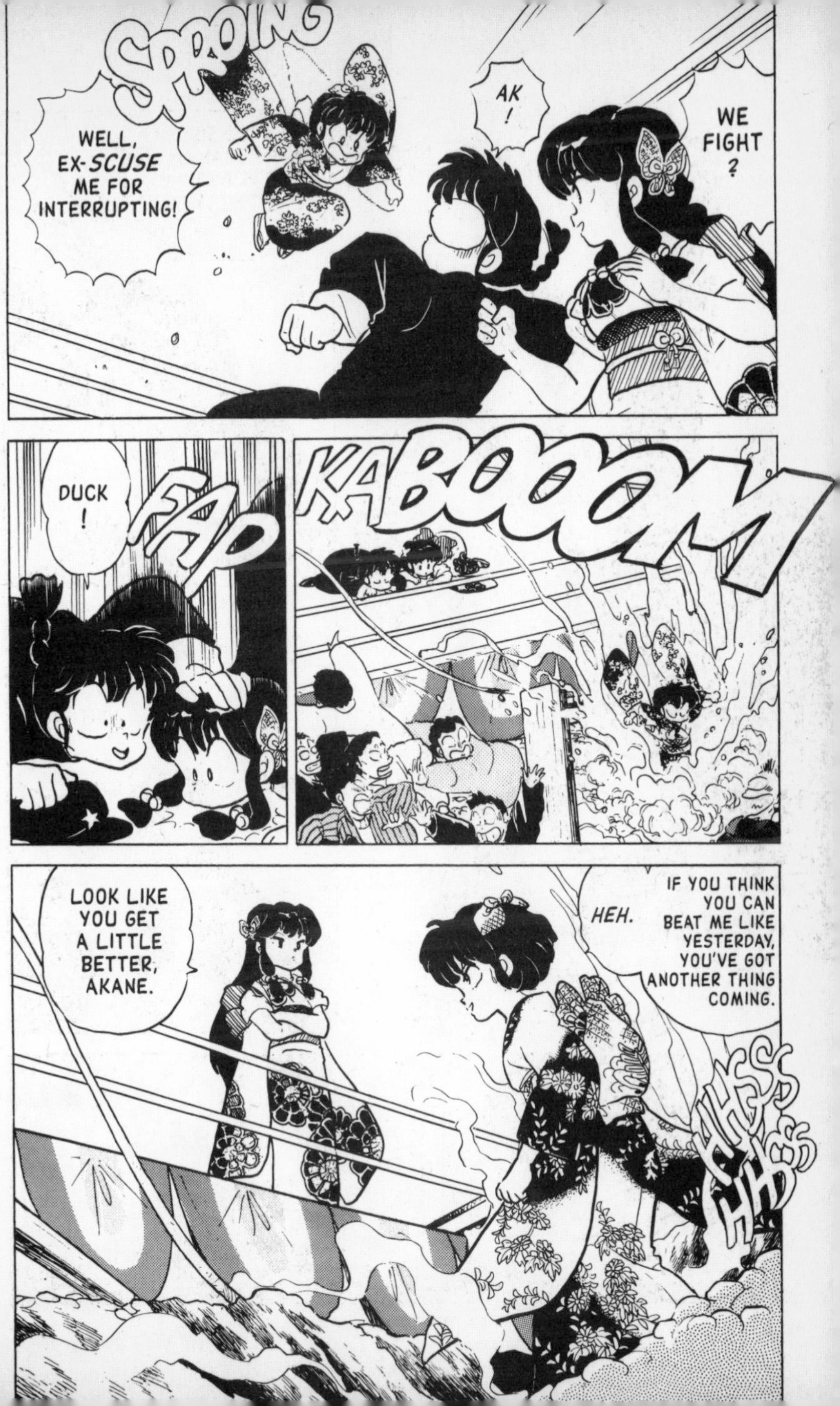
SPROING
WELL, EX-SCUSE ME FOR INTERRUPTING!
AK!
WE FIGHT?
DUCK!
FAP
KABOOOM
LOOK LIKE YOU GET A LITTLE BETTER, AKANE.
HEH.
IF YOU THINK YOU CAN BEAT ME LIKE YESTERDAY, YOU'VE GOT ANOTHER THING COMING.
HSSS
HSSS
HH

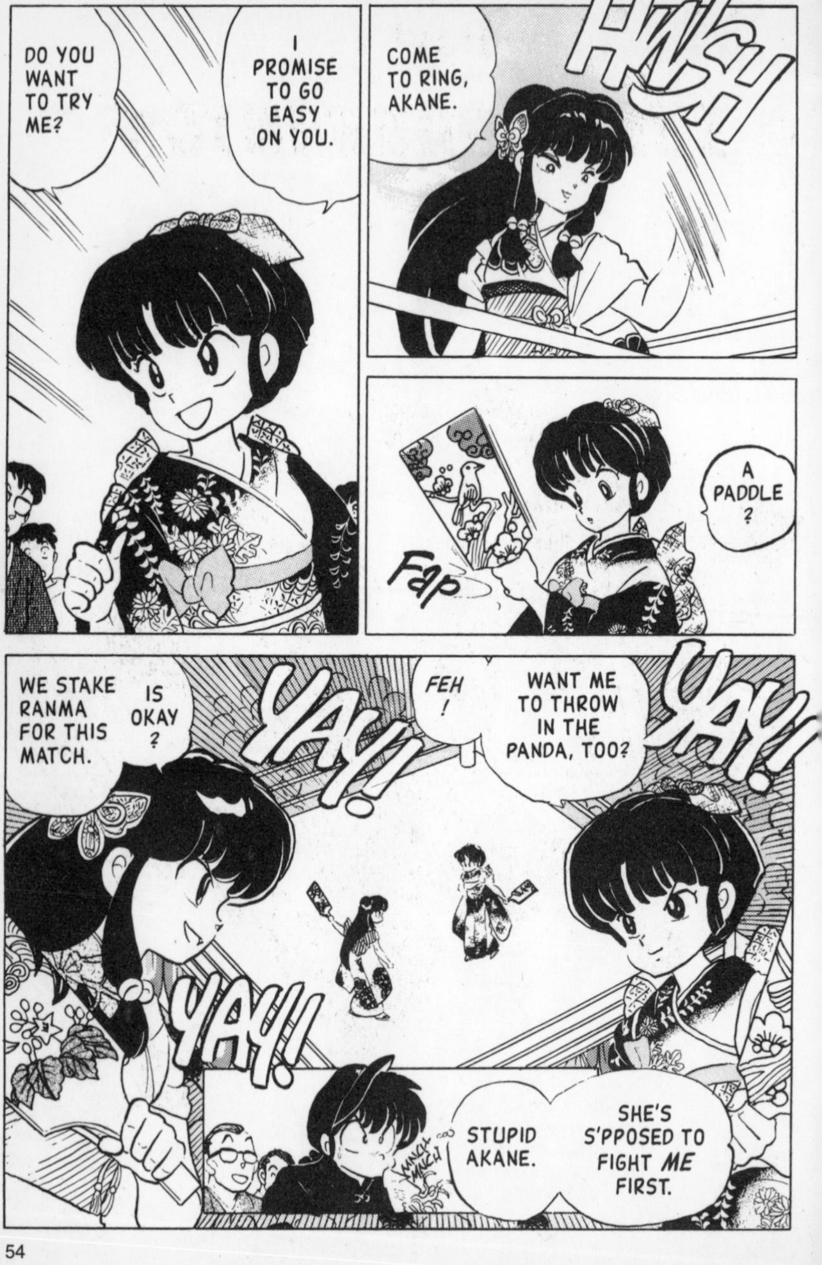

DO YOU WANT TO TRY ME?
I PROMISE TO GO EASY ON YOU.
COME TO RING, AKANE.
HWSH
Fap
A PADDLE?
WE STAKE RANMA FOR THIS MATCH.
IS OKAY?
YAY!
FEH!
WANT ME TO THROW IN THE PANDA, TOO?
YAY!
YAY!
MUNCH MUNCH
STUPID AKANE.
SHE'S S'PPOSED TO FIGHT *ME* FIRST.

Part 4
SUPER BADMINTON

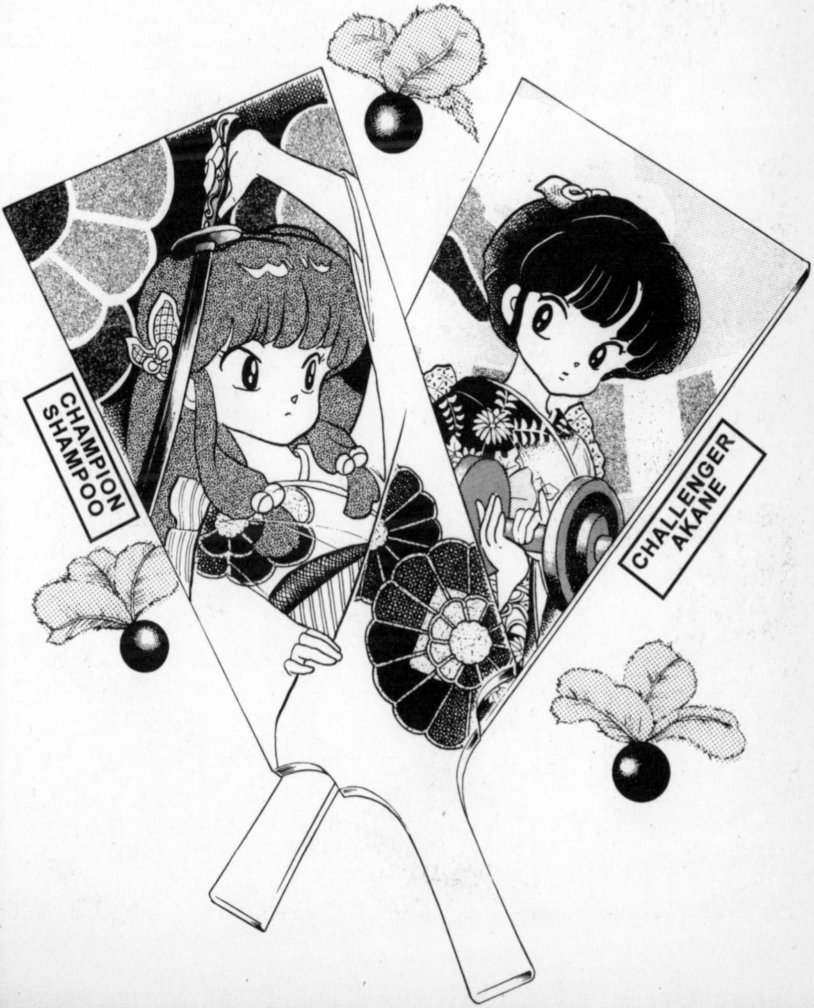
CHAMPION SHAMPOO
CHALLENGER AKANE

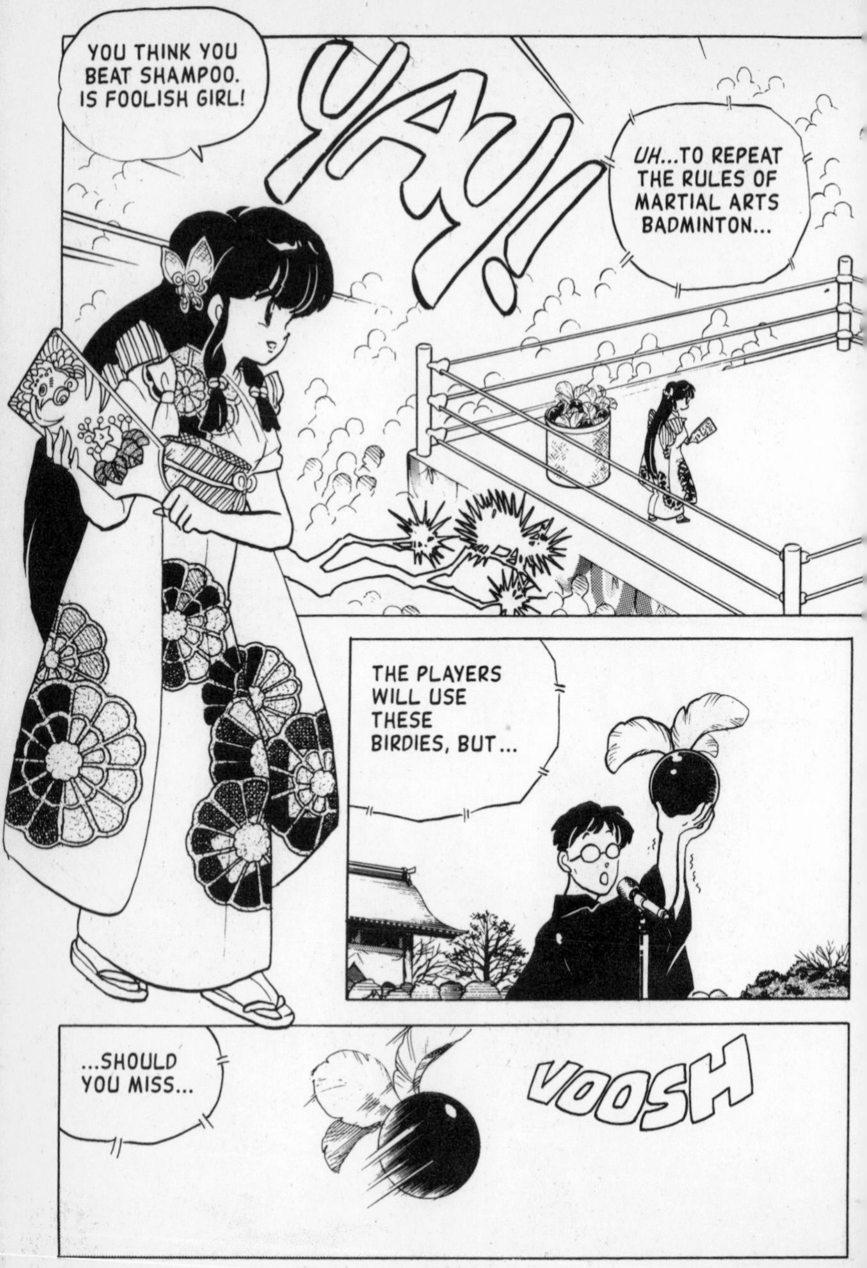
YOU THINK YOU BEAT SHAMPOO. IS FOOLISH GIRL!
YAY!!
UH...TO REPEAT THE RULES OF MARTIAL ARTS BADMINTON...
THE PLAYERS WILL USE THESE BIRDIES, BUT...
...SHOULD YOU MISS...
VOOSH

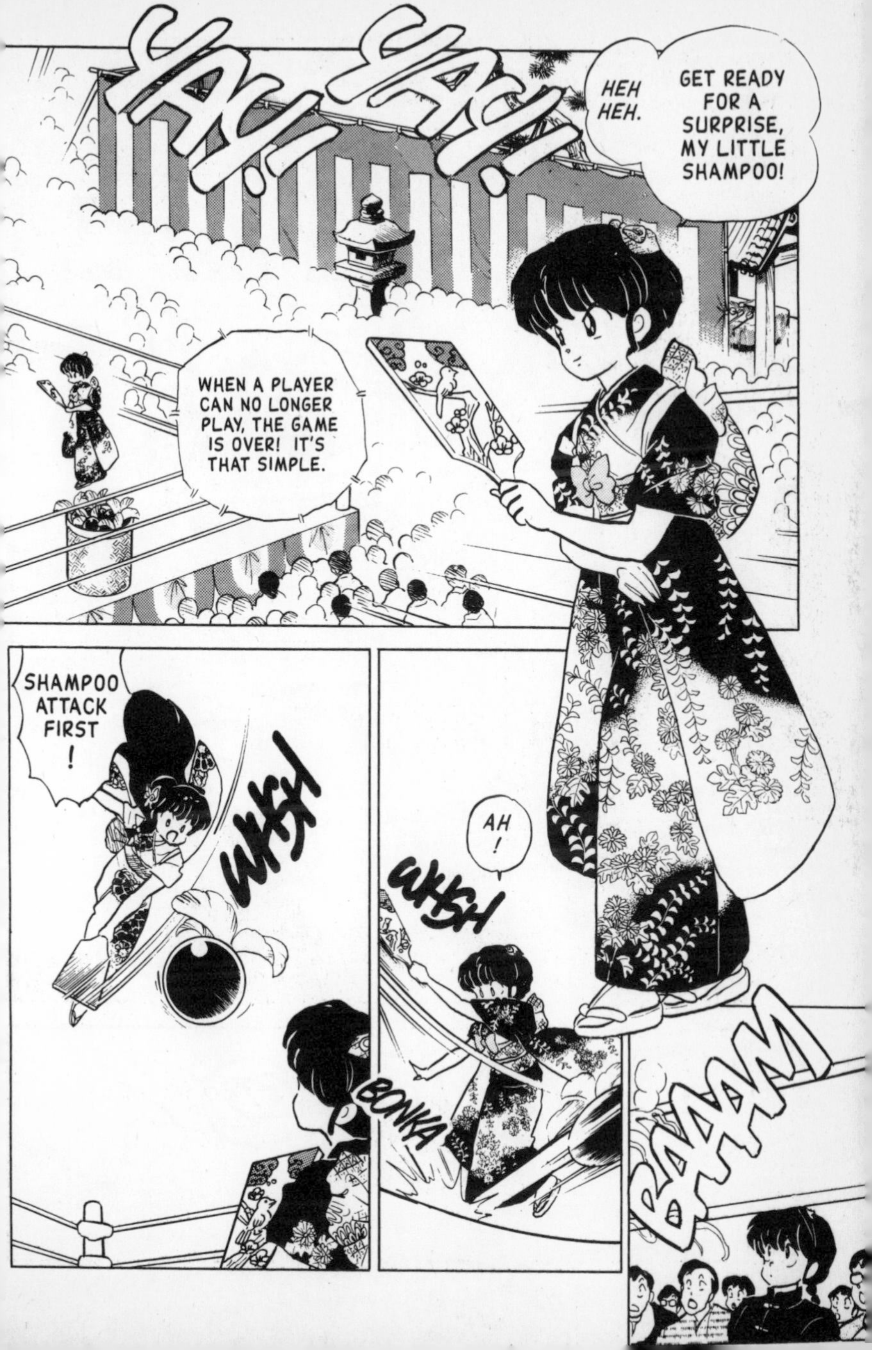
YAY! YAY!
HEH HEH.
GET READY FOR A SURPRISE, MY LITTLE SHAMPOO!
WHEN A PLAYER CAN NO LONGER PLAY, THE GAME IS OVER! IT'S THAT SIMPLE.
SHAMPOO ATTACK FIRST !
WHSH
AH !
WHSH
BONKA
BAAAM

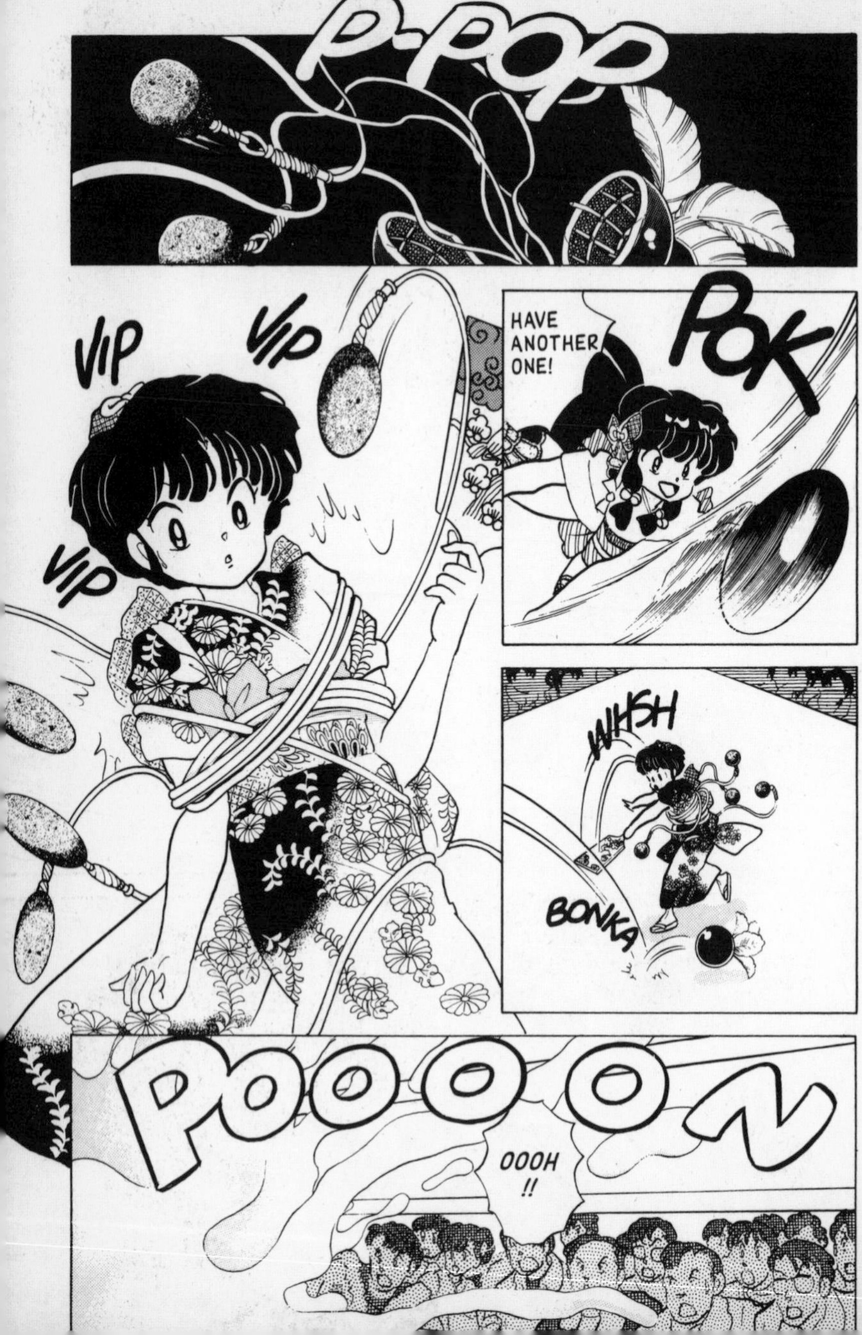
P-POP
VIP
VIP
VIP
HAVE ANOTHER ONE!
POK
WHSH
BONKA
POOOON
OOOH !!

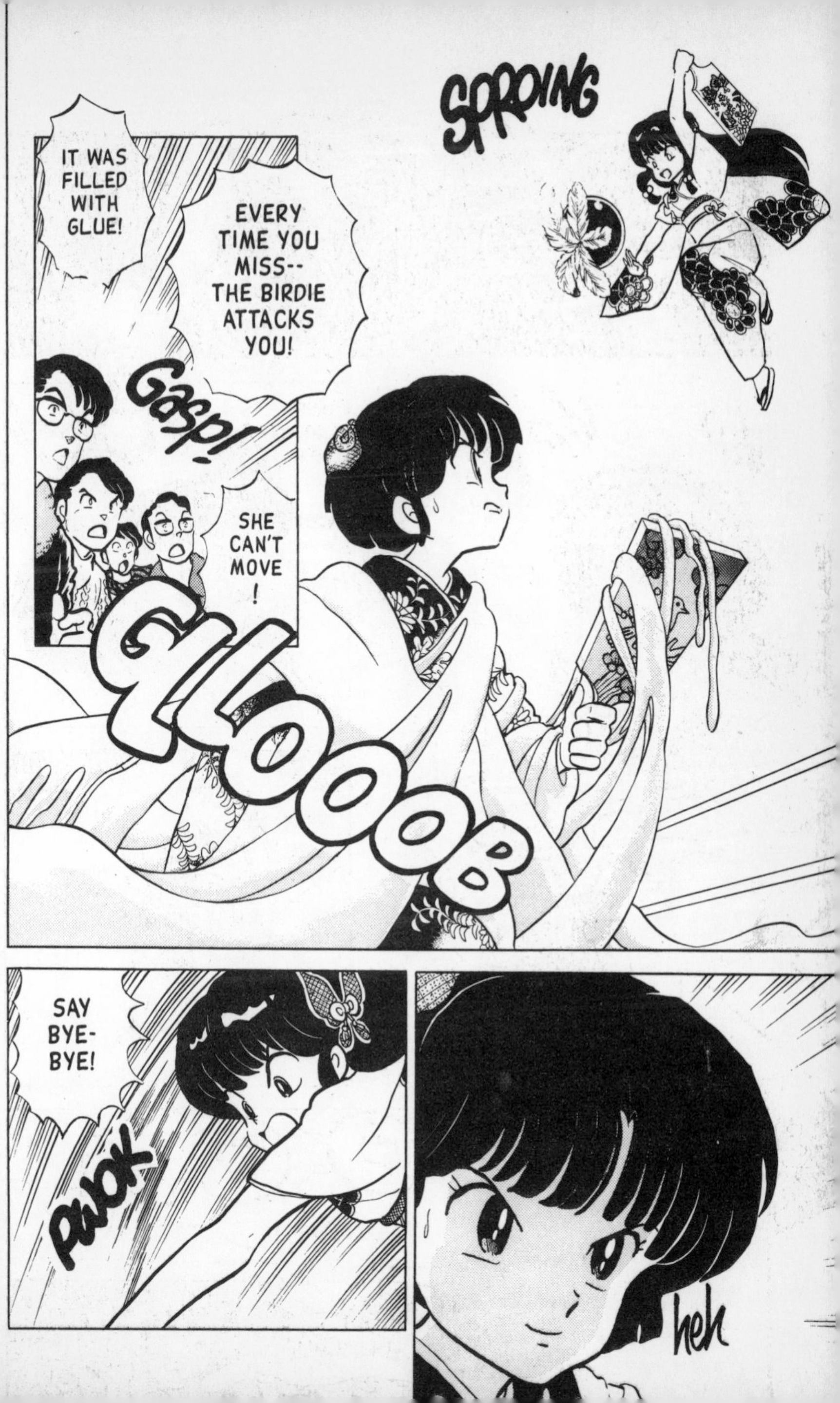
IT WAS FILLED WITH GLUE!
SPROING
EVERY TIME YOU MISS-- THE BIRDIE ATTACKS YOU!
GASP!
SHE CAN'T MOVE!
GLOOOOB
SAY BYE-BYE!
PWOK
heh

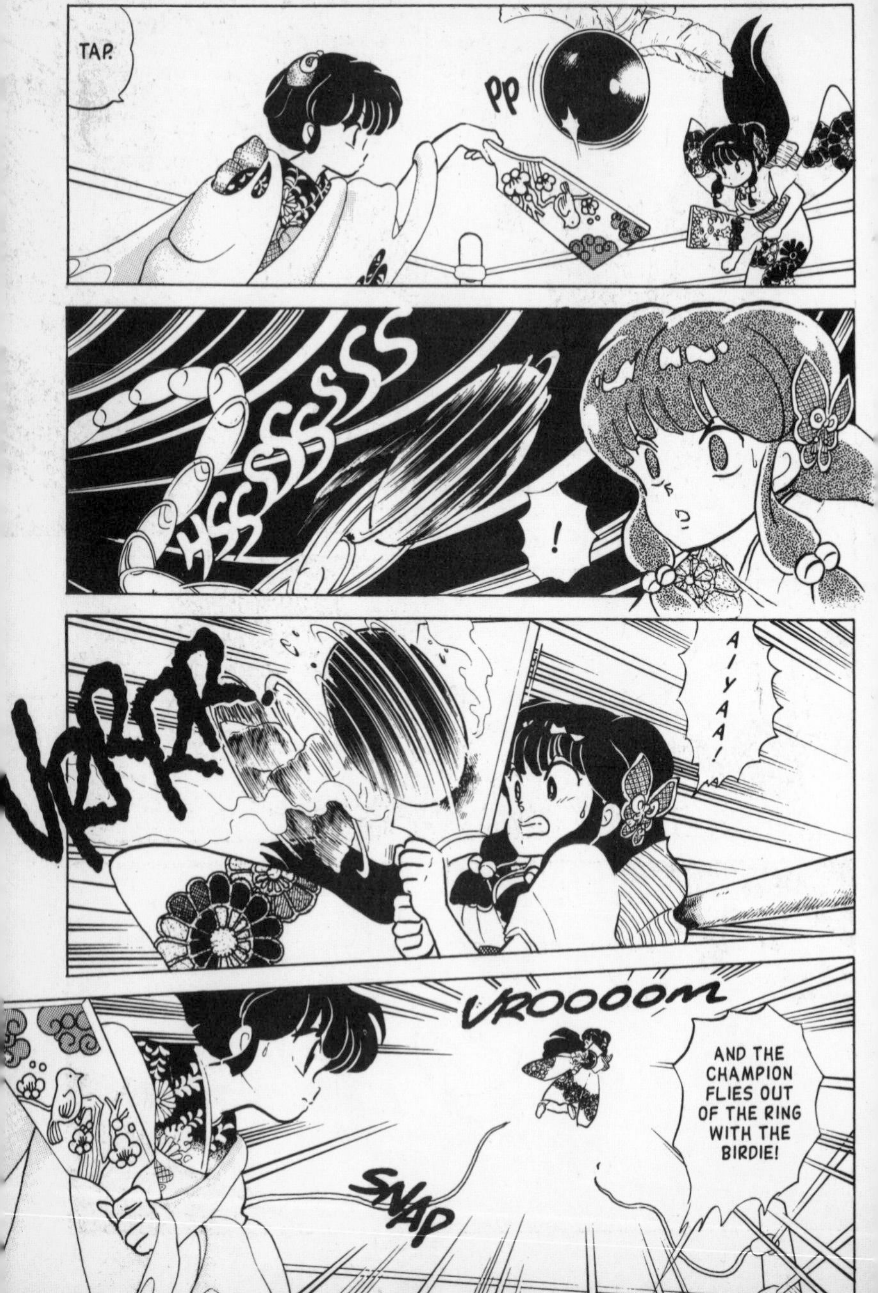
TAP.
PP
HSSSSSSS
!
VRRR
AIYAA!
VROOOOM
AND THE CHAMPION FLIES OUT OF THE RING WITH THE BIRDIE!
SNAP

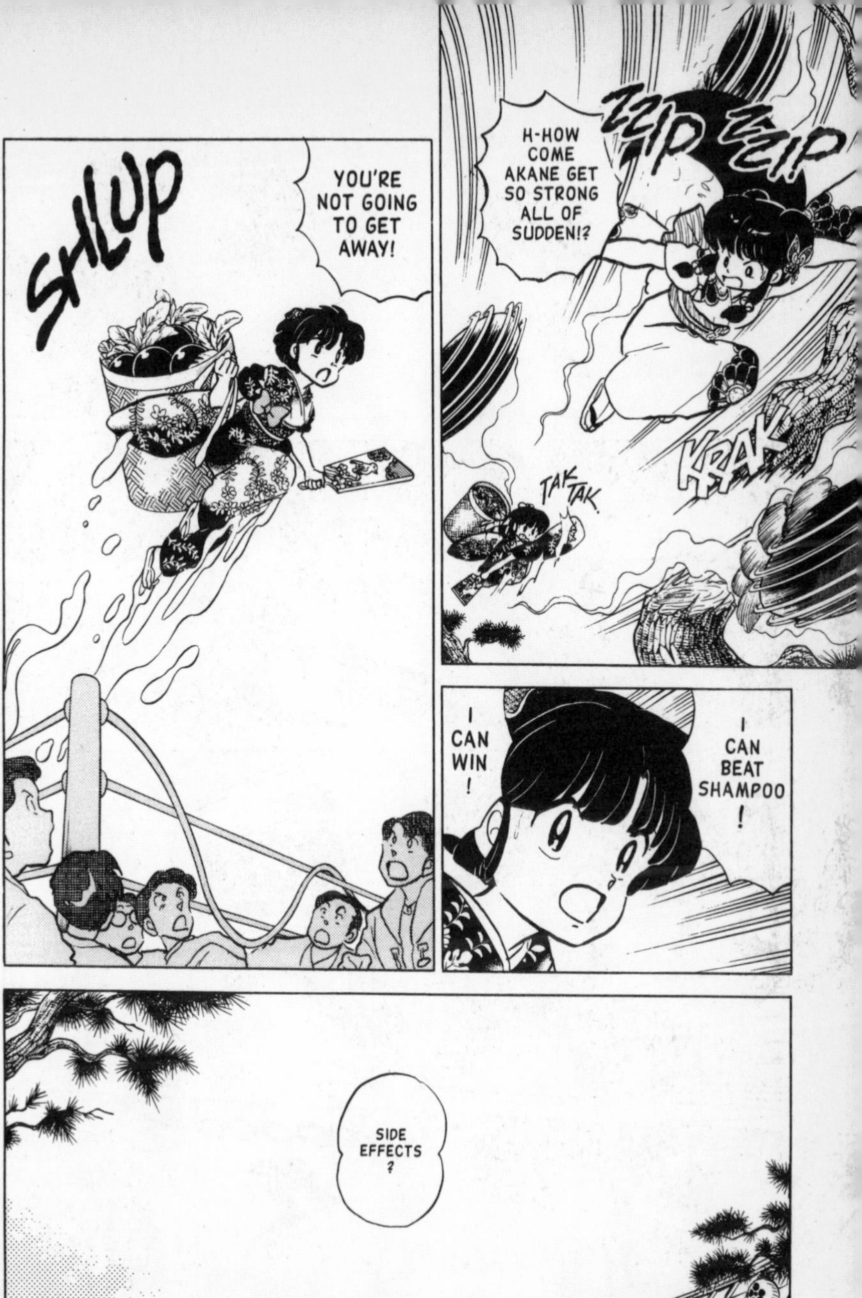
SHLUP
YOU'RE NOT GOING TO GET AWAY!
H-HOW COME AKANE GET SO STRONG ALL OF SUDDEN!?
ZZIP ZZIP
KRAK
TAK TAK
I CAN WIN!
I CAN BEAT SHAMPOO!
SIDE EFFECTS?

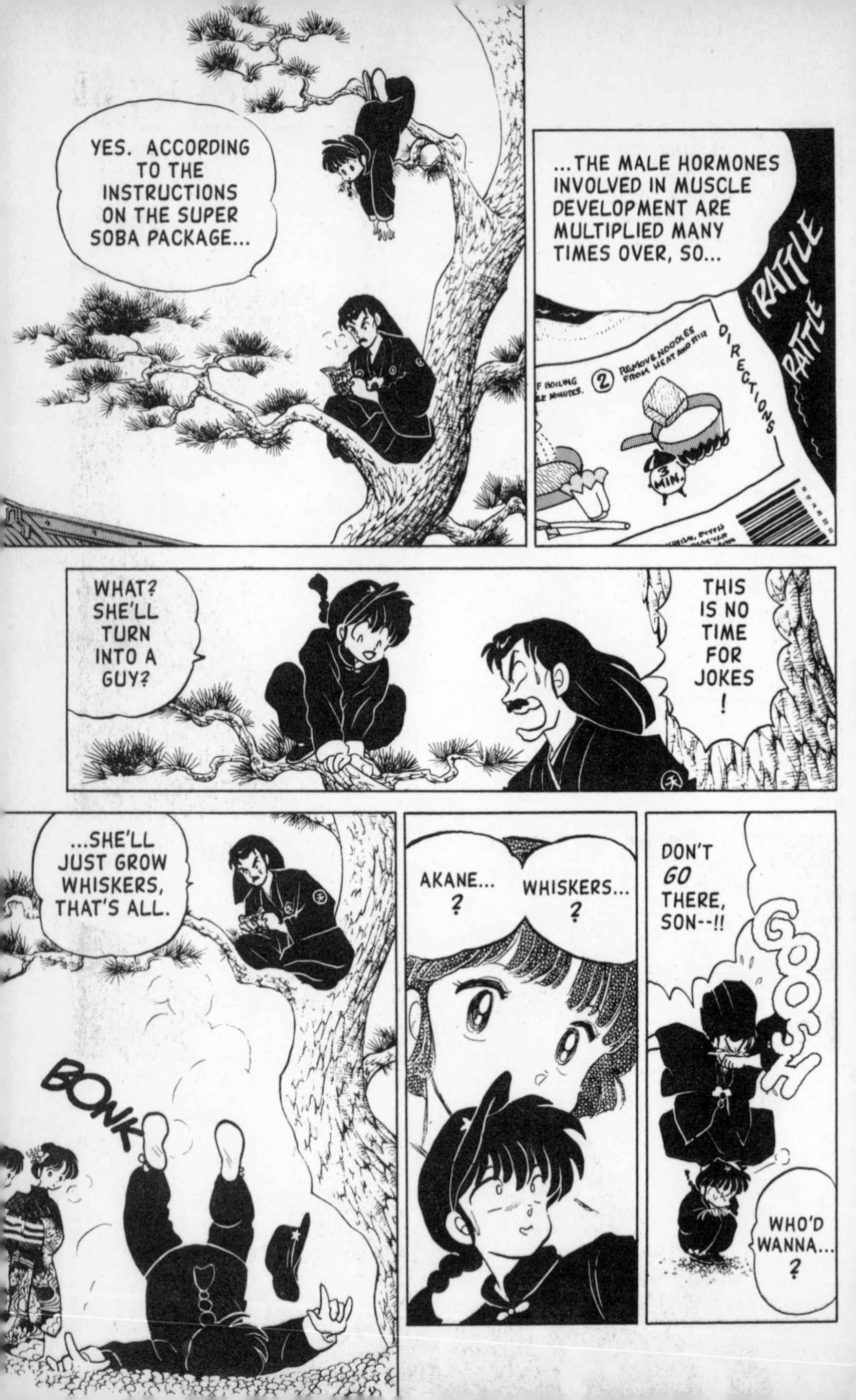
YES. ACCORDING TO THE INSTRUCTIONS ON THE SUPER SOBA PACKAGE...
...THE MALE HORMONES INVOLVED IN MUSCLE DEVELOPMENT ARE MULTIPLIED MANY TIMES OVER, SO...
RATTLE RATTLE
DIRECTIONS
REMOVE NOODLES FROM HEAT AND STIR
3 MIN.
WHAT? SHE'LL TURN INTO A GUY?
THIS IS NO TIME FOR JOKES!
...SHE'LL JUST GROW WHISKERS, THAT'S ALL.
BONK
AKANE...?
WHISKERS...?
DON'T *GO* THERE, SON--!!
GOOSH
WHO'D WANNA...?

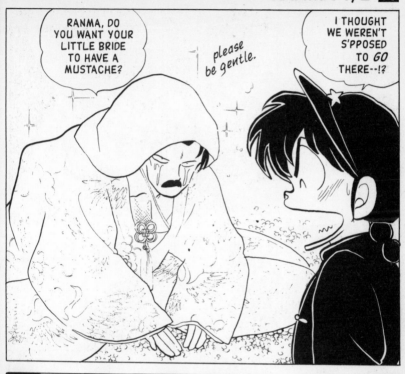

RANMA, DO YOU WANT YOUR LITTLE BRIDE TO HAVE A MUSTACHE?

please be gentle.

I THOUGHT WE WEREN'T S'PPOSED TO *GO* THERE--!?

HERE IN MY HANDS...

...IS THE ANTIDOTE.

PLEASE GET AKANE TO TAKE IT... *SNIF*... IMMEDIATELY!

SOB SOB SOB SOB

PEH. NO PROBLEM.

FLIP

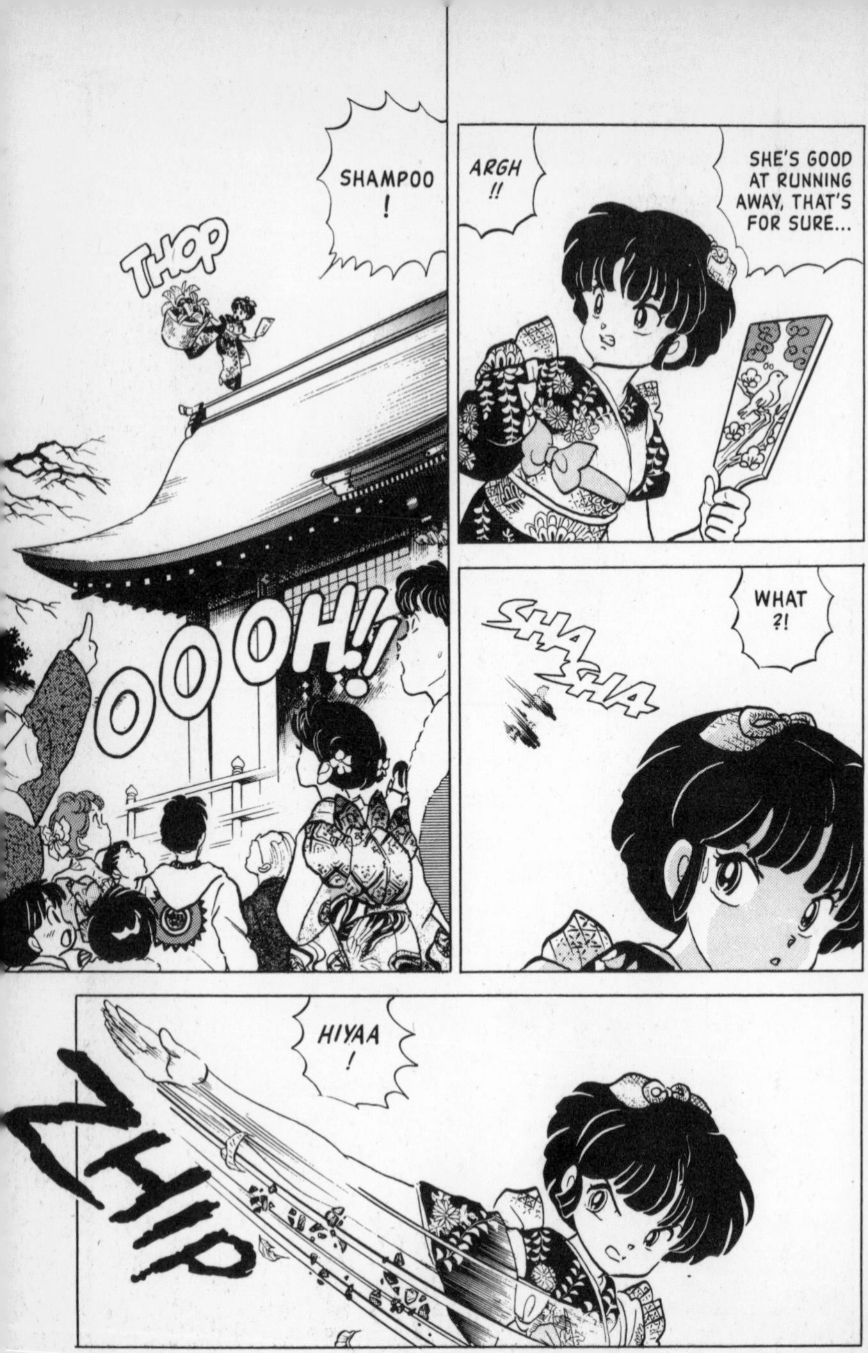
SHAMPOO !
THOP
OOOOH!!
ARGH !!
SHE'S GOOD AT RUNNING AWAY, THAT'S FOR SURE...
SHA SHA
WHAT ?!
HIYAA !
ZHIP

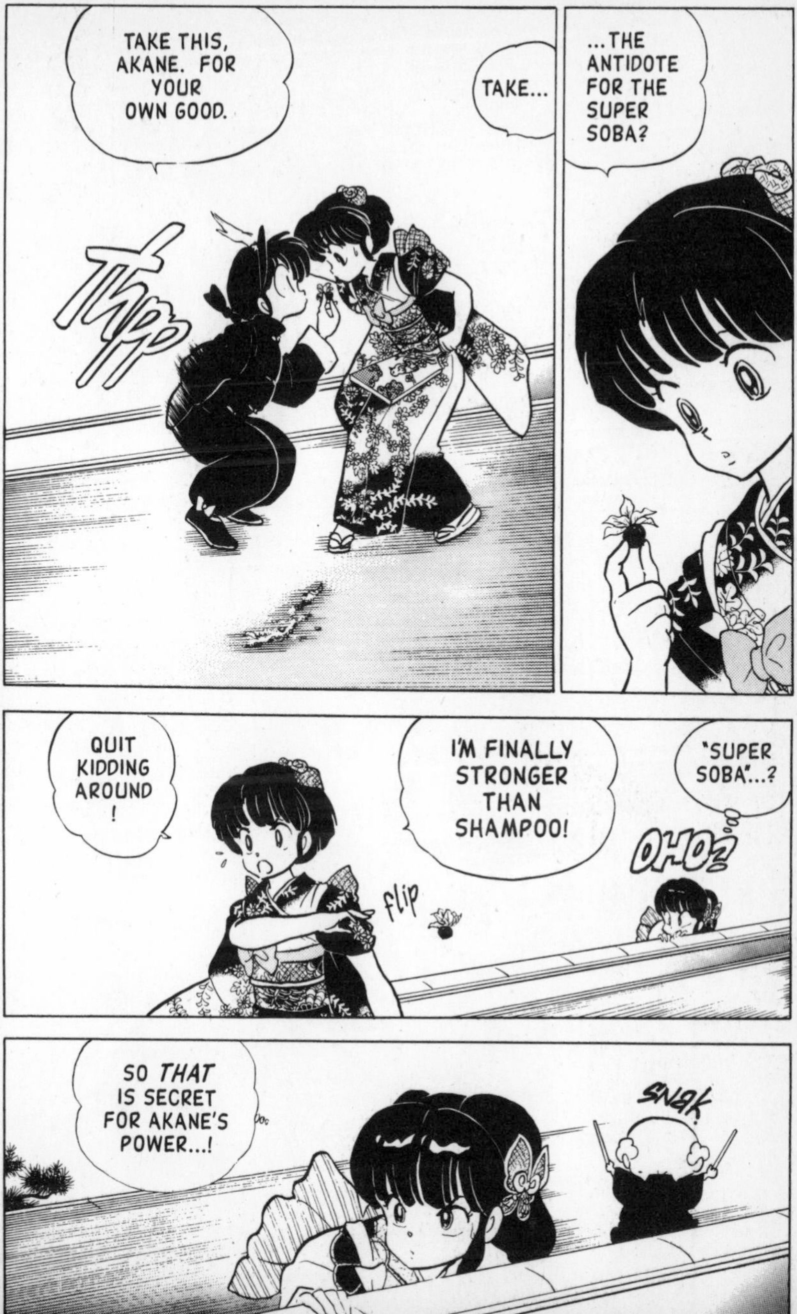
TAKE THIS, AKANE. FOR YOUR OWN GOOD.
THPP
TAKE...
...THE ANTIDOTE FOR THE SUPER SOBA?
QUIT KIDDING AROUND!
I'M FINALLY STRONGER THAN SHAMPOO!
flip
"SUPER SOBA"...?
OHO?
SO *THAT* IS SECRET FOR AKANE'S POWER...!
SNAK

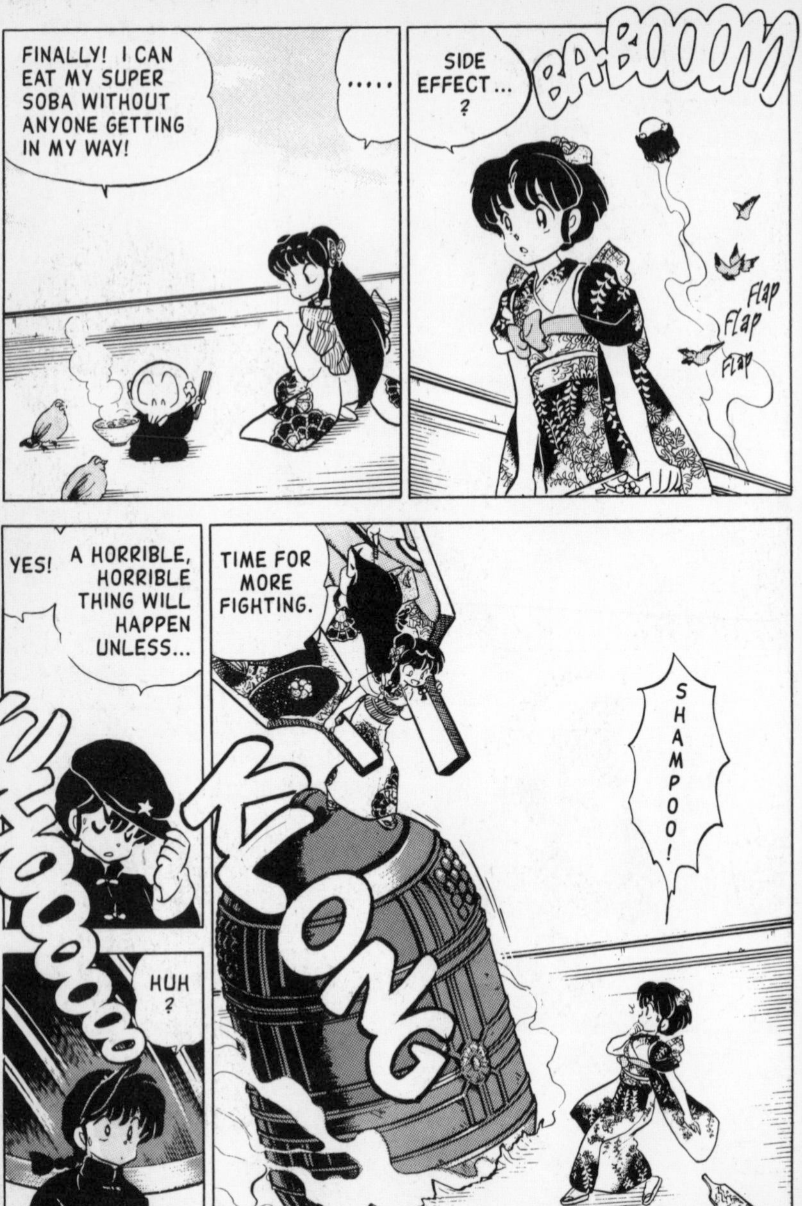
FINALLY! I CAN EAT MY SUPER SOBA WITHOUT ANYONE GETTING IN MY WAY!
.....
SIDE EFFECT... ?
BA-BOOOM
Flap
Flap
Flap
YES!
A HORRIBLE, HORRIBLE THING WILL HAPPEN UNLESS...
WHOOOOOO
HUH ?
TIME FOR MORE FIGHTING.
KLONG
SHAMPOO!

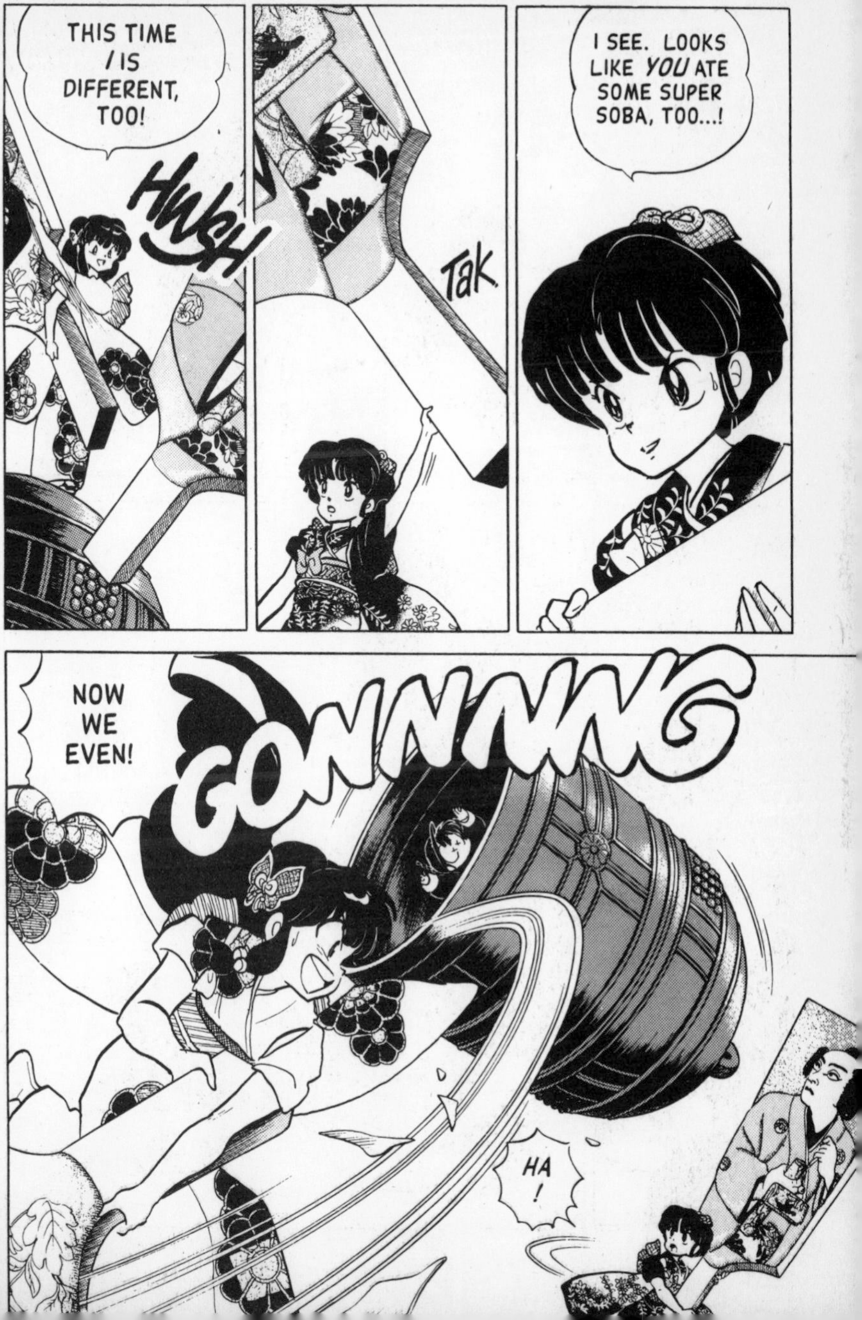
THIS TIME / IS DIFFERENT, TOO!
HWAGH
TAK
I SEE. LOOKS LIKE YOU ATE SOME SUPER SOBA, TOO...!
NOW WE EVEN!
GONNNNG
HA !

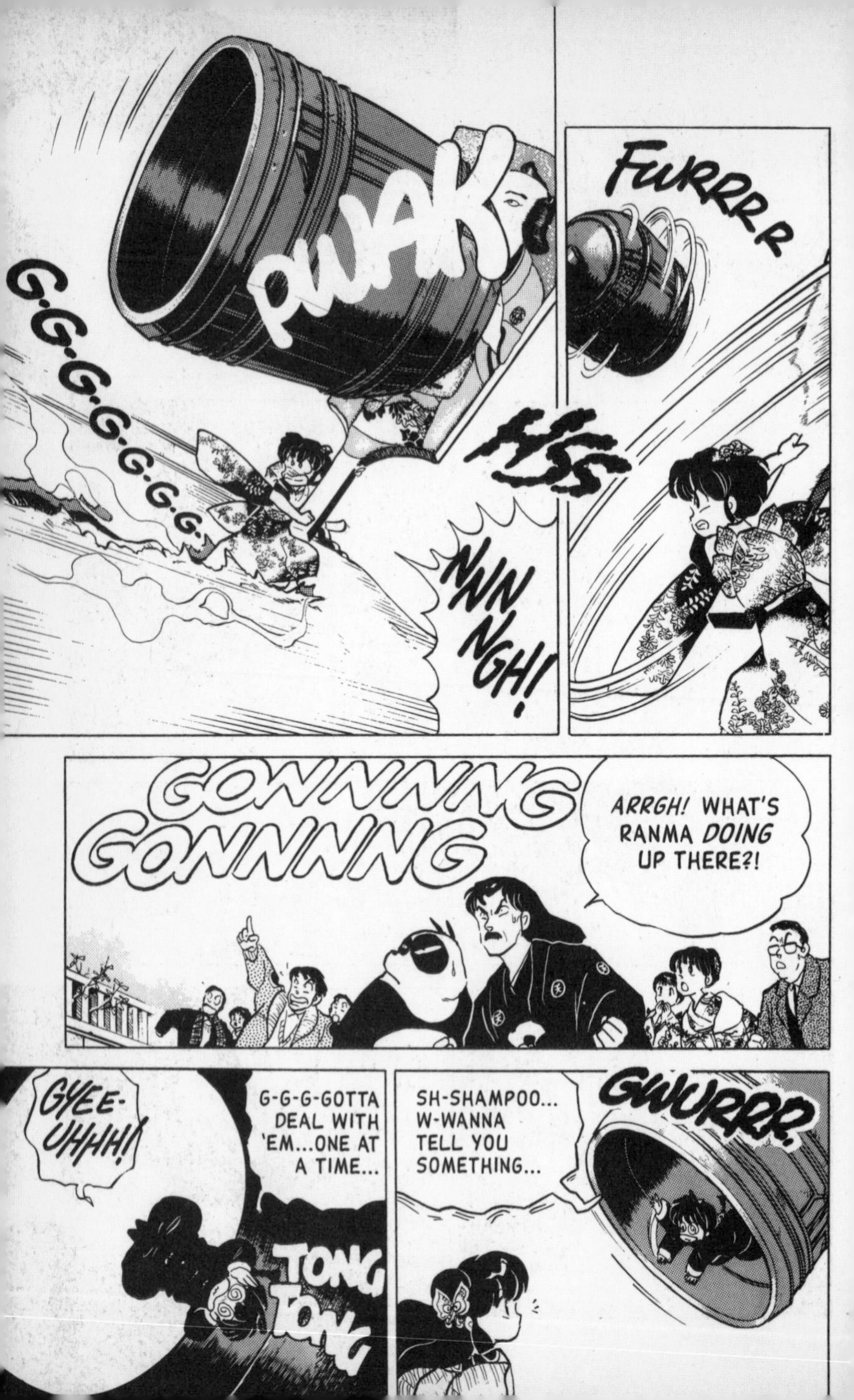
PWAK!
G-G-G-G-G-G-G
HSS
NNN NGH!
FURRRR
GONNNNG
GONNNNG
ARRGH! WHAT'S RANMA *DOING* UP THERE?!
GYEE-UHHH!
G-G-G-GOTTA DEAL WITH 'EM...ONE AT A TIME...
TONG
TONG
SH-SHAMPOO... W-WANNA TELL YOU SOMETHING...
GWURRR

WHAT IS IT, RANMA?

KWONNNG

TEE HEE!

W-WELL... YOU SEE, I...

...HAVE THE ANTIDOTE!

pip

ANTIDOTE?

Gulp

NNNNGH!

SHAMPOO LIFT THIS BEFORE! WHAT HAPPEN?

ONE DOWN.

AND NOW FOR AKANE...

AK!

I CAN'T GET OUT!

NNNGH!

WE ALL ALONE IN THIS DARK.

GOOF

PRRR RRR

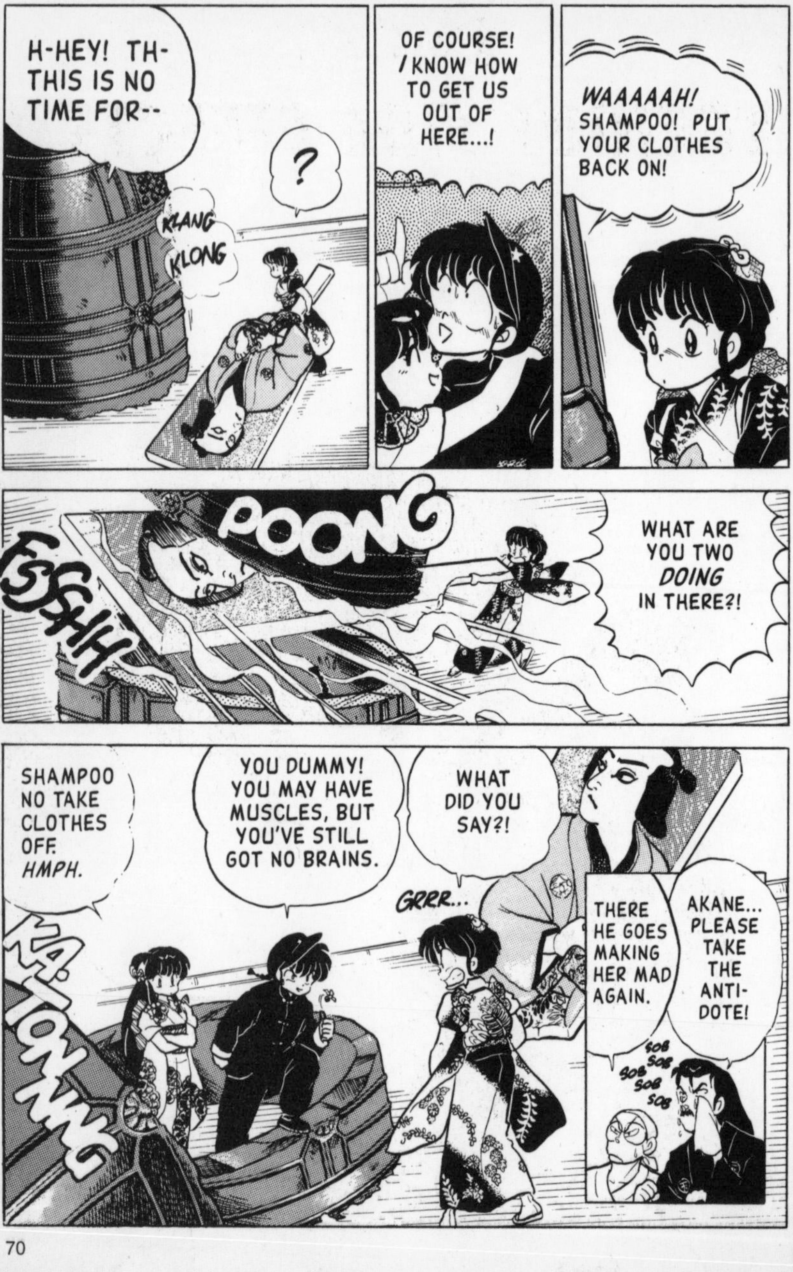
H-HEY! TH-THIS IS NO TIME FOR--
KLANG
KLONG
?
OF COURSE! I KNOW HOW TO GET US OUT OF HERE...!
WAAAAAH! SHAMPOO! PUT YOUR CLOTHES BACK ON!
FSSHHH
POONG
WHAT ARE YOU TWO DOING IN THERE?!
SHAMPOO NO TAKE CLOTHES OFF. HMPH.
YOU DUMMY! YOU MAY HAVE MUSCLES, BUT YOU'VE STILL GOT NO BRAINS.
WHAT DID YOU SAY?!
GRRR...
KA-TONNNG
THERE HE GOES MAKING HER MAD AGAIN.
AKANE... PLEASE TAKE THE ANTI-DOTE!
SOB SOB SOB SOB SOB

Part 5

SERIOUS SIDE EFFECTS

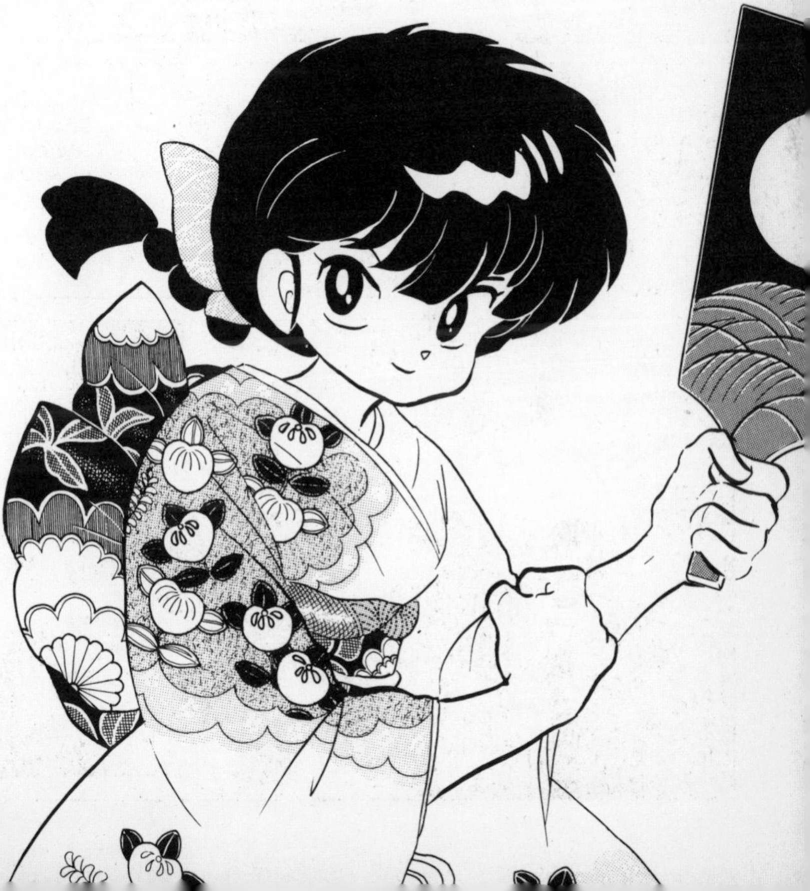

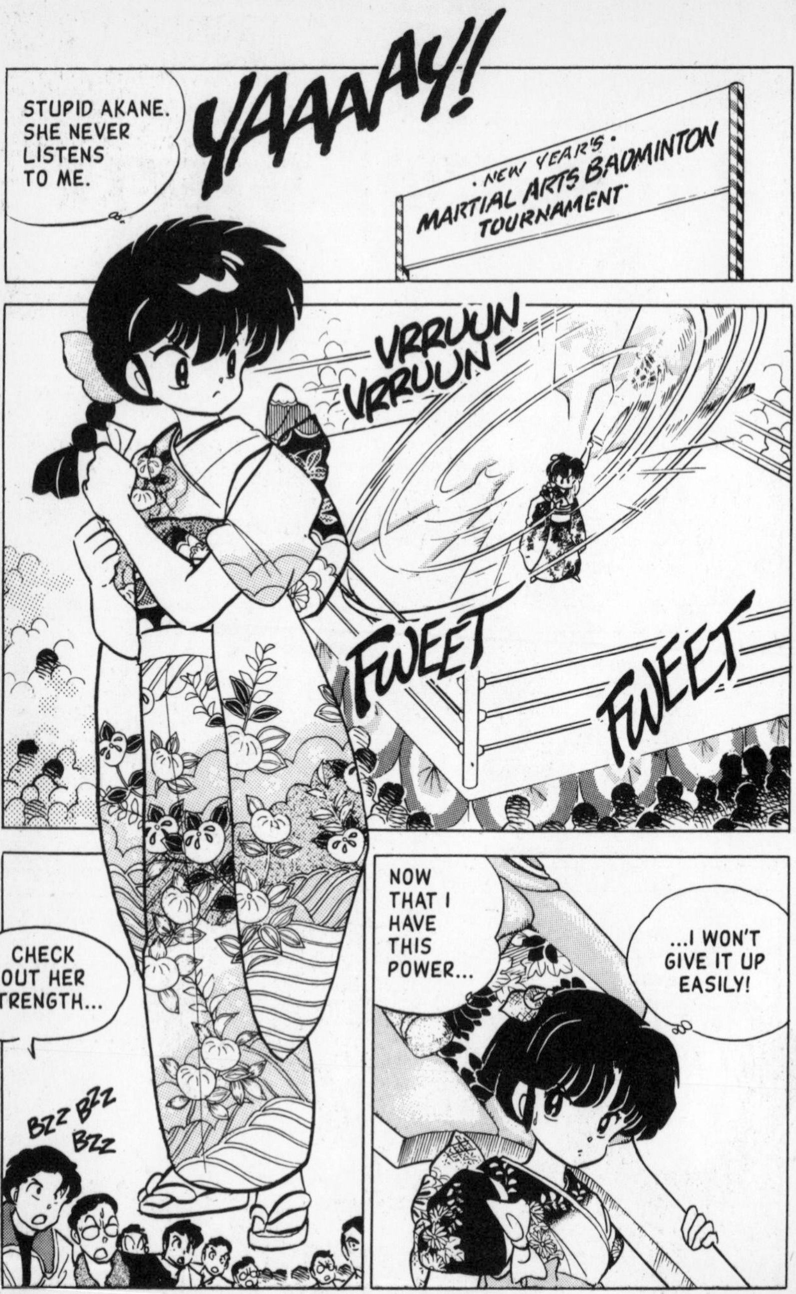

STUPID AKANE. SHE NEVER LISTENS TO ME.
YAAAAY!
·NEW YEAR'S· MARTIAL ARTS BADMINTON TOURNAMENT
VRRUUN VRRUUN
FWEET
FWEET
CHECK OUT HER STRENGTH...
BZZ BZZ BZZ
NOW THAT I HAVE THIS POWER...
...I WON'T GIVE IT UP EASILY!

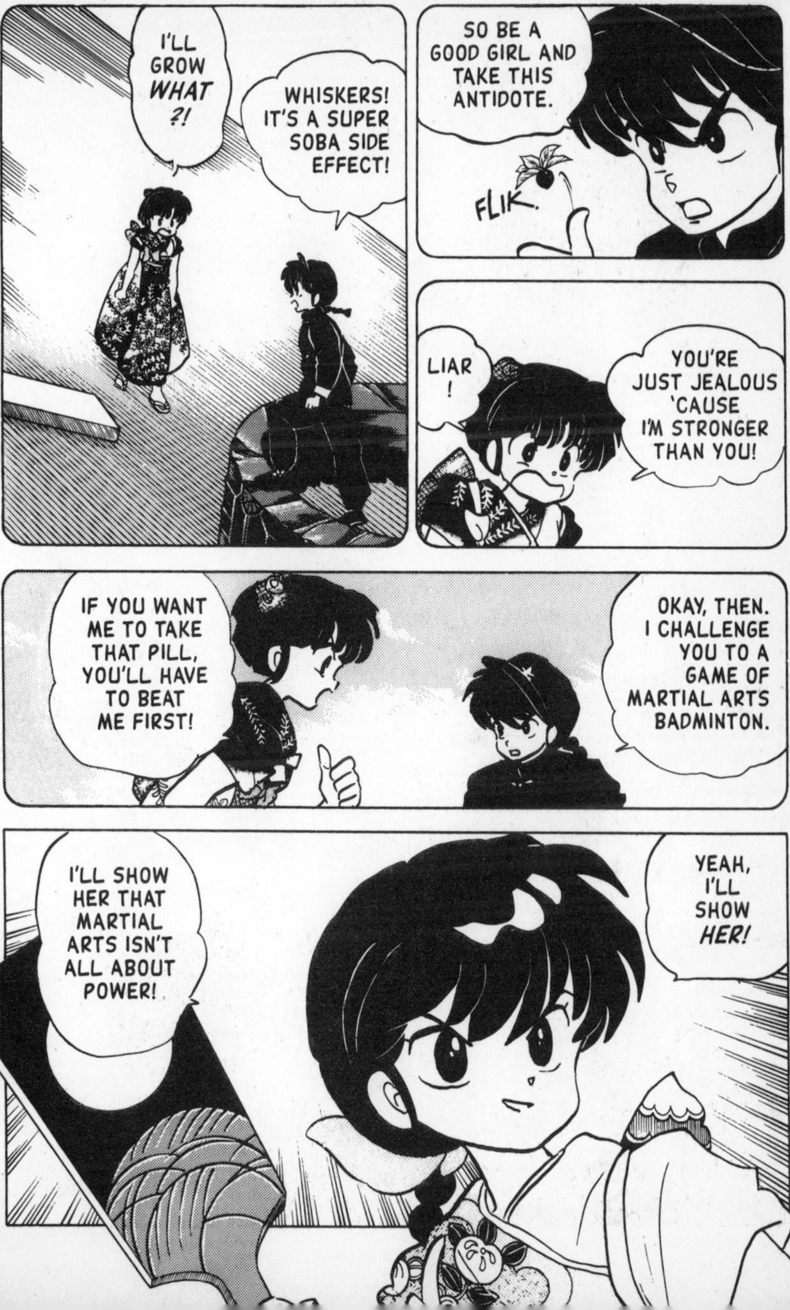
I'LL GROW *WHAT* ?!
WHISKERS! IT'S A SUPER SOBA SIDE EFFECT!
SO BE A GOOD GIRL AND TAKE THIS ANTIDOTE.
FLIK
LIAR!
YOU'RE JUST JEALOUS 'CAUSE I'M STRONGER THAN YOU!
IF YOU WANT ME TO TAKE THAT PILL, YOU'LL HAVE TO BEAT ME FIRST!
OKAY, THEN. I CHALLENGE YOU TO A GAME OF MARTIAL ARTS BADMINTON.
I'LL SHOW HER THAT MARTIAL ARTS ISN'T ALL ABOUT POWER!
YEAH, I'LL SHOW *HER!*

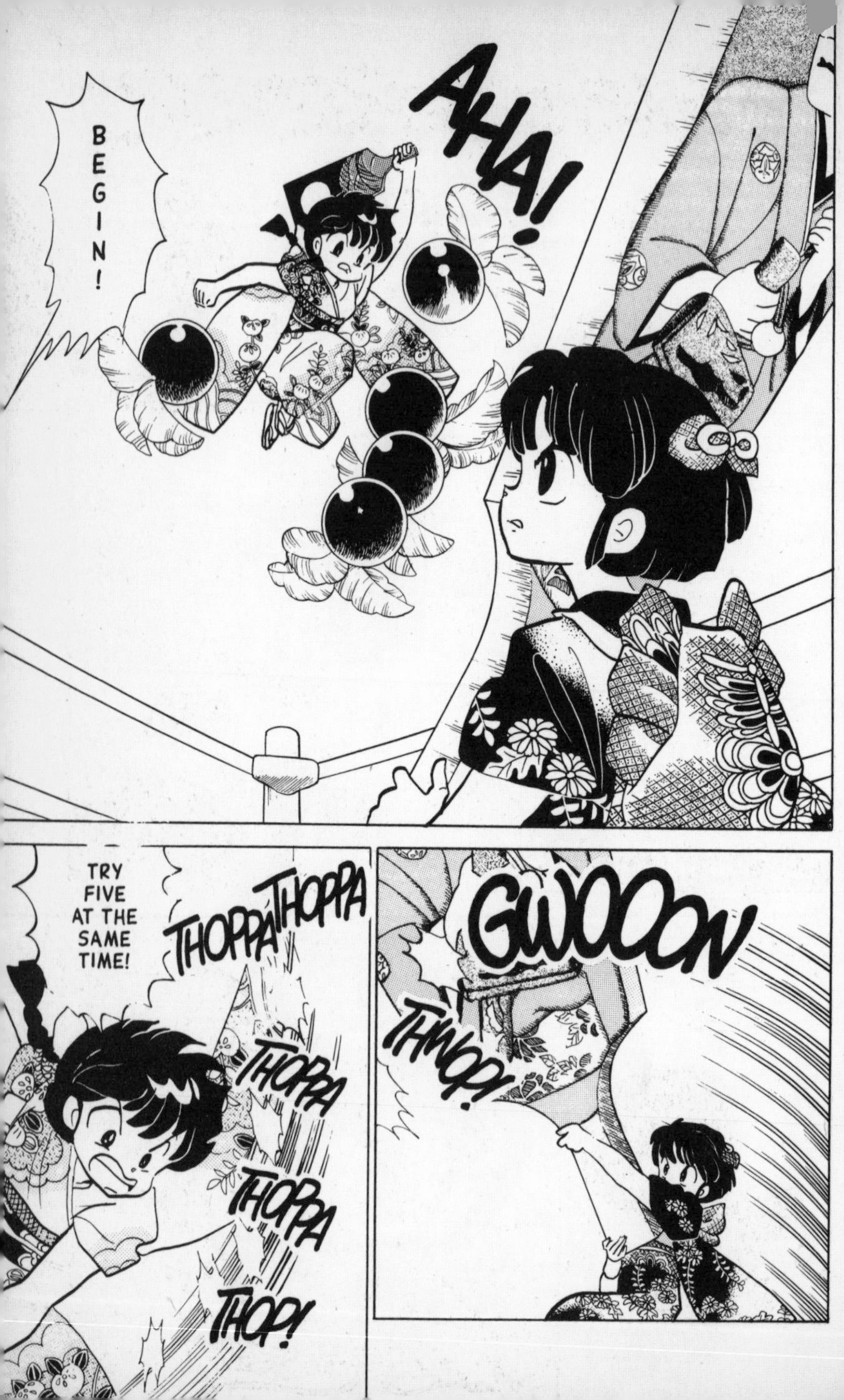
BEGIN!
AHA!
TRY FIVE AT THE SAME TIME!
THOPPA THOPPA
THOPPA
THOPPA
THOP!
GWOOOON
THWOP!

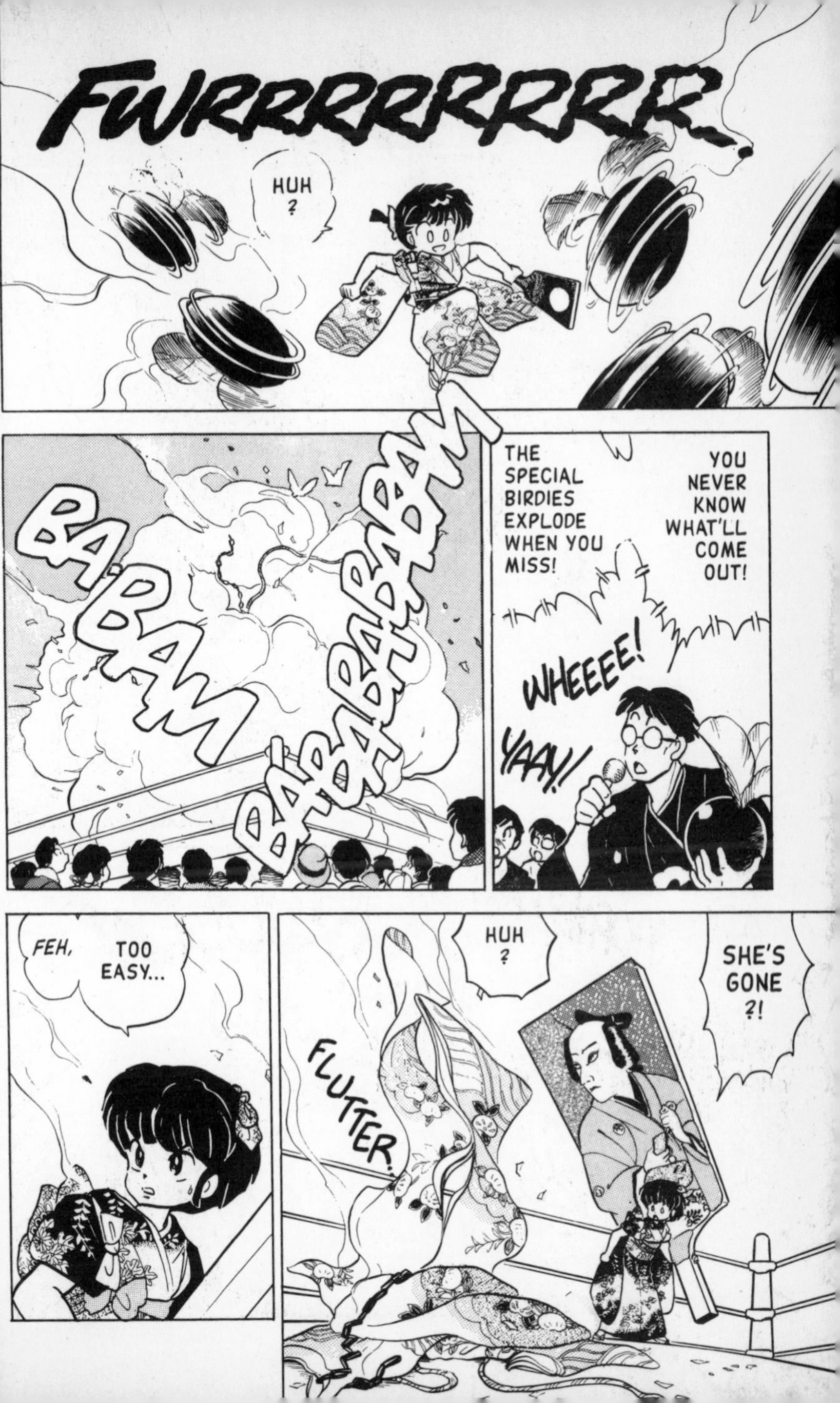
FWRRRRRRRR
HUH ?
BABAM
BABABABABAM
THE SPECIAL BIRDIES EXPLODE WHEN YOU MISS!
YOU NEVER KNOW WHAT'LL COME OUT!
WHEEEE!
YAAY!
FEH, TOO EASY...
HUH ?
FLUTTER
SHE'S GONE ?!

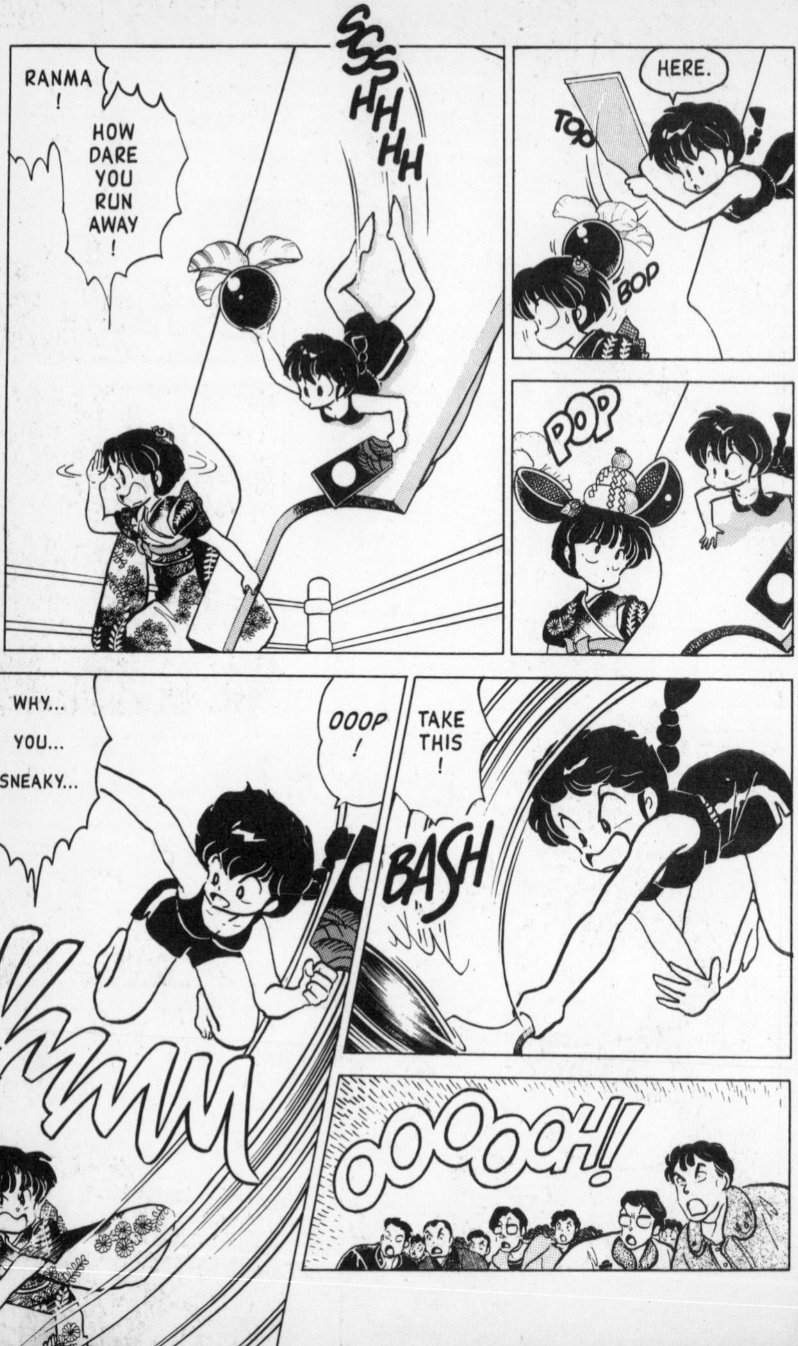
RANMA!
HOW DARE YOU RUN AWAY!
SSSHHHHH
HERE.
TOP
BOP
POP
WHY... YOU... SNEAKY...
OOOP!
TAKE THIS!
BASH
VMMM
OOOOOH!

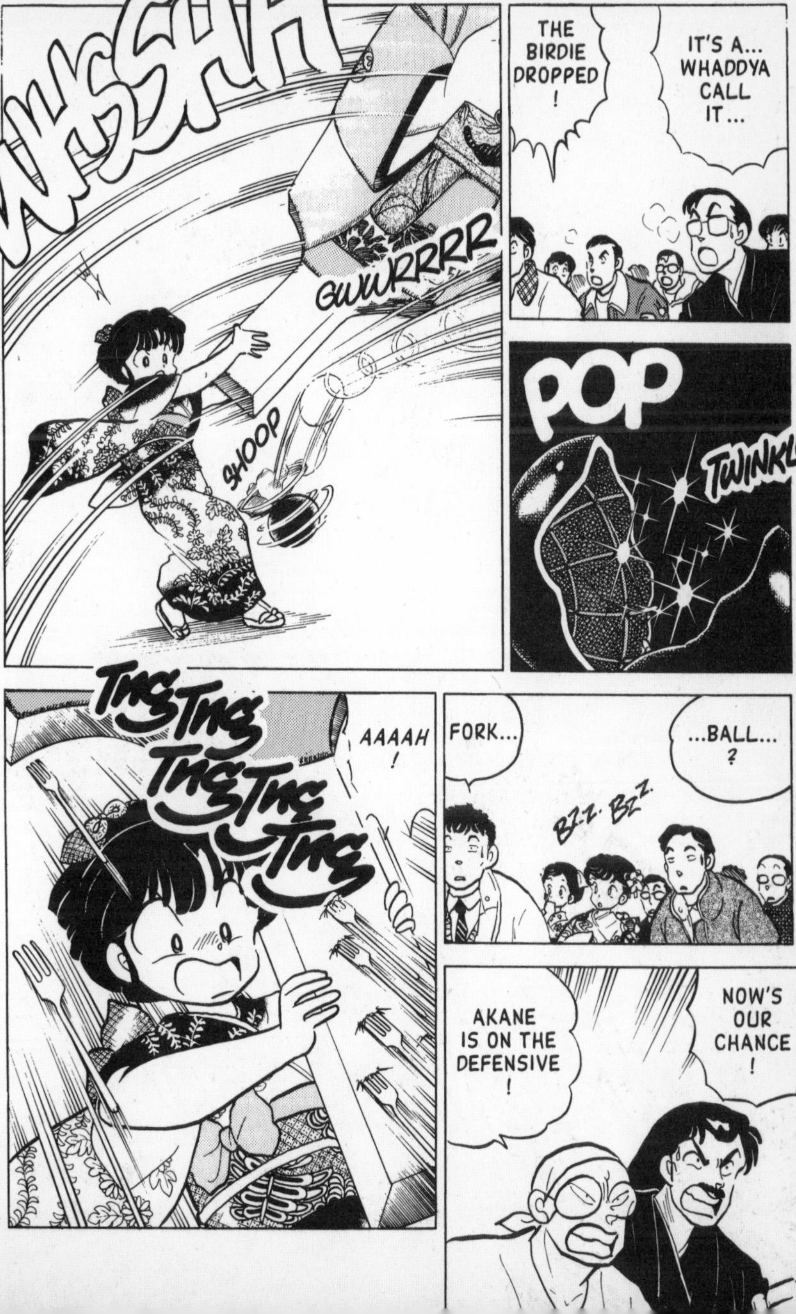
WHSSHH
GWWRRRR
SHOOP
THE BIRDIE DROPPED!
IT'S A... WHADDYA CALL IT...
POP
TWINKLE
TING TING TING TING TING
AAAAH!
FORK...
...BALL...?
BZ-Z. BZ-Z.
AKANE IS ON THE DEFENSIVE!
NOW'S OUR CHANCE!

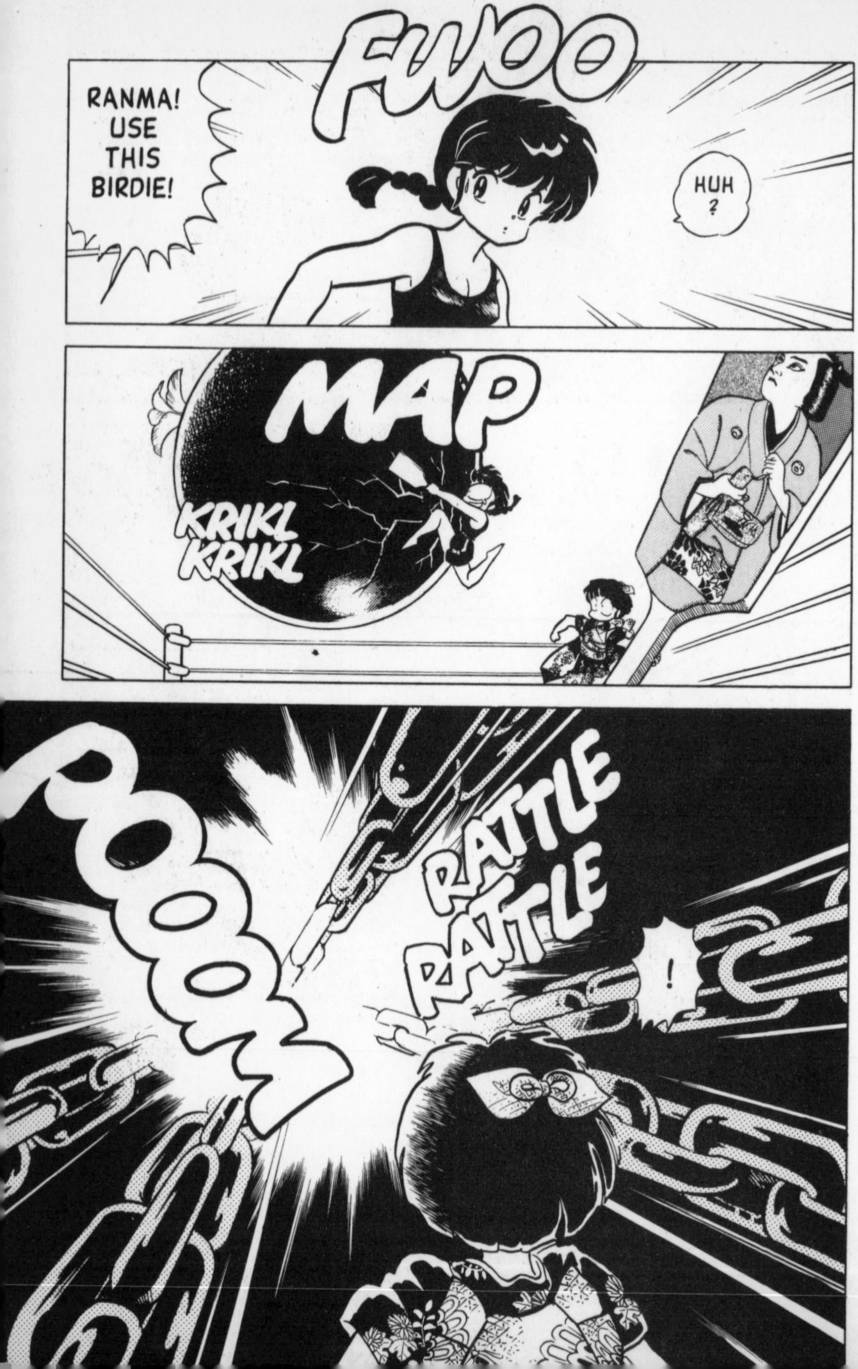
FWOO
RANMA! USE THIS BIRDIE!
HUH?
MAP
KRIKL KRIKL
ROOOM
RATTLE RATTLE
!

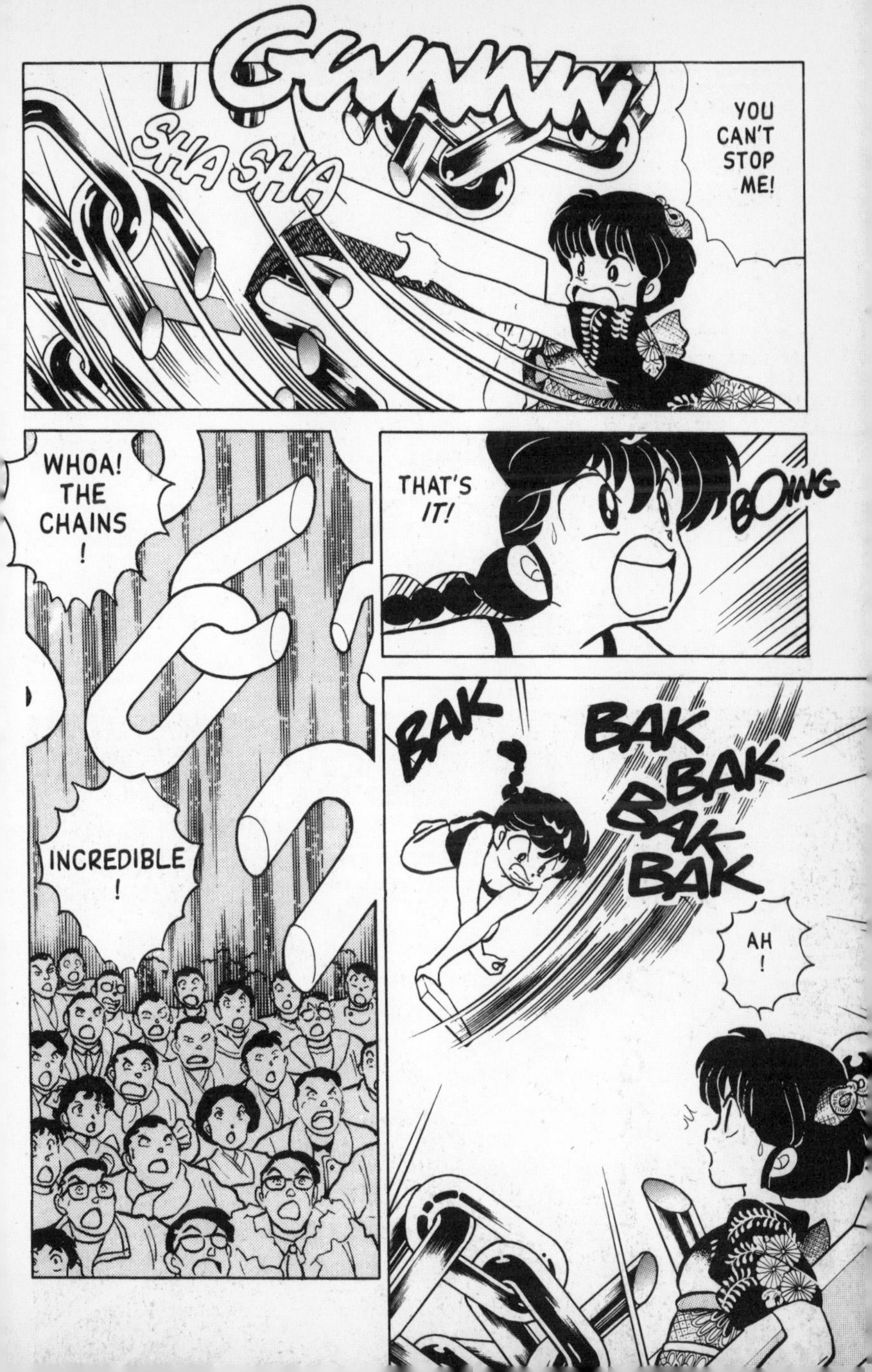
GUNNN
SHA SHA
YOU CAN'T STOP ME!
WHOA! THE CHAINS!
INCREDIBLE!
THAT'S IT!
BOING
BAK
BAK BAK BAK BAK
AH!

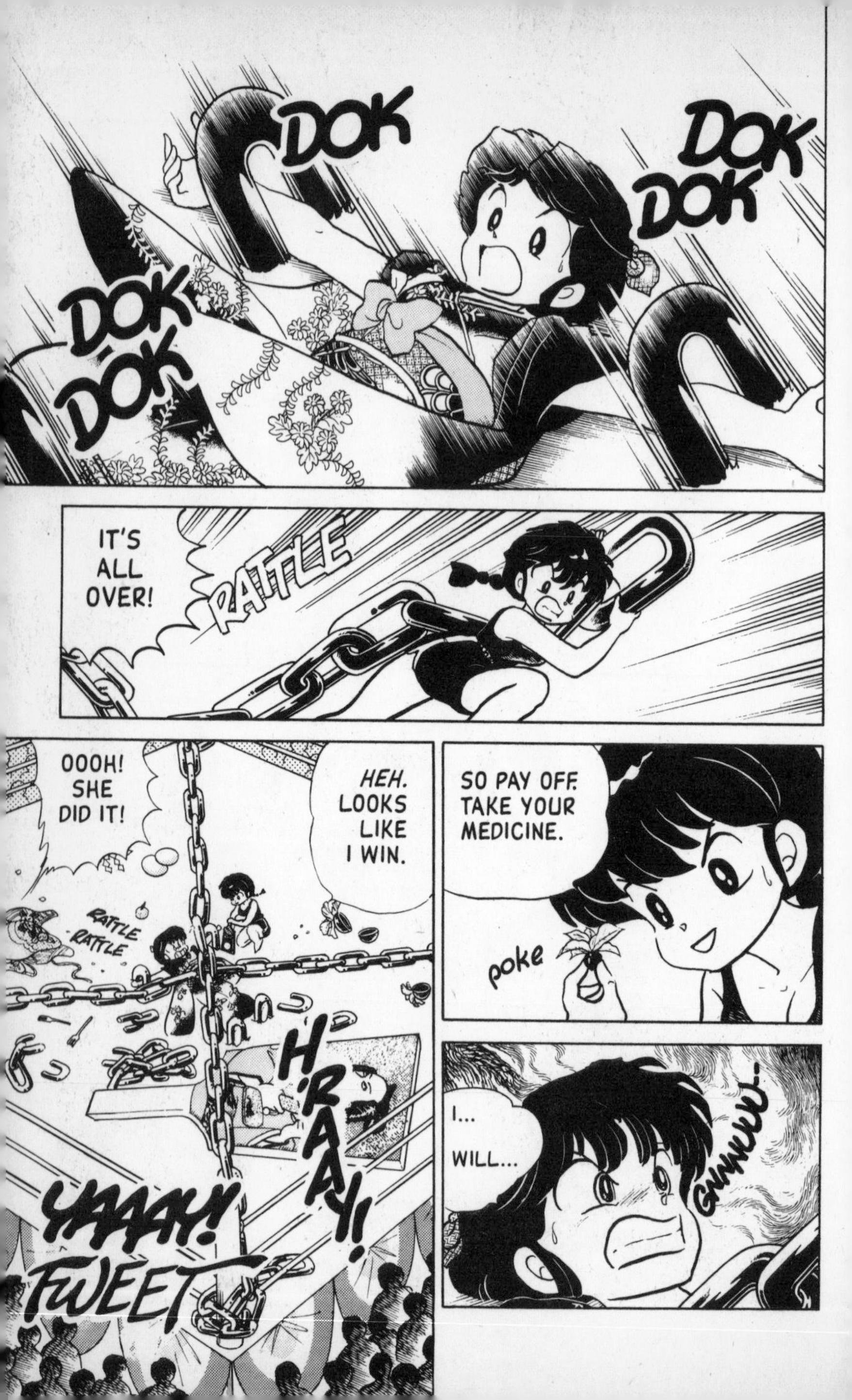
DOK
DOK DOK
DOK DOK
IT'S ALL OVER!
RATTLE
OOOH! SHE DID IT!
HEH. LOOKS LIKE I WIN.
RATTLE RATTLE
H'RAAY!
YAAAY!
TWEET
SO PAY OFF. TAKE YOUR MEDICINE.
poke
I...
WILL...
GNNNNN...

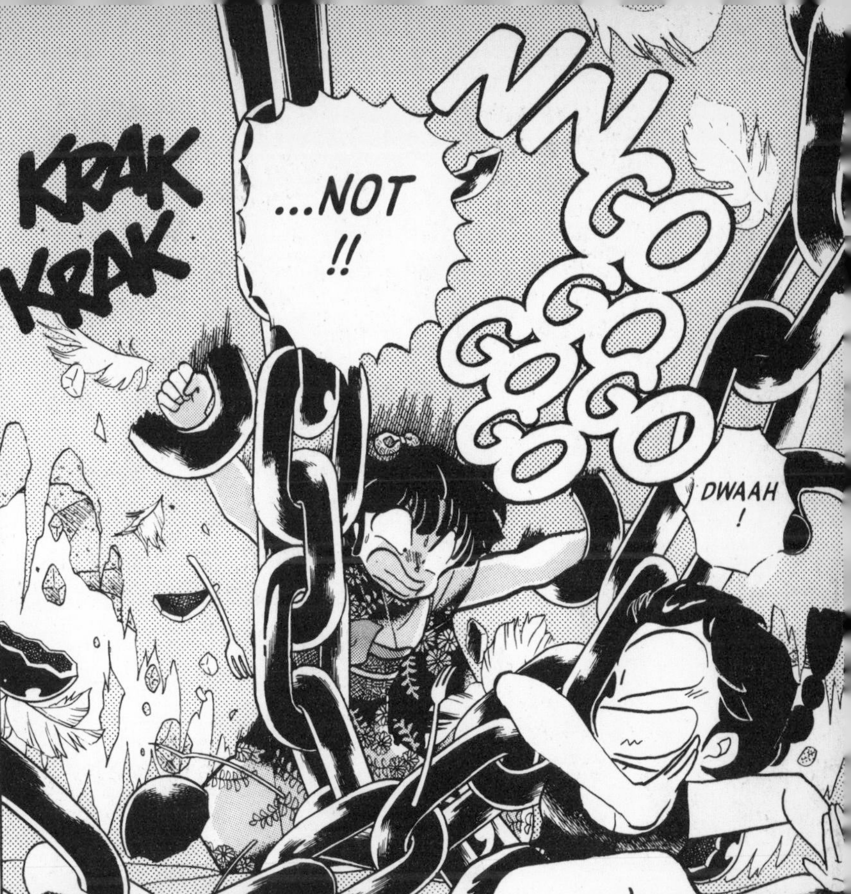
KRAK
KRAK
...NOT !!
NNGO GO GO GO GO
DWAAH !
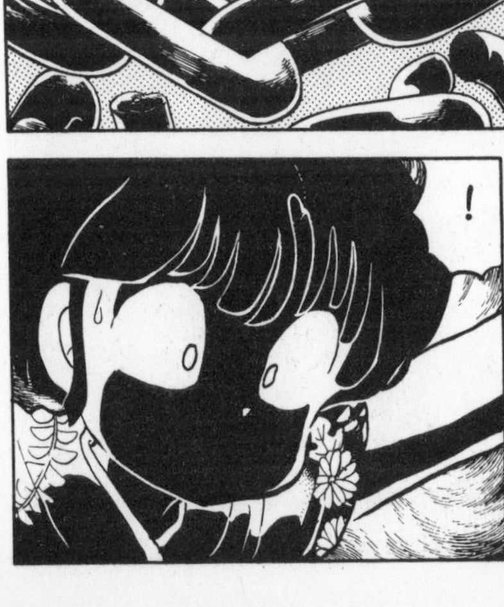
!
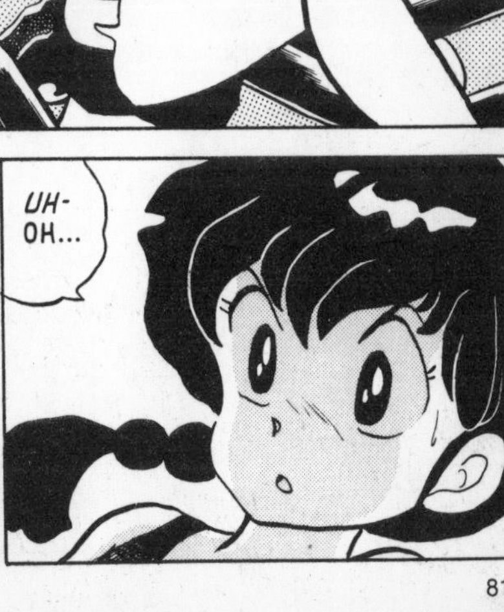
UH-OH...

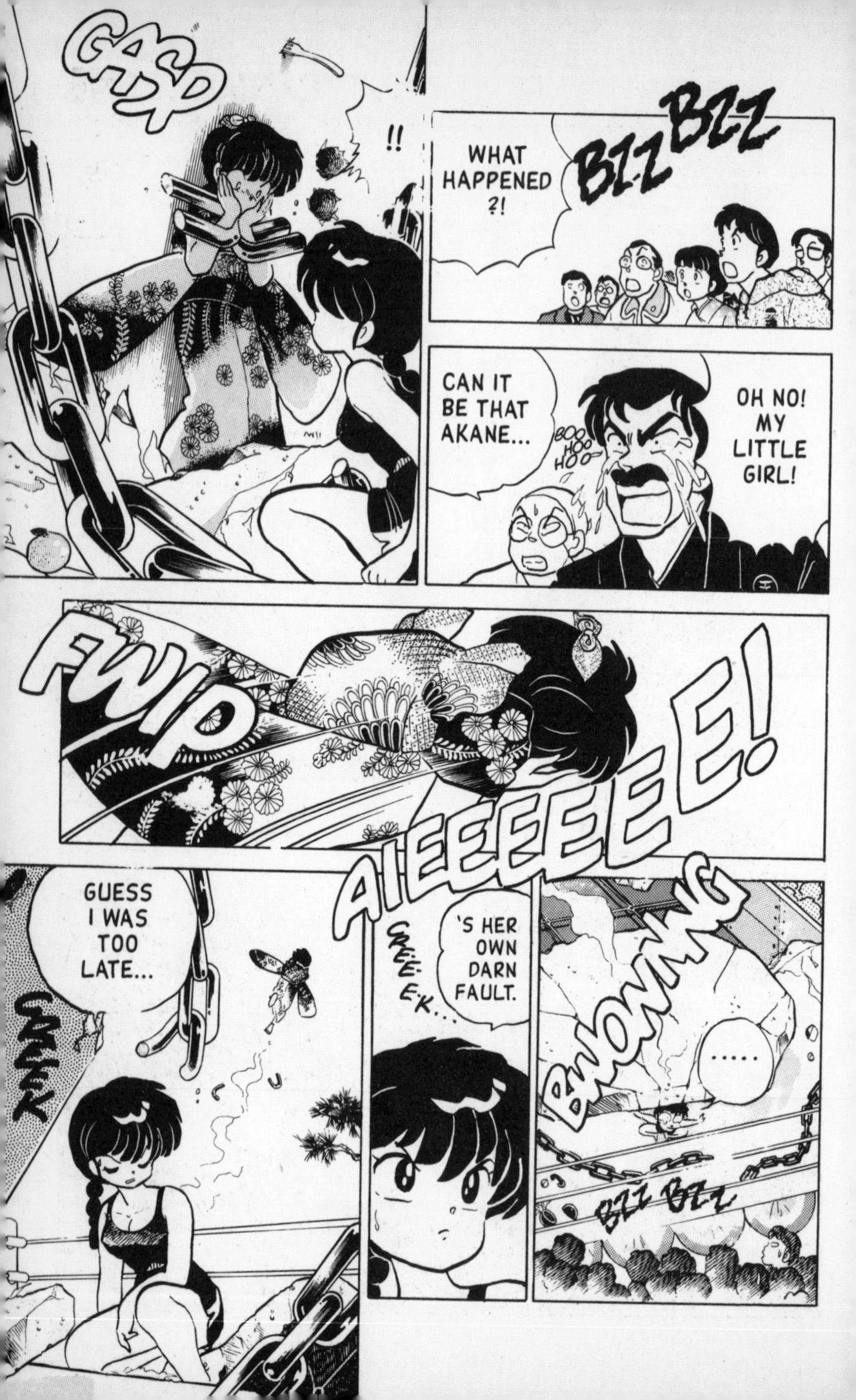
GASP
!!
WHAT HAPPENED ?!
BZZ BZZ
CAN IT BE THAT AKANE...
BOO HOO HOO
OH NO! MY LITTLE GIRL!
FWIP
AIEEEEEEE!
GUESS I WAS TOO LATE...
'S HER OWN DARN FAULT.
.....
BZZ BZZ

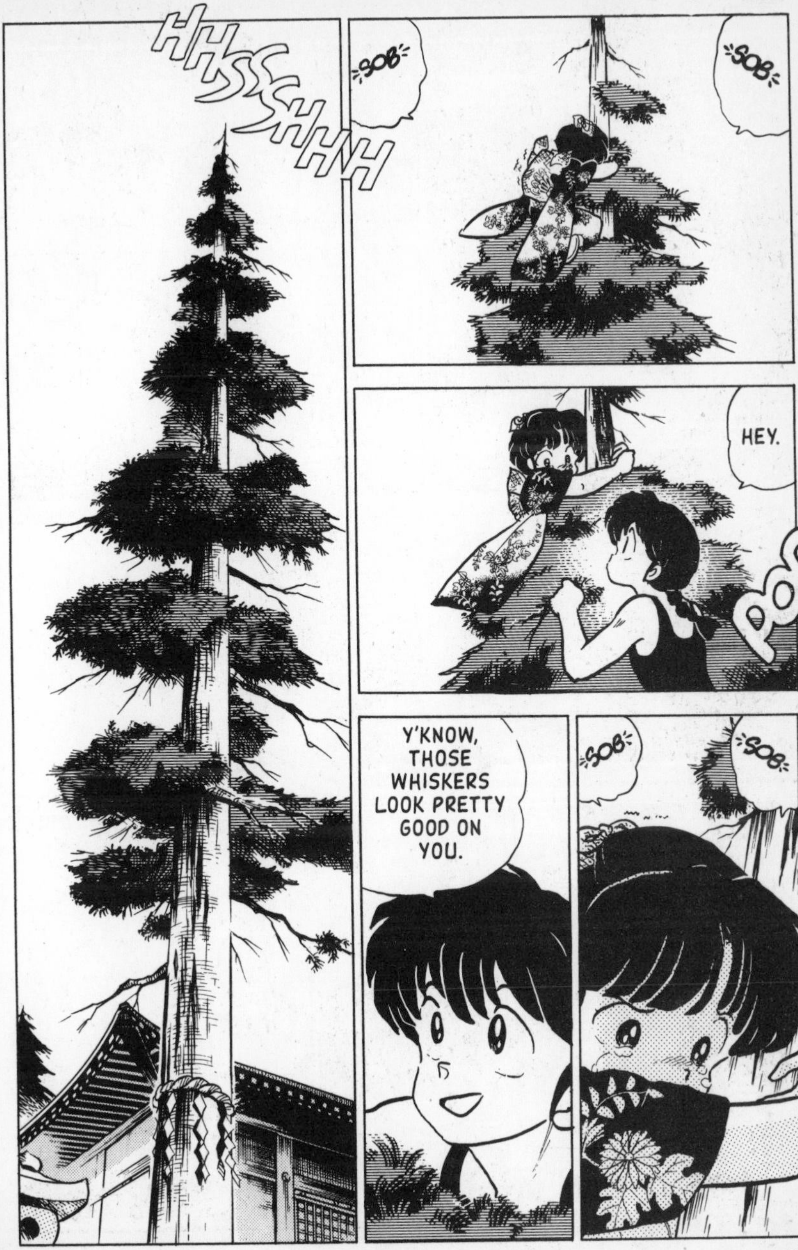
HHSSSHHHH
SOB
SOB
HEY.
POP
Y'KNOW, THOSE WHISKERS LOOK PRETTY GOOD ON YOU.
SOB
SOB

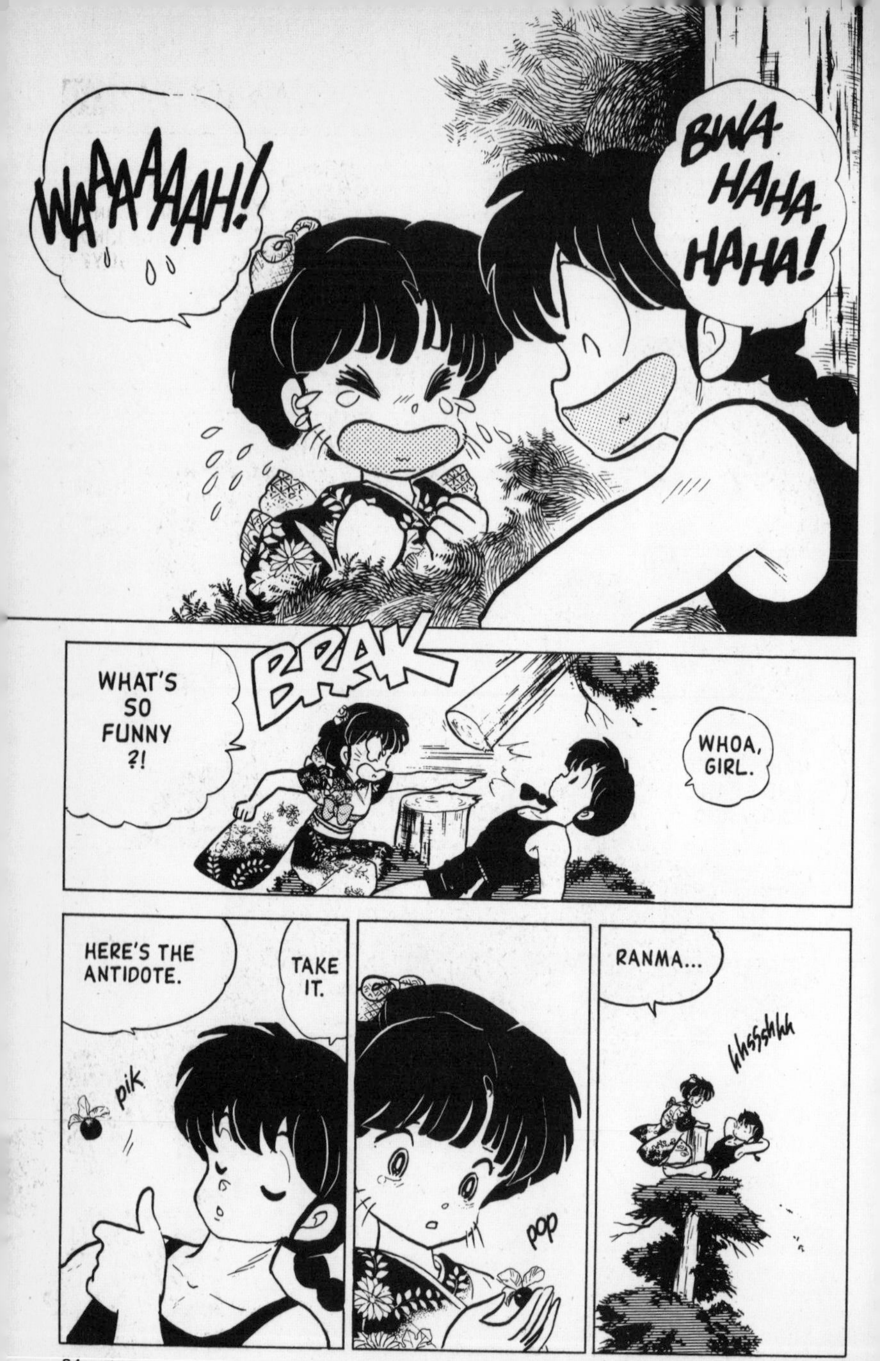
WAAAAAAH!
BWA HAHA HAHA HAHA!
BRAK
WHAT'S SO FUNNY ?!
WHOA, GIRL.
HERE'S THE ANTIDOTE.
pik
TAKE IT.
pop
RANMA...
hhssshhh

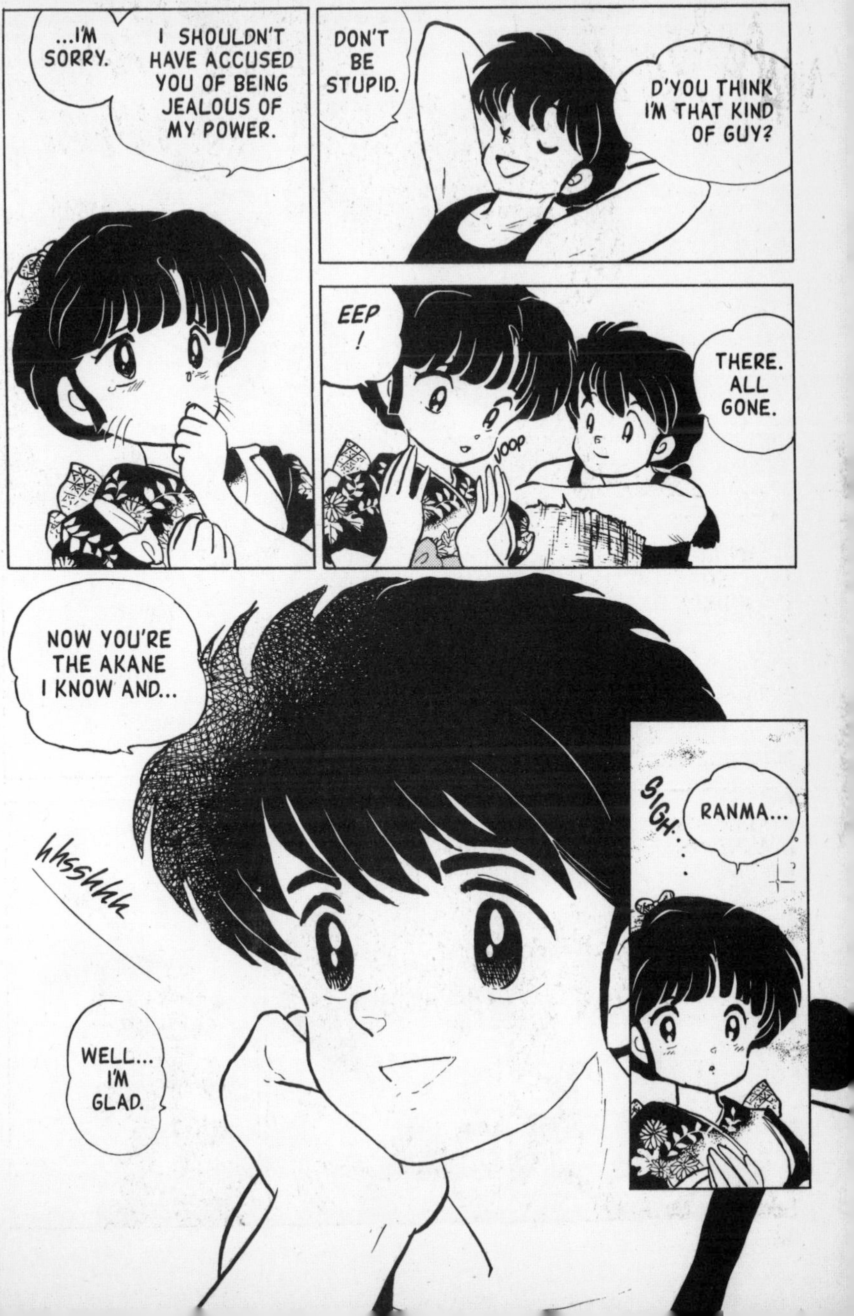
...I'M SORRY.
I SHOULDN'T HAVE ACCUSED YOU OF BEING JEALOUS OF MY POWER.
DON'T BE STUPID.
D'YOU THINK I'M THAT KIND OF GUY?
EEP!
VOOP
THERE. ALL GONE.
NOW YOU'RE THE AKANE I KNOW AND...
hhsshhh
WELL... I'M GLAD.
SIGH...
RANMA...

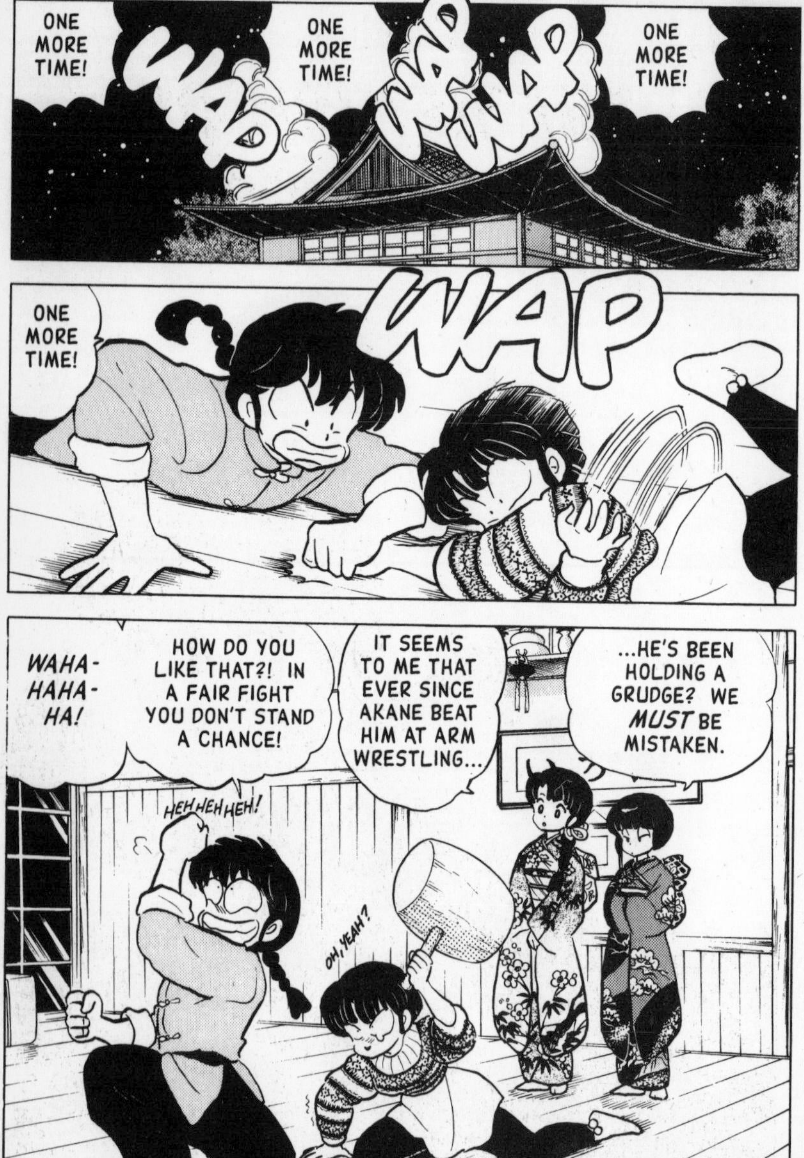
ONE MORE TIME!
WAP
ONE MORE TIME!
WAP WAP
ONE MORE TIME!
ONE MORE TIME!
WAP
WAHA-HAHA-HA!
HOW DO YOU LIKE THAT?! IN A FAIR FIGHT YOU DON'T STAND A CHANCE!
HEH HEH HEH!
IT SEEMS TO ME THAT EVER SINCE AKANE BEAT HIM AT ARM WRESTLING...
...HE'S BEEN HOLDING A GRUDGE? WE *MUST* BE MISTAKEN.
OH, YEAH?

Part 6

THE RETURN OF THE PRINCIPAL

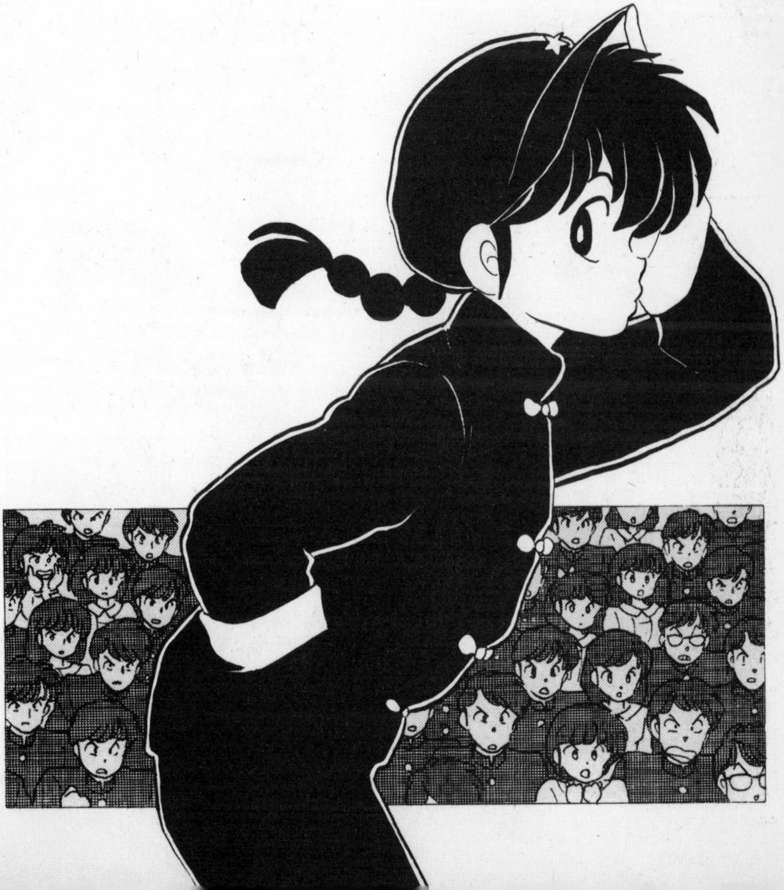

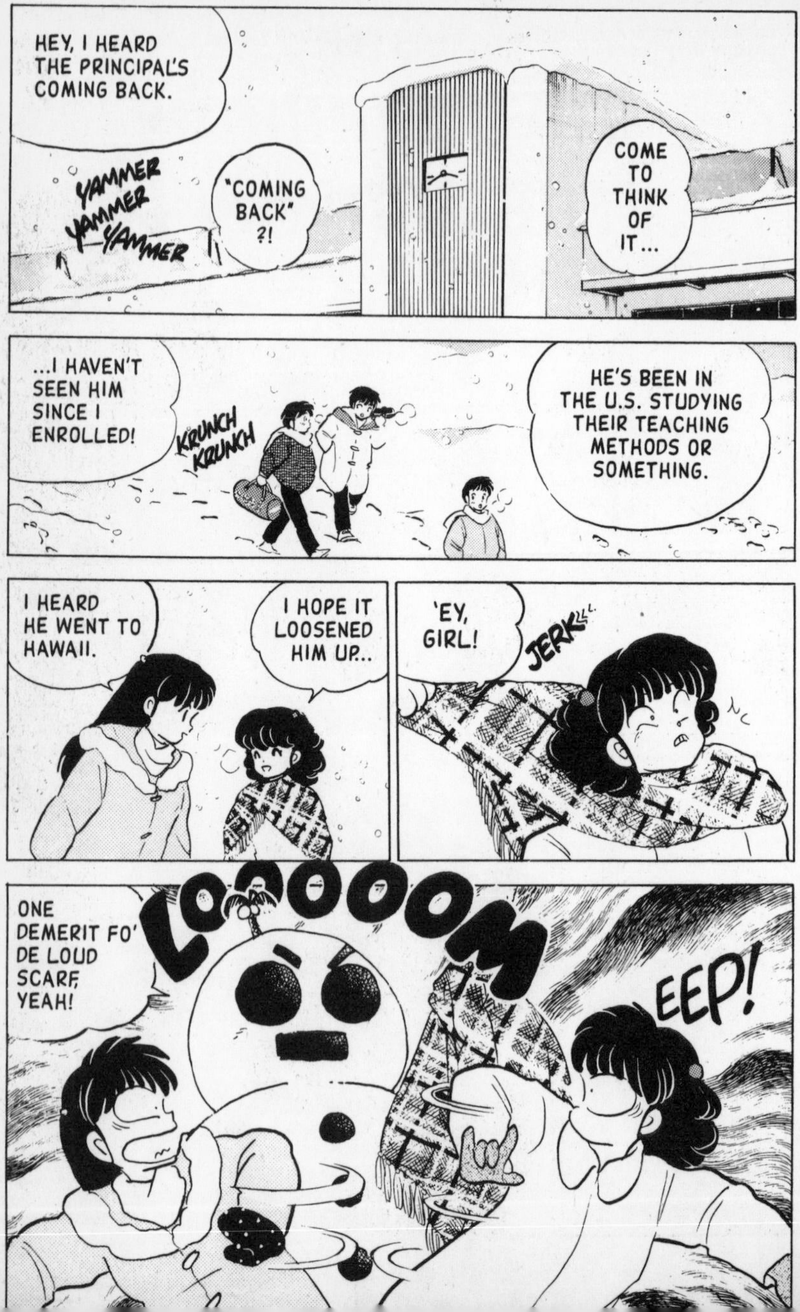
HEY, I HEARD THE PRINCIPAL'S COMING BACK.
YAMMER YAMMER YAMMER
"COMING BACK" ?!
COME TO THINK OF IT...
...I HAVEN'T SEEN HIM SINCE I ENROLLED!
KRUNCH KRUNCH
HE'S BEEN IN THE U.S. STUDYING THEIR TEACHING METHODS OR SOMETHING.
I HEARD HE WENT TO HAWAII.
I HOPE IT LOOSENED HIM UP...
'EY, GIRL!
JERK
ONE DEMERIT FO' DE LOUD SCARF, YEAH!
LOOOOOM
EEP!

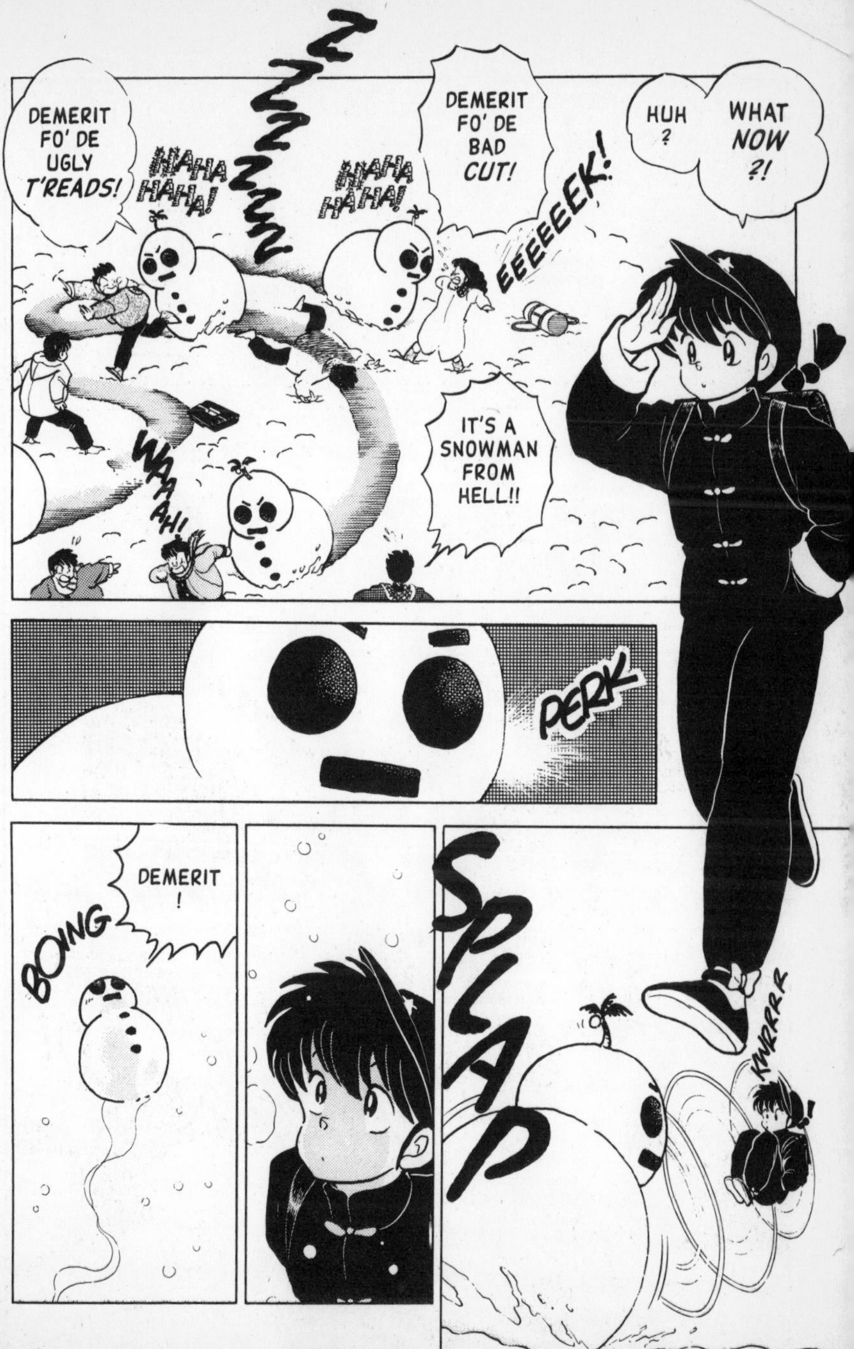

DEMERIT FO' DE UGLY T'READS!
HAHA HAHA!
ZZZZZZZ
HAHA HAHA!
DEMERIT FO' DE BAD CUT!
EEEEEEK!
HUH ?
WHAT NOW ?!
WAAAAH!
IT'S A SNOWMAN FROM HELL!!
PERK
DEMERIT !
BOING
SPLAP
KWRRRR

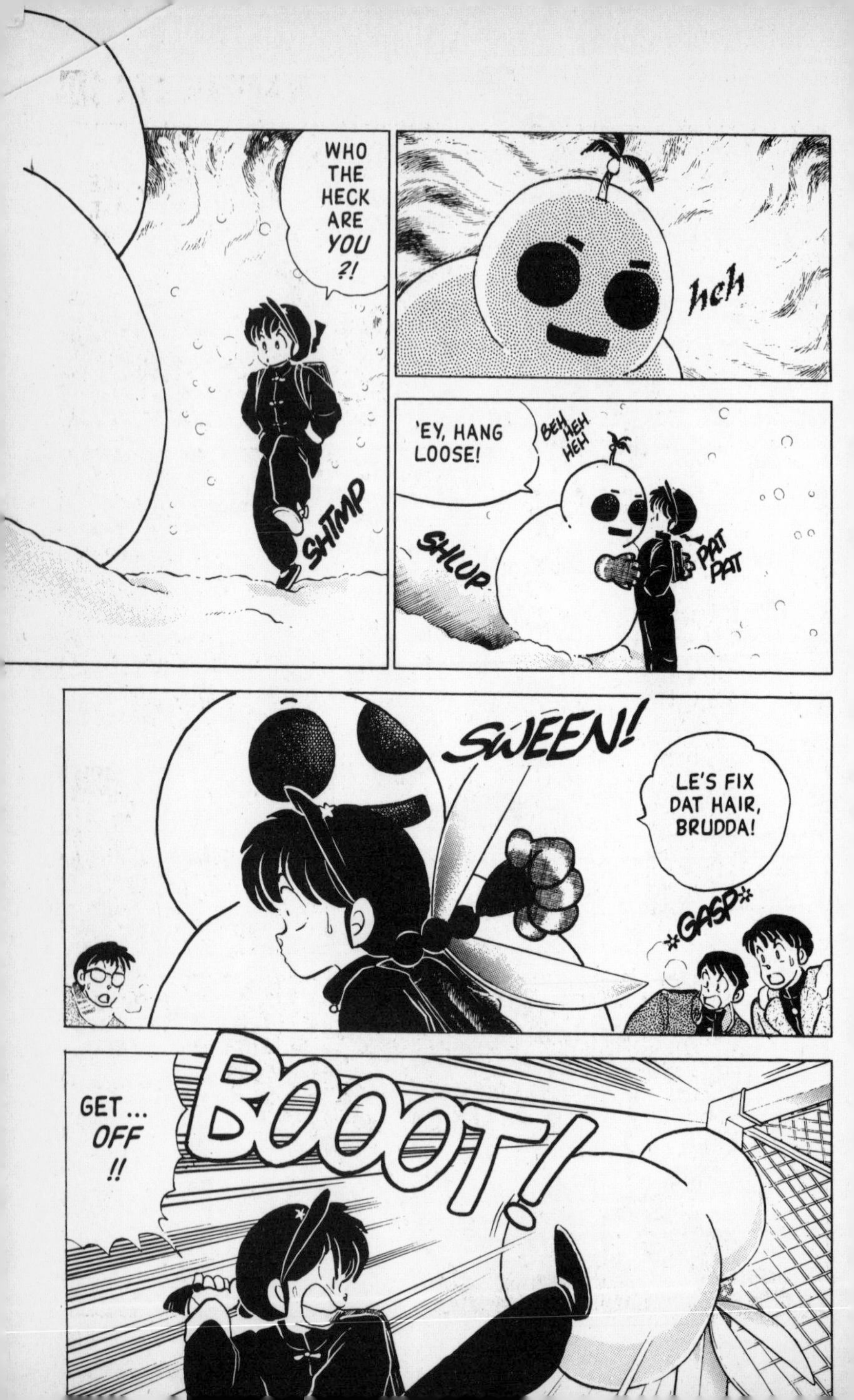
WHO THE HECK ARE YOU ?!
SHTMP
heh
'EY, HANG LOOSE!
BEH HEH HEH
SHLUP
PAT PAT
SWEEN!
LE'S FIX DAT HAIR, BRUDDA!
GASP
GET... OFF !!
BOOOT!

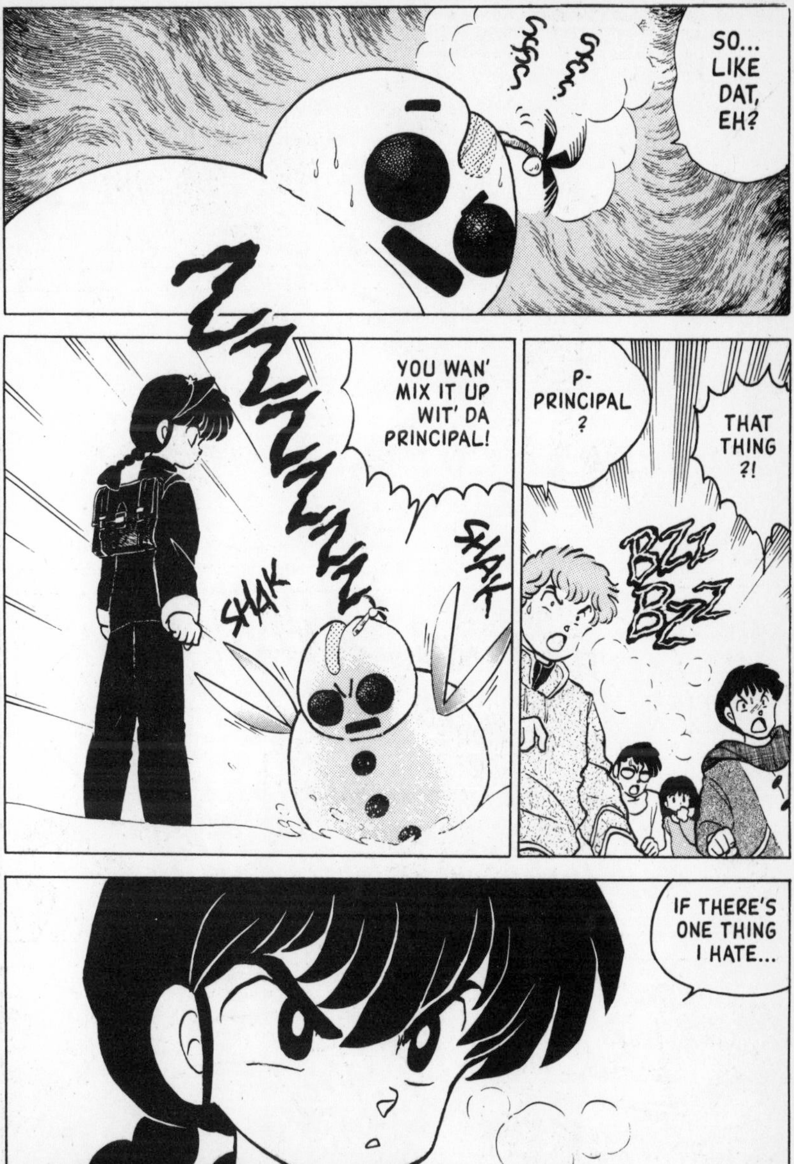
SO... LIKE DAT, EH?
ZZZZZZZZZZZ
YOU WAN' MIX IT UP WIT' DA PRINCIPAL!
SHAK
SHAK
P-PRINCIPAL?
THAT THING?!
BZZ BZZ
IF THERE'S ONE THING I HATE...

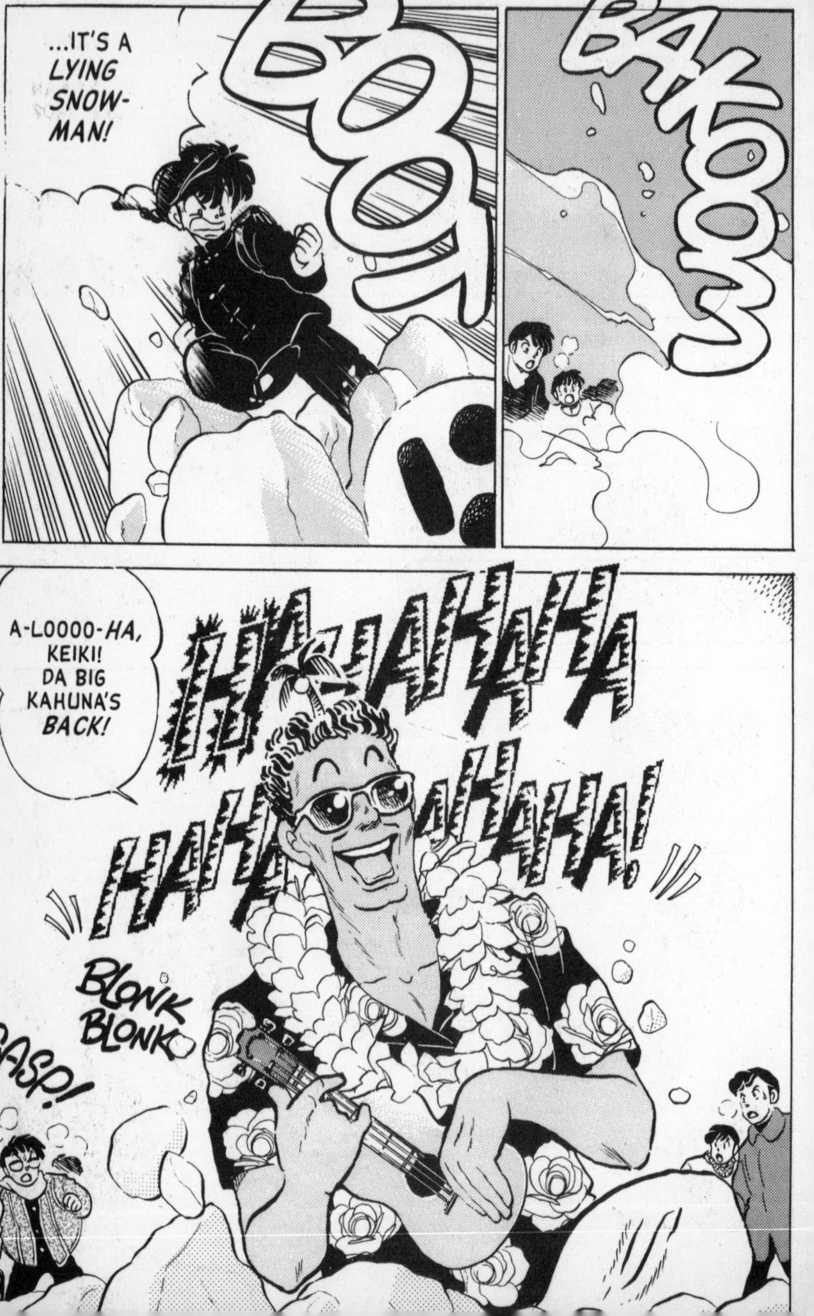
...IT'S A LYING SNOWMAN!
BOOOT
BAKOOM
A-LOOOO-HA, KEIKI! DA BIG KAHUNA'S BACK!
HAHAHAHAHA
HAHAHAHAHAHA!
BLONK BLONK
GASP!

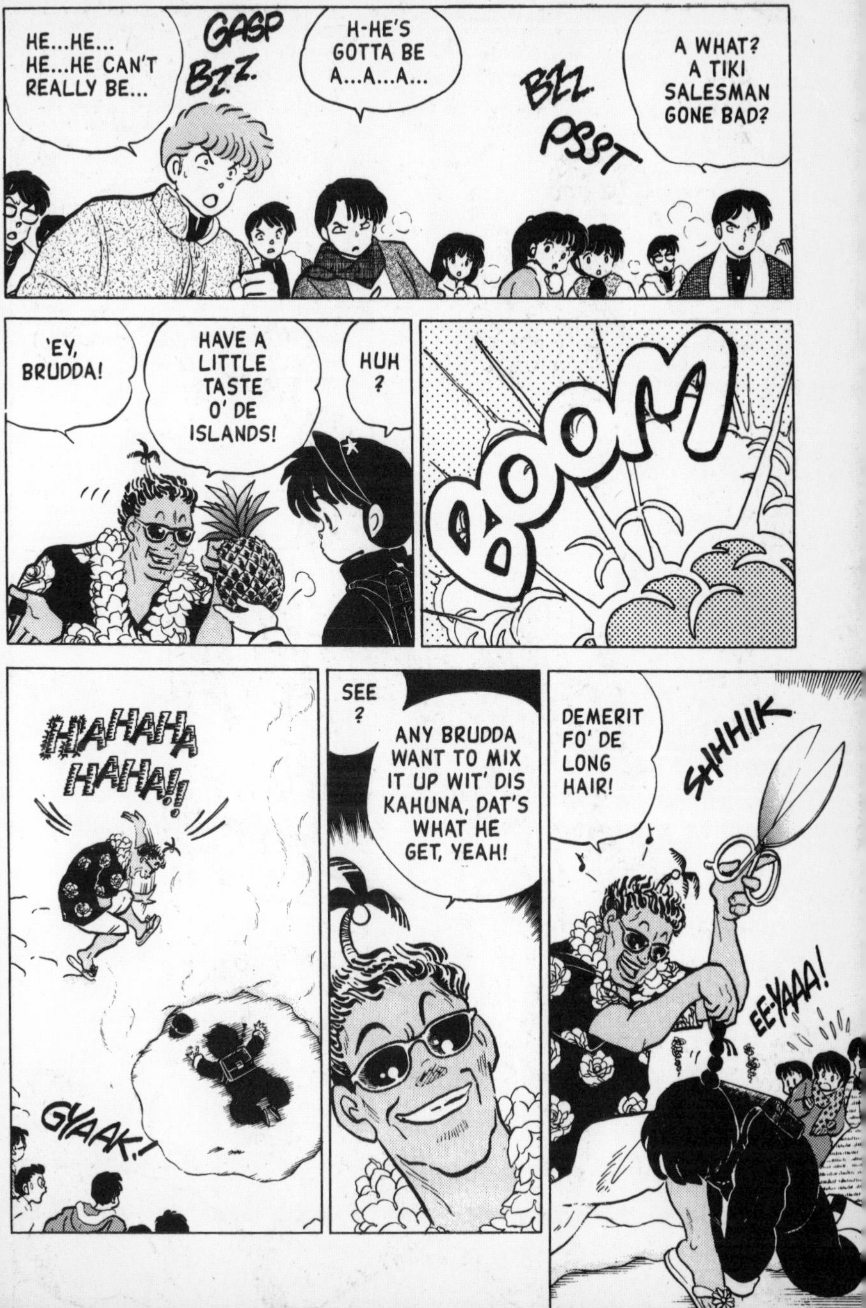
HE...HE...
HE...HE CAN'T REALLY BE...
GASP
BZZ
H-HE'S GOTTA BE A...A...A...
BZZ
PSST
A WHAT? A TIKI SALESMAN GONE BAD?
'EY, BRUDDA!
HAVE A LITTLE TASTE O' DE ISLANDS!
HUH?
BOOM
HAHAHA HAHA!
GYAAK!
SEE?
ANY BRUDDA WANT TO MIX IT UP WIT' DIS KAHUNA, DAT'S WHAT HE GET, YEAH!
DEMERIT FO' DE LONG HAIR!
SHHHIK
EE-YAAA!

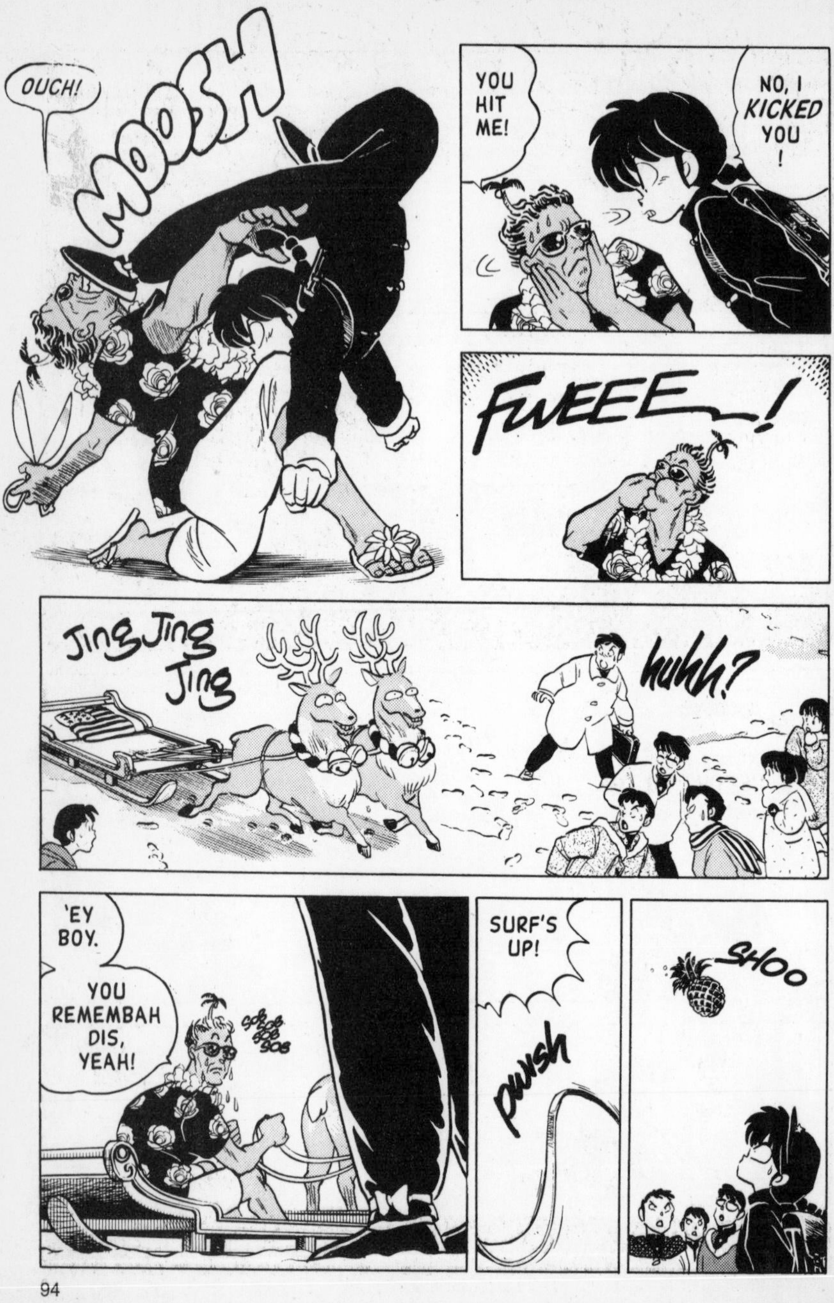
OUCH!
MOOSH
YOU HIT ME!
NO, I KICKED YOU!
FWEEE—!
Jing Jing Jing
huhh?
'EY BOY.
YOU REMEMBAH DIS, YEAH!
SURF'S UP!
push
SHOO

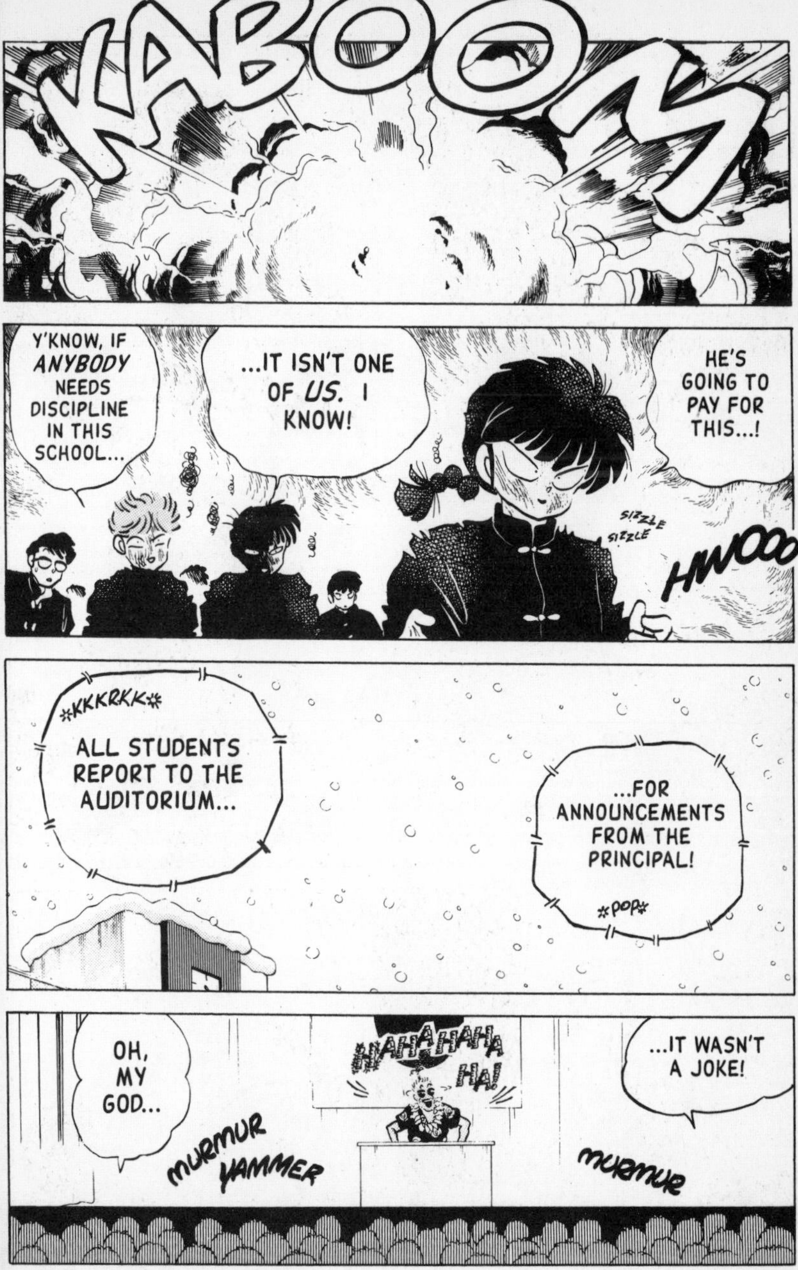
KABOOM
Y'KNOW, IF ANYBODY NEEDS DISCIPLINE IN THIS SCHOOL...
...IT ISN'T ONE OF US. I KNOW!
HE'S GOING TO PAY FOR THIS...!
SIZZLE SIZZLE
HWOOOOO...
KKKRKK
ALL STUDENTS REPORT TO THE AUDITORIUM...
...FOR ANNOUNCEMENTS FROM THE PRINCIPAL!
POP
OH, MY GOD...
HAHAHAHA HA!
...IT WASN'T A JOKE!
MURMUR YAMMER
MURMUR

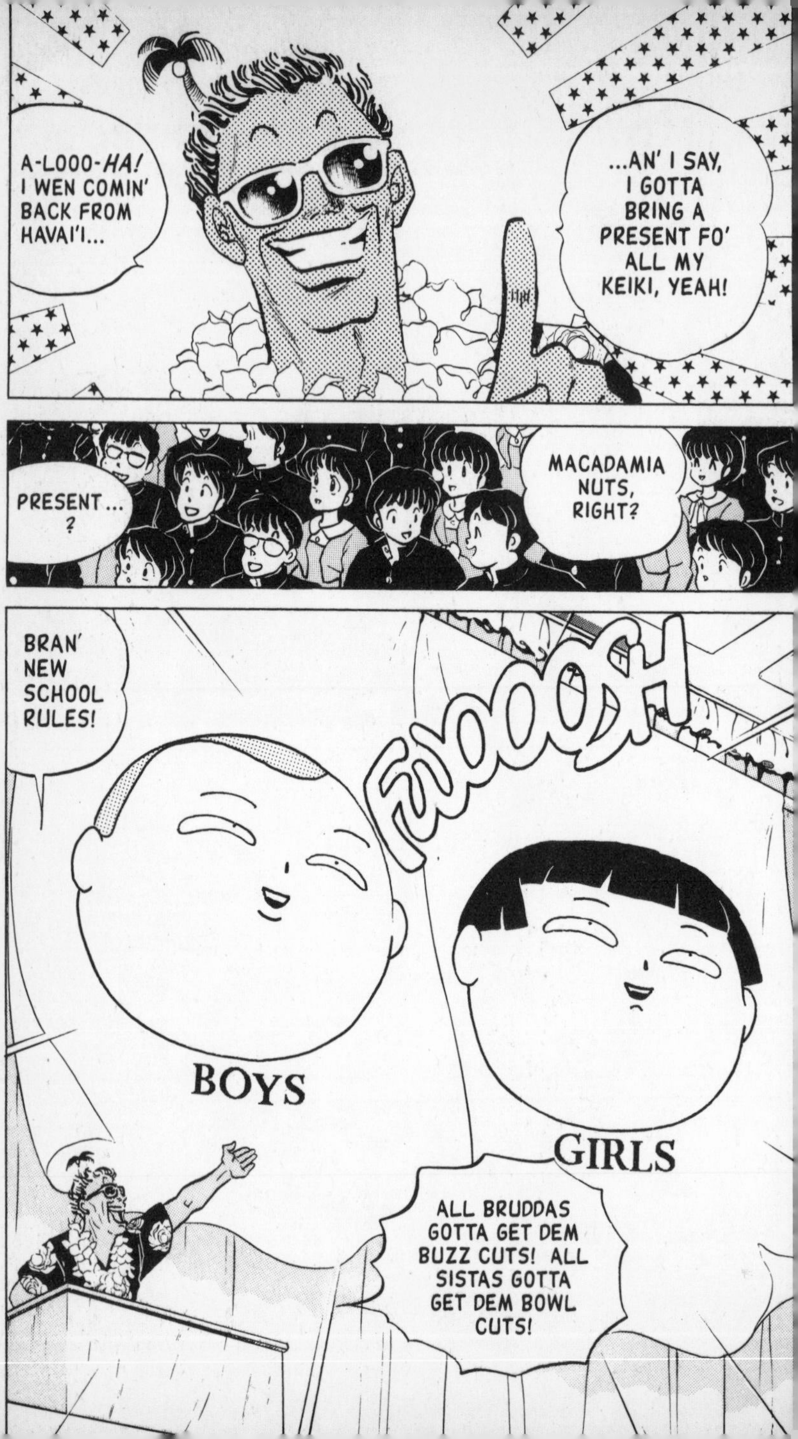
A-LOOO-*HA!* I WEN COMIN' BACK FROM HAVAI'I...
...AN' I SAY, I GOTTA BRING A PRESENT FO' ALL MY KEIKI, YEAH!
PRESENT... ?
MACADAMIA NUTS, RIGHT?
BRAN' NEW SCHOOL RULES!
FWOOOSH
BOYS
GIRLS
ALL BRUDDAS GOTTA GET DEM BUZZ CUTS! ALL SISTAS GOTTA GET DEM BOWL CUTS!

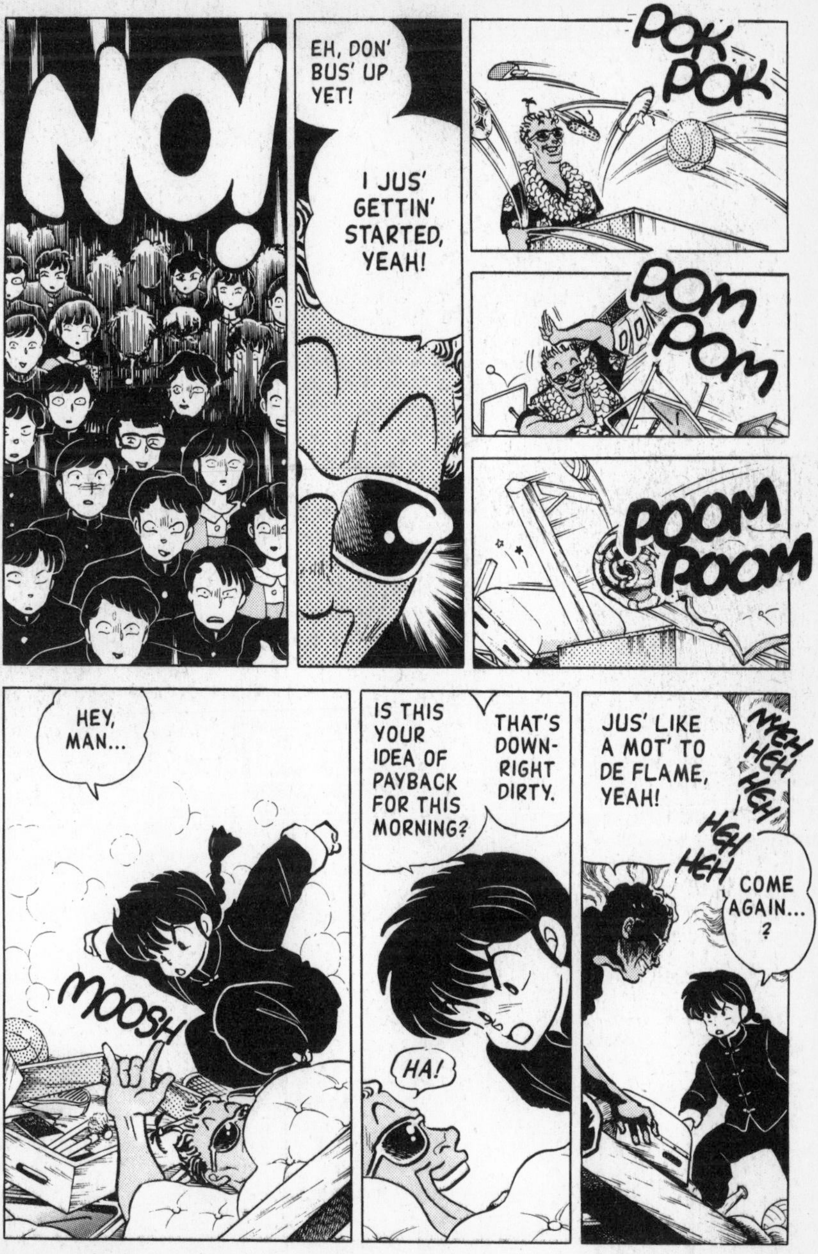

NO!
EH, DON' BUS' UP YET!
I JUS' GETTIN' STARTED, YEAH!
POK POK POK
POM POM
POOM POOM
HEY, MAN...
MOOSH
IS THIS YOUR IDEA OF PAYBACK FOR THIS MORNING?
THAT'S DOWN-RIGHT DIRTY.
HA!
JUS' LIKE A MOT' TO DE FLAME, YEAH!
NYEH HEH HEH HEH HEH HEH
COME AGAIN...?

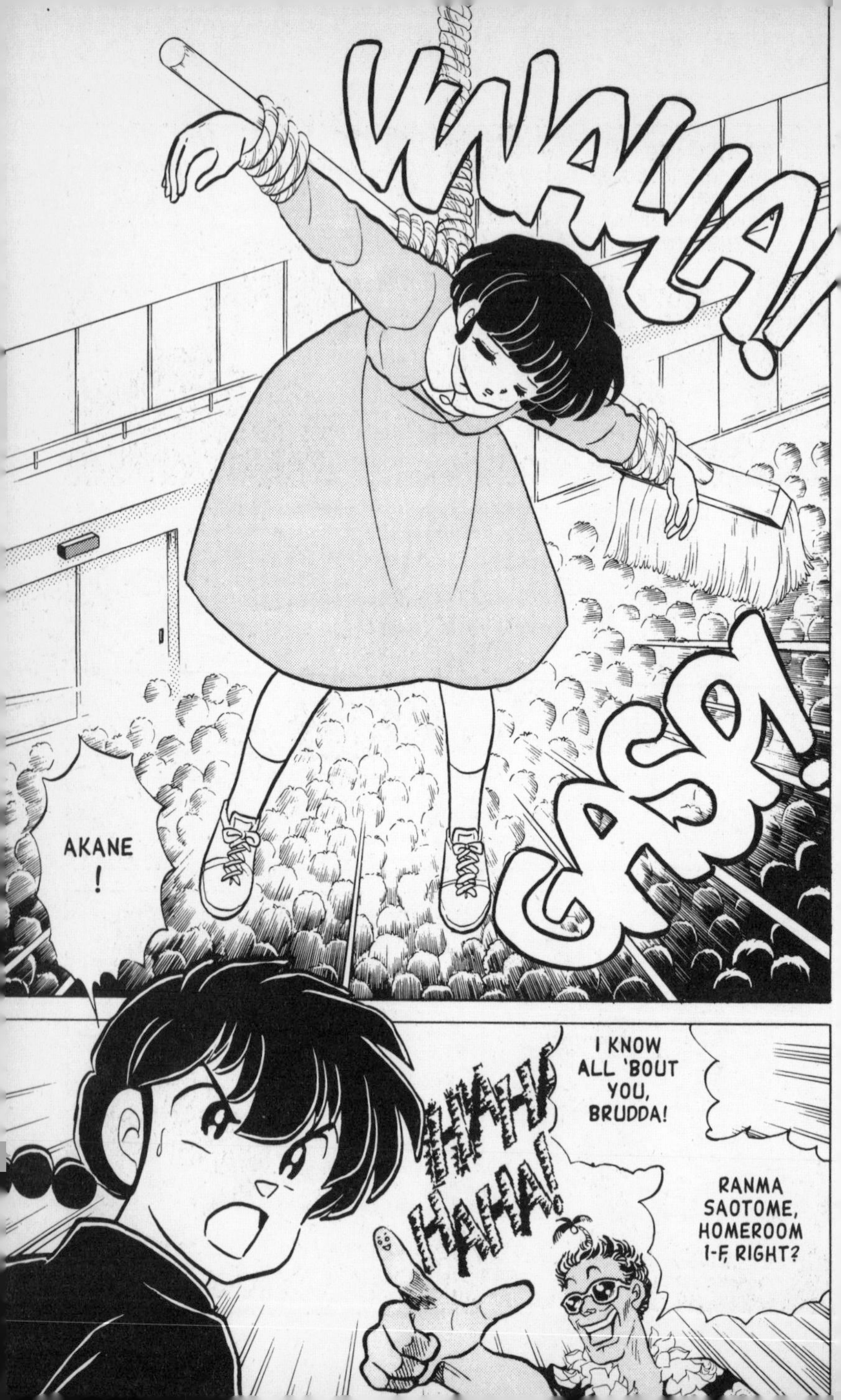
WHAM!
AKANE
!
I KNOW
ALL 'BOUT
YOU,
BRUDDA!
HAHA!
RANMA
SAOTOME,
HOMEROOM
1-F, RIGHT?

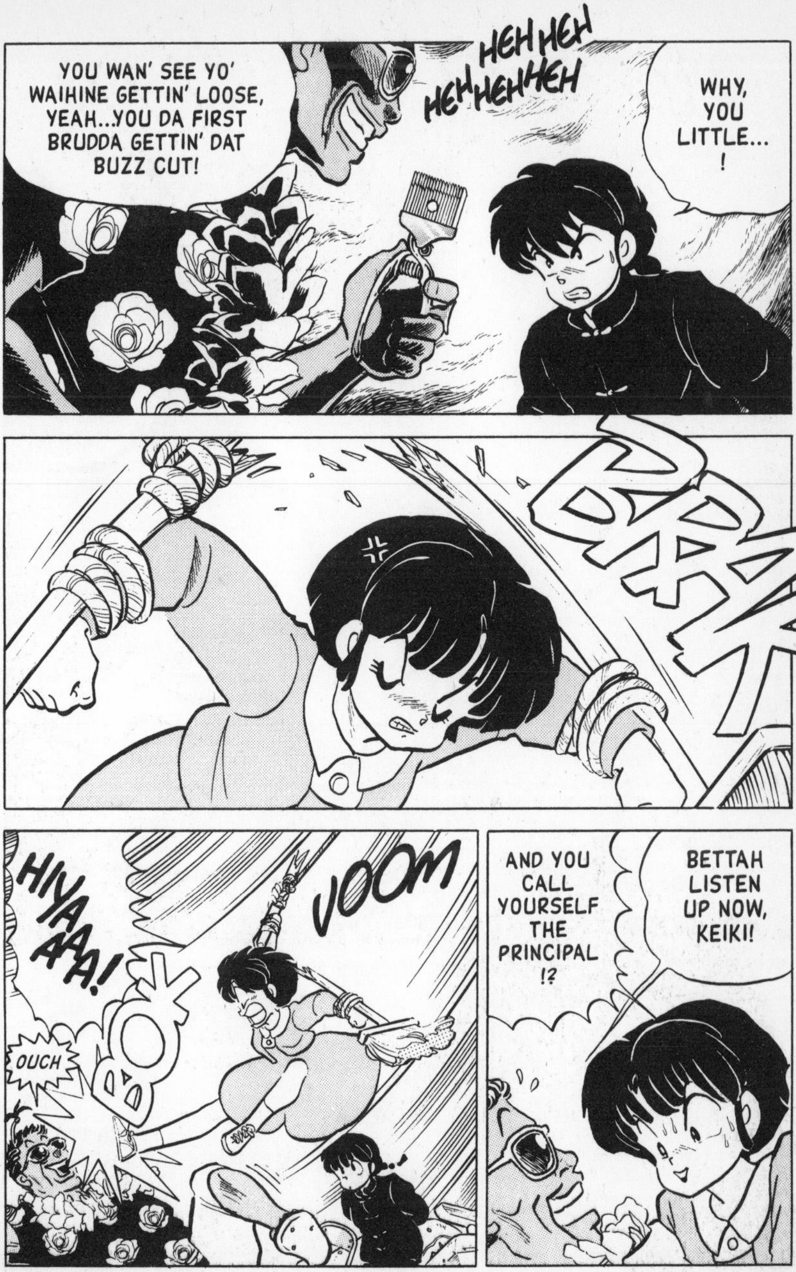
YOU WAN' SEE YO' WAIHINE GETTIN' LOOSE, YEAH...YOU DA FIRST BRUDDA GETTIN' DAT BUZZ CUT!
HEH HEH HEH HEH HEH HEH
WHY, YOU LITTLE...!
DRAK
HIYAAAAA!
VOOM
BOK
OUCH
AND YOU CALL YOURSELF THE PRINCIPAL!?
BETTAH LISTEN UP NOW, KEIKI!

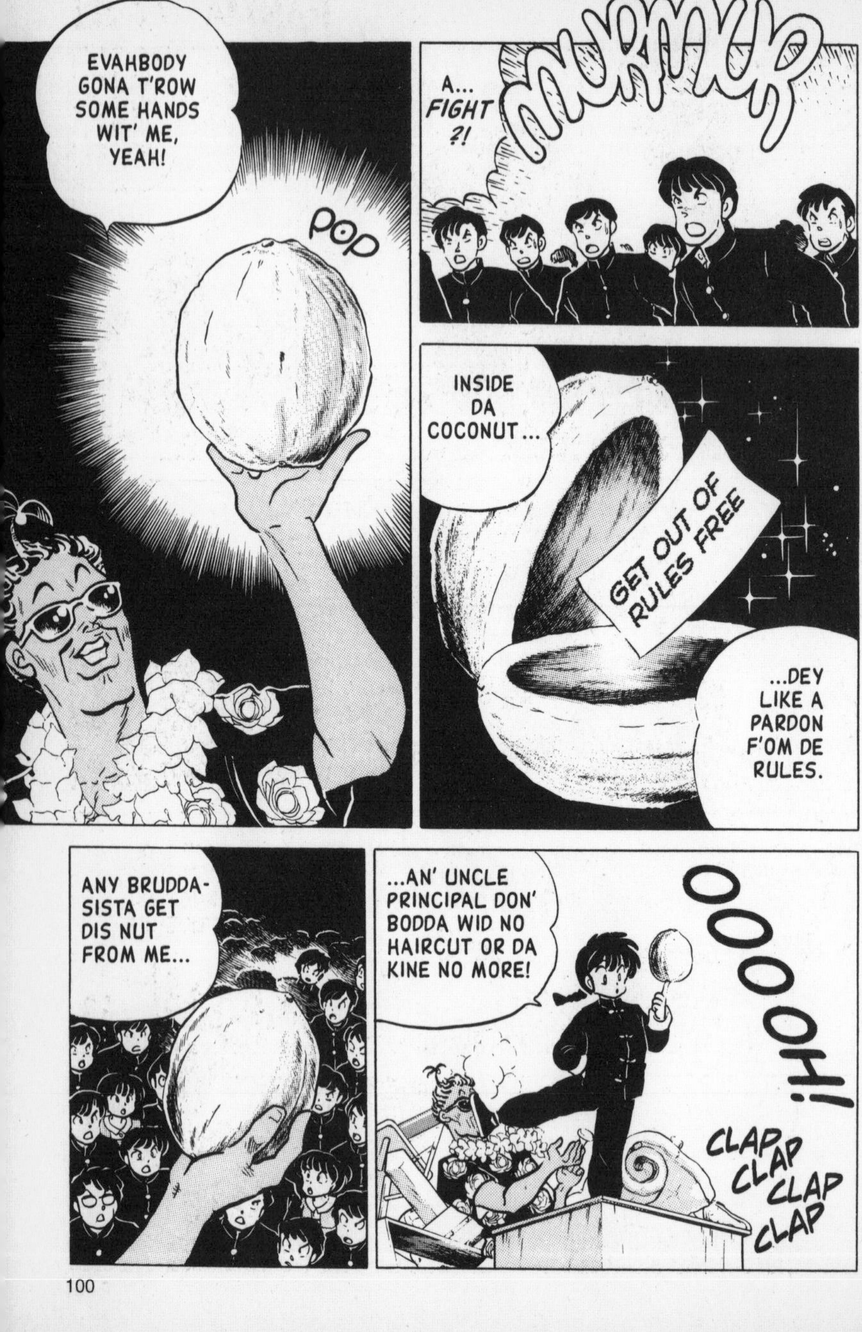
EVAHBODY GONA T'ROW SOME HANDS WIT' ME, YEAH!
POP
A... FIGHT ?!
MURMUR
INSIDE DA COCONUT...
GET OUT OF RULES FREE
...DEY LIKE A PARDON F'OM DE RULES.
ANY BRUDDA-SISTA GET DIS NUT FROM ME...
...AN' UNCLE PRINCIPAL DON' BODDA WID NO HAIRCUT OR DA KINE NO MORE!
OOOOOH!
CLAP CLAP CLAP CLAP

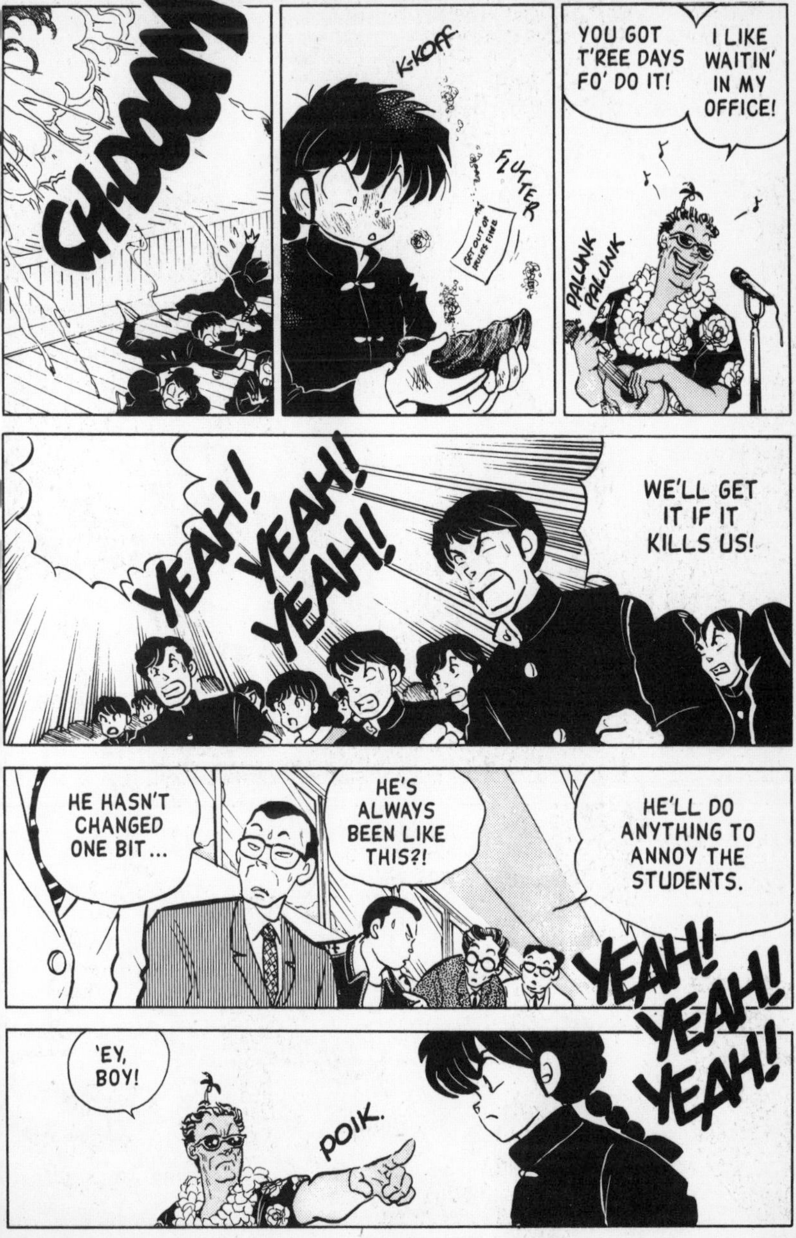
CHDOOM
K-KOFF
FLUTTER
GET OUT OF
YOU GOT T'REE DAYS FO' DO IT!
I LIKE WAITIN' IN MY OFFICE!
PALUNK PALUNK
YEAH! YEAH! YEAH!
WE'LL GET IT IF IT KILLS US!
HE HASN'T CHANGED ONE BIT...
HE'S ALWAYS BEEN LIKE THIS?!
HE'LL DO ANYTHING TO ANNOY THE STUDENTS.
YEAH! YEAH! YEAH!
'EY, BOY!
POIK.

DAT HAIR GON' LOOK REALLY PRETTY ON DE FLOOR! SNIP SNIP!

YOU SHOULDA STAYED IN HAWAII AND BEEN A LIFE-GUARD, DUDE.

AND SO BEGINS THE DUEL FOR THE SCHOOL RULES PARDON!

HAHAHAHAHAHAHAHAHA!

BOYS

GIRLS

Part 7

JOURNEY INTO THE PRINCIPAL'S OFFICE

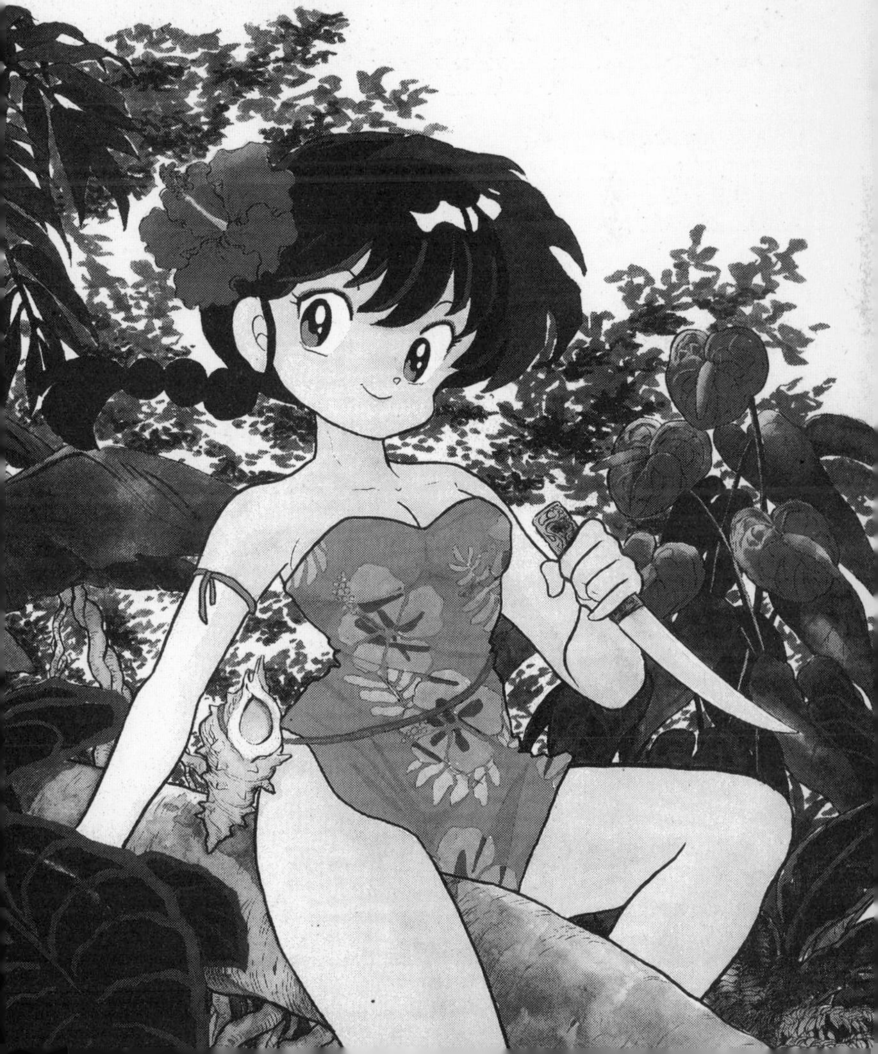

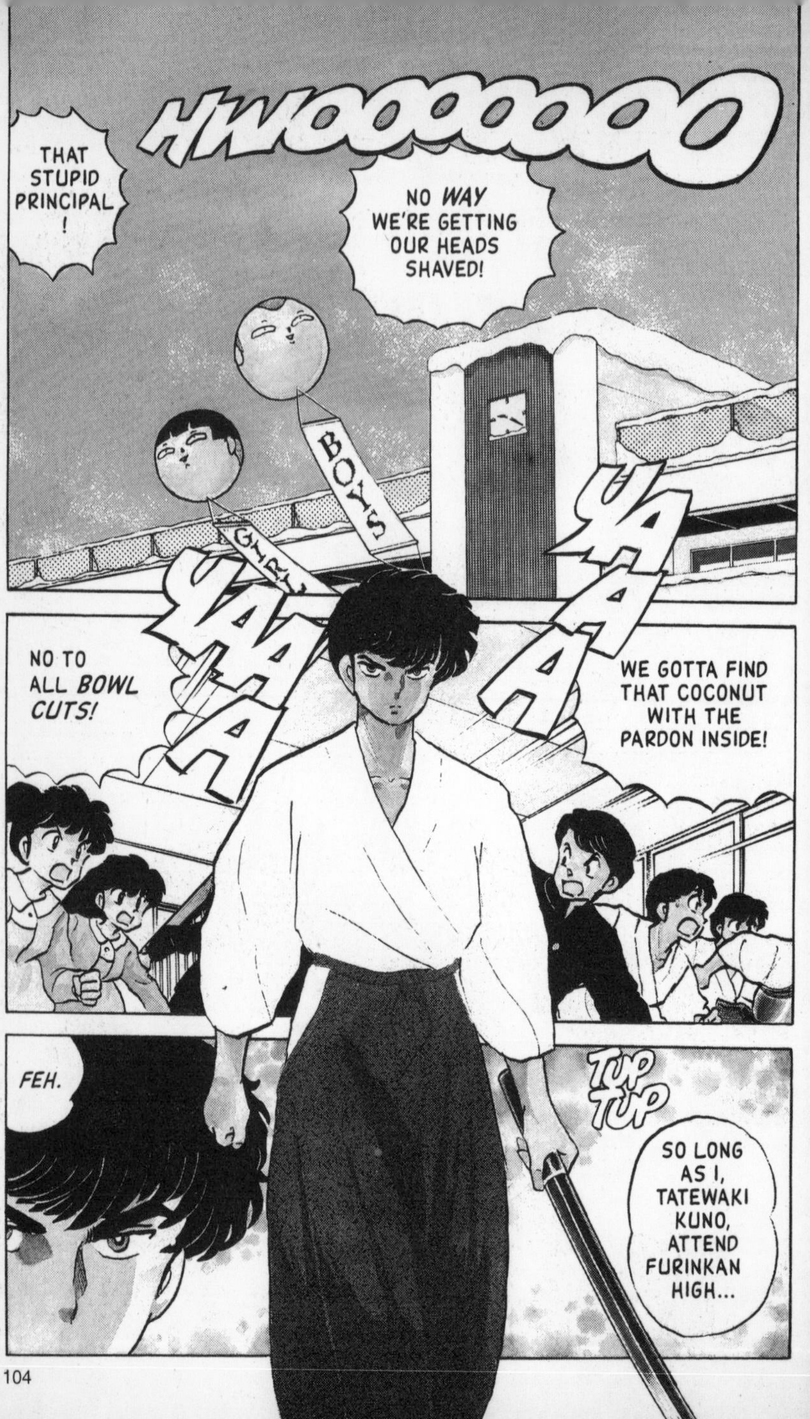
HWOOOOOOO
THAT STUPID PRINCIPAL!
NO *WAY* WE'RE GETTING OUR HEADS SHAVED!
BOYS
YAAA
YAAA
NO TO ALL *BOWL CUTS!*
WE GOTTA FIND THAT COCONUT WITH THE PARDON INSIDE!
FEH.
TUP TUP
SO LONG AS I, TATEWAKI KUNO, ATTEND FURINKAN HIGH...

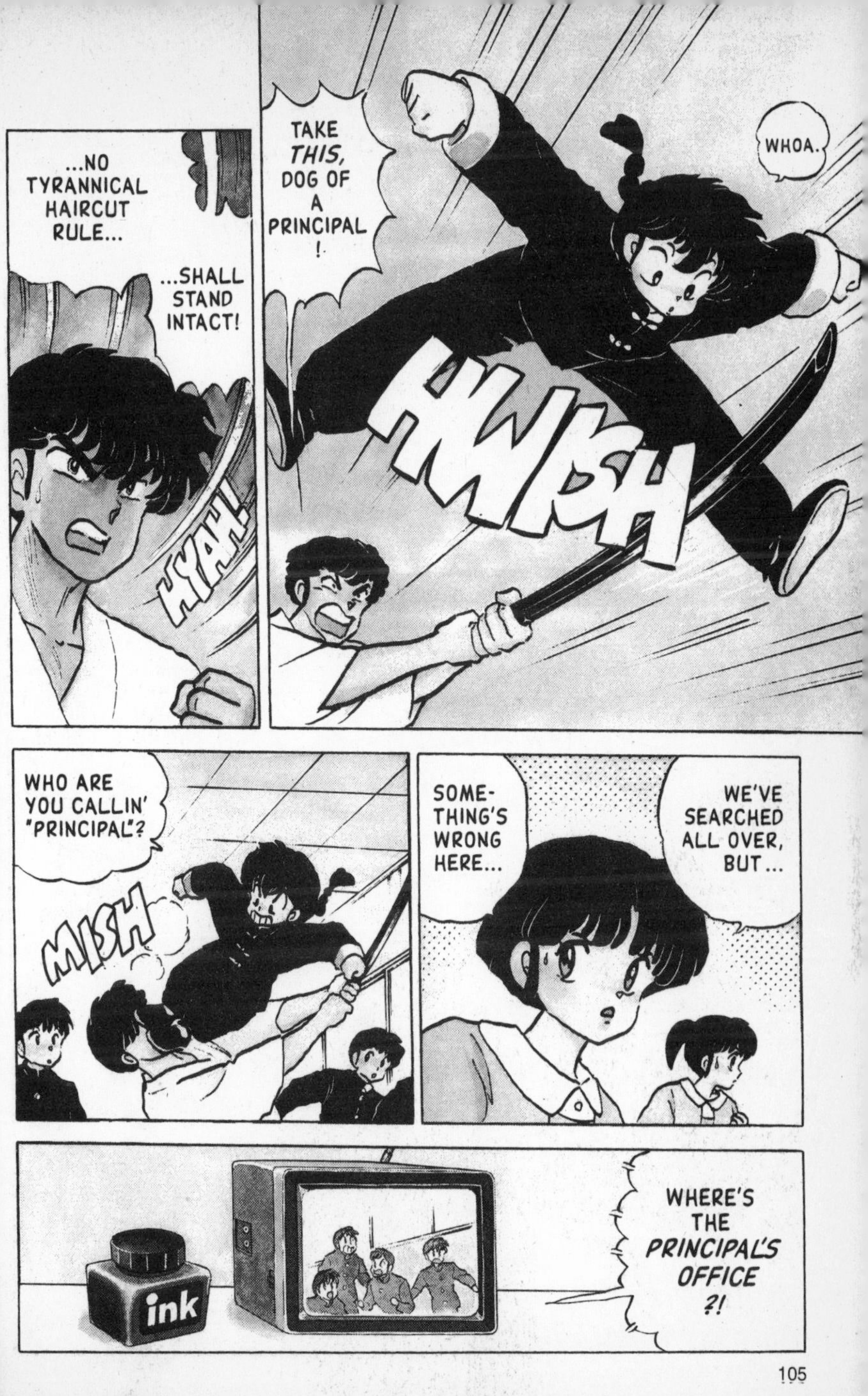
...NO TYRANNICAL HAIRCUT RULE...
...SHALL STAND INTACT!
HYAH!
TAKE THIS, DOG OF A PRINCIPAL!
WHOA.
HWISH
WHO ARE YOU CALLIN' "PRINCIPAL"?
MISH
SOME-THING'S WRONG HERE...
WE'VE SEARCHED ALL OVER, BUT...
ink
WHERE'S THE PRINCIPAL'S OFFICE ?!

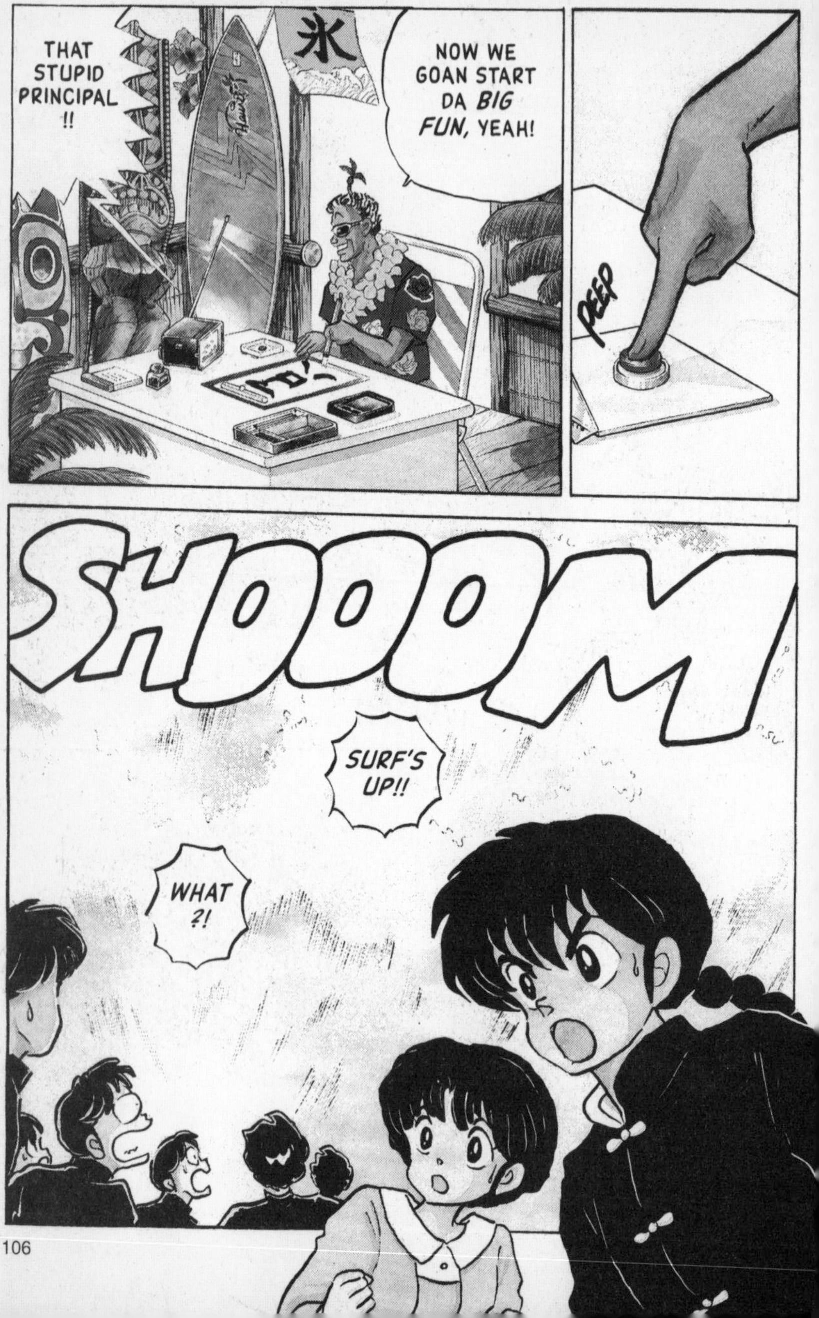
THAT STUPID PRINCIPAL !!
NOW WE GOAN START DA BIG FUN, YEAH!
PEEP
SHOOOM
SURF'S UP!!
WHAT ?!

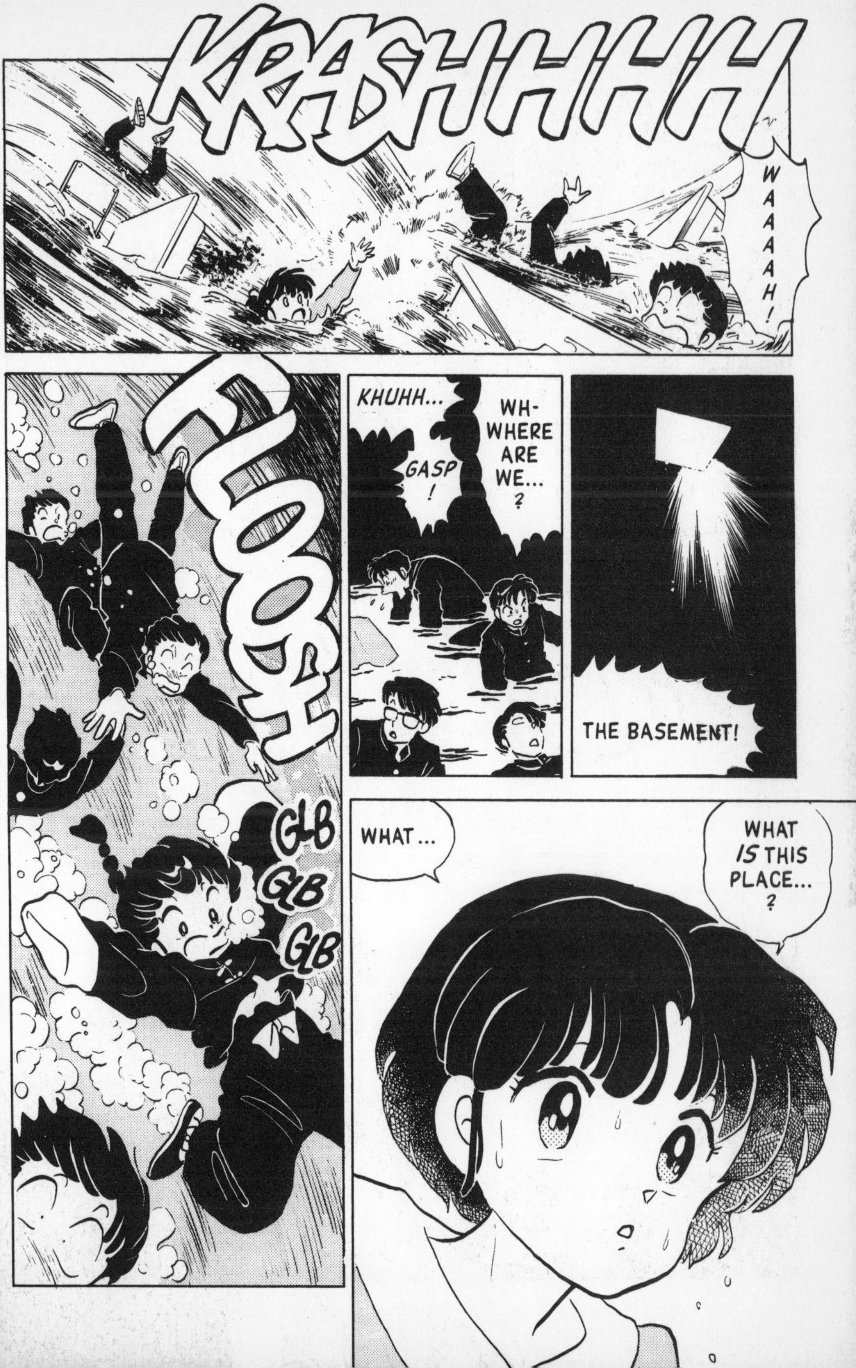
KRASHHHHH
WAAAAAH!
FLOOSH
GLB
GLB
GLB
KHUHH...
GASP!
WH-WHERE ARE WE...?
THE BASEMENT!
WHAT...
WHAT IS THIS PLACE...?

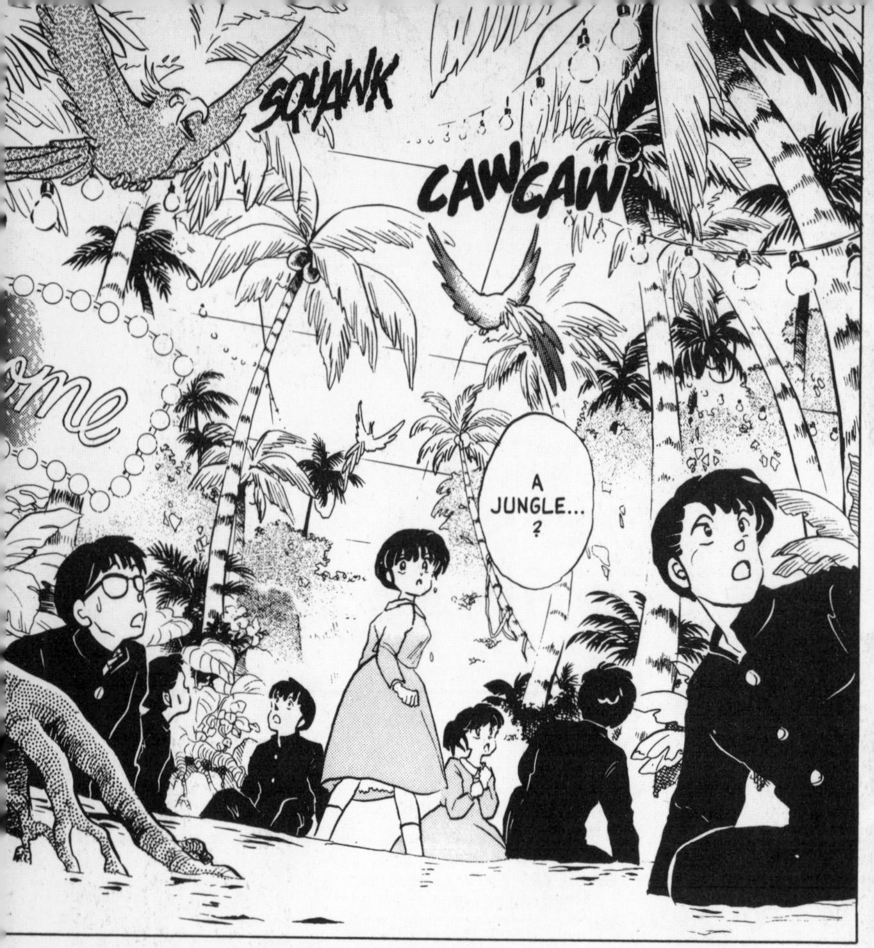
SQUAWK
CAW CAW
A JUNGLE...?
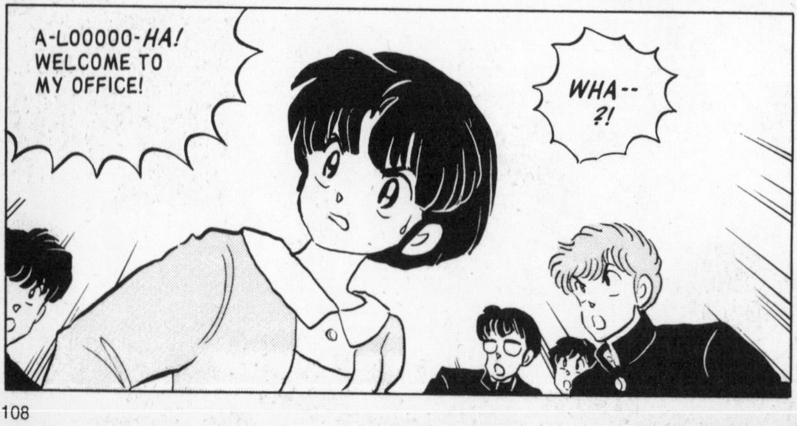
A-LOOOOO-HA! WELCOME TO MY OFFICE!
WHA--?!

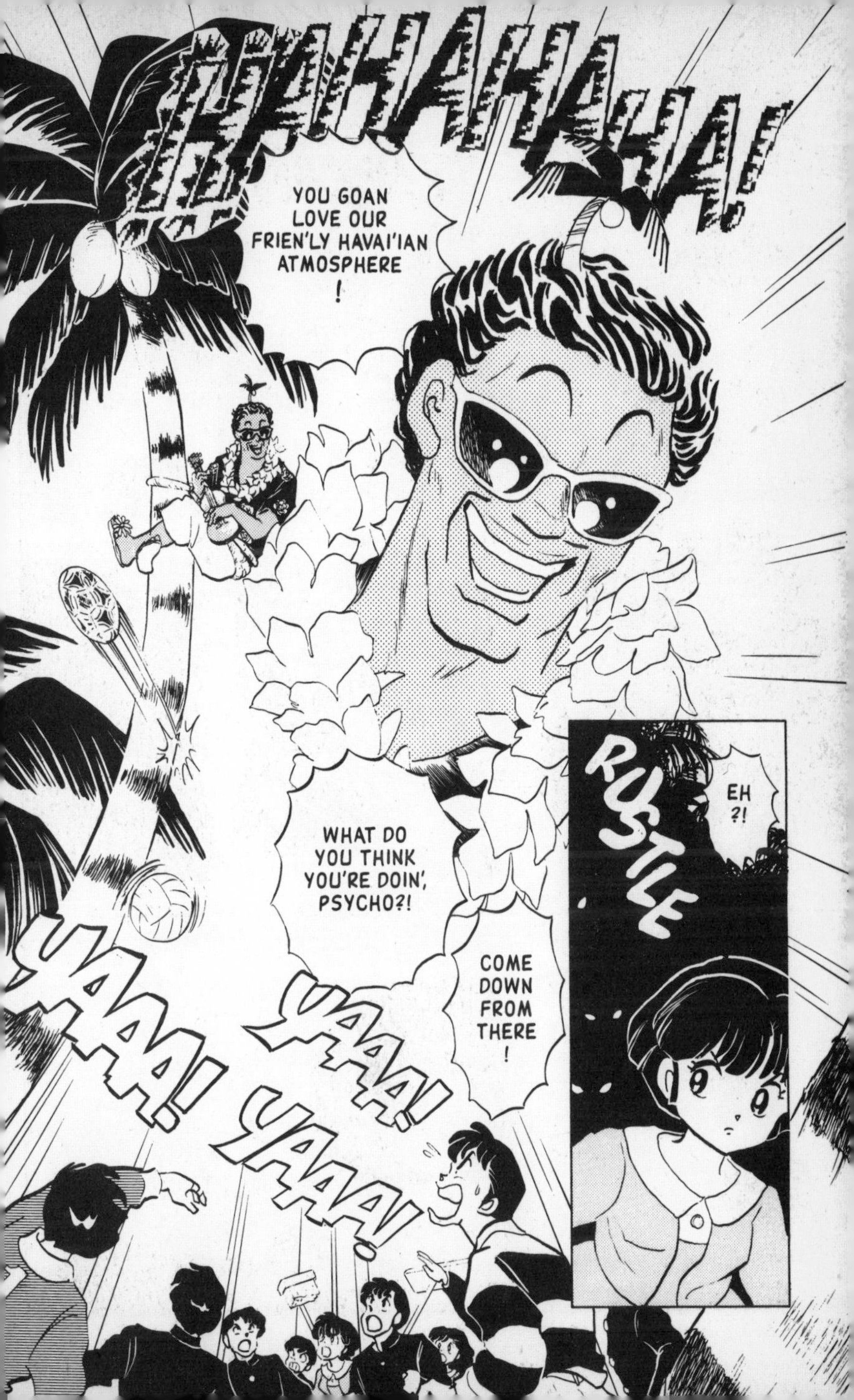
HAHAHAHA!
YOU GOAN LOVE OUR FRIEN'LY HAVAI'IAN ATMOSPHERE!
WHAT DO YOU THINK YOU'RE DOIN', PSYCHO?!
COME DOWN FROM THERE!
YAAA! YAAA! YAAA! YAAA!
RUSTLE
EH?!

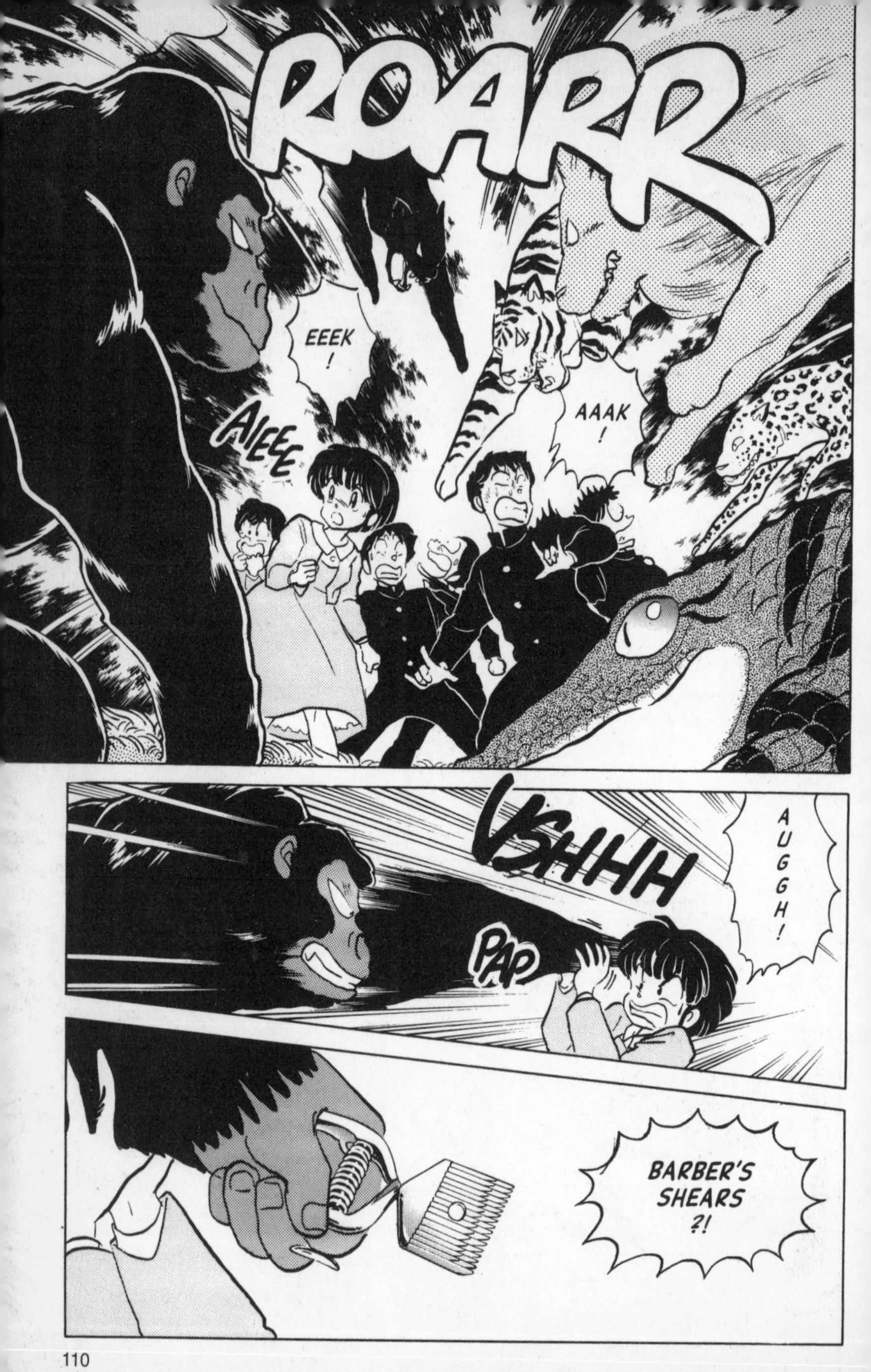
ROARR
EEEK!
AIEEE
AAAK!
VSHHH
PAP
AUGGH!
BARBER'S SHEARS ?!

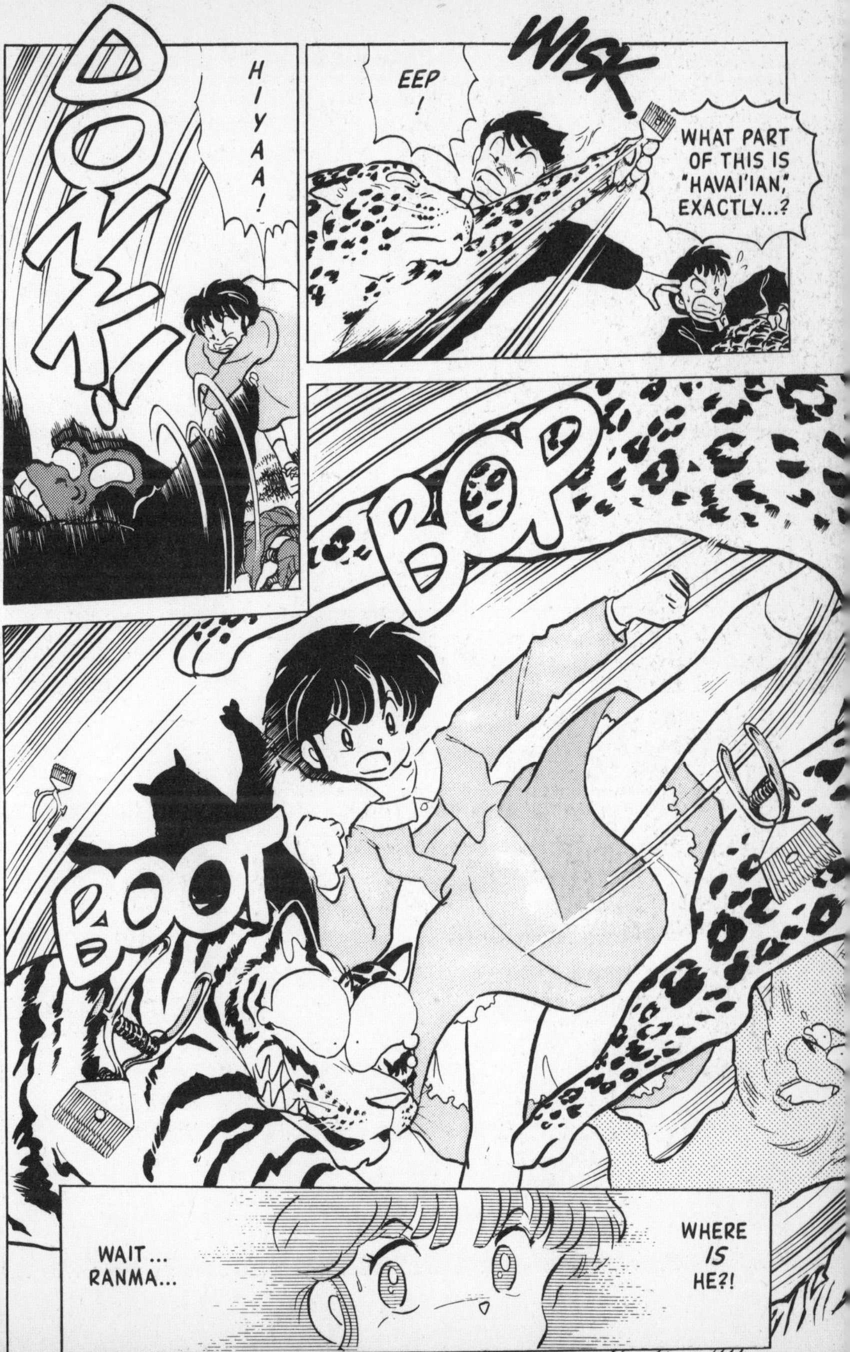
WISK
EEP!
WHAT PART OF THIS IS "HAVAI'IAN," EXACTLY...?
BOP
HIYAA!
DONK!
BOOT
WHERE IS HE?!
WAIT... RANMA...

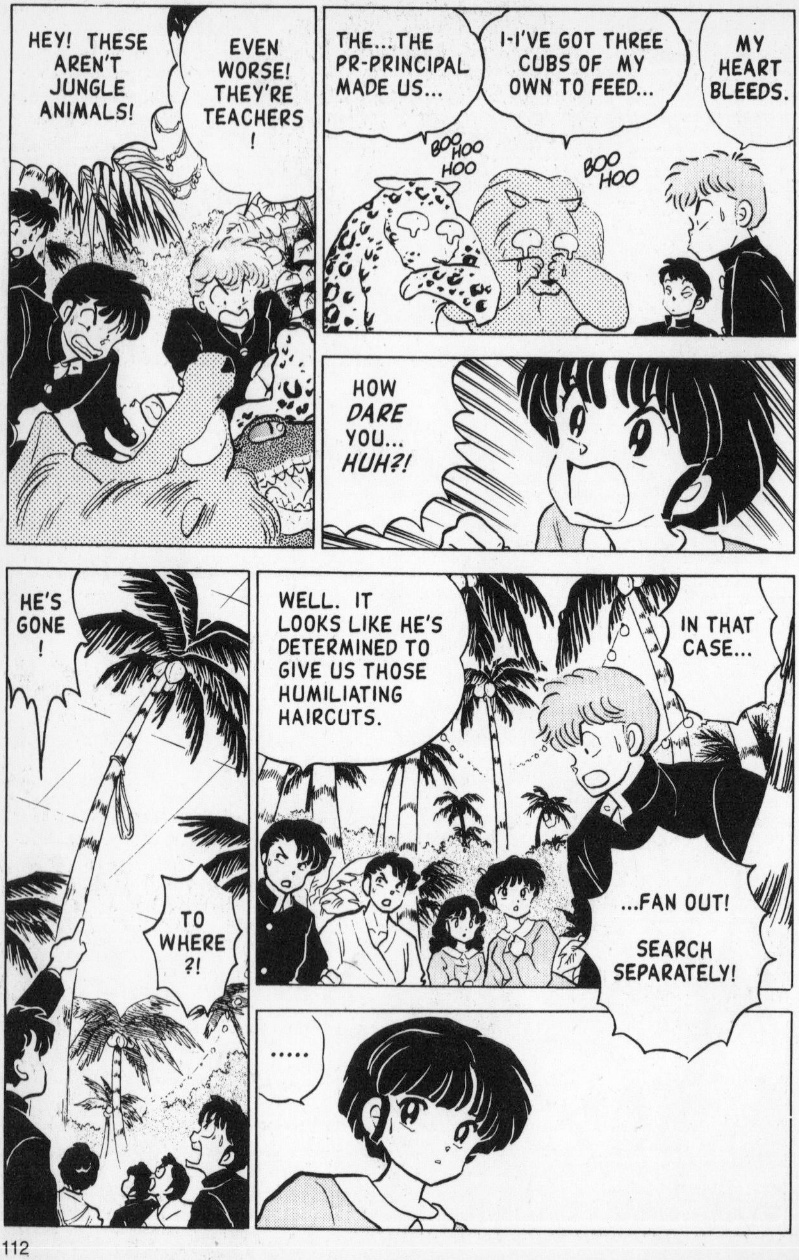
HEY! THESE AREN'T JUNGLE ANIMALS!
EVEN WORSE! THEY'RE TEACHERS!
THE... THE PR-PRINCIPAL MADE US...
BOO HOO HOO
I-I'VE GOT THREE CUBS OF MY OWN TO FEED...
BOO HOO
MY HEART BLEEDS.
HOW DARE YOU... HUH?!
HE'S GONE!
TO WHERE?!
WELL. IT LOOKS LIKE HE'S DETERMINED TO GIVE US THOSE HUMILIATING HAIRCUTS.
IN THAT CASE...
...FAN OUT!
SEARCH SEPARATELY!
.....

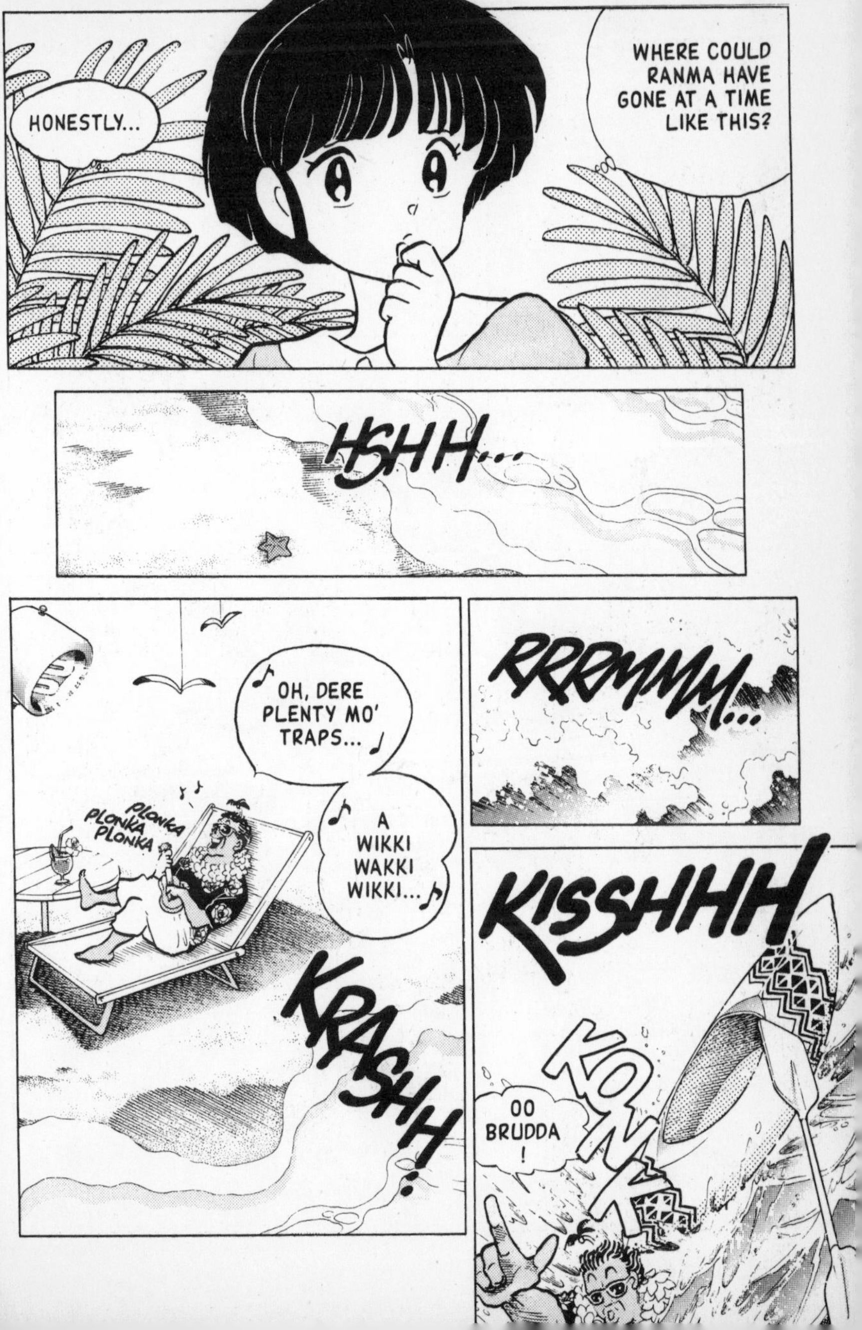
HONESTLY...
WHERE COULD RANMA HAVE GONE AT A TIME LIKE THIS?
HSHH...
OH, DERE PLENTY MO' TRAPS...
A WIKKI WAKKI WIKKI...
PLONKA PLONKA PLONKA
KRASHH...
RRRMMM...
KISSHHH
KONK
OO BRUDDA!

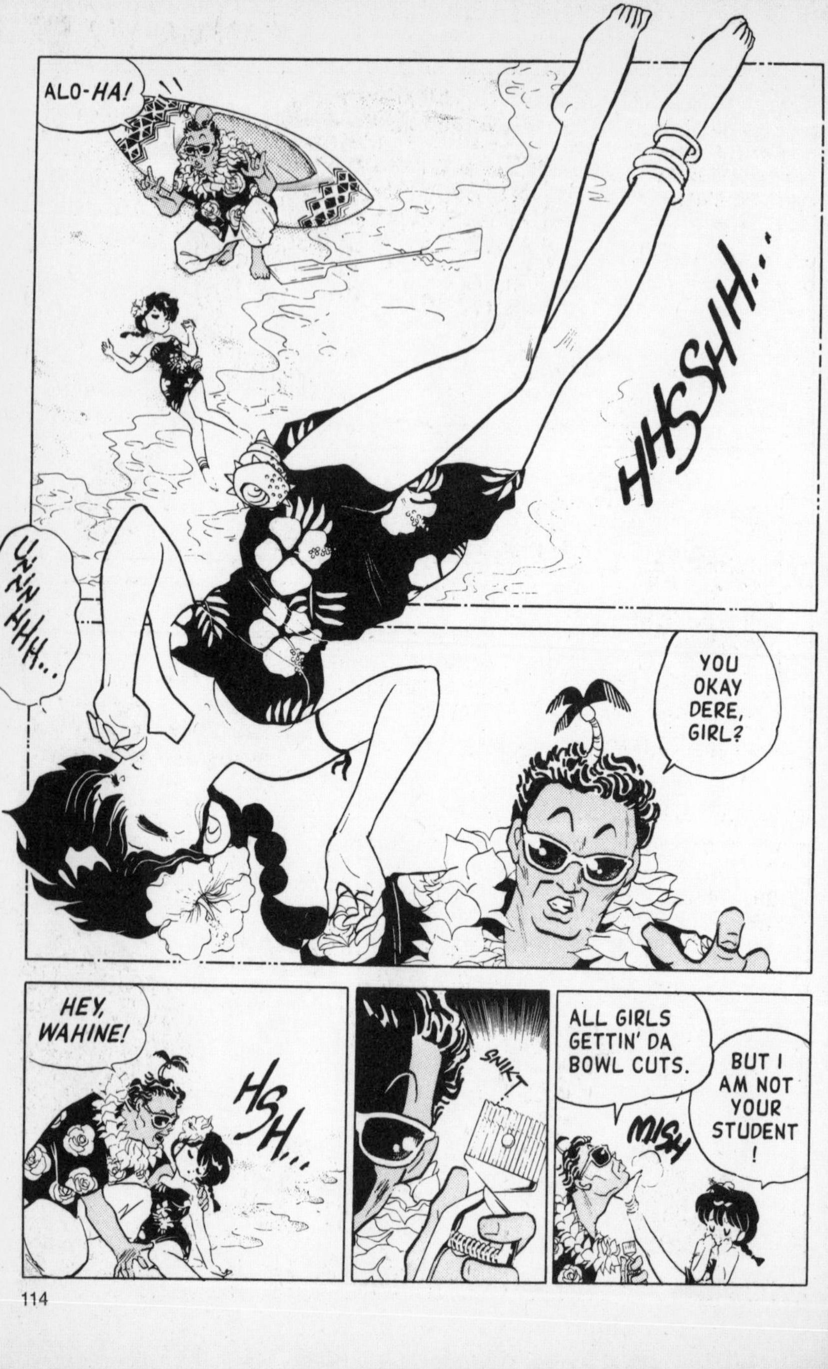
ALO-HA!
HHSHH...
U'N'N HHH...
YOU OKAY DERE, GIRL?
HEY, WAHINE!
HSH...
SNIKT
ALL GIRLS GETTIN' DA BOWL CUTS.
MISH
BUT I AM NOT YOUR STUDENT !

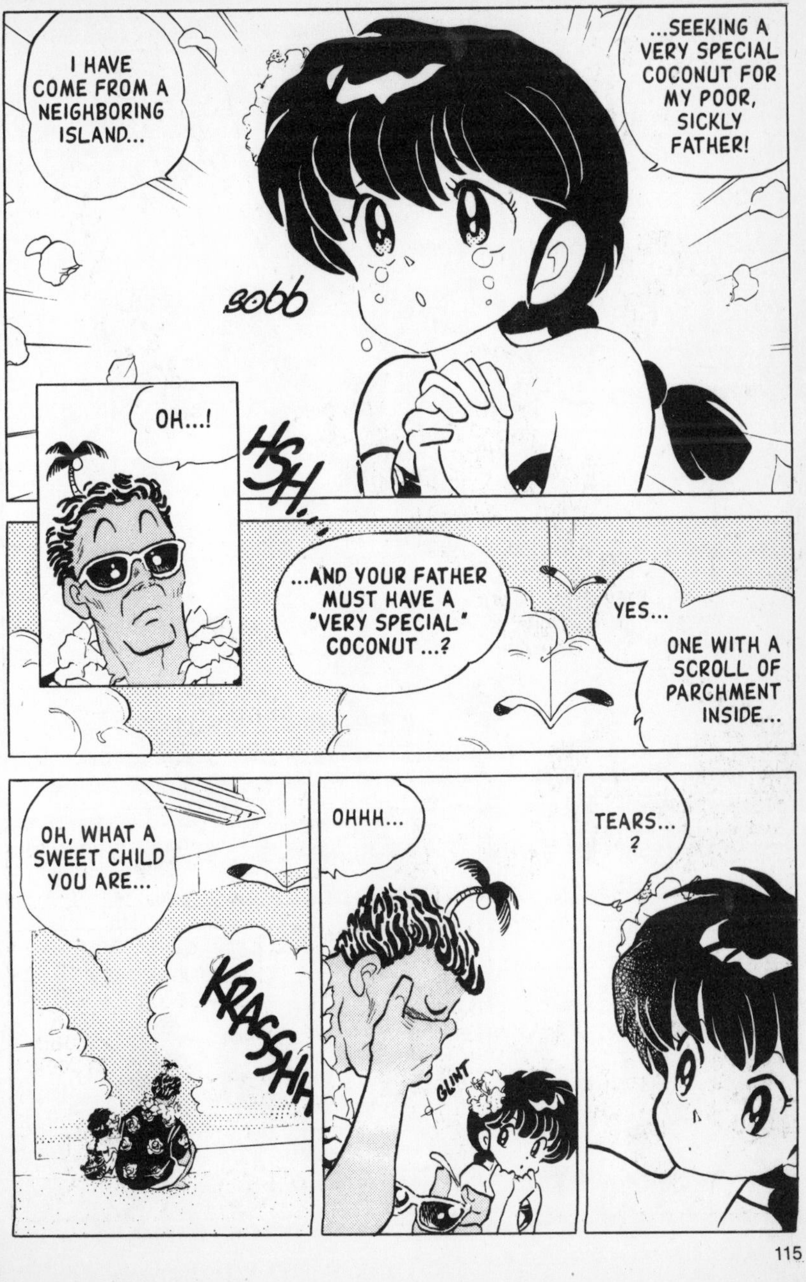
I HAVE COME FROM A NEIGHBORING ISLAND...
...SEEKING A VERY SPECIAL COCONUT FOR MY POOR, SICKLY FATHER!
sobb
OH...!
HSH...
...AND YOUR FATHER MUST HAVE A "VERY SPECIAL" COCONUT...?
YES...
ONE WITH A SCROLL OF PARCHMENT INSIDE...
OH, WHAT A SWEET CHILD YOU ARE...
KRASSHH
OHHH...
GLINT
TEARS...?

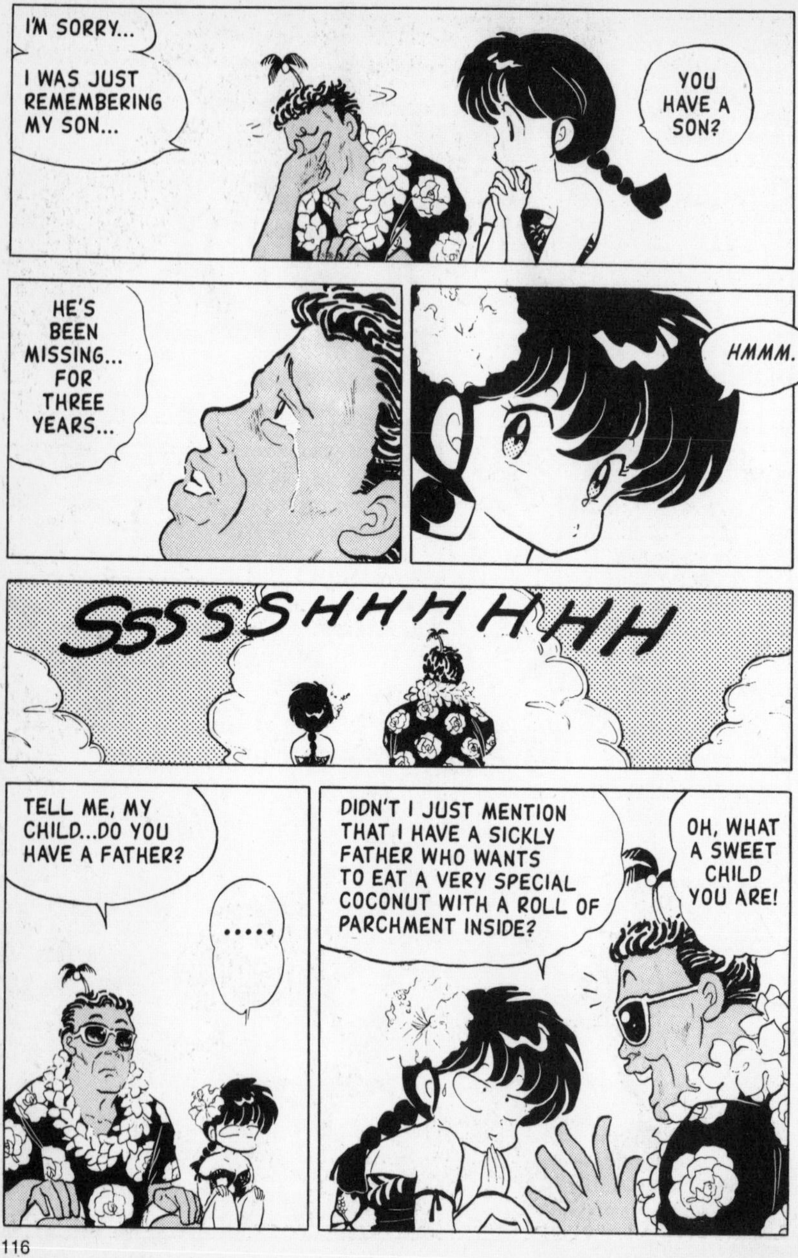
I'M SORRY...
I WAS JUST REMEMBERING MY SON...
YOU HAVE A SON?
HE'S BEEN MISSING... FOR THREE YEARS...
HMMM.
SSSSHHHHHH
TELL ME, MY CHILD...DO YOU HAVE A FATHER?
.....
DIDN'T I JUST MENTION THAT I HAVE A SICKLY FATHER WHO WANTS TO EAT A VERY SPECIAL COCONUT WITH A ROLL OF PARCHMENT INSIDE?
OH, WHAT A SWEET CHILD YOU ARE!

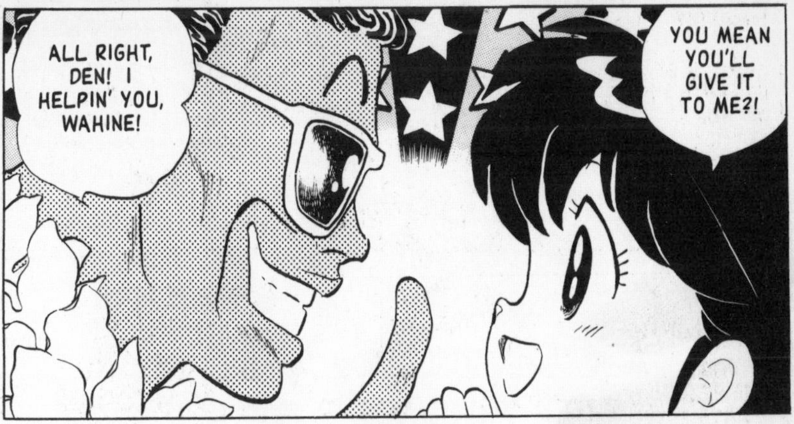
ALL RIGHT, DEN! I HELPIN' YOU, WAHINE!
YOU MEAN YOU'LL GIVE IT TO ME?!

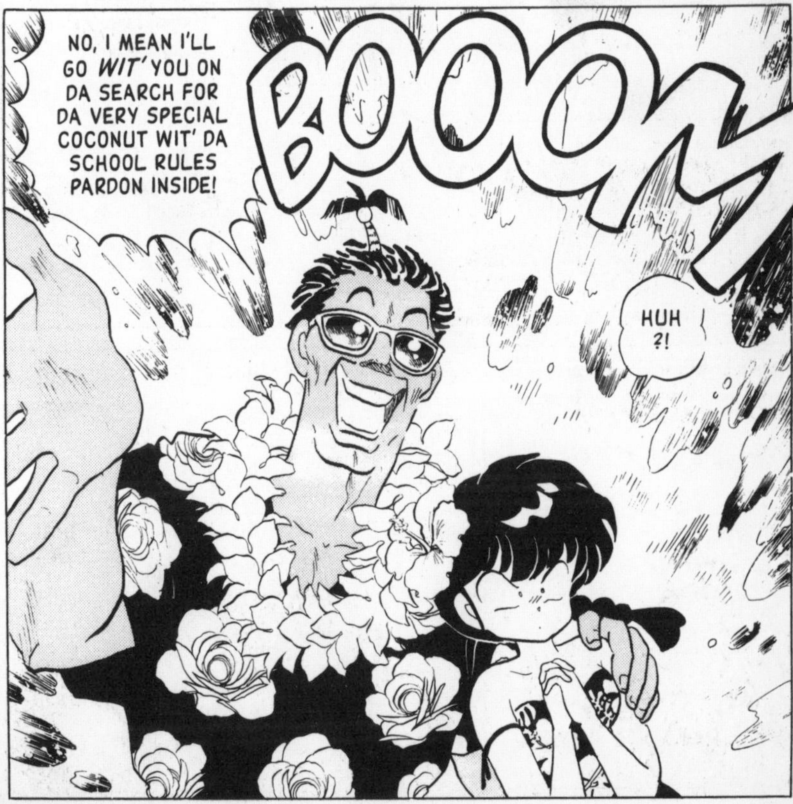
NO, I MEAN I'LL GO *WIT'* YOU ON DA SEARCH FOR DA VERY SPECIAL COCONUT WIT' DA SCHOOL RULES PARDON INSIDE!
BOOOM
HUH ?!

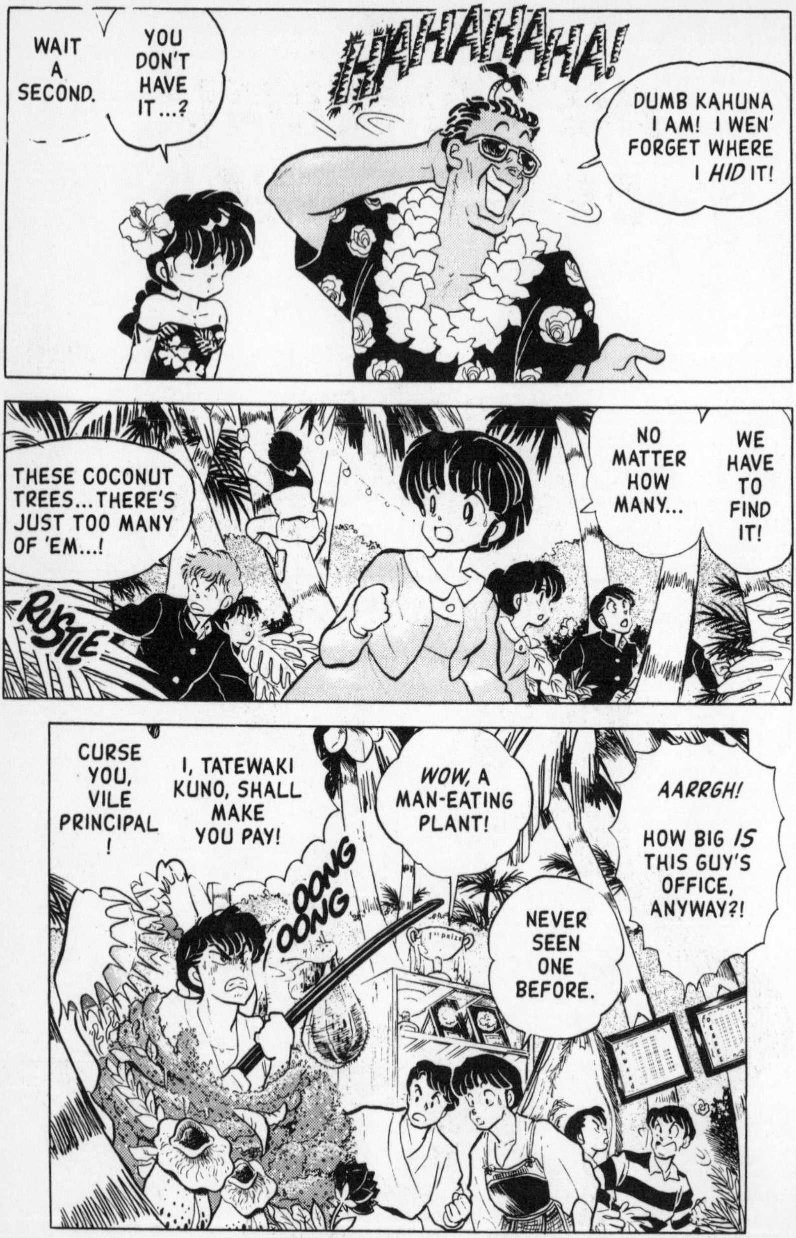
WAIT A SECOND.
YOU DON'T HAVE IT...?
HAHAHAHA!
DUMB KAHUNA I AM! I WEN' FORGET WHERE I *HID* IT!
THESE COCONUT TREES...THERE'S JUST TOO MANY OF 'EM...!
RUSTLE
NO MATTER HOW MANY...
WE HAVE TO FIND IT!
CURSE YOU, VILE PRINCIPAL!
I, TATEWAKI KUNO, SHALL MAKE YOU PAY!
WOW, A MAN-EATING PLANT!
DOONG DOONG
NEVER SEEN ONE BEFORE.
AARRGH!
HOW BIG *IS* THIS GUY'S OFFICE, ANYWAY?!

Part 8

THE PRINCIPAL OF THE THING

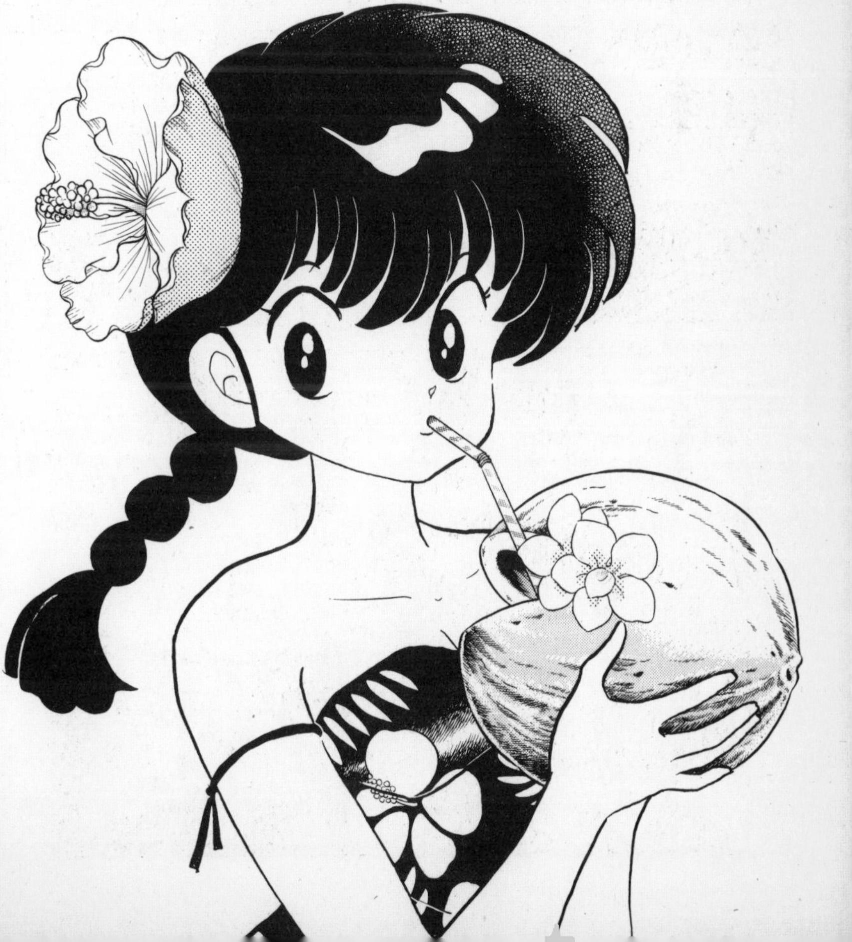

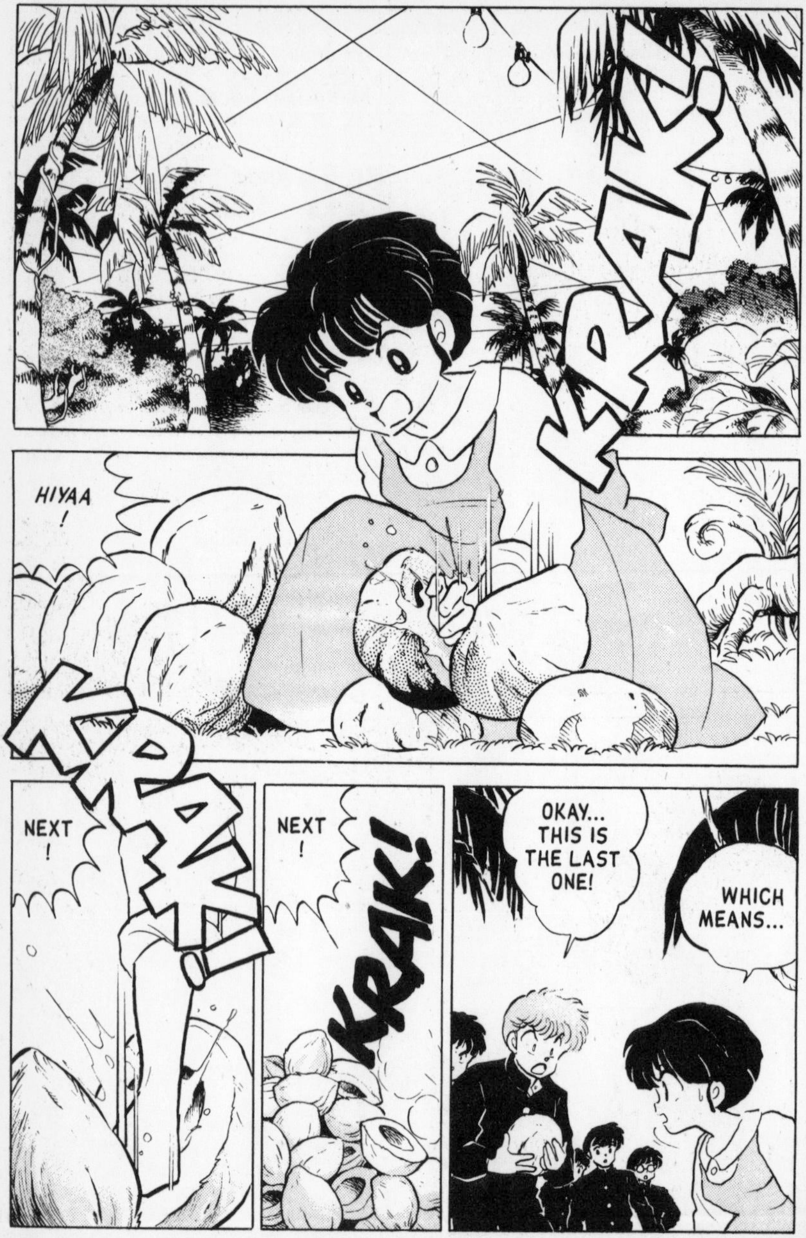
KRAK!
HIYAA!
KRAK!
NEXT!
NEXT!
KRAK!
OKAY... THIS IS THE LAST ONE!
WHICH MEANS...

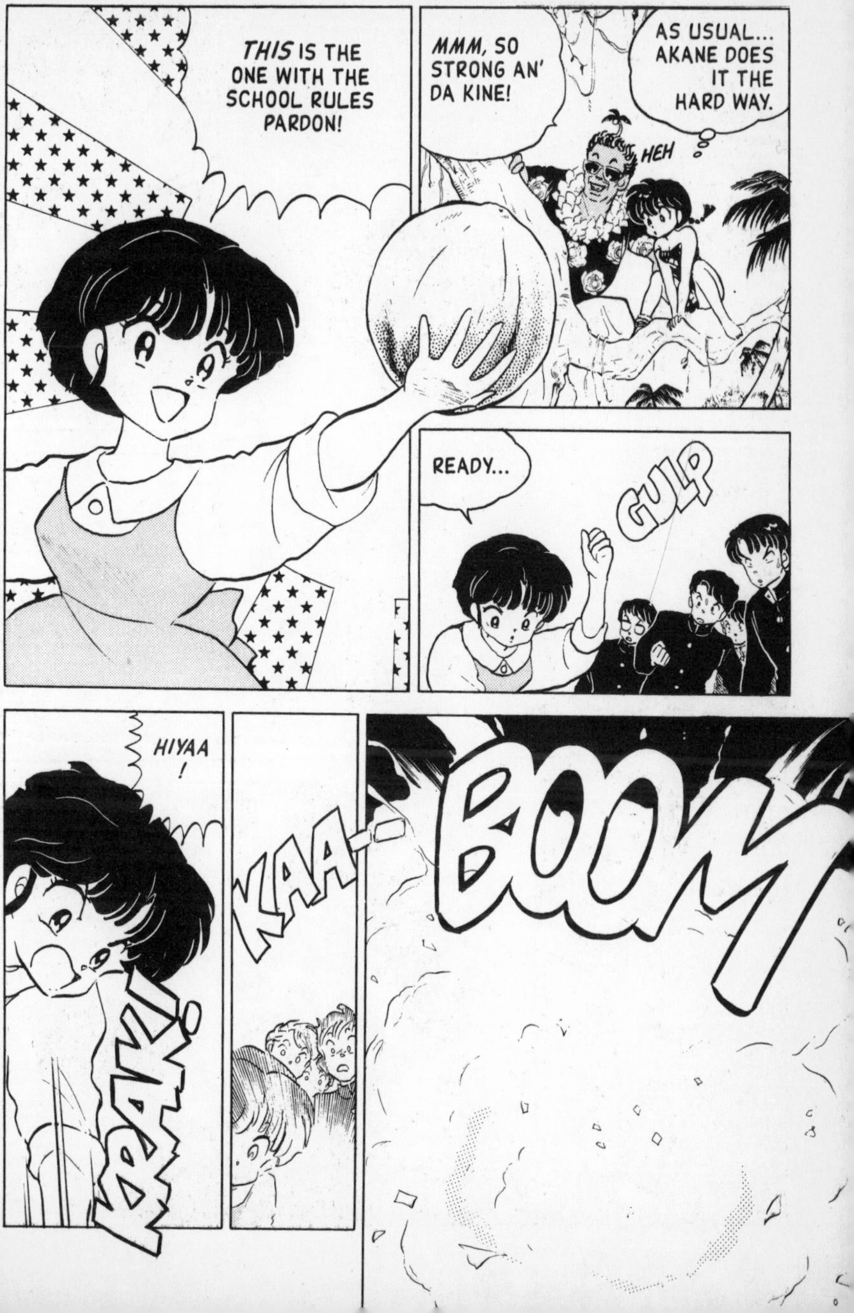
THIS IS THE ONE WITH THE SCHOOL RULES PARDON!
MMM, SO STRONG AN' DA KINE!
AS USUAL... AKANE DOES IT THE HARD WAY.
HEH
READY...
GULP
HIYAA !
KRAAK!
KAA-
BOOM

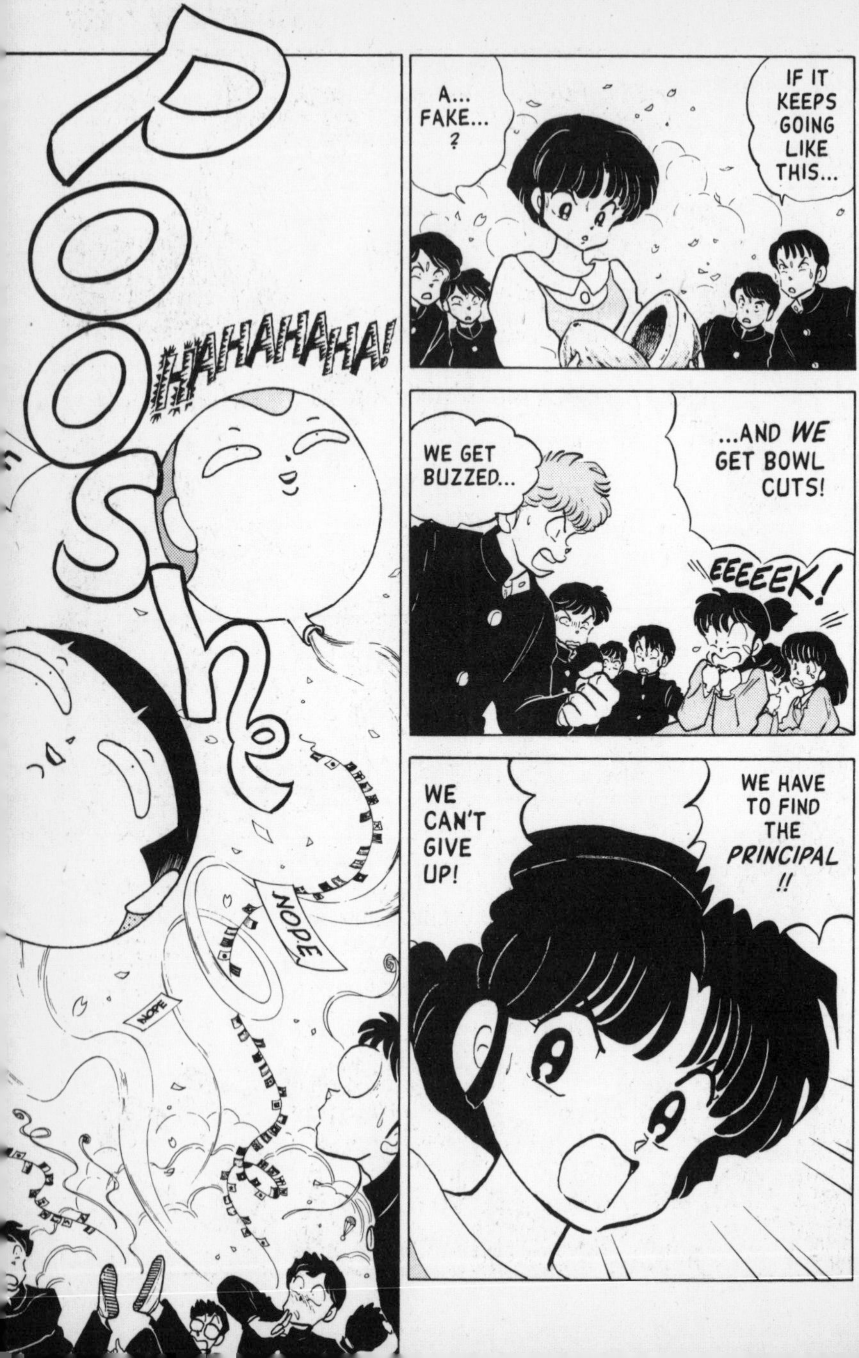
POOOSH
HAHAHAHA!
NOPE
NOPE
A... FAKE...?
IF IT KEEPS GOING LIKE THIS...
WE GET BUZZED...
...AND WE GET BOWL CUTS!
EEEEEK!
WE CAN'T GIVE UP!
WE HAVE TO FIND THE PRINCIPAL!!

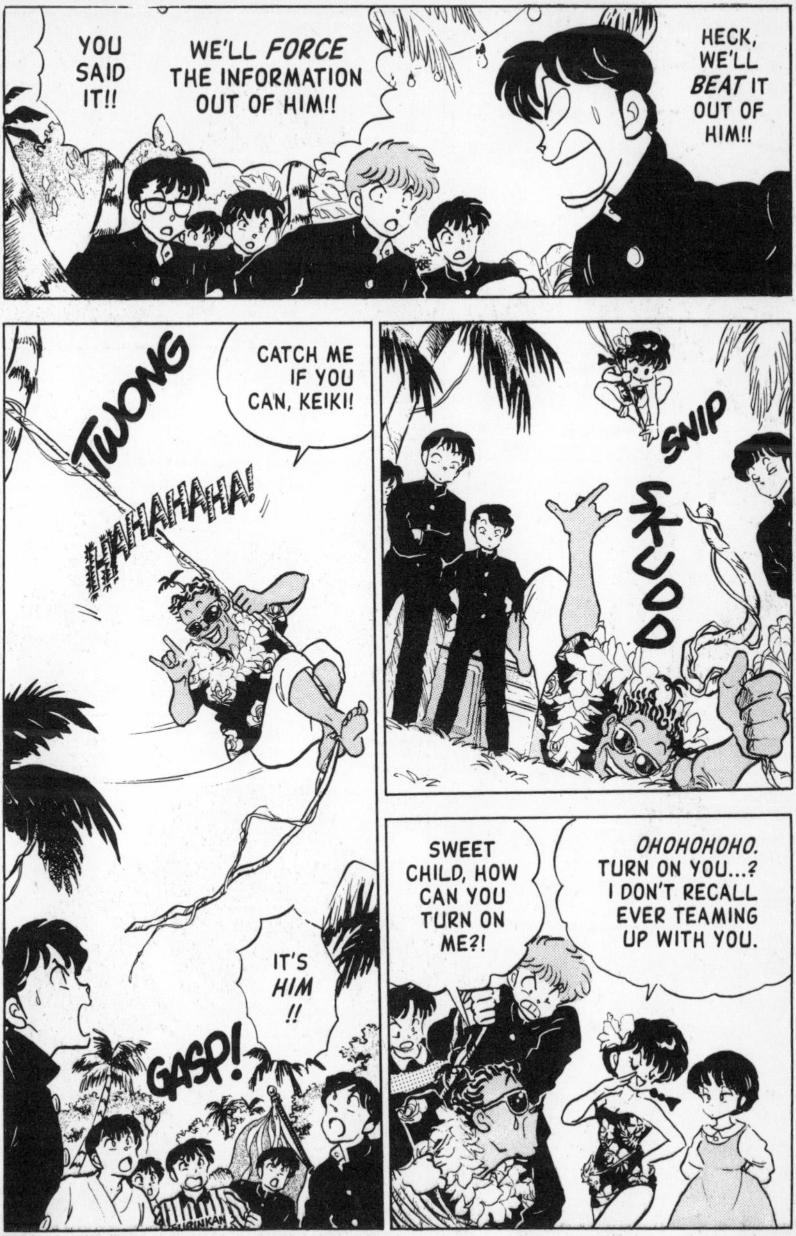
YOU SAID IT!!
WE'LL *FORCE* THE INFORMATION OUT OF HIM!!
HECK, WE'LL *BEAT* IT OUT OF HIM!!
TWONG
CATCH ME IF YOU CAN, KEIKI!
HAHAHAHA!
IT'S *HIM* !!
GASP!
SNIP
SKUDD
SWEET CHILD, HOW CAN YOU TURN ON ME?!
OHOHOHOHO. TURN ON YOU...? I DON'T RECALL EVER TEAMING UP WITH YOU.

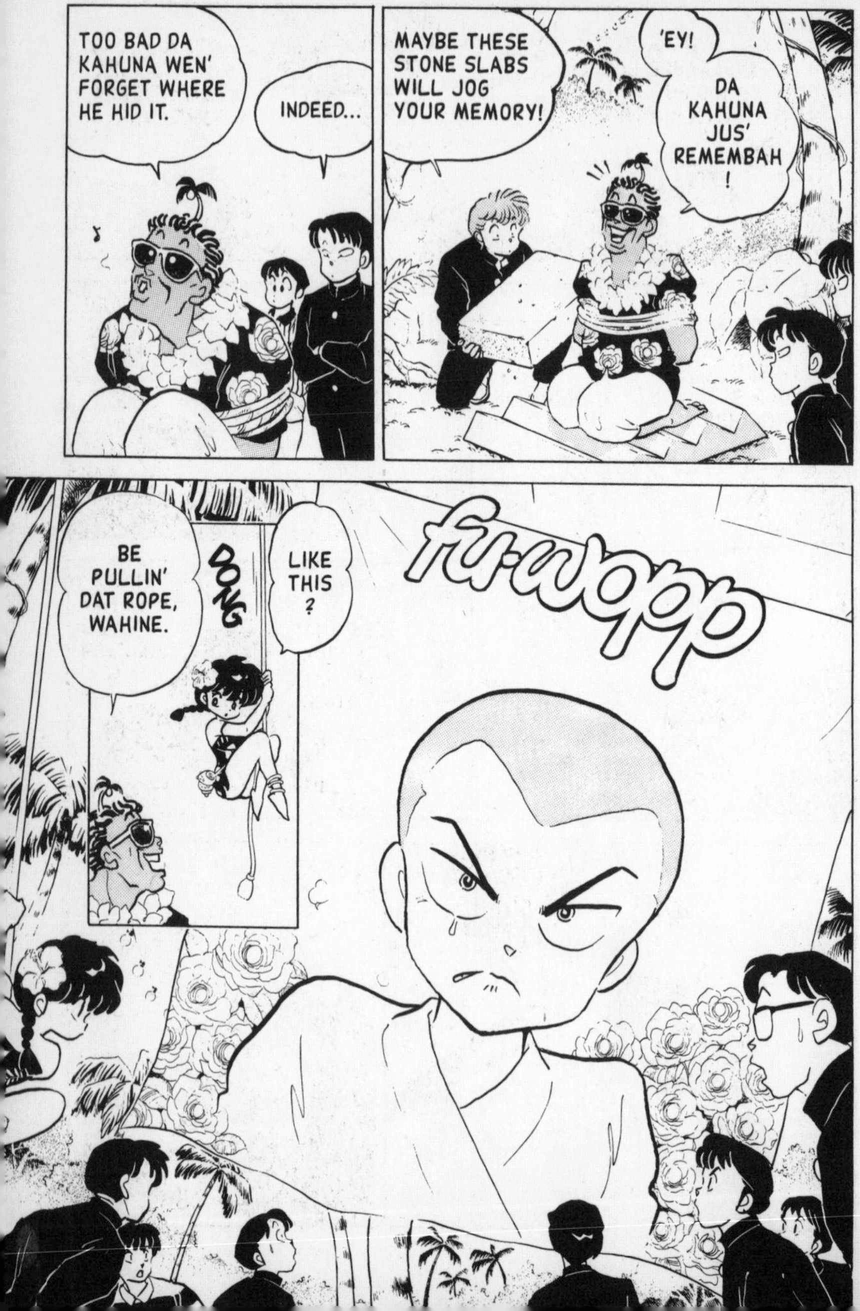
TOO BAD DA KAHUNA WEN' FORGET WHERE HE HID IT.
INDEED...
MAYBE THESE STONE SLABS WILL JOG YOUR MEMORY!
'EY!
DA KAHUNA JUS' REMEMBAH!
BE PULLIN' DAT ROPE, WAHINE.
DONG
LIKE THIS?
fu-wopp

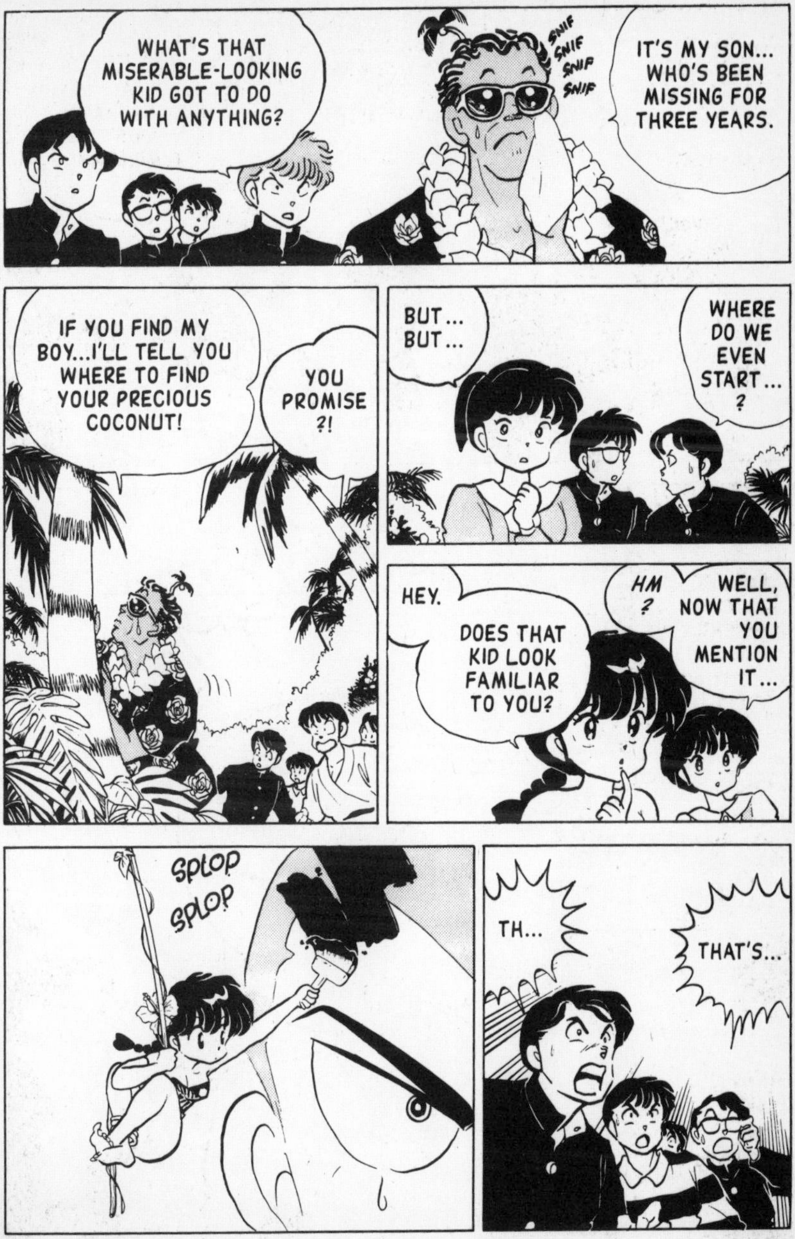
WHAT'S THAT MISERABLE-LOOKING KID GOT TO DO WITH ANYTHING?
SNIF SNIF SNIF SNIF
IT'S MY SON... WHO'S BEEN MISSING FOR THREE YEARS.
IF YOU FIND MY BOY...I'LL TELL YOU WHERE TO FIND YOUR PRECIOUS COCONUT!
YOU PROMISE ?!
BUT... BUT...
WHERE DO WE EVEN START... ?
HEY.
DOES THAT KID LOOK FAMILIAR TO YOU?
HM ?
WELL, NOW THAT YOU MENTION IT...
SPLOP SPLOP
TH...
THAT'S...

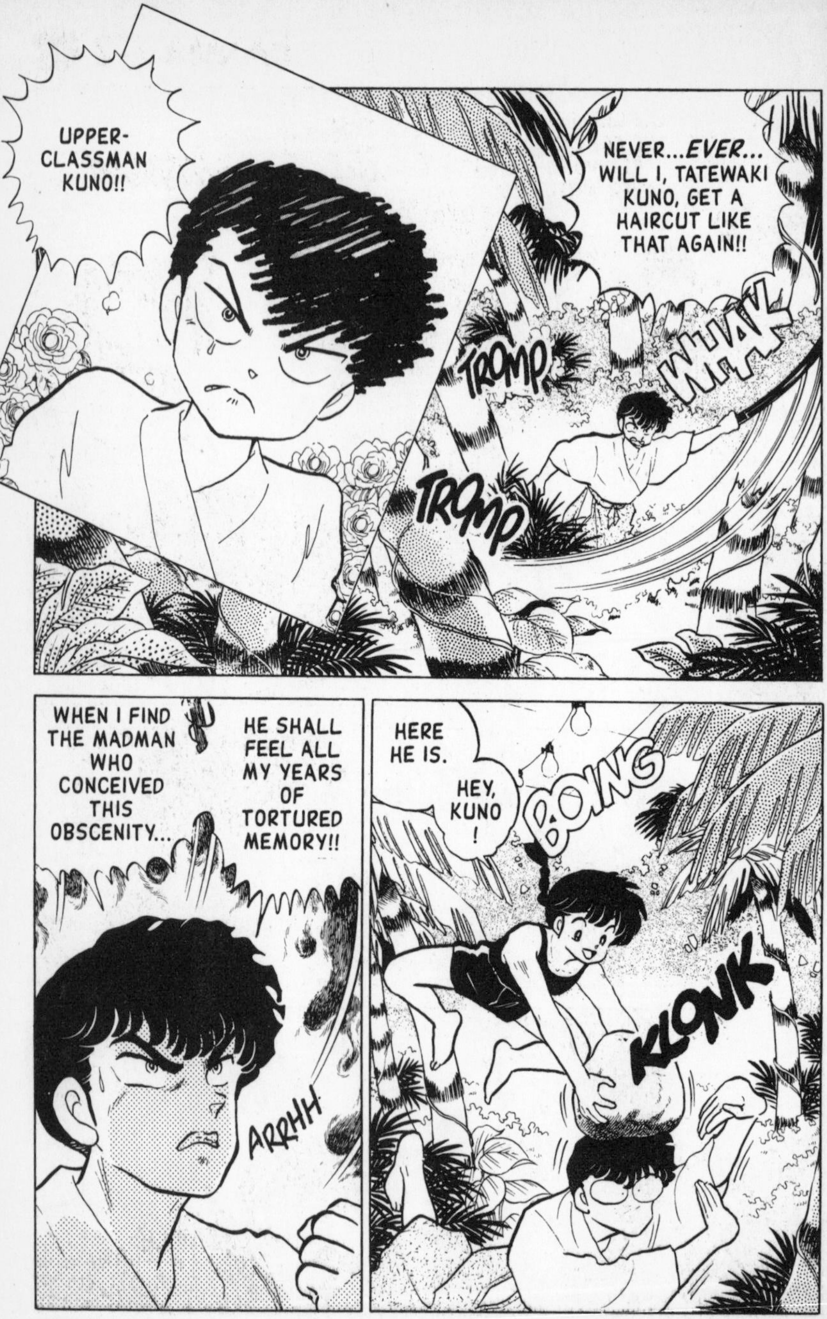
UPPER-CLASSMAN KUNO!!
NEVER...*EVER*... WILL I, TATEWAKI KUNO, GET A HAIRCUT LIKE THAT AGAIN!!
TROMP
WHAK
TROMP
WHEN I FIND THE MADMAN WHO CONCEIVED THIS OBSCENITY...
HE SHALL FEEL ALL MY YEARS OF TORTURED MEMORY!!
ARRHH
HERE HE IS.
HEY, KUNO!
BOING
KLONK

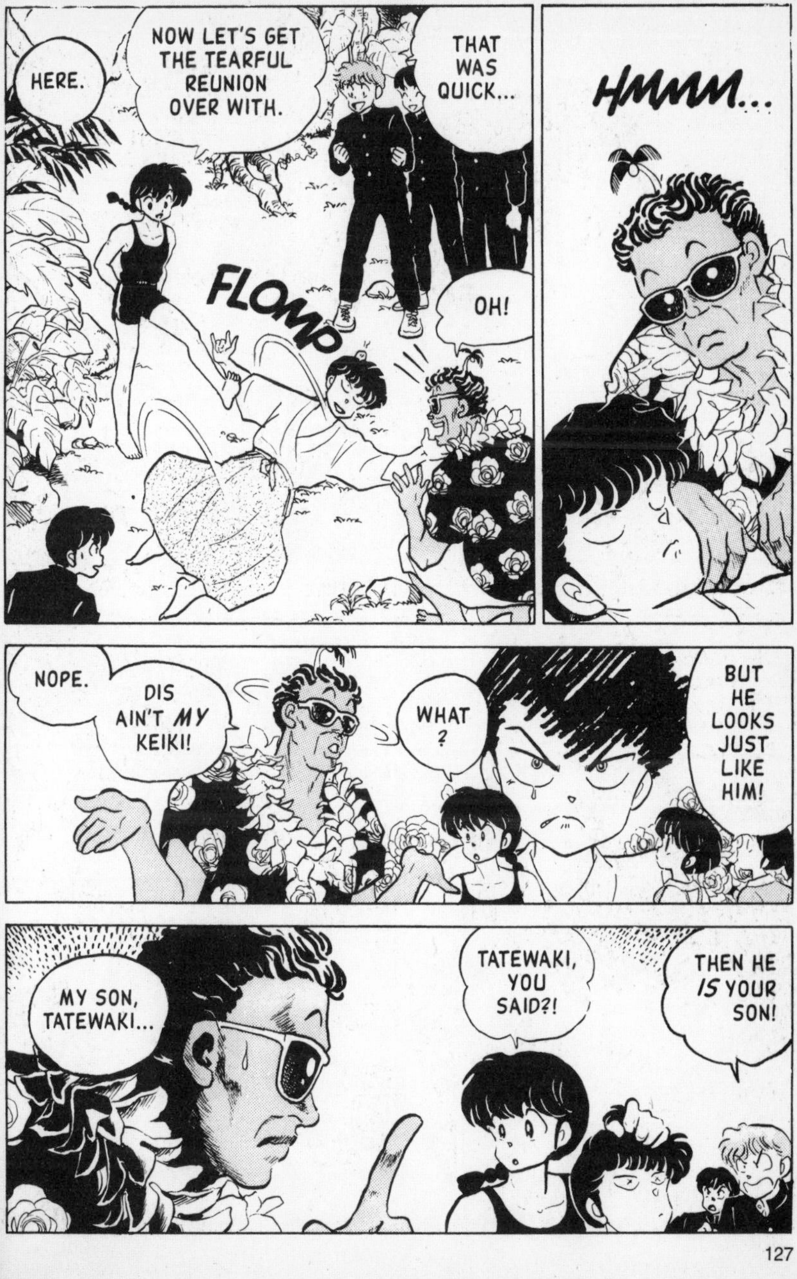
HERE.
NOW LET'S GET THE TEARFUL REUNION OVER WITH.
THAT WAS QUICK...
FLOMP
OH!
HMMM...
NOPE.
DIS AIN'T *MY* KEIKI!
WHAT?
BUT HE LOOKS JUST LIKE HIM!
MY SON, TATEWAKI...
TATEWAKI, YOU SAID?!
THEN HE *IS* YOUR SON!

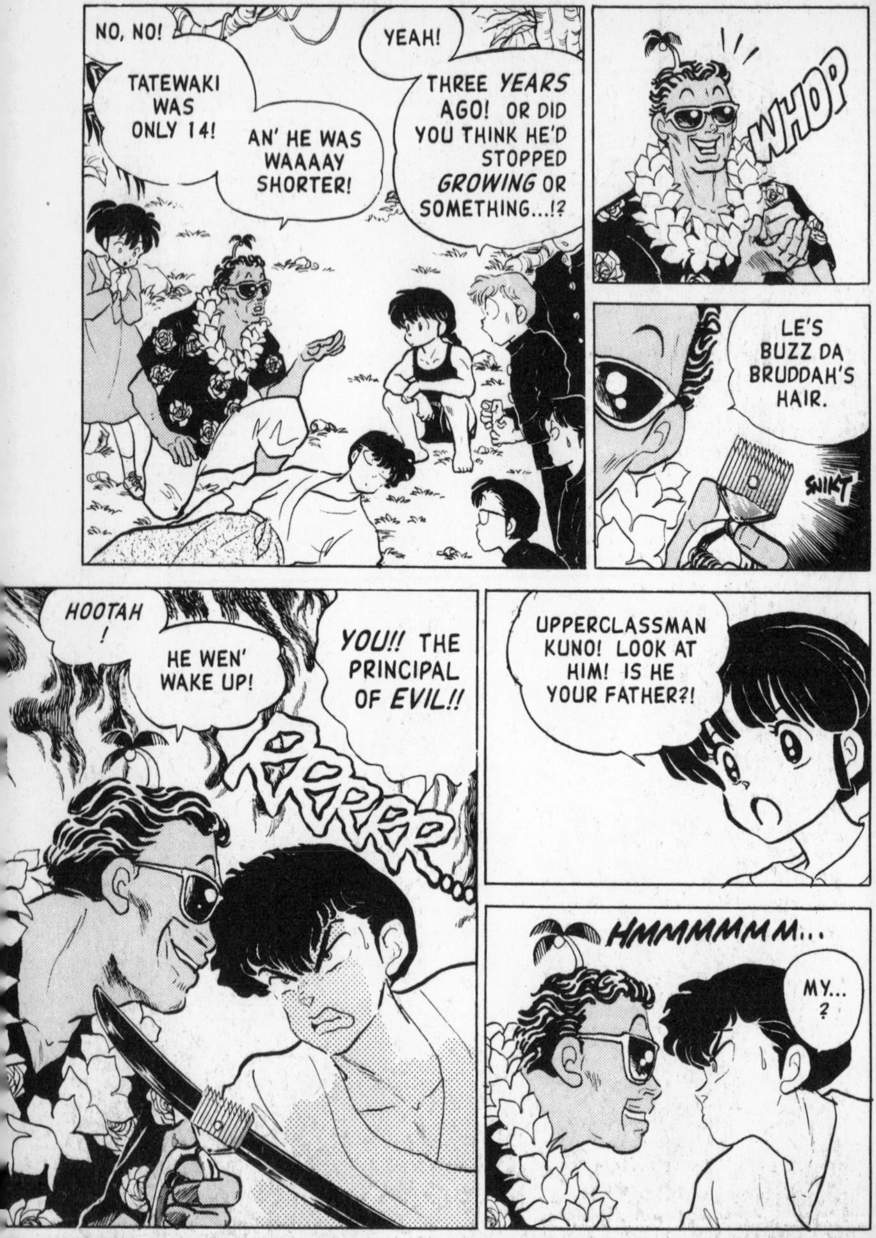
NO, NO!
TATEWAKI WAS ONLY 14!
AN' HE WAS WAAAAY SHORTER!
YEAH!
THREE *YEARS* AGO! OR DID YOU THINK HE'D STOPPED *GROWING* OR SOMETHING...!?
WHOP
LE'S BUZZ DA BRUDDAH'S HAIR.
SNIKT
HOOTAH!
HE WEN' WAKE UP!
YOU!! THE PRINCIPAL OF *EVIL!!*
BZZZZZ
UPPERCLASSMAN KUNO! LOOK AT HIM! IS HE YOUR FATHER?!
HMMMMMM...
MY...?

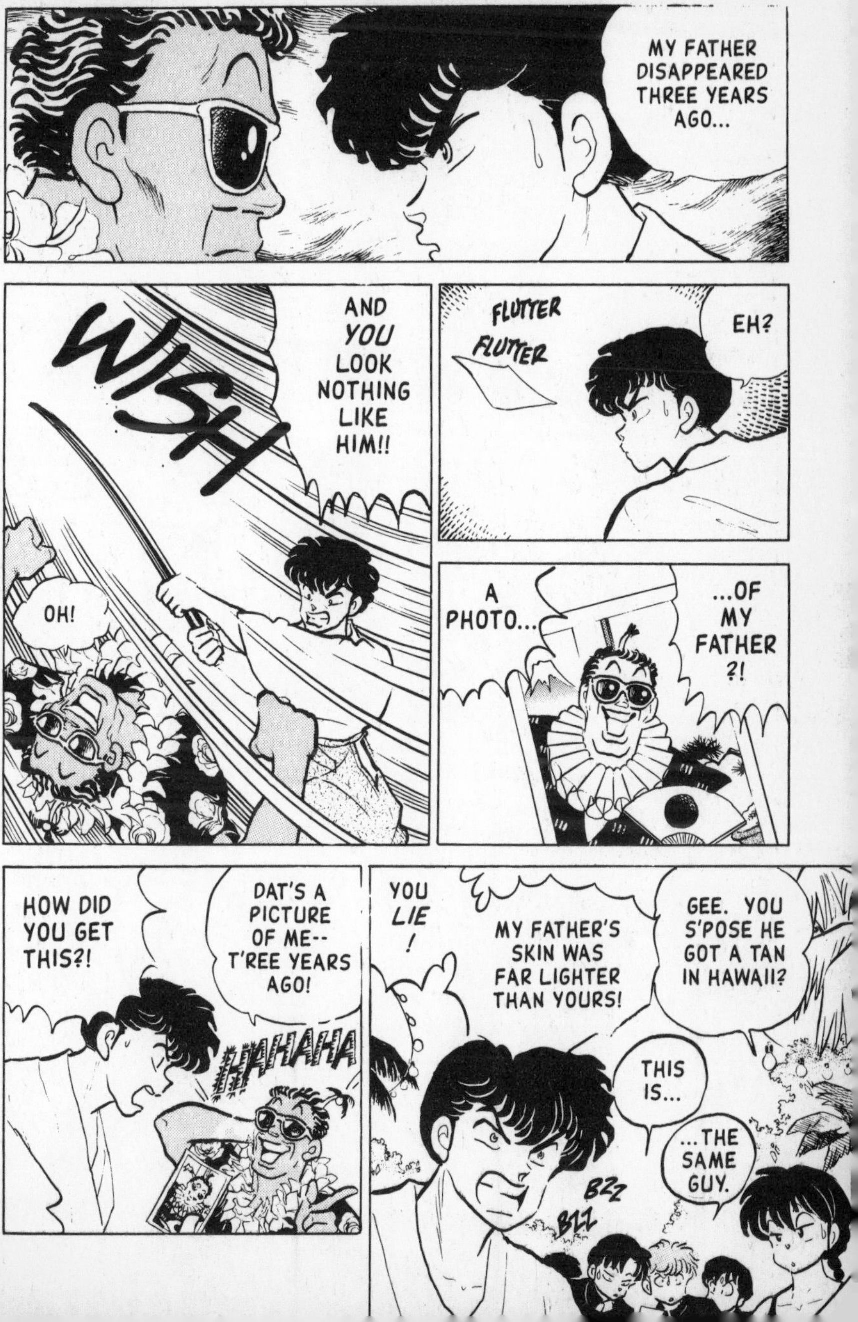
MY FATHER DISAPPEARED THREE YEARS AGO...
WISH
AND YOU LOOK NOTHING LIKE HIM!!
OH!
FLUTTER
FLUTTER
EH?
A PHOTO...
...OF MY FATHER ?!
HOW DID YOU GET THIS?!
DAT'S A PICTURE OF ME-- T'REE YEARS AGO!
HAHAHA
YOU LIE !
MY FATHER'S SKIN WAS FAR LIGHTER THAN YOURS!
GEE. YOU S'POSE HE GOT A TAN IN HAWAII?
THIS IS...
...THE SAME GUY.
BZZ
BZZ

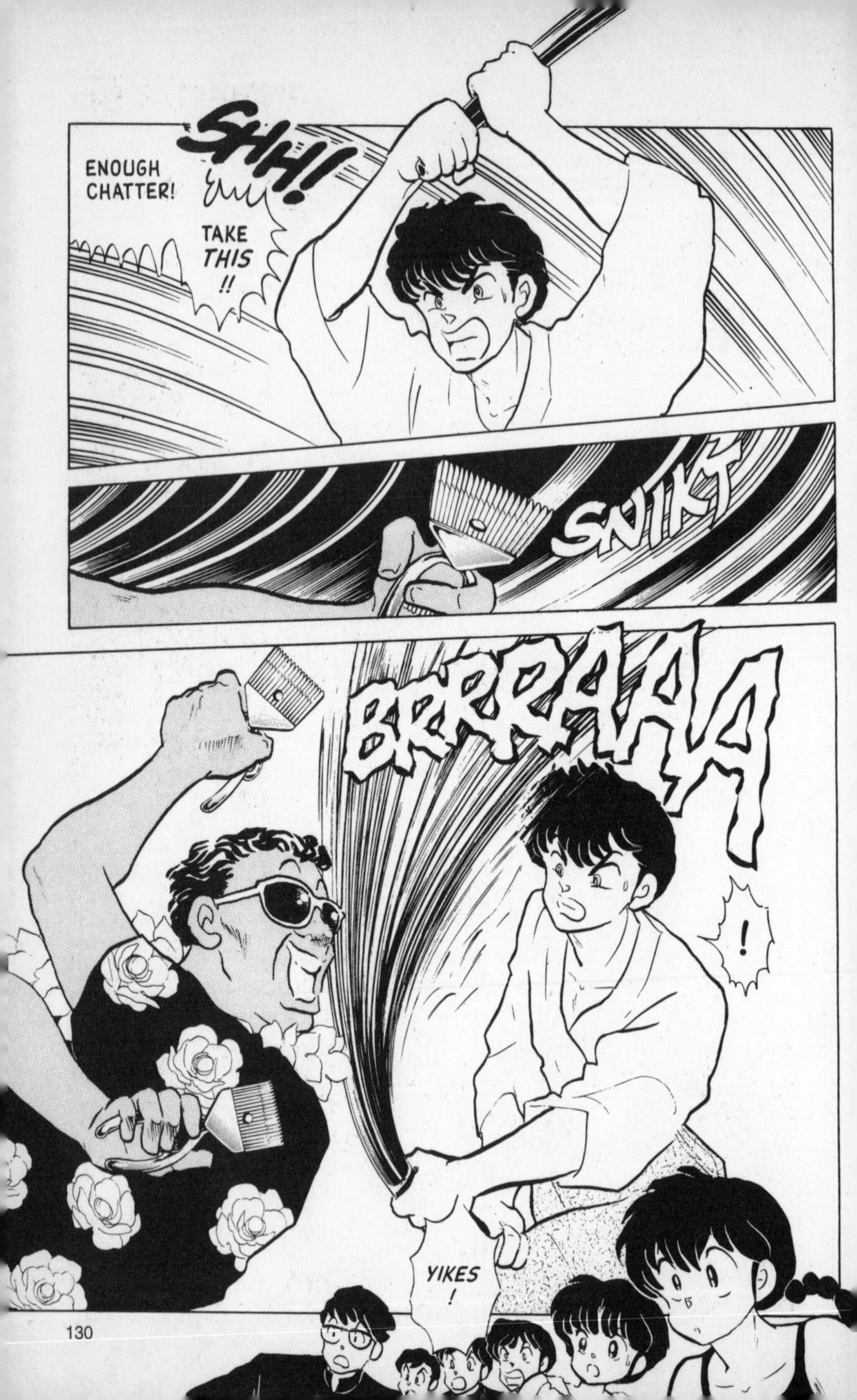
SHH!
ENOUGH CHATTER!
TAKE THIS !!
SNIKT
BRRRAAAA
!
YIKES !

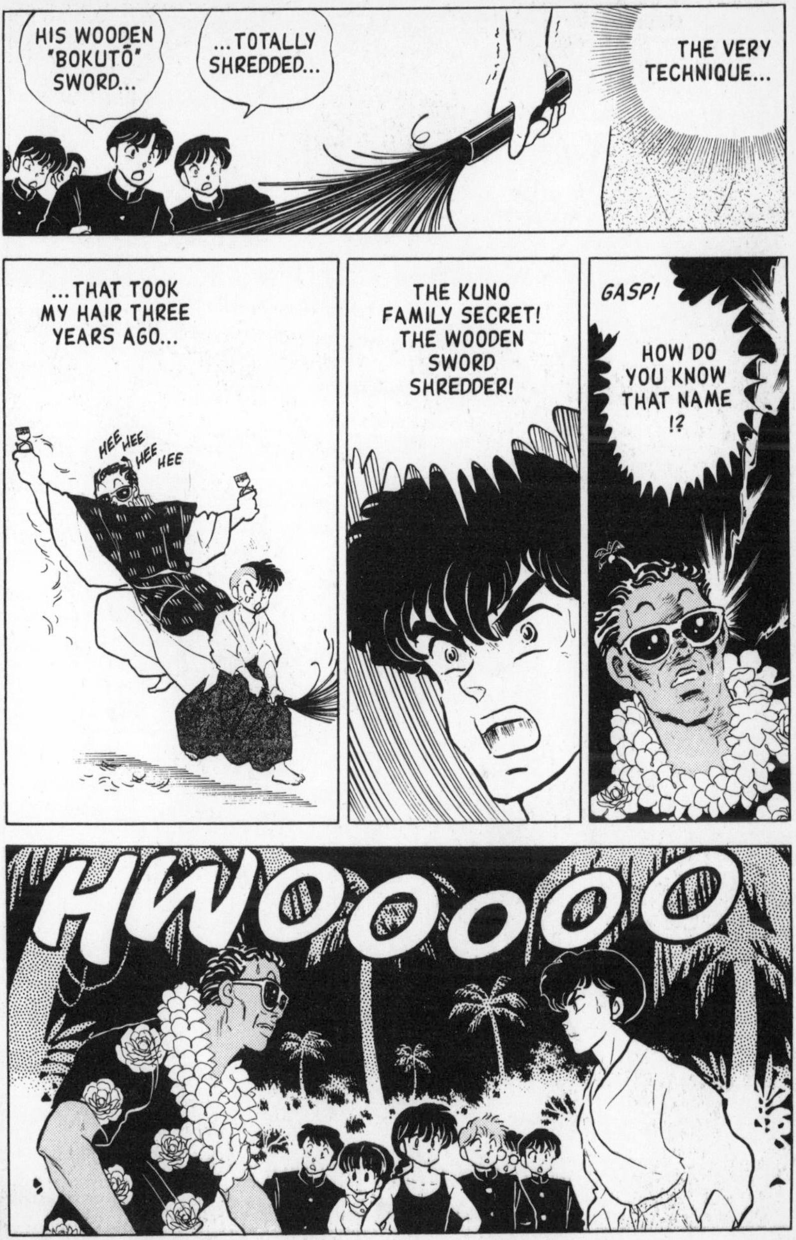
HIS WOODEN "BOKUTŌ" SWORD...
...TOTALLY SHREDDED...
THE VERY TECHNIQUE...
...THAT TOOK MY HAIR THREE YEARS AGO...
HEE HEE HEE HEE
THE KUNO FAMILY SECRET! THE WOODEN SWORD SHREDDER!
GASP!
HOW DO YOU KNOW THAT NAME !?
HWOOOOO

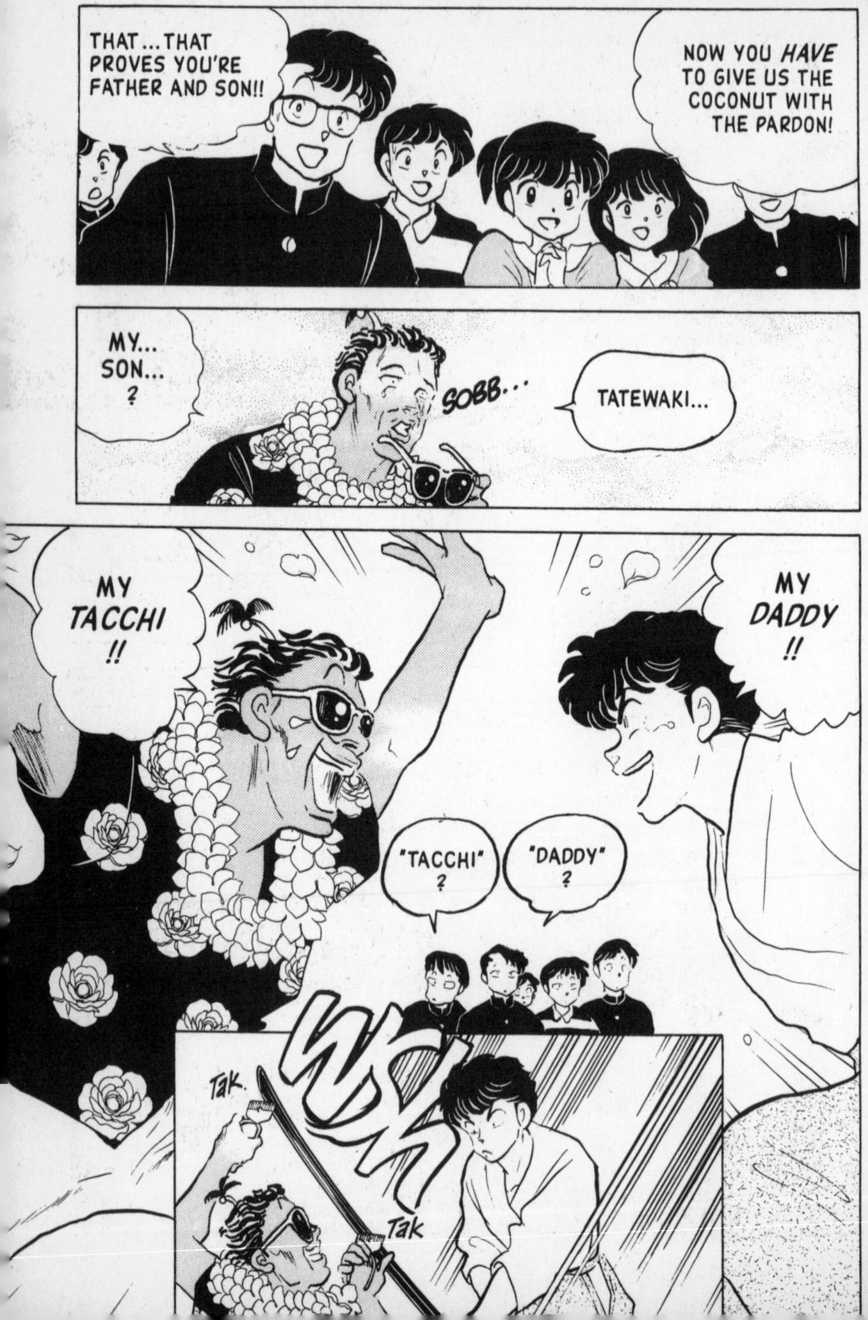
THAT... THAT PROVES YOU'RE FATHER AND SON!!
NOW YOU *HAVE* TO GIVE US THE COCONUT WITH THE PARDON!
MY... SON... ?
SOBB...
TATEWAKI...
MY *TACCHI* !!
MY *DADDY* !!
"TACCHI" ?
"DADDY" ?
TAK.
TAK

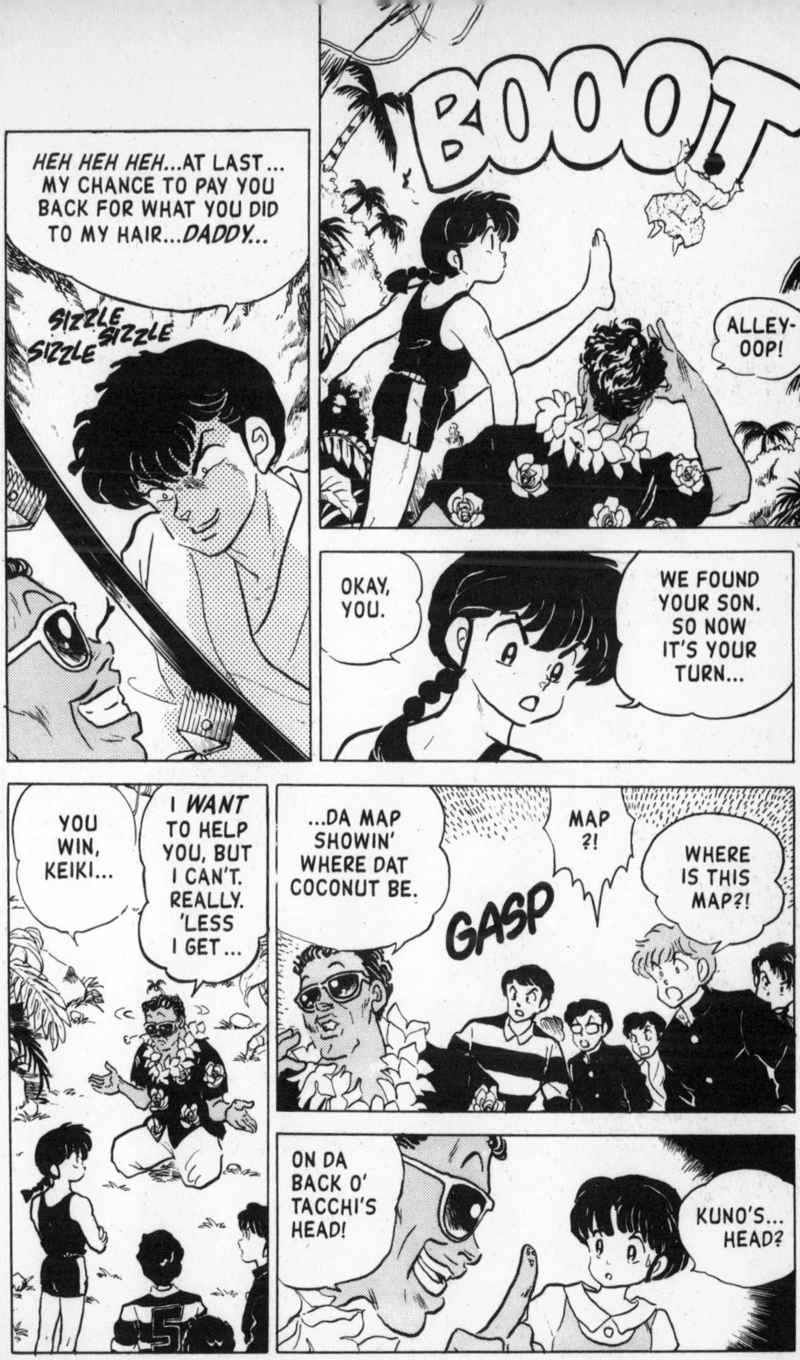
HEH HEH HEH...AT LAST... MY CHANCE TO PAY YOU BACK FOR WHAT YOU DID TO MY HAIR...*DADDY*...
SIZZLE SIZZLE SIZZLE
BOOOT
ALLEY-OOP!
OKAY, YOU.
WE FOUND YOUR SON. SO NOW IT'S YOUR TURN...
YOU WIN, KEIKI...
I *WANT* TO HELP YOU, BUT I CAN'T. REALLY. 'LESS I GET...
...DA MAP SHOWIN' WHERE DAT COCONUT BE.
GASP
MAP ?!
WHERE IS THIS MAP?!
ON DA BACK O' TACCHI'S HEAD!
KUNO'S... HEAD?

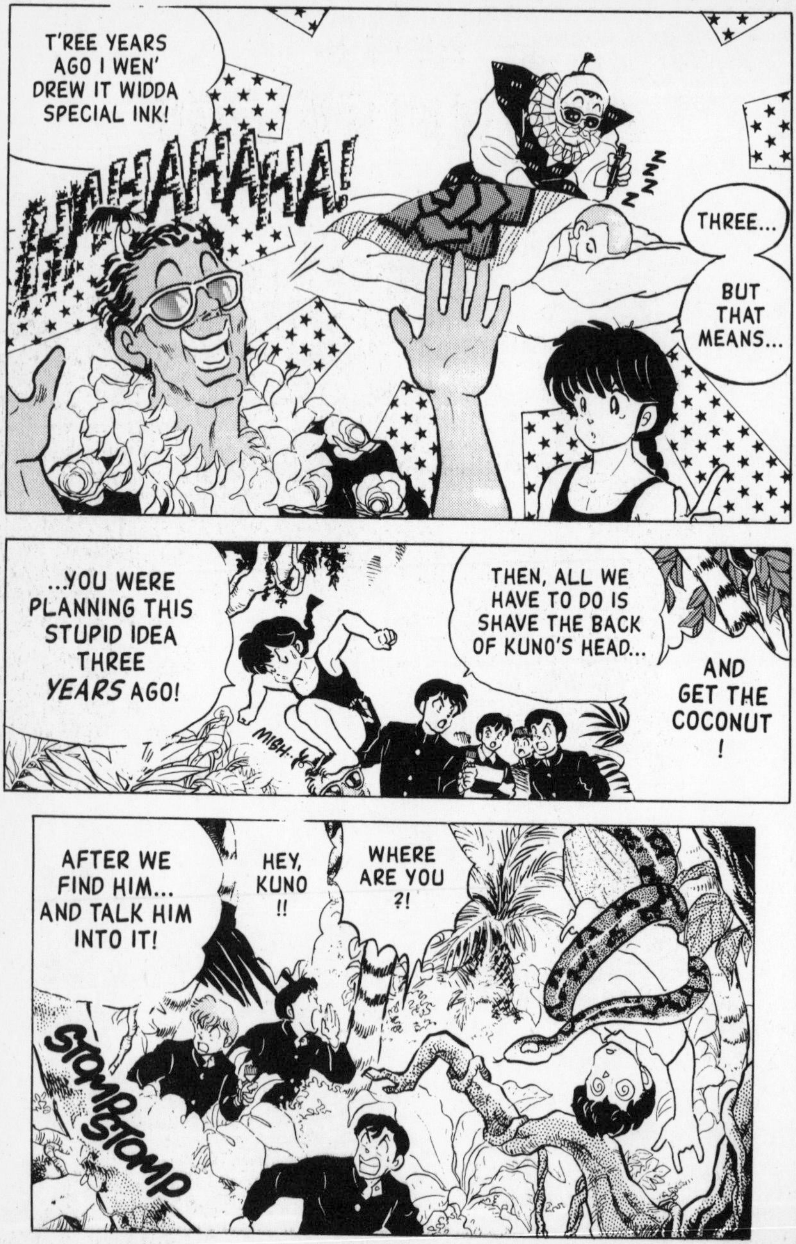
T'REE YEARS AGO I WEN' DREW IT WIDDA SPECIAL INK!
HAHAHAHA!
THREE...
BUT THAT MEANS...
...YOU WERE PLANNING THIS STUPID IDEA THREE YEARS AGO!
MISH...
THEN, ALL WE HAVE TO DO IS SHAVE THE BACK OF KUNO'S HEAD...
AND GET THE COCONUT!
AFTER WE FIND HIM... AND TALK HIM INTO IT!
HEY, KUNO!!
WHERE ARE YOU?!
STOMP STOMP

Part 9
ONE HAIRY DAY

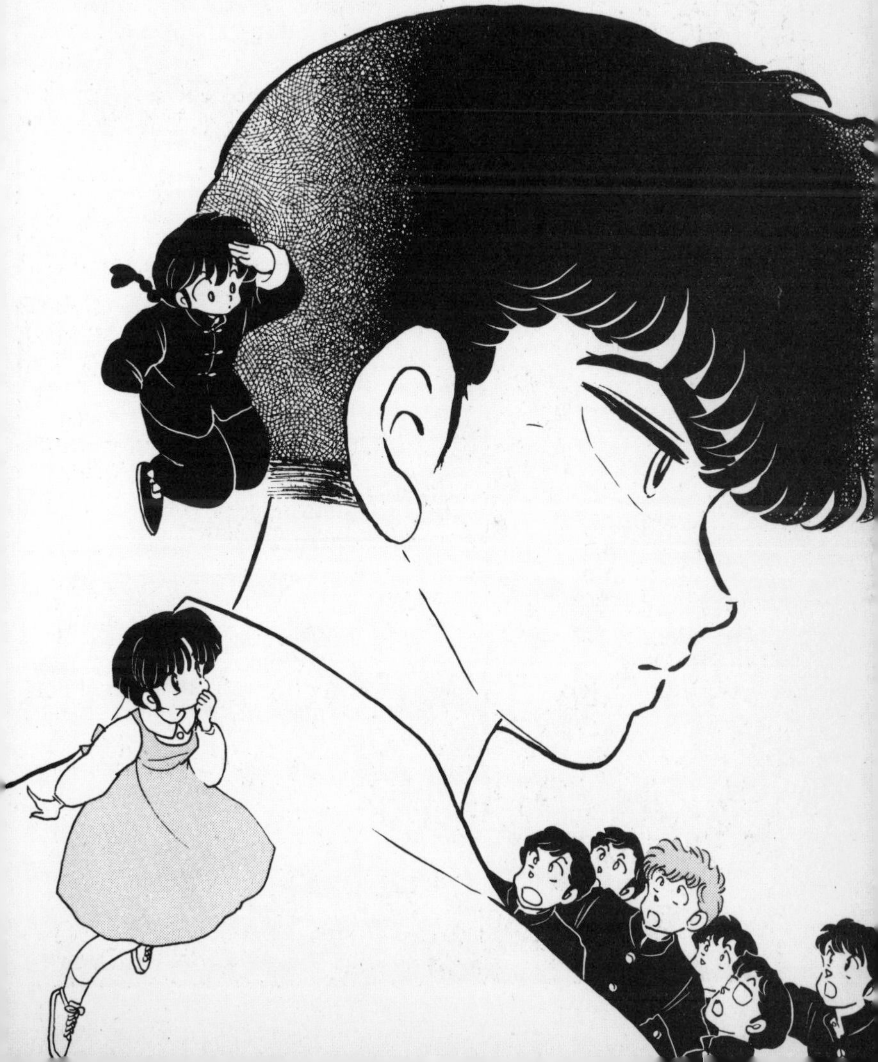

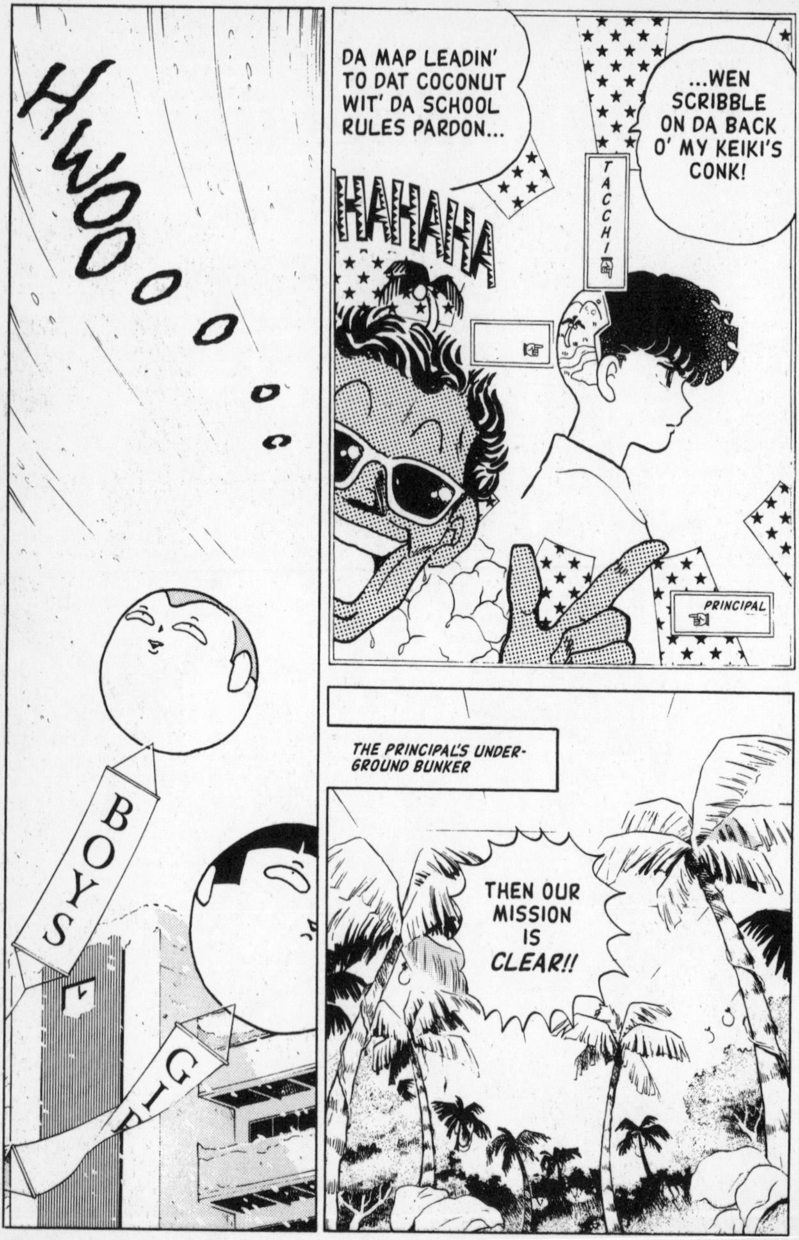
HWOOOOOO
BOYS
DA MAP LEADIN' TO DAT COCONUT WIT' DA SCHOOL RULES PARDON...
HAHAHA
...WEN SCRIBBLE ON DA BACK O' MY KEIKI'S CONK!
TACCHI
PRINCIPAL
THE PRINCIPAL'S UNDER-GROUND BUNKER
THEN OUR MISSION IS *CLEAR!!*

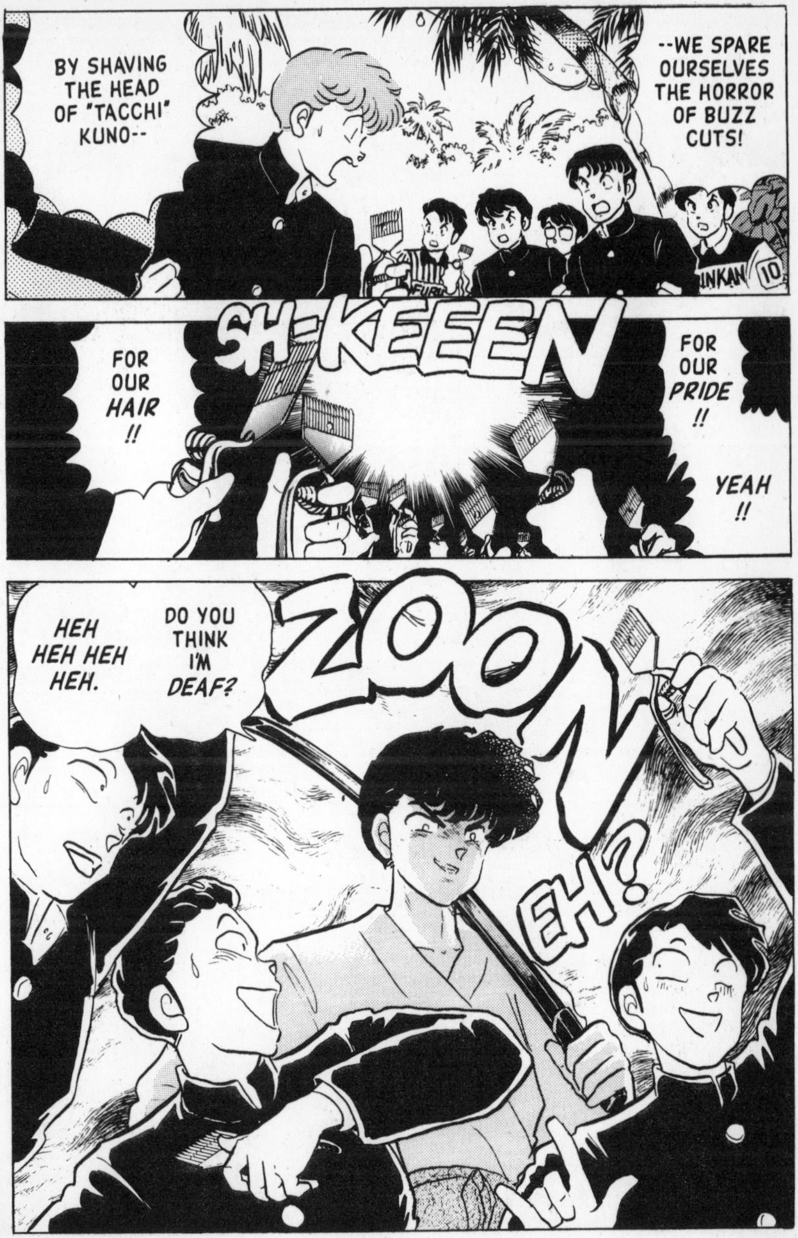
BY SHAVING THE HEAD OF "TACCHI" KUNO--
--WE SPARE OURSELVES THE HORROR OF BUZZ CUTS!
SH-KEEEN
FOR OUR HAIR !!
FOR OUR PRIDE !!
YEAH !!
HEH HEH HEH HEH.
DO YOU THINK I'M DEAF?
ZOOON
EH?

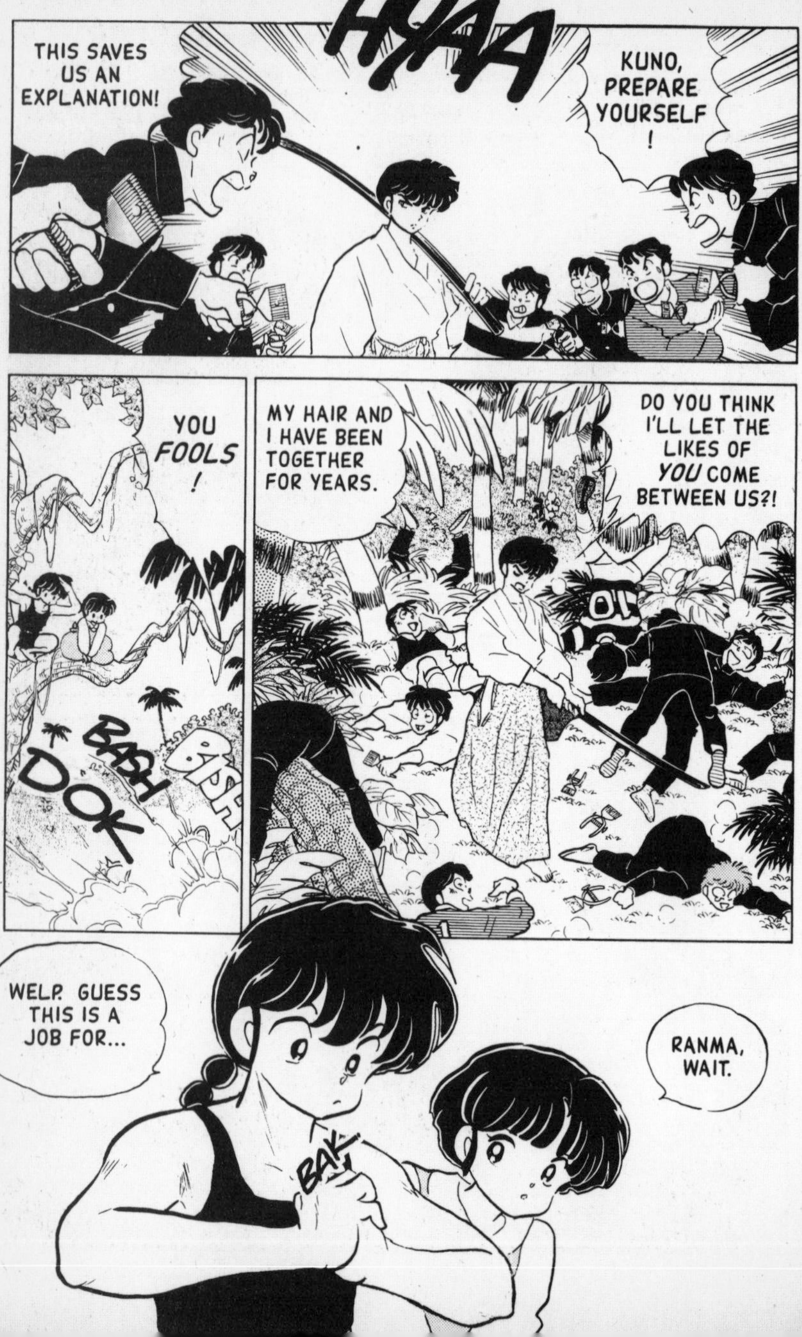
THIS SAVES US AN EXPLANATION!
HYAA
KUNO, PREPARE YOURSELF!
YOU FOOLS!
BASH
DOK
BISH
MY HAIR AND I HAVE BEEN TOGETHER FOR YEARS.
DO YOU THINK I'LL LET THE LIKES OF *YOU* COME BETWEEN US?!
WELP. GUESS THIS IS A JOB FOR...
BAK
RANMA, WAIT.

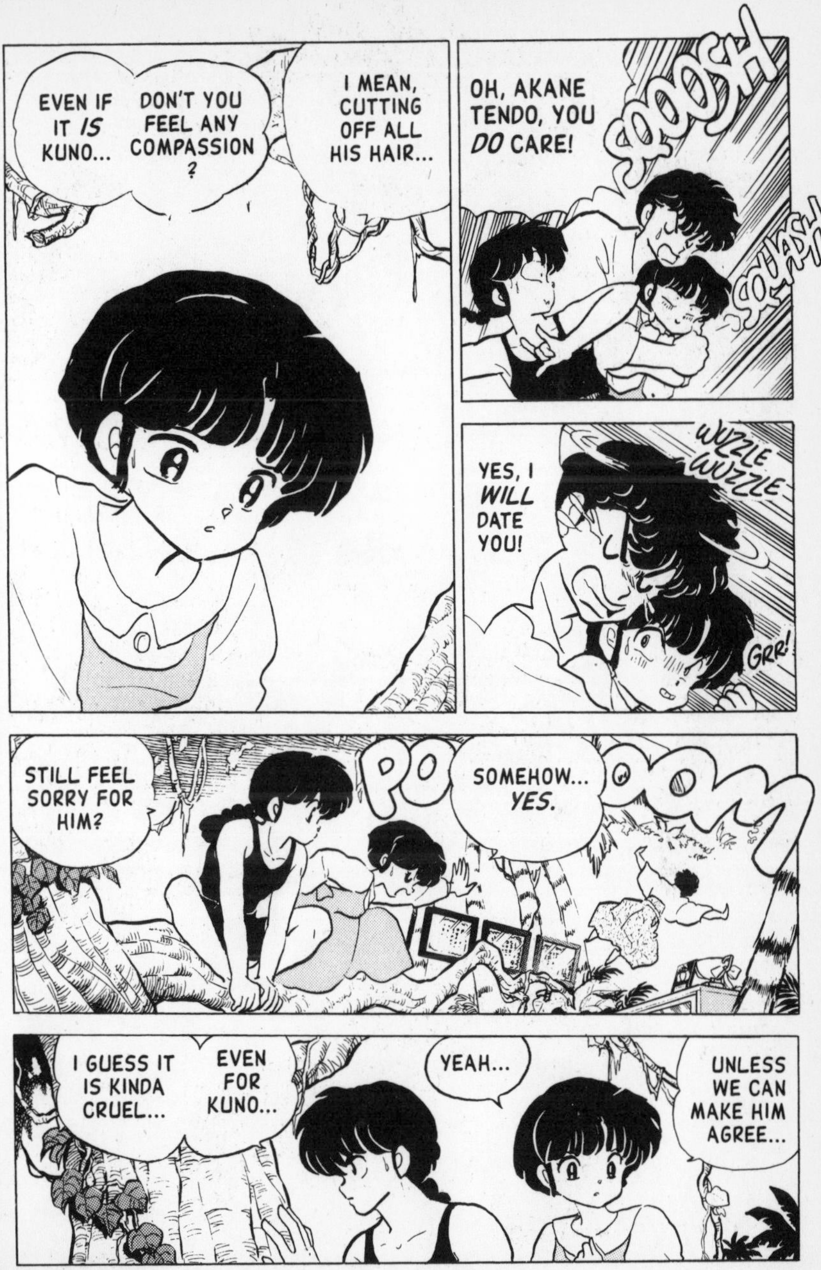
EVEN IF IT IS KUNO...
DON'T YOU FEEL ANY COMPASSION?
I MEAN, CUTTING OFF ALL HIS HAIR...
SOOOSH
OH, AKANE TENDO, YOU DO CARE!
SQUASH
WUZZLE WUZZLE
YES, I WILL DATE YOU!
GRR!
STILL FEEL SORRY FOR HIM?
POOOM
SOMEHOW... YES.
I GUESS IT IS KINDA CRUEL...
EVEN FOR KUNO...
YEAH...
UNLESS WE CAN MAKE HIM AGREE...

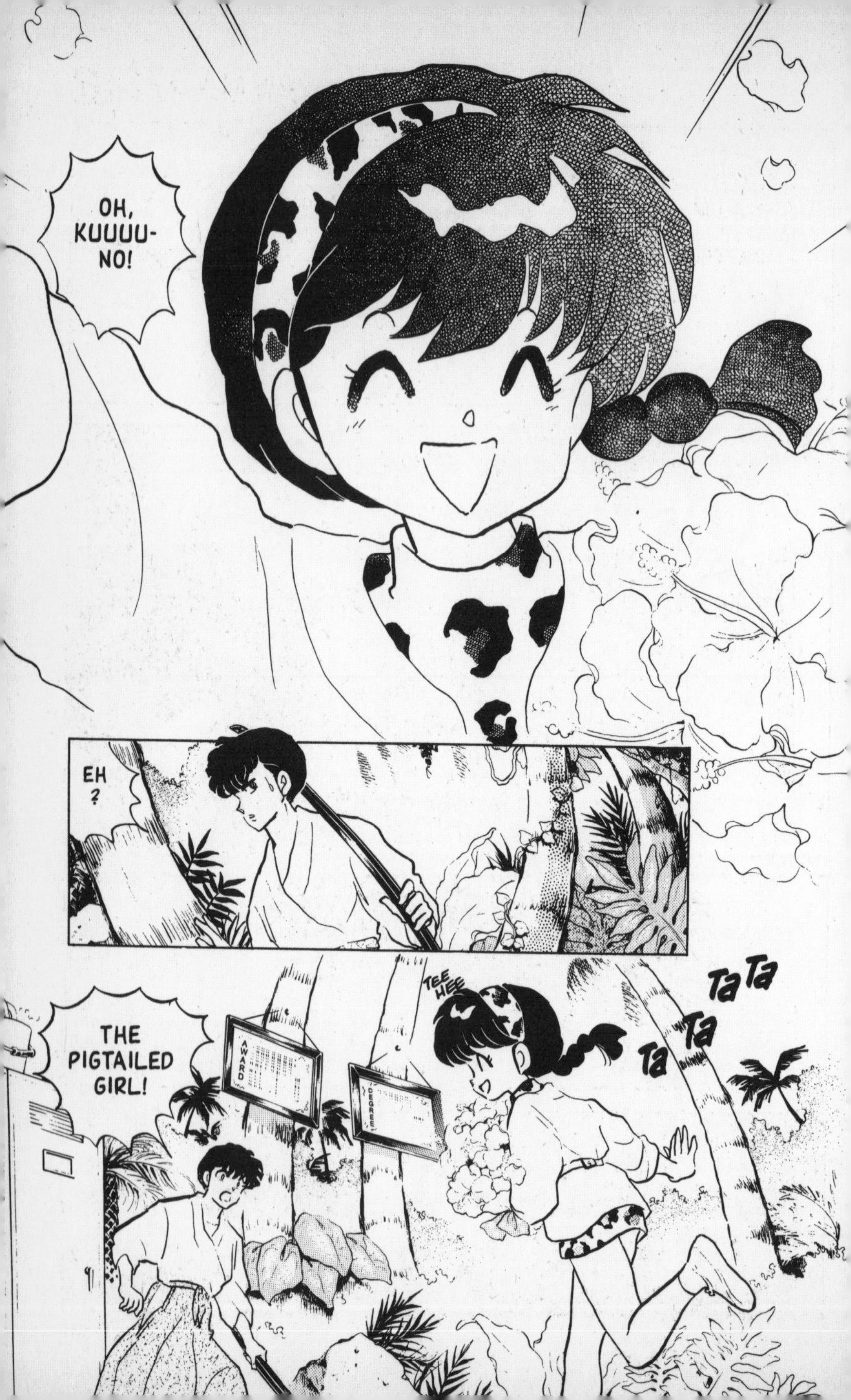
OH, KUUUU-NO!
EH?
THE PIGTAILED GIRL!
TEE HEE
AWARD
DEGREE
TA TA TA TA

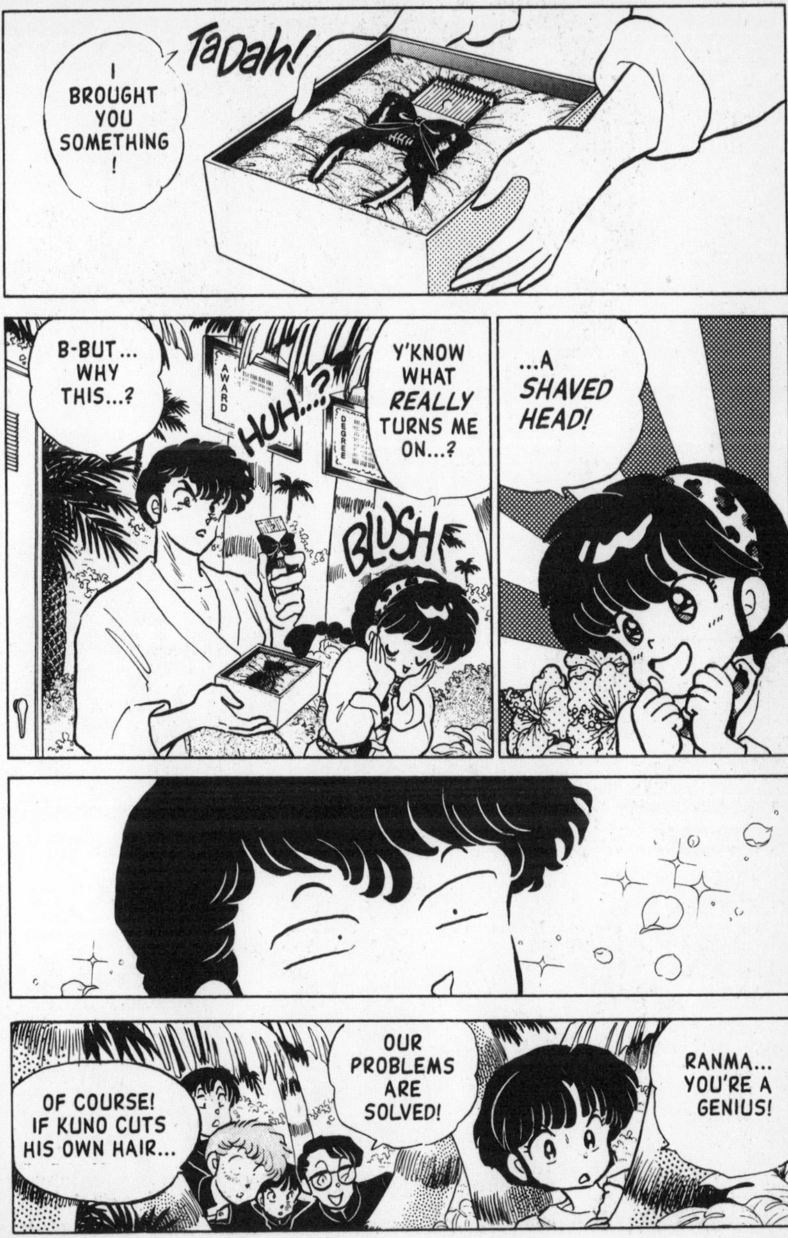
I BROUGHT YOU SOMETHING!
TaDah!
B-BUT... WHY THIS...?
AWARD
HUH...?
DEGREE
Y'KNOW WHAT REALLY TURNS ME ON...?
BLUSH
...A SHAVED HEAD!
OF COURSE! IF KUNO CUTS HIS OWN HAIR...
OUR PROBLEMS ARE SOLVED!
RANMA... YOU'RE A GENIUS!

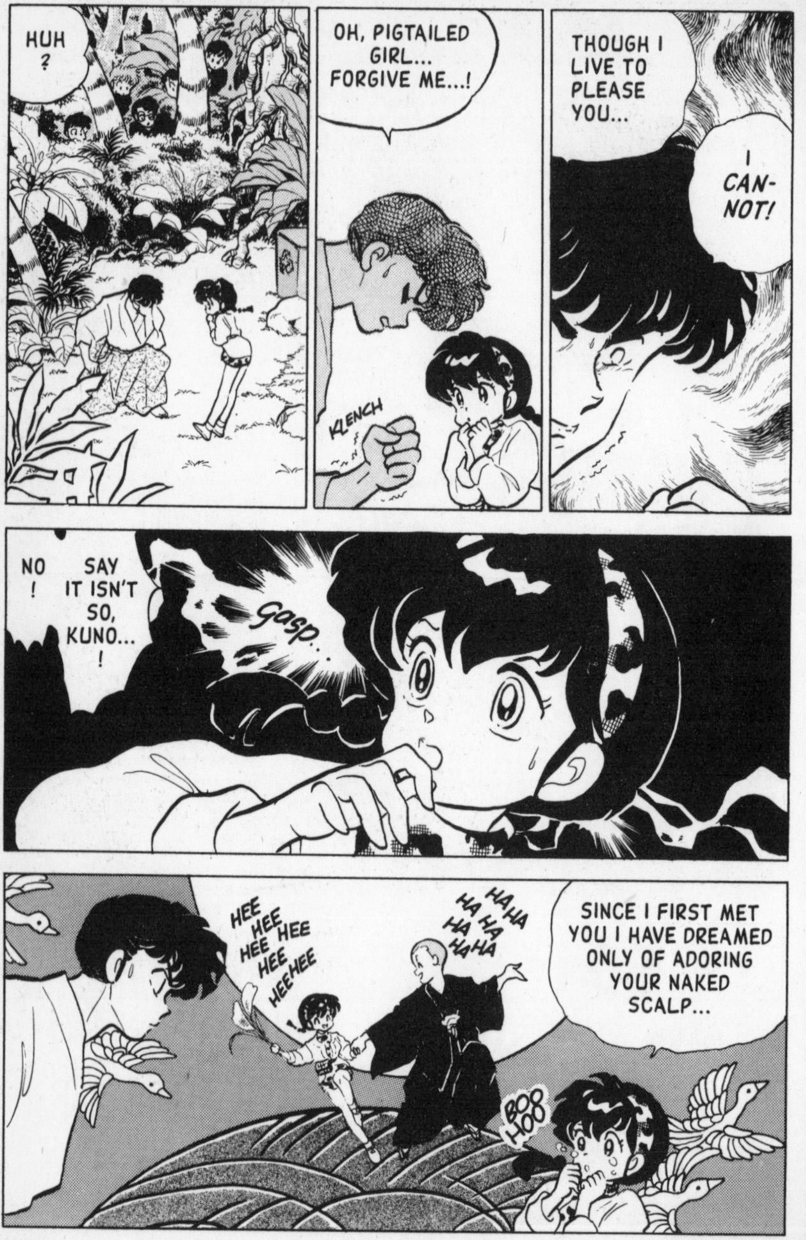
HUH ?
OH, PIGTAILED GIRL... FORGIVE ME...!
KLENCH
THOUGH I LIVE TO PLEASE YOU...
I CAN-NOT!
NO !
SAY IT ISN'T SO, KUNO... !
Gasp...
HEE HEE HEE HEE HEE HEEHEE
HA HA HA HA HA HA HA
SINCE I FIRST MET YOU I HAVE DREAMED ONLY OF ADORING YOUR NAKED SCALP...
BOO HOO

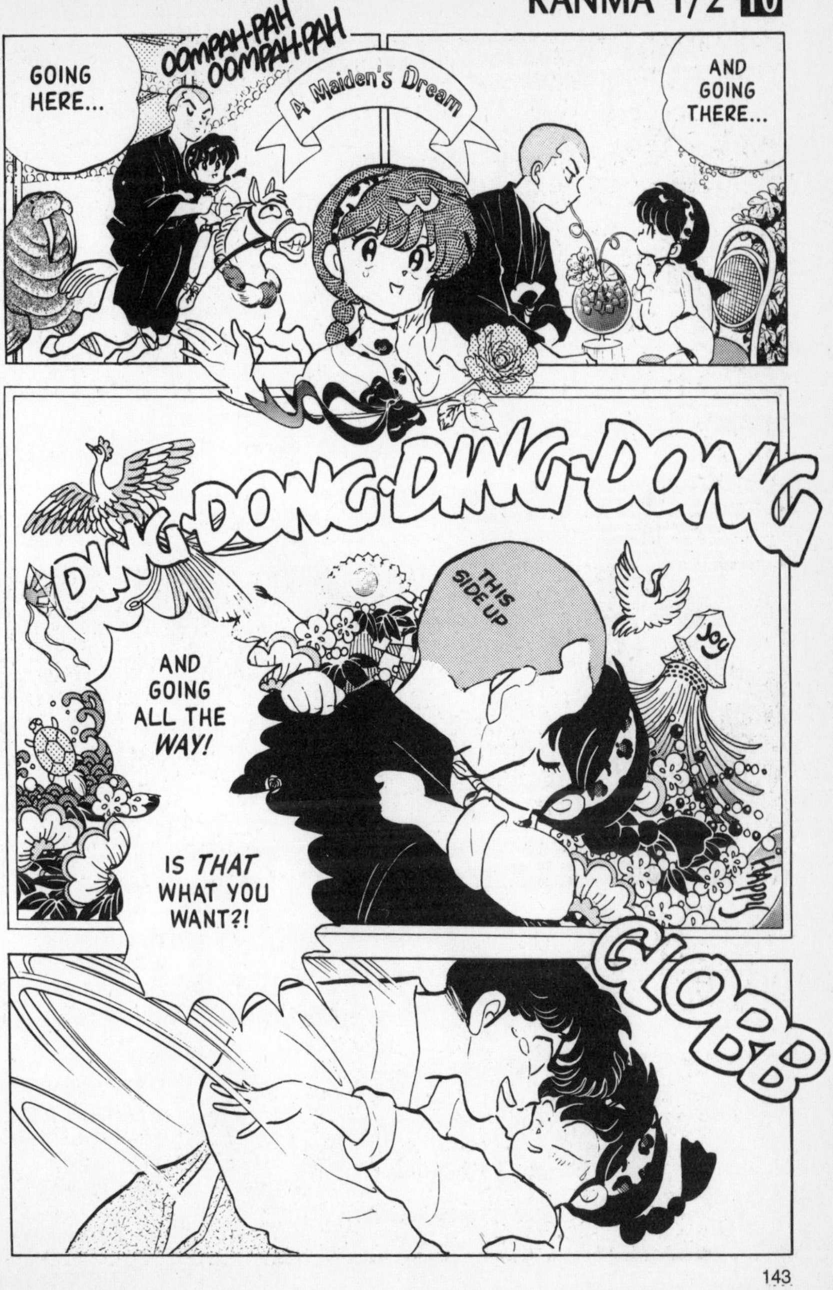
GOING HERE...
OOMPAH-PAH OOMPAH-PAH
A Maiden's Dream
AND GOING THERE...
DING-DONG-DING-DONG
THIS SIDE UP
JOY
AND GOING ALL THE WAY!
IS THAT WHAT YOU WANT?!
HAPPY
GLOBB

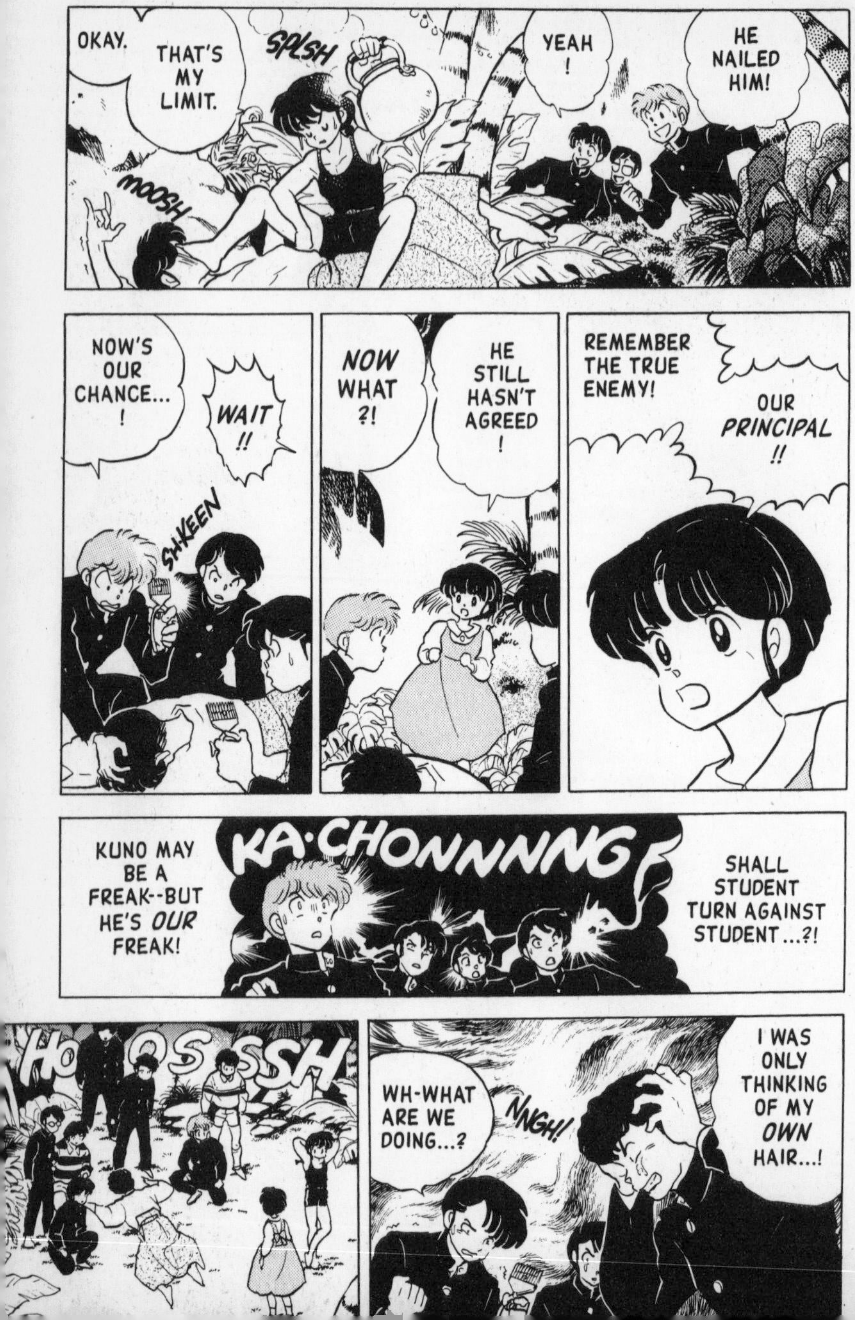
OKAY.
THAT'S MY LIMIT.
SPLSH
MOOSH
YEAH !
HE NAILED HIM!
NOW'S OUR CHANCE... !
WAIT !!
SHKEEN
NOW WHAT ?!
HE STILL HASN'T AGREED !
REMEMBER THE TRUE ENEMY!
OUR PRINCIPAL !!
KUNO MAY BE A FREAK--BUT HE'S OUR FREAK!
KA·CHONNNNG
SHALL STUDENT TURN AGAINST STUDENT...?!
HO OS SSH
WH-WHAT ARE WE DOING...?
NNGH!
I WAS ONLY THINKING OF MY OWN HAIR...!

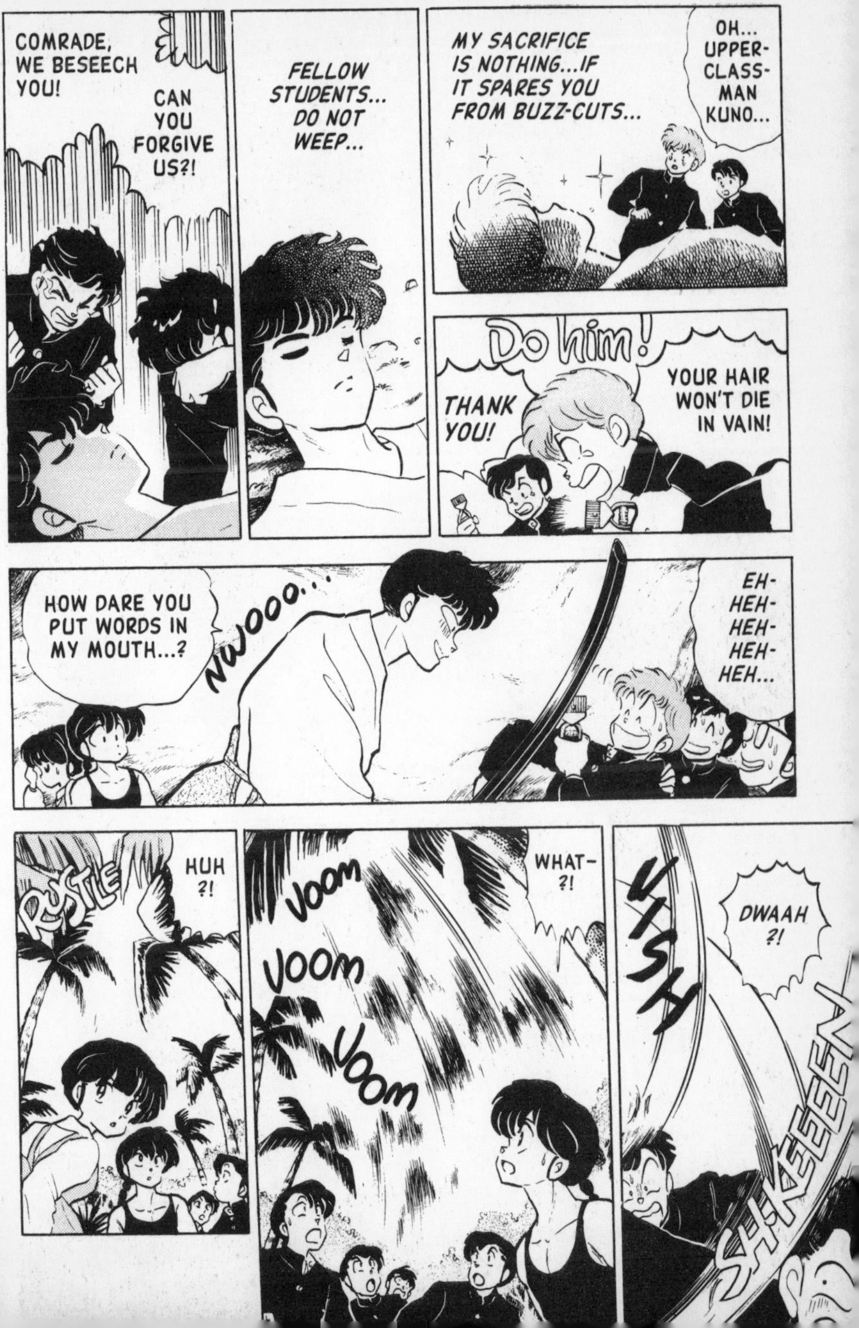
COMRADE, WE BESEECH YOU!
CAN YOU FORGIVE US?!
FELLOW STUDENTS... DO NOT WEEP...
MY SACRIFICE IS NOTHING...IF IT SPARES YOU FROM BUZZ-CUTS...
OH... UPPER-CLASS-MAN KUNO...
Do him!
THANK YOU!
YOUR HAIR WON'T DIE IN VAIN!
HOW DARE YOU PUT WORDS IN MY MOUTH...?
NWOOO...
EH-HEH-HEH-HEH-HEH...
RUSTLE
HUH ?!
WHAT- ?!
VOOM
VOOM
VOOM
VISH
DWAAH ?!
SHKEEEEN

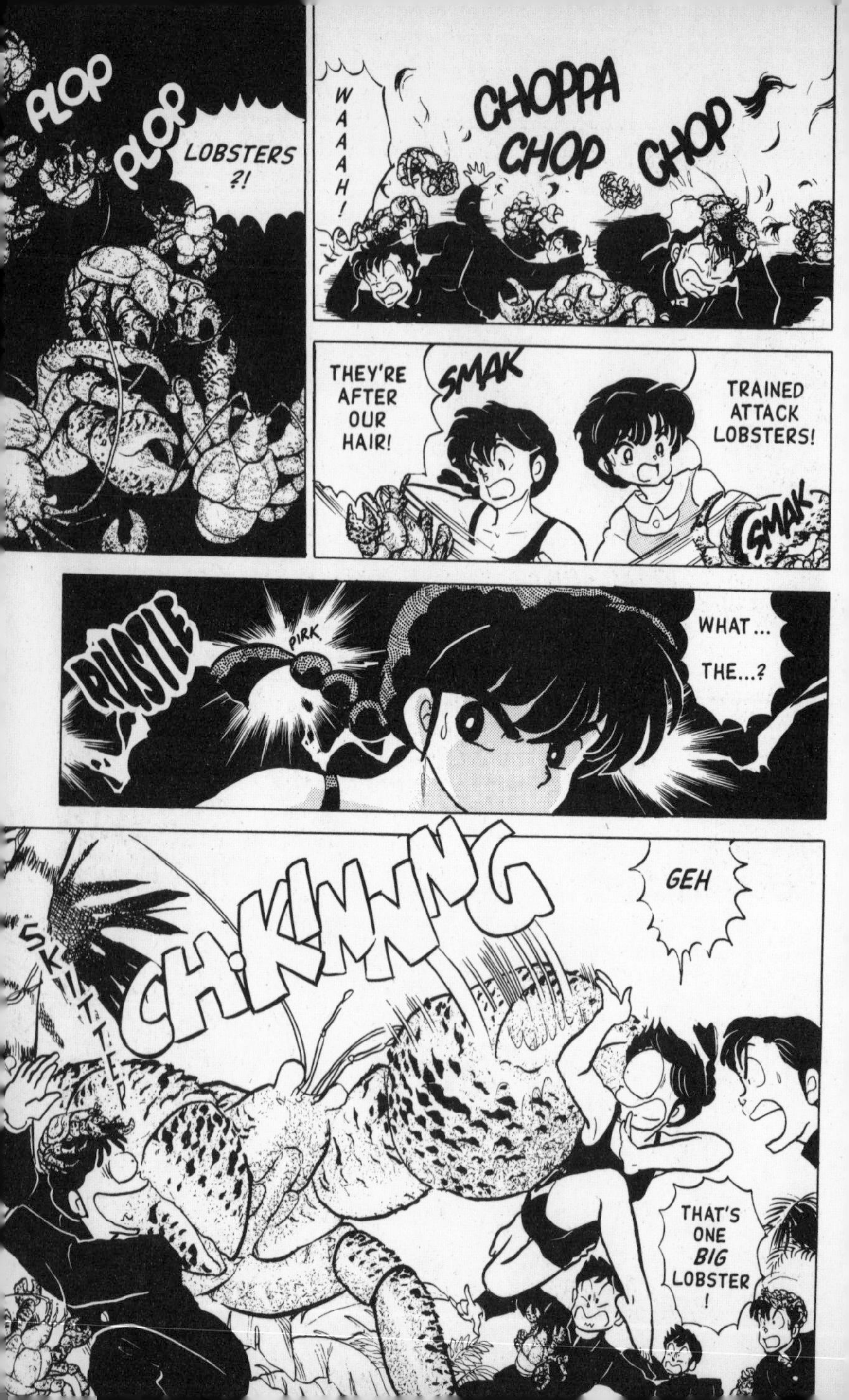
PLOP PLOP
LOBSTERS ?!
WAAAAH!
CHOPPA CHOP CHOP
THEY'RE AFTER OUR HAIR!
SMAK
TRAINED ATTACK LOBSTERS!
SMAK
RUSTLE
PIRK
WHAT... THE...?
SKITTTER
CHKINNNG
GEH
THAT'S ONE *BIG* LOBSTER!

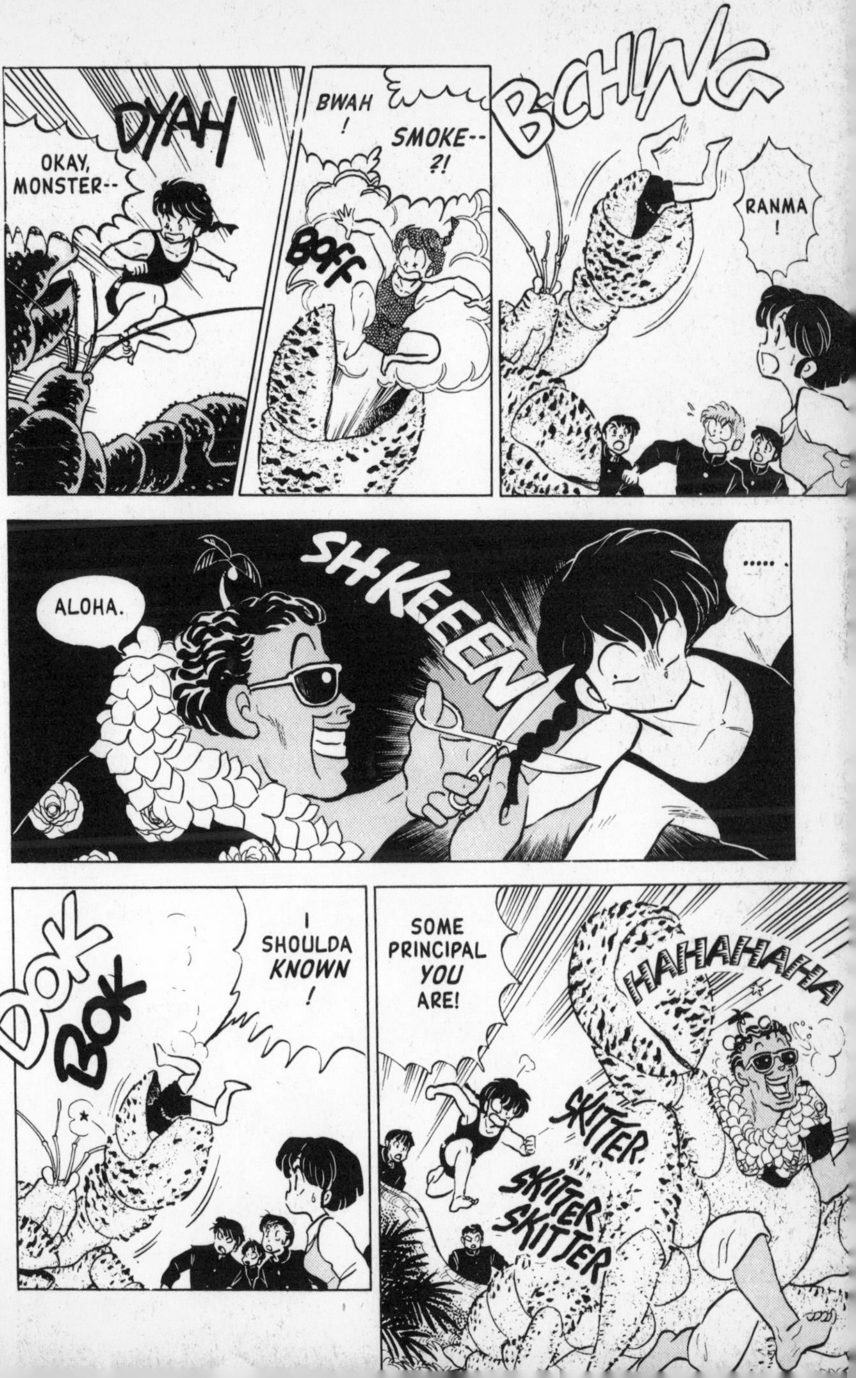
OKAY, MONSTER--
DYAH
BWAH!
SMOKE--?!
BOFF
B-CHING
RANMA!
ALOHA.
SHKEEEN
......
DOK BOK
I SHOULDA KNOWN!
SOME PRINCIPAL YOU ARE!
HAHAHAHAHA
SKITTER
SKITTER SKITTER

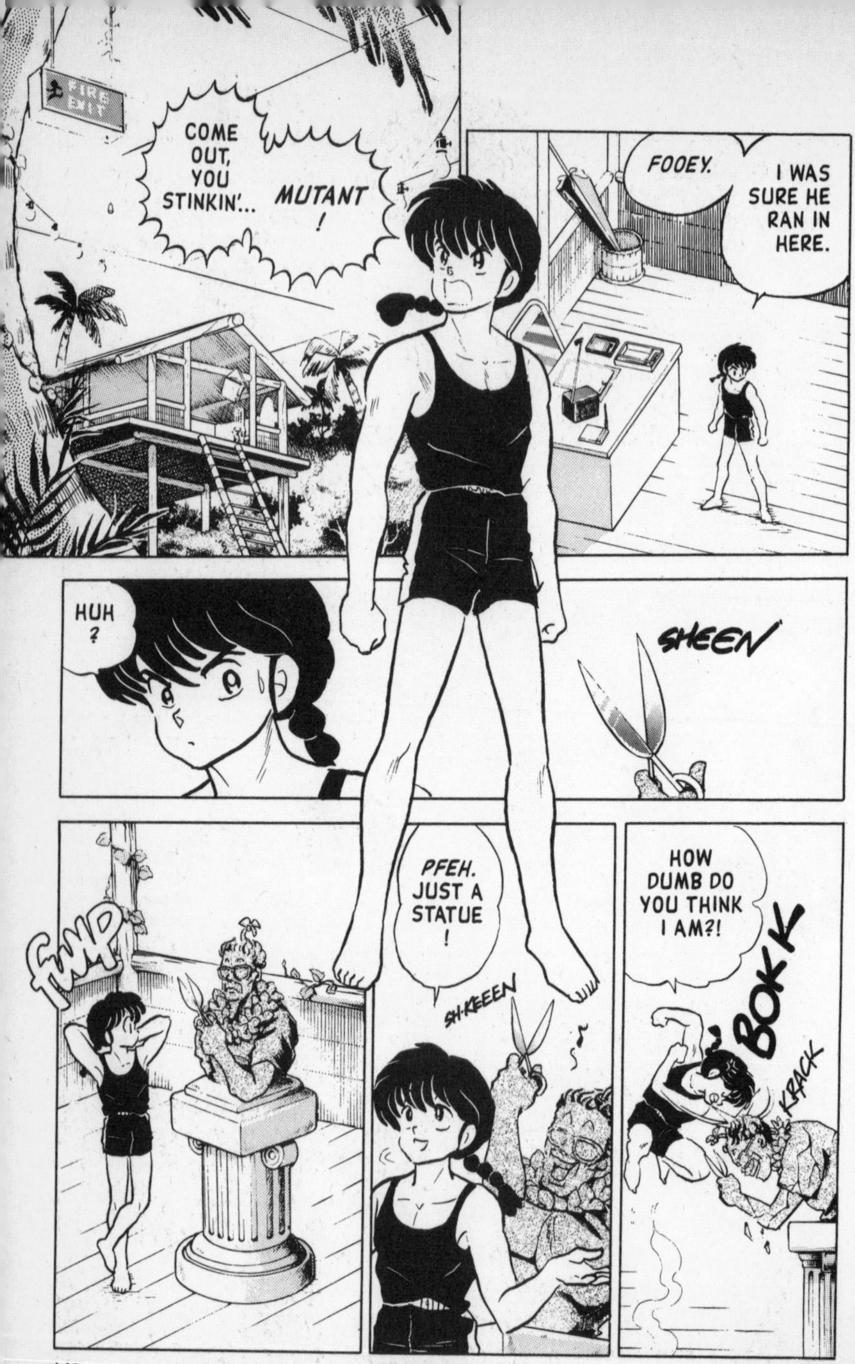
FIRE EXIT
COME OUT, YOU STINKIN'...
MUTANT!
FOOEY.
I WAS SURE HE RAN IN HERE.
HUH?
SHEEN
FWIP
PFEH. JUST A STATUE!
SH-KEEEN
HOW DUMB DO YOU THINK I AM?!
BOKK
KRACK

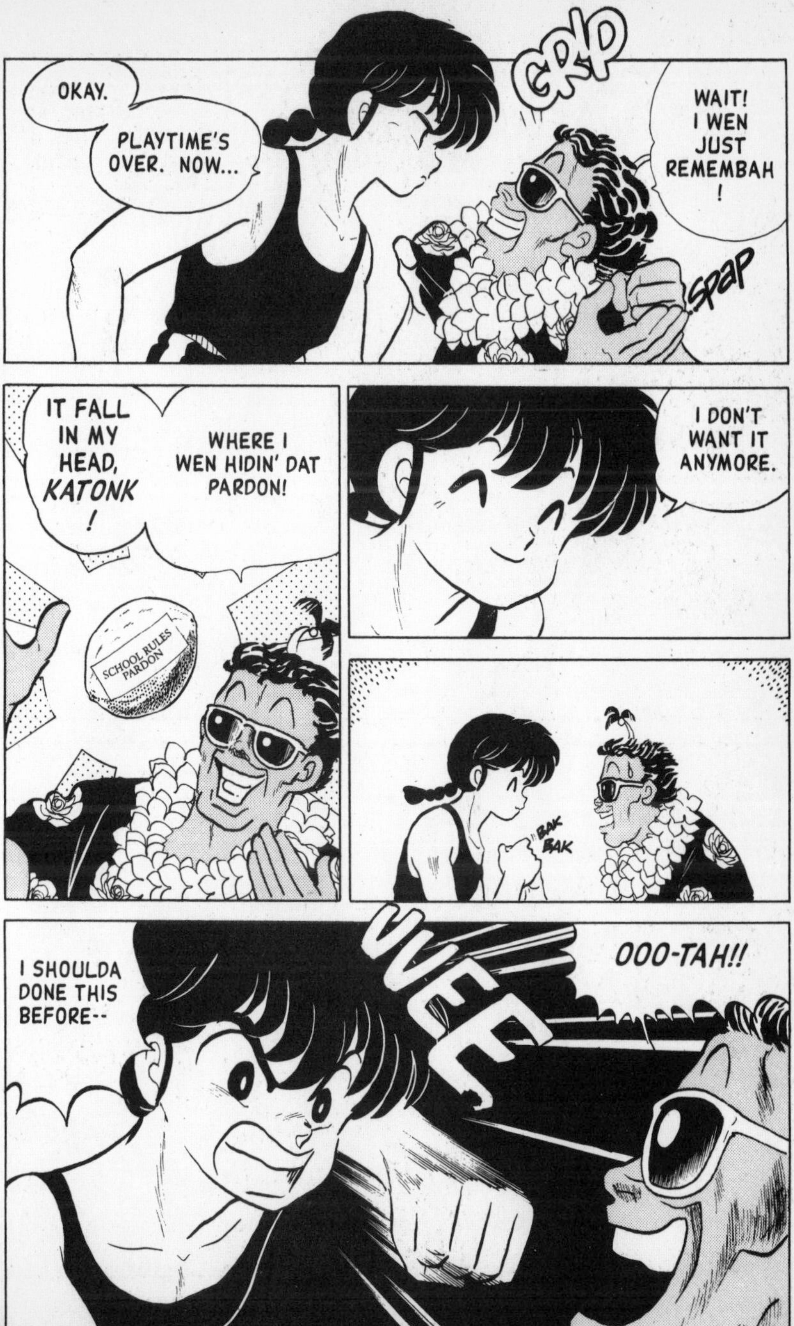
OKAY.
PLAYTIME'S OVER. NOW...
GRIP
WAIT! I WEN JUST REMEMBAH!
SPAP
IT FALL IN MY HEAD, KATONK!
WHERE I WEN HIDIN' DAT PARDON!
SCHOOL RULES PARDON
I DON'T WANT IT ANYMORE.
BAK BAK
I SHOULDA DONE THIS BEFORE--
OOO-TAH!!

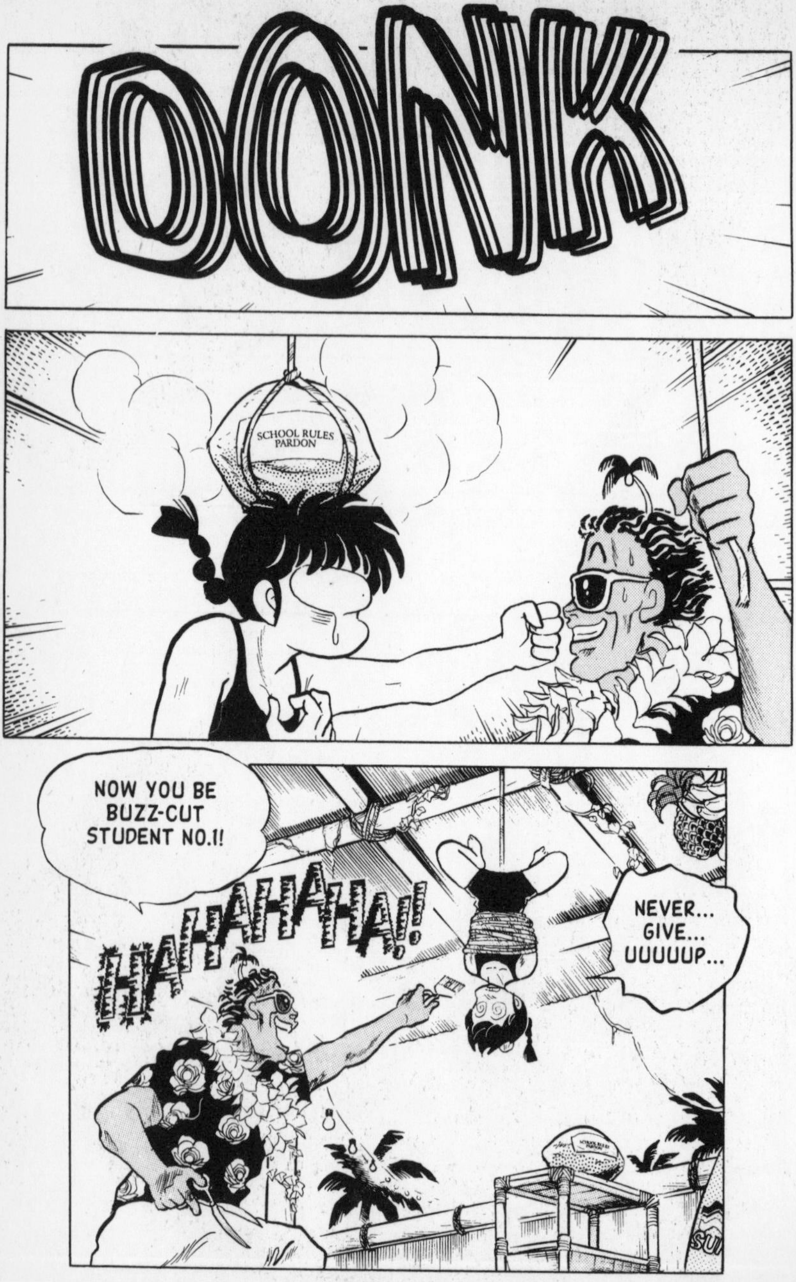
DONK
SCHOOL RULES PARDON
NOW YOU BE BUZZ-CUT STUDENT NO.1!
HAHAHAHA!
NEVER... GIVE... UUUUUP...

Part 10
SHEAR FOLLY

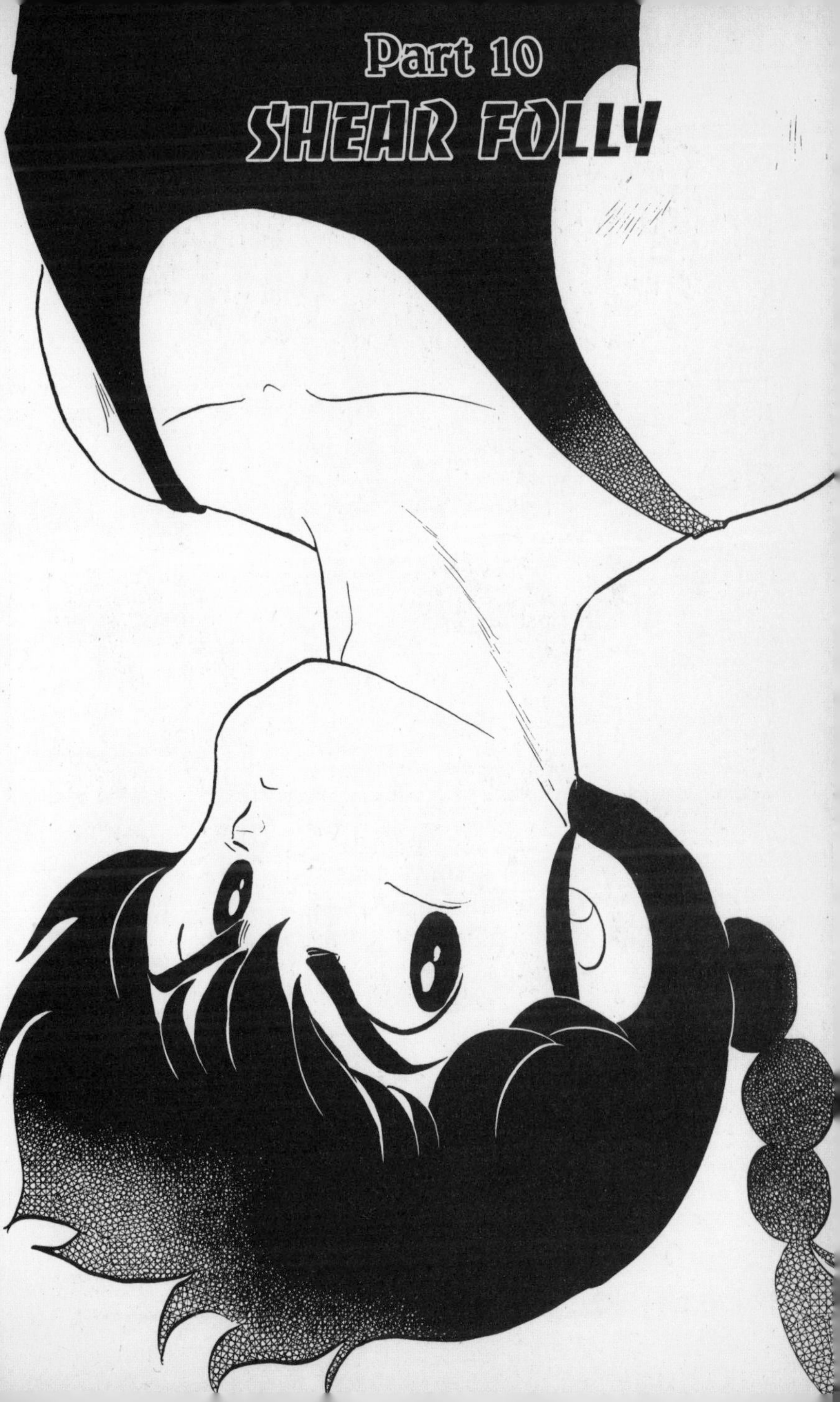

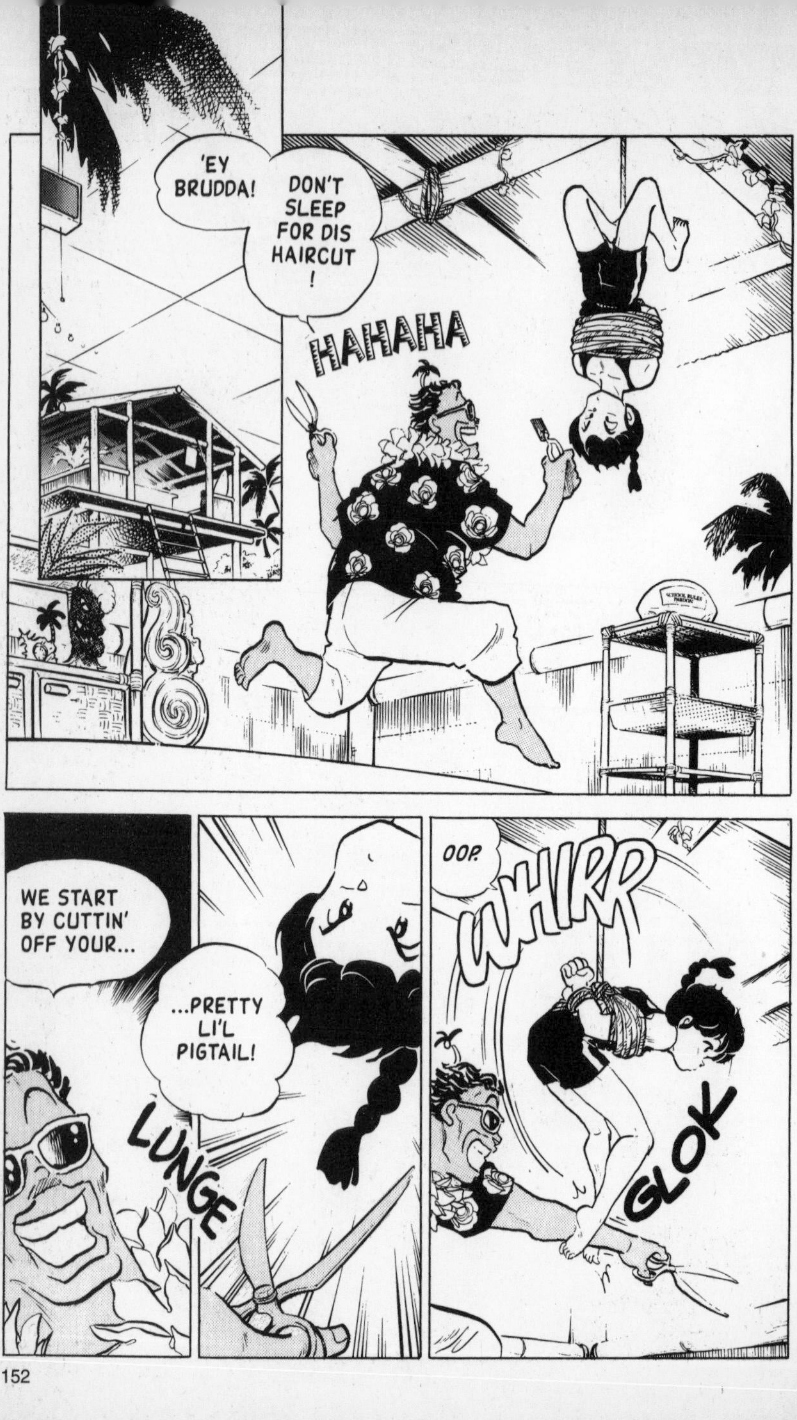
'EY BRUDDA!
DON'T SLEEP FOR DIS HAIRCUT!
HAHAHA
WE START BY CUTTIN' OFF YOUR...
LUNGE
...PRETTY LI'L PIGTAIL!
OOP.
WHIRR
GLOK

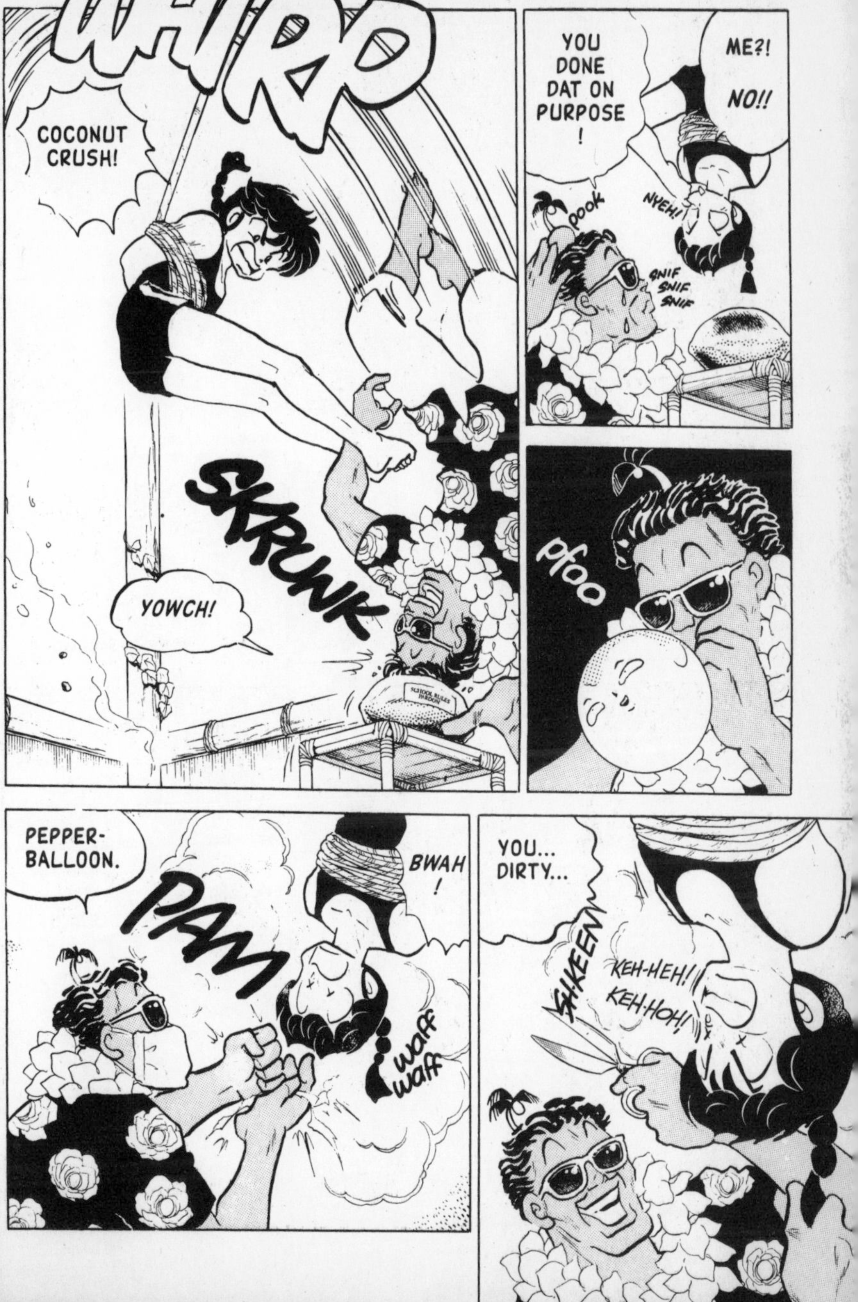
WHIRP
COCONUT CRUSH!
SKRUNK
YOWCH!
YOU DONE DAT ON PURPOSE!
ME?!
NO!!
pook
NYEH!
SNIF SNIF SNIF
pfoo
PEPPER-BALLOON.
PAM
BWAH!
waff waff
YOU... DIRTY...
SHKEEN
KEH-HEH!
KEH-HOH!

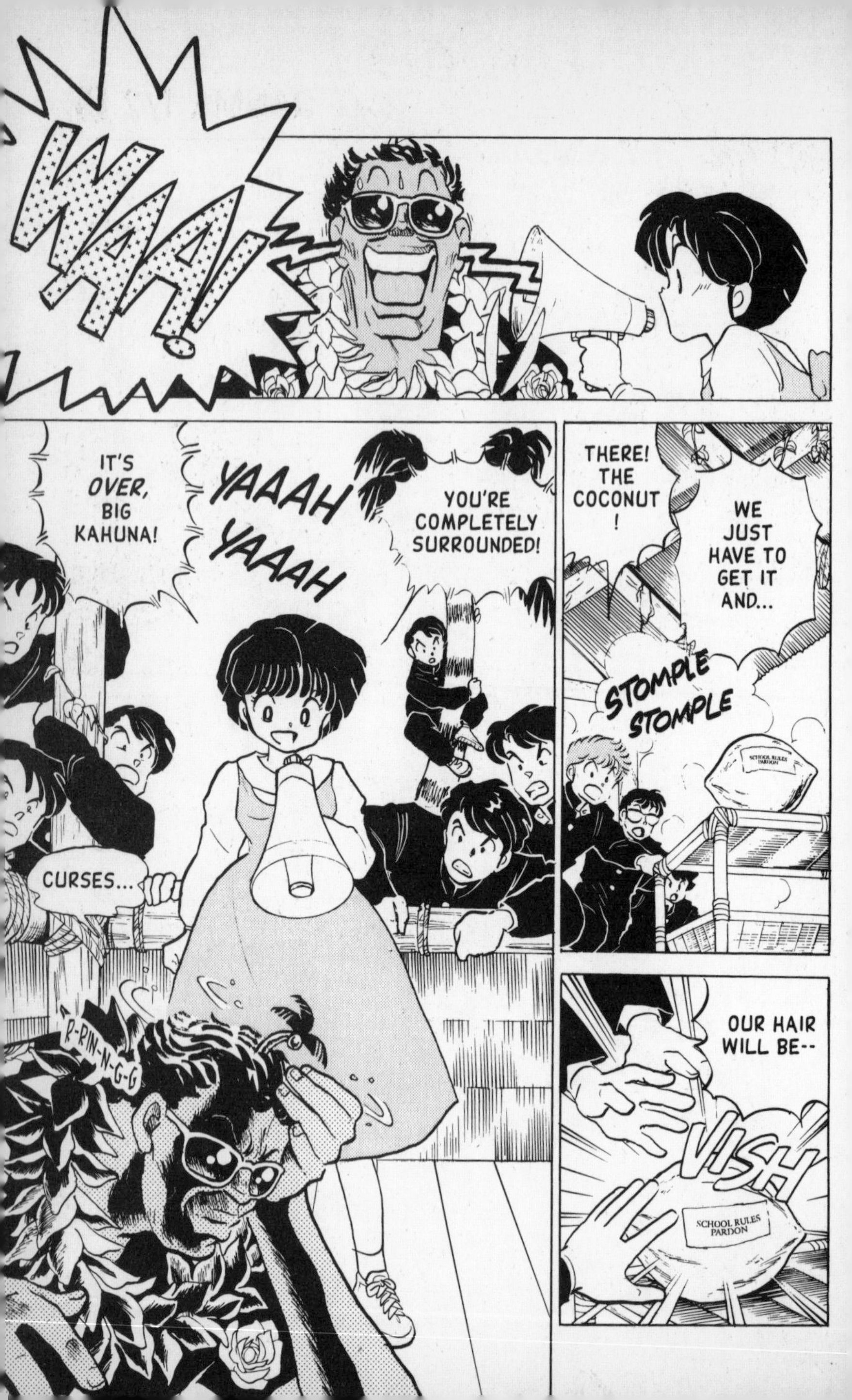
WAA!
IT'S OVER, BIG KAHUNA!
YAAAH YAAAH
YOU'RE COMPLETELY SURROUNDED!
CURSES...
R-RIN-N-G-G
THERE! THE COCONUT!
WE JUST HAVE TO GET IT AND...
STOMPLE STOMPLE
SCHOOL RULES PARDON
OUR HAIR WILL BE--
VISH
SCHOOL RULES PARDON

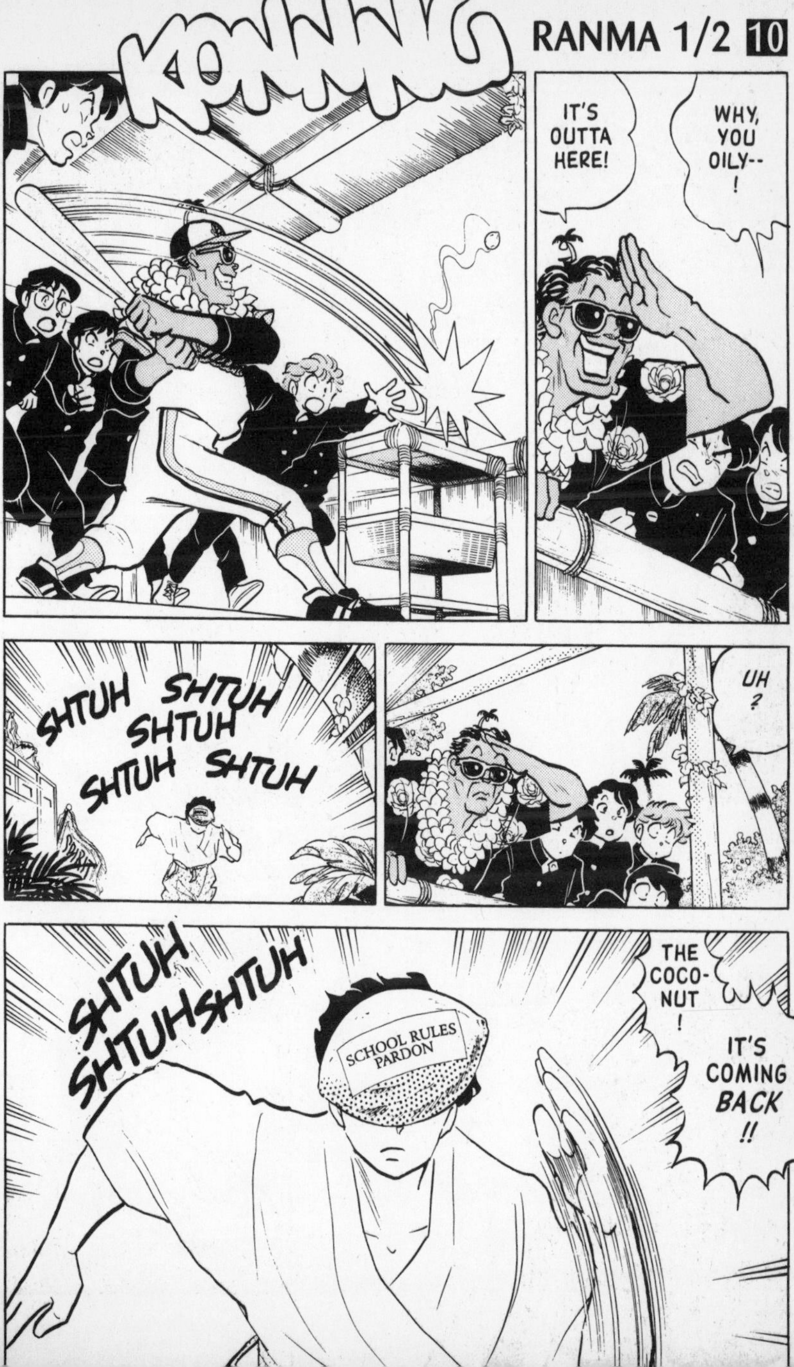
KONNNG
IT'S OUTTA HERE!
WHY, YOU OILY-- !
SHTUH SHTUH SHTUH SHTUH SHTUH
UH ?
SHTUH SHTUHSHTUH
SCHOOL RULES PARDON
THE COCONUT !
IT'S COMING BACK !!

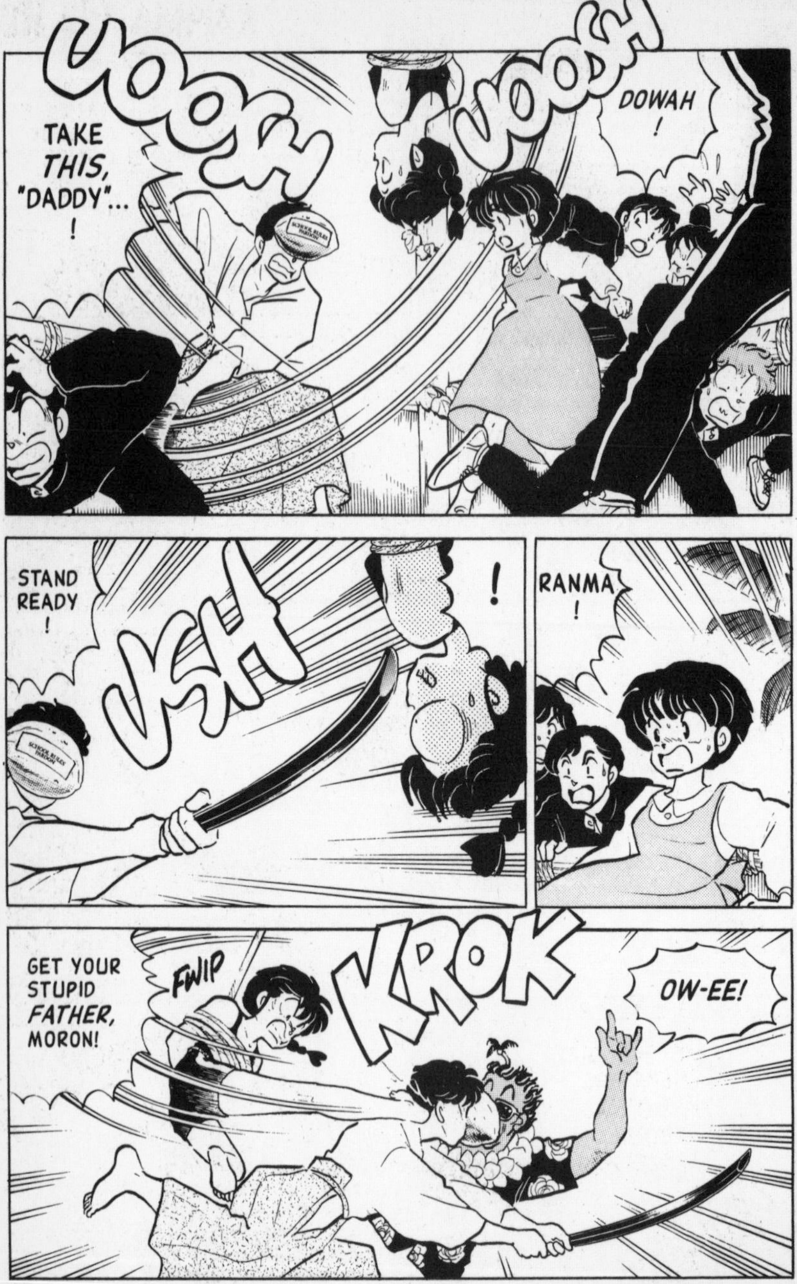
VOOSH
TAKE THIS, "DADDY"... !
VOOSH
DOWAH !
STAND READY !
VSH
!
RANMA !
GET YOUR STUPID FATHER, MORON!
FWIP
KROK
OW-EE!

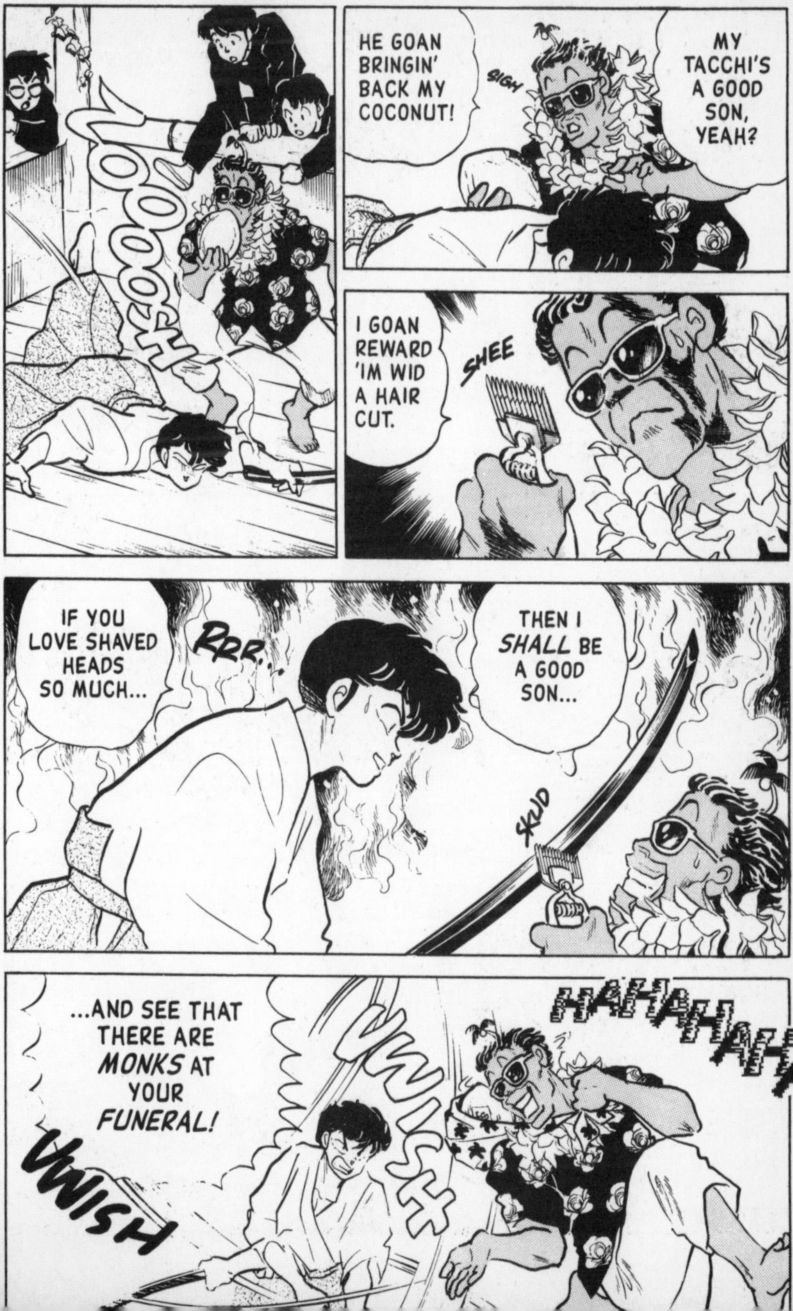
WHOOOOOSH
SIGH
HE GOAN BRINGIN' BACK MY COCONUT!
MY TACCHI'S A GOOD SON, YEAH?
I GOAN REWARD 'IM WID A HAIR CUT.
SHEE
IF YOU LOVE SHAVED HEADS SO MUCH...
RRR...
THEN I *SHALL* BE A GOOD SON...
SKUD
...AND SEE THAT THERE ARE *MONKS* AT YOUR *FUNERAL*!
HAHAHAHAHA
VWISH
VWISH

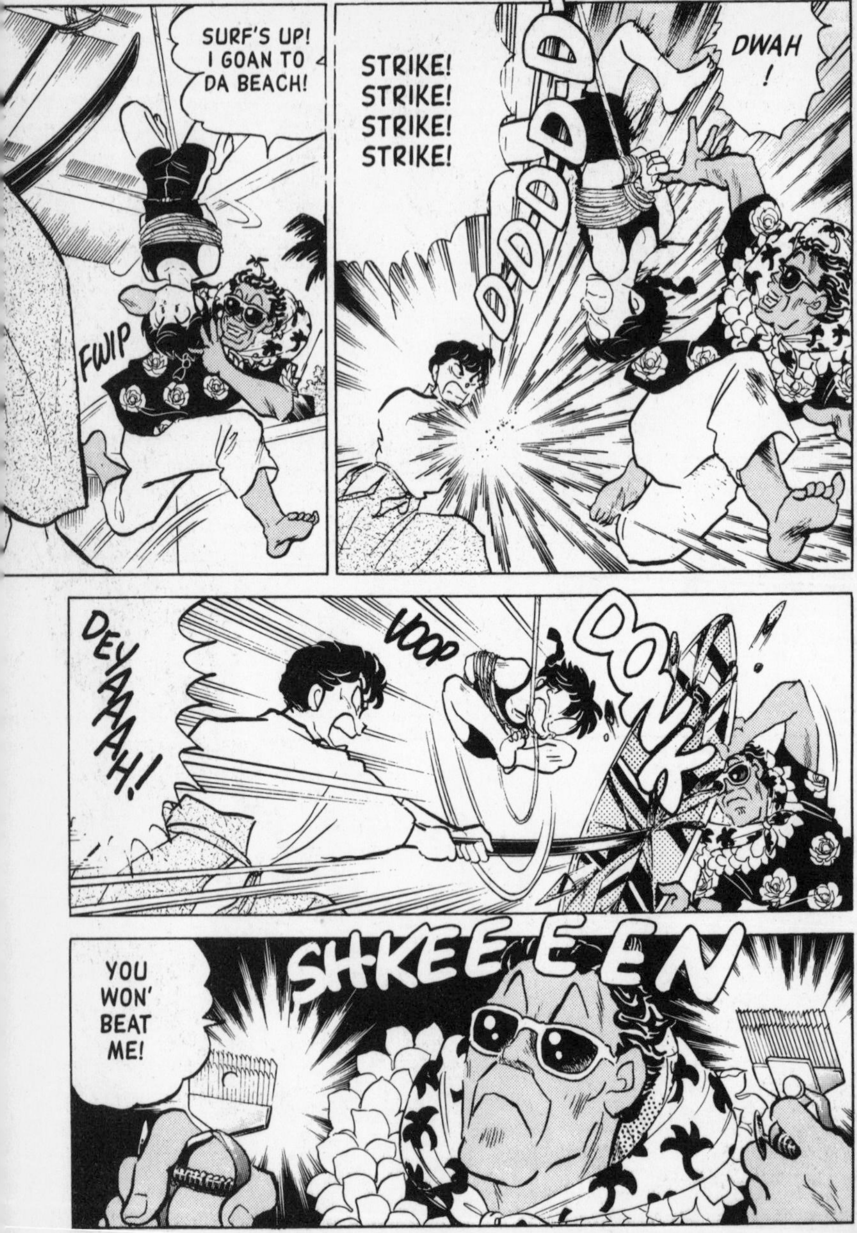
SURF'S UP! I GOAN TO DA BEACH!
FWIP
STRIKE! STRIKE! STRIKE! STRIKE!
DDDDD
DWAH!
DEYAAAAH!
VOOP
DONK!
YOU WON' BEAT ME!
SHKEEEEN

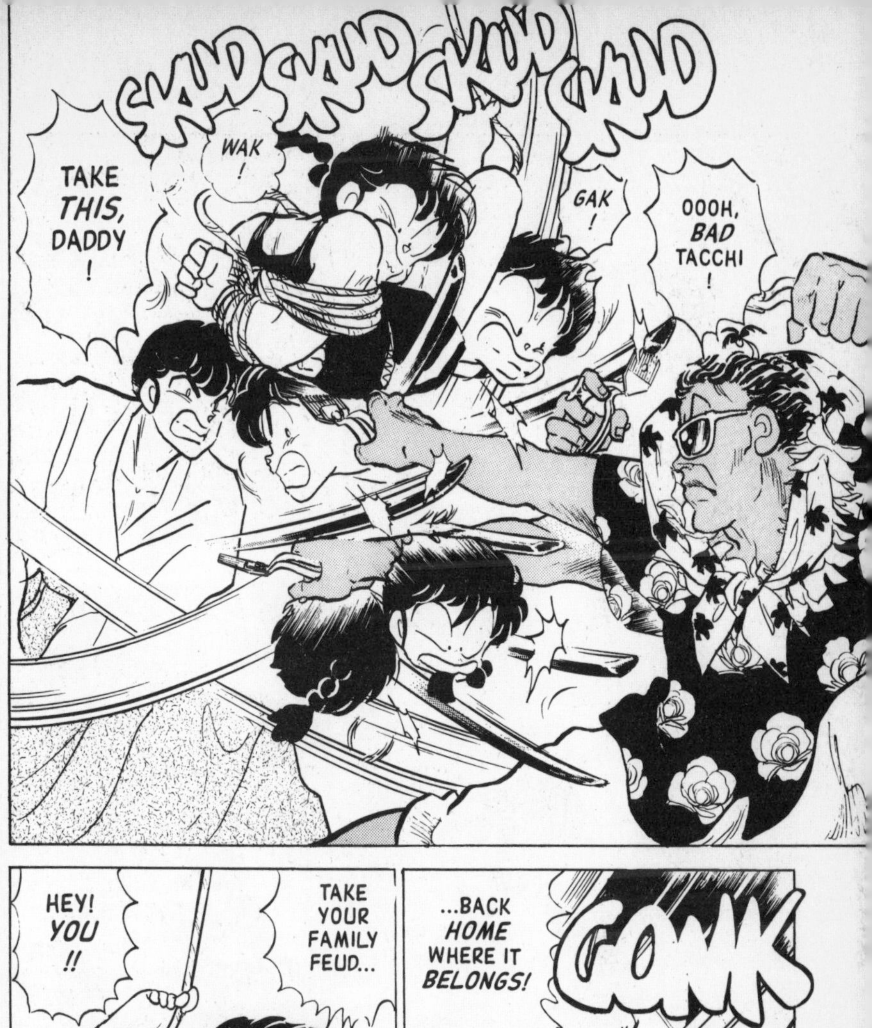
SKUD SKUD SKUD SKUD
TAKE THIS, DADDY!
WAK!
GAK!
OOOH, BAD TACCHI!

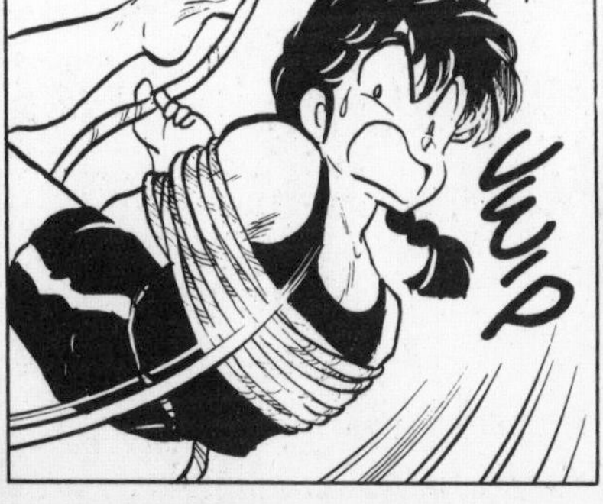
HEY! YOU!!
TAKE YOUR FAMILY FEUD...
WWIP

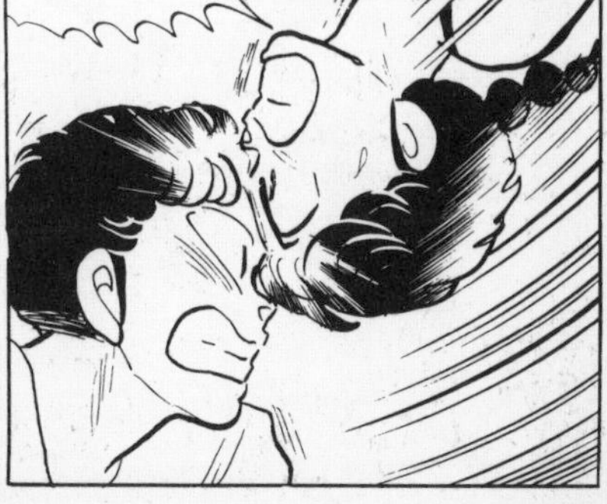
...BACK HOME WHERE IT BELONGS!
GONK

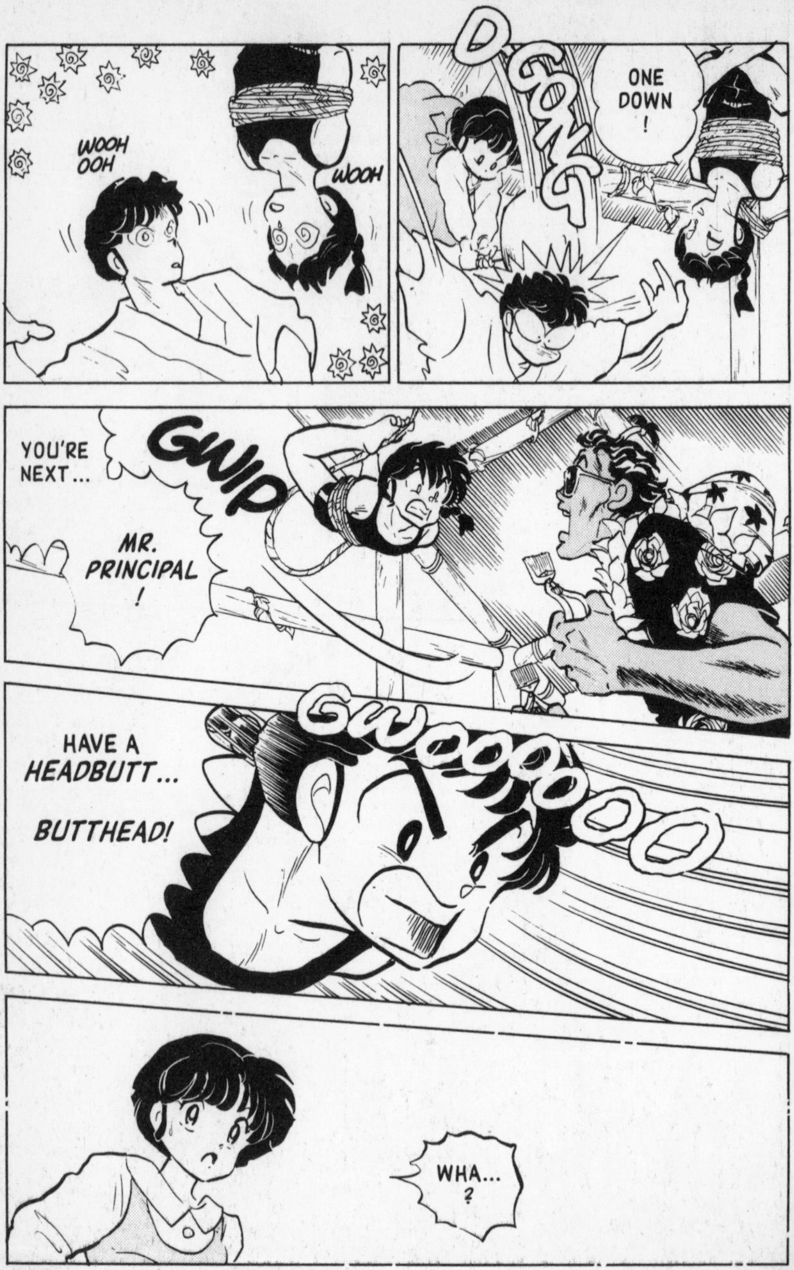
WOOH
OOH
WOOH
D GONG
ONE DOWN !
YOU'RE NEXT...
GWIP
MR. PRINCIPAL !
HAVE A HEADBUTT...
BUTTHEAD!
GWOOOOOOO
WHA... ?

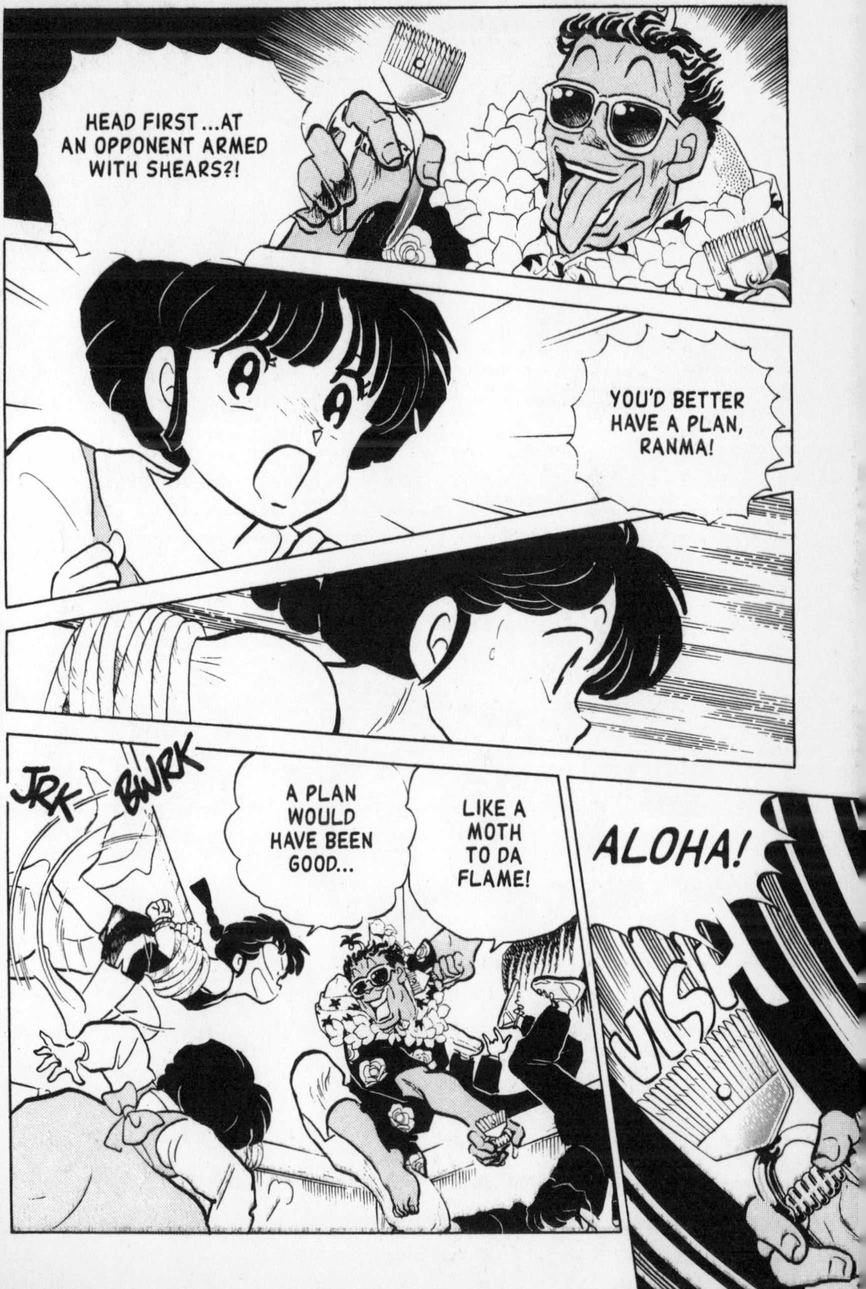
HEAD FIRST...AT AN OPPONENT ARMED WITH SHEARS?!
YOU'D BETTER HAVE A PLAN, RANMA!
JRK
BWRK
A PLAN WOULD HAVE BEEN GOOD...
LIKE A MOTH TO DA FLAME!
ALOHA!
VISH

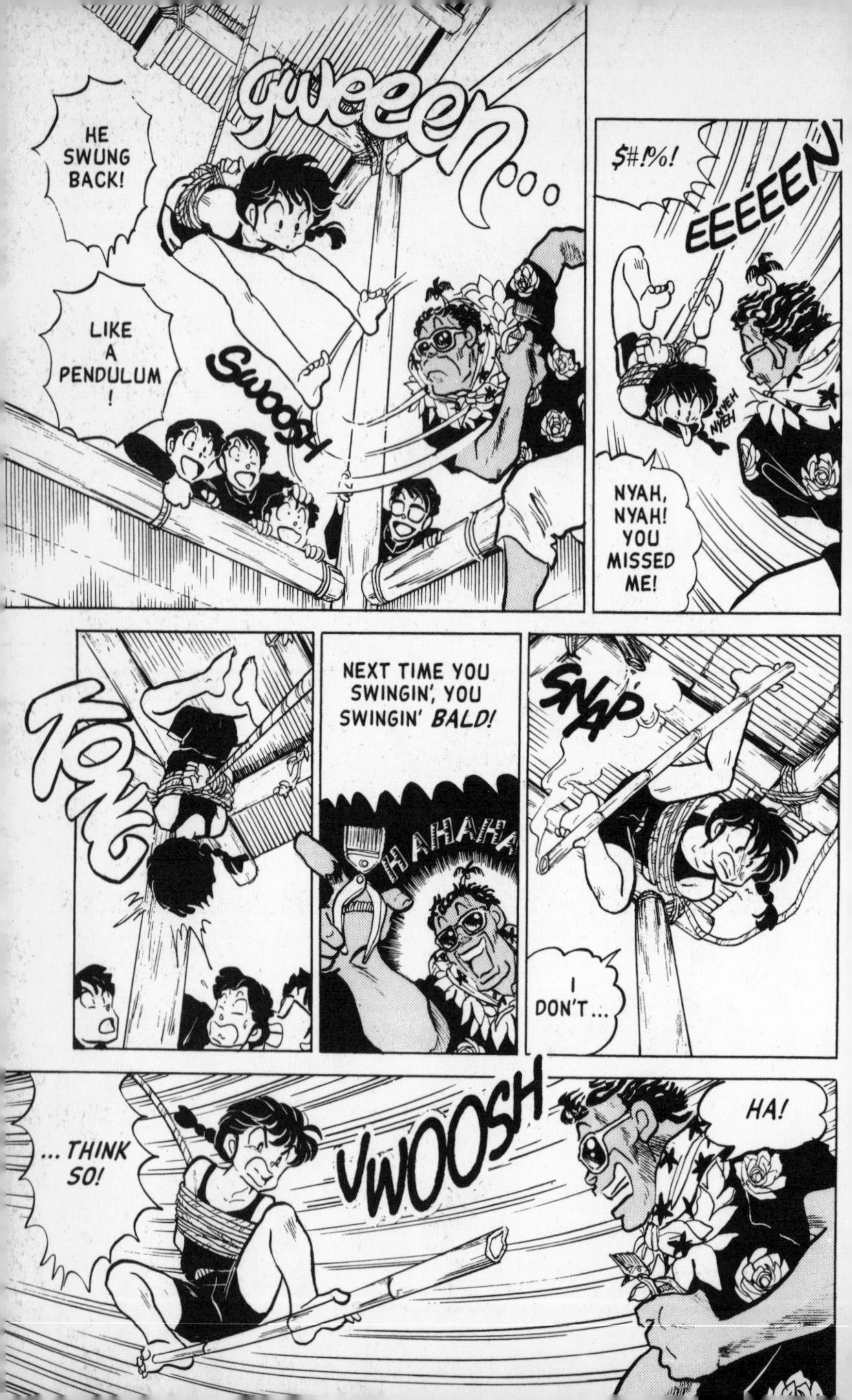
GWEEEN
OOO
HE SWUNG BACK!
LIKE A PENDULUM!
SWOOSH
$#!%!
EEEEEN
NYEH NYEH
NYAH, NYAH! YOU MISSED ME!
KONG
NEXT TIME YOU SWINGIN', YOU SWINGIN' BALD!
HAHAHA
SNAP
I DON'T...
...THINK SO!
VWOOSH
HA!

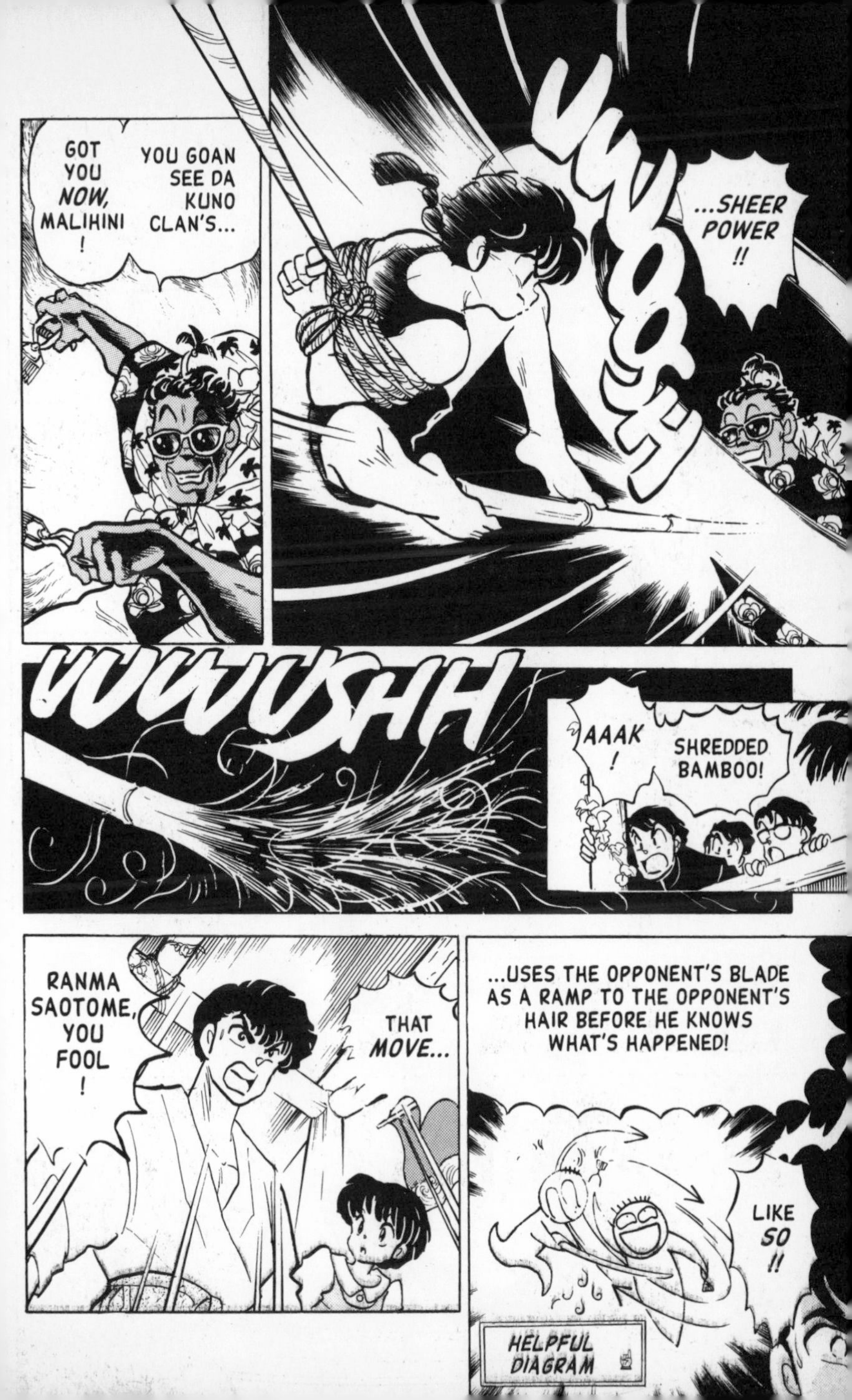
GOT YOU NOW, MALIHINI !
YOU GOAN SEE DA KUNO CLAN'S...
VVOOSH
...SHEER POWER !!
VVVUSHH
AAAK !
SHREDDED BAMBOO!
RANMA SAOTOME, YOU FOOL !
THAT MOVE...
...USES THE OPPONENT'S BLADE AS A RAMP TO THE OPPONENT'S HAIR BEFORE HE KNOWS WHAT'S HAPPENED!
LIKE SO !!
HELPFUL DIAGRAM

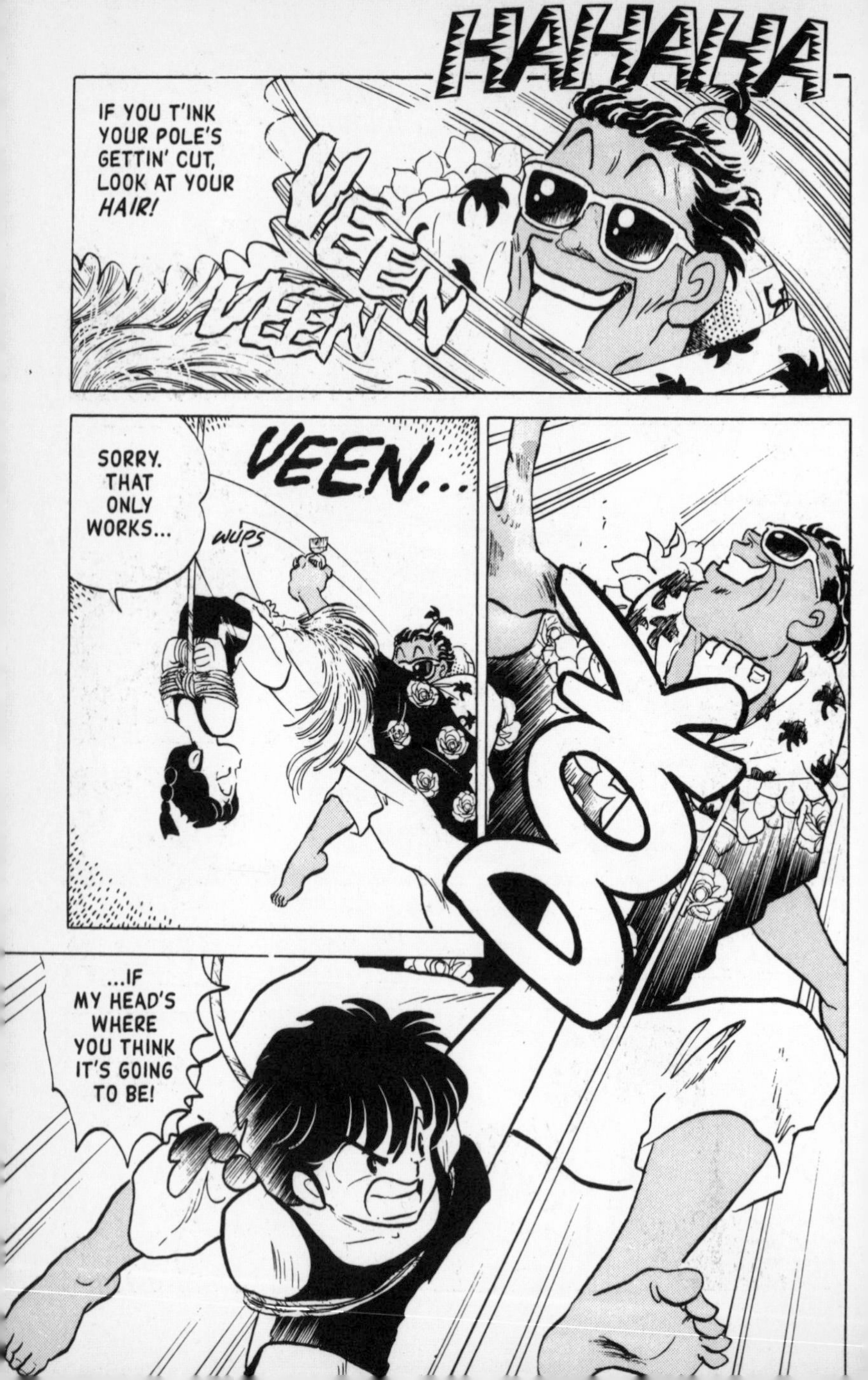
HAHAHA
IF YOU T'INK YOUR POLE'S GETTIN' CUT, LOOK AT YOUR *HAIR!*
VEEN VEEN
SORRY. THAT ONLY WORKS...
VEEN...
WUPS
DOK
...IF MY HEAD'S WHERE YOU THINK IT'S GOING TO BE!

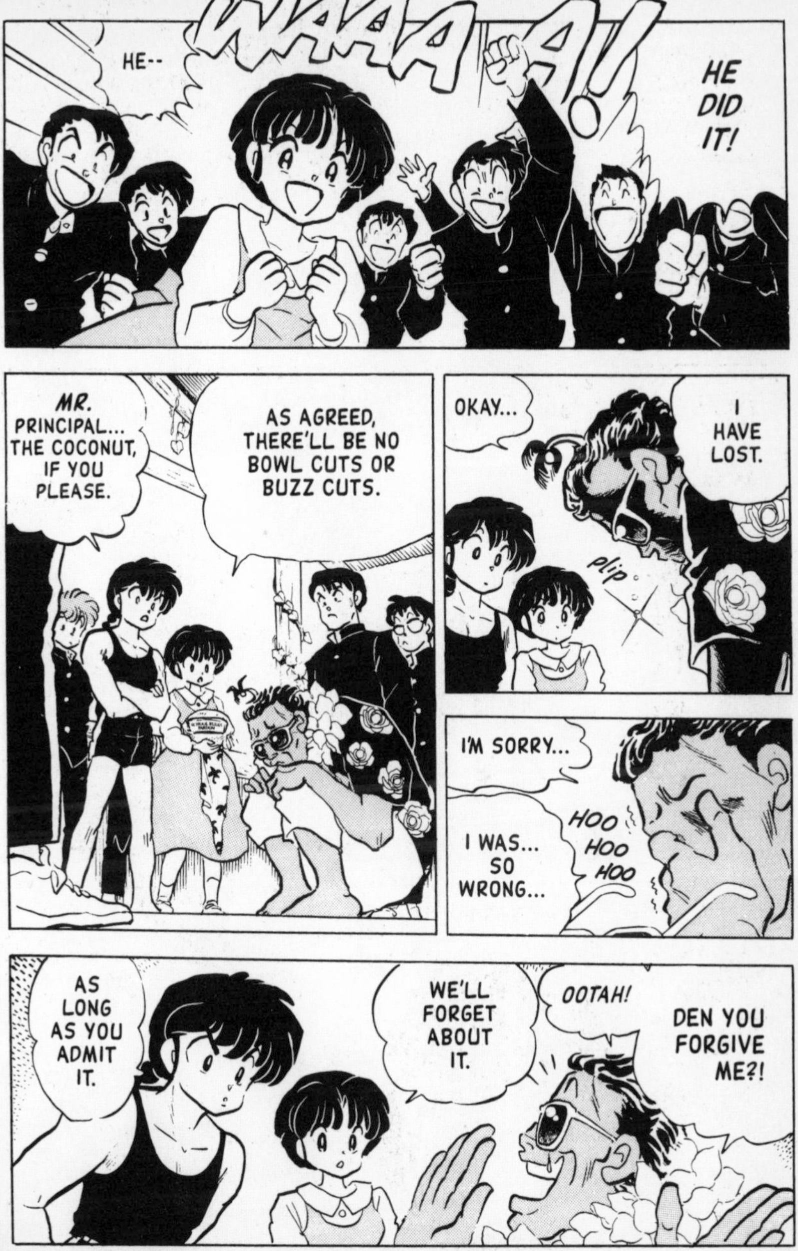
HE--
WAAAA!
HE DID IT!
MR. PRINCIPAL... THE COCONUT, IF YOU PLEASE.
AS AGREED, THERE'LL BE NO BOWL CUTS OR BUZZ CUTS.
OKAY...
I HAVE LOST.
plip
I'M SORRY...
I WAS... SO WRONG...
HOO HOO HOO
AS LONG AS YOU ADMIT IT.
WE'LL FORGET ABOUT IT.
OOTAH!
DEN YOU FORGIVE ME?!

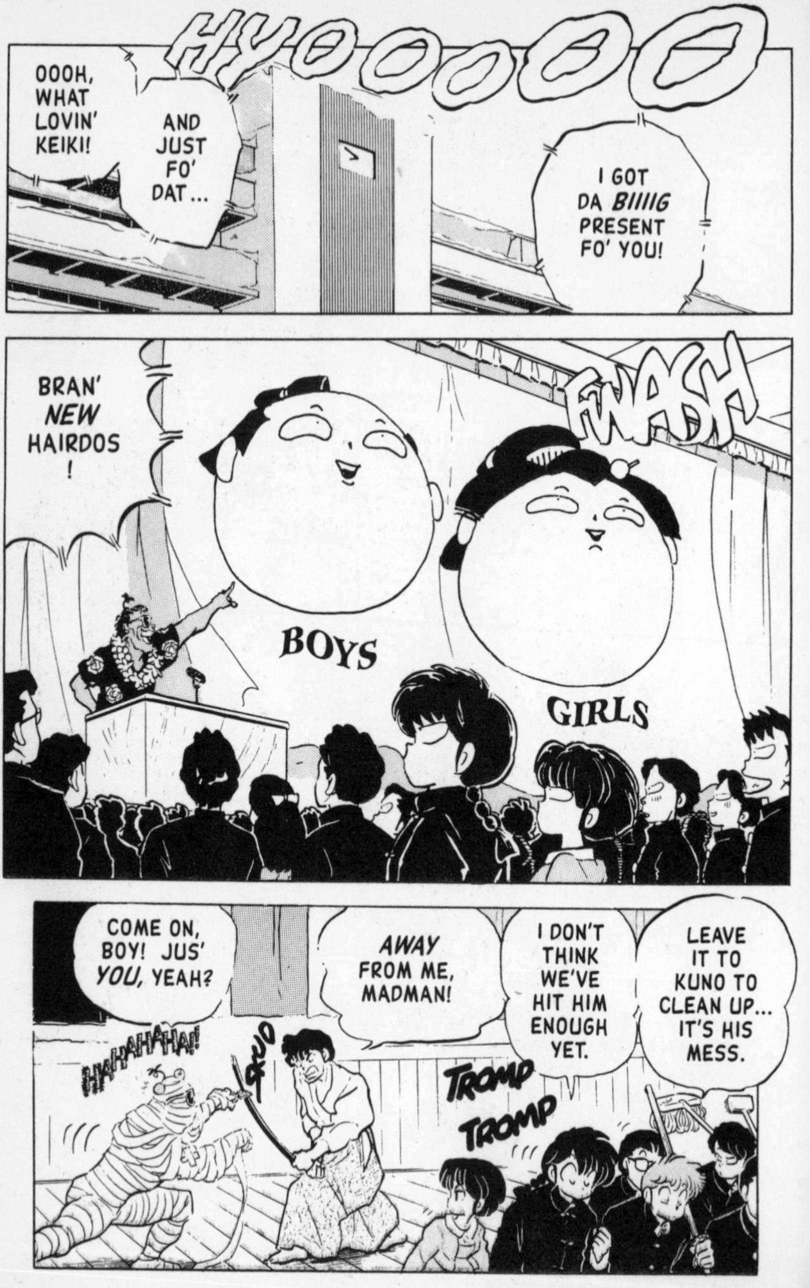
HYOOOOOO
OOOH, WHAT LOVIN' KEIKI!
AND JUST FO' DAT...
I GOT DA BIIIIG PRESENT FO' YOU!
FWASH
BRAN' NEW HAIRDOS !
BOYS
GIRLS
COME ON, BOY! JUS' YOU, YEAH?
HAHAHAHAHA!
AWAY FROM ME, MADMAN!
TROMP
TROMP
I DON'T THINK WE'VE HIT HIM ENOUGH YET.
LEAVE IT TO KUNO TO CLEAN UP... IT'S HIS MESS.

Part 11

GONNA MAKE YOU TARDY!

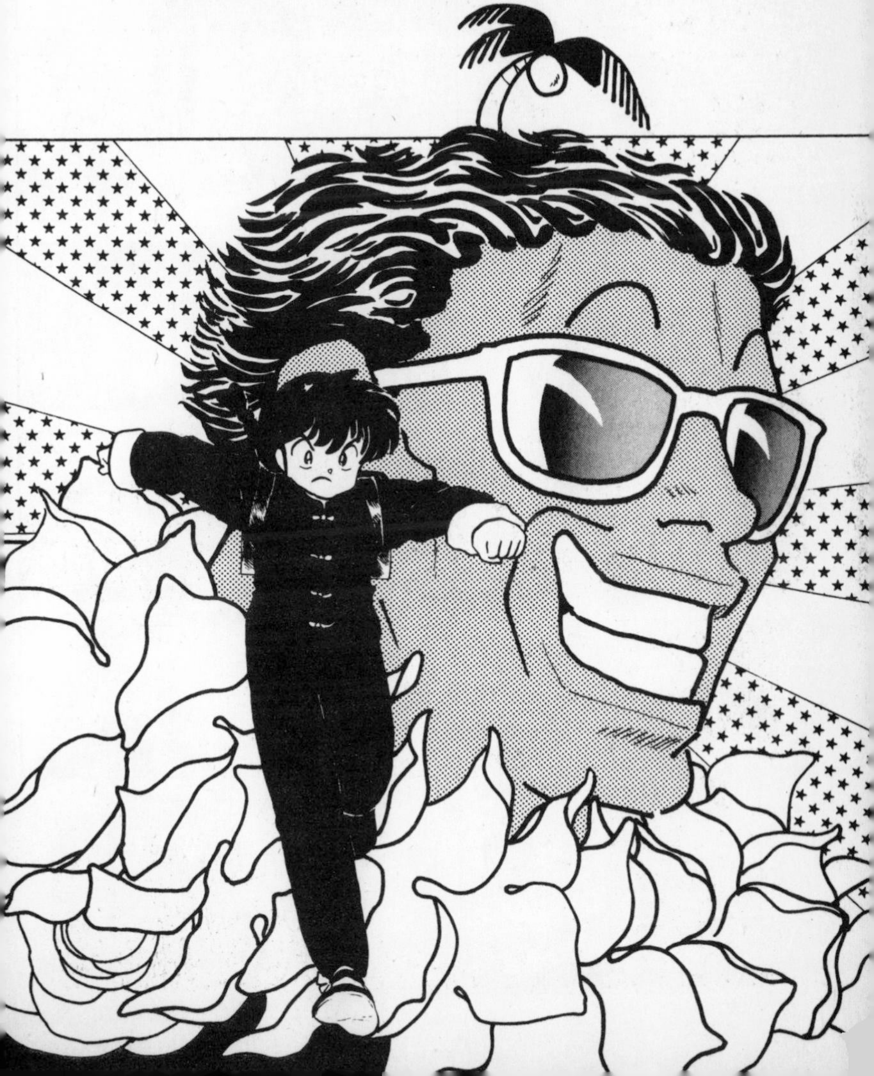

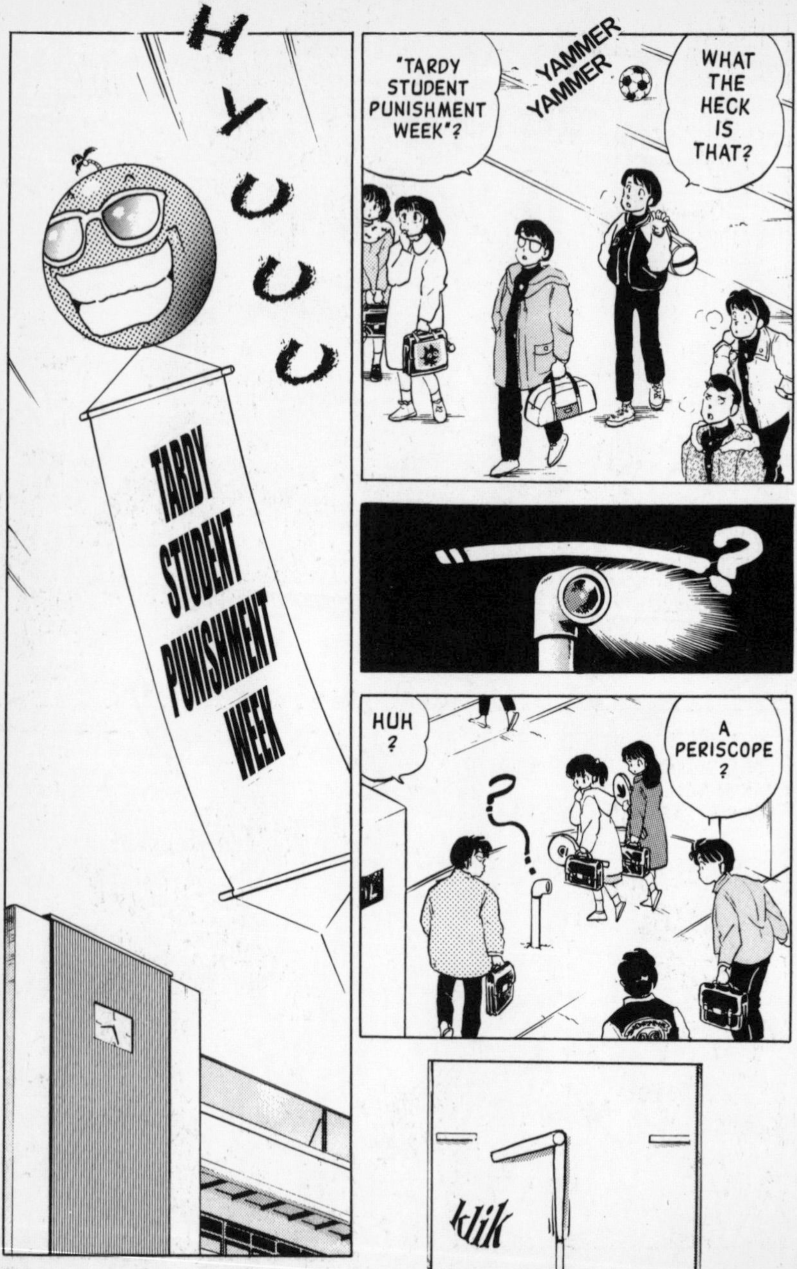
HYUUUU
TARDY STUDENT PUNISHMENT WEEK
"TARDY STUDENT PUNISHMENT WEEK"?
YAMMER YAMMER
WHAT THE HECK IS THAT?
?
HUH ?
A PERISCOPE ?
?
klik

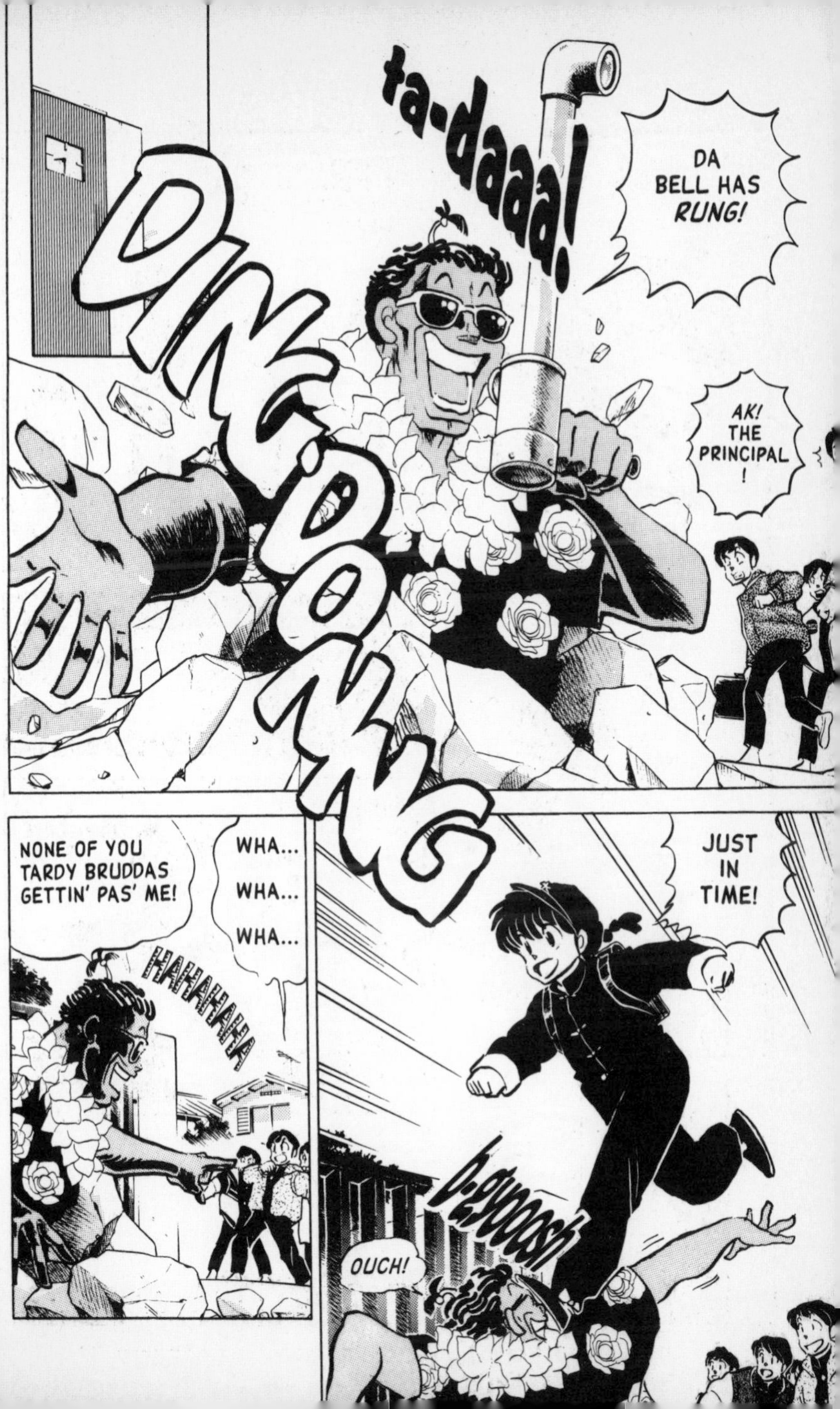
ta-daaa!
DING-DONG
DA BELL HAS RUNG!
AK! THE PRINCIPAL!
NONE OF YOU TARDY BRUDDAS GETTIN' PAS' ME!
HAHAHAHAHA
WHA... WHA... WHA...
JUST IN TIME!
b-gyooosh
OUCH!

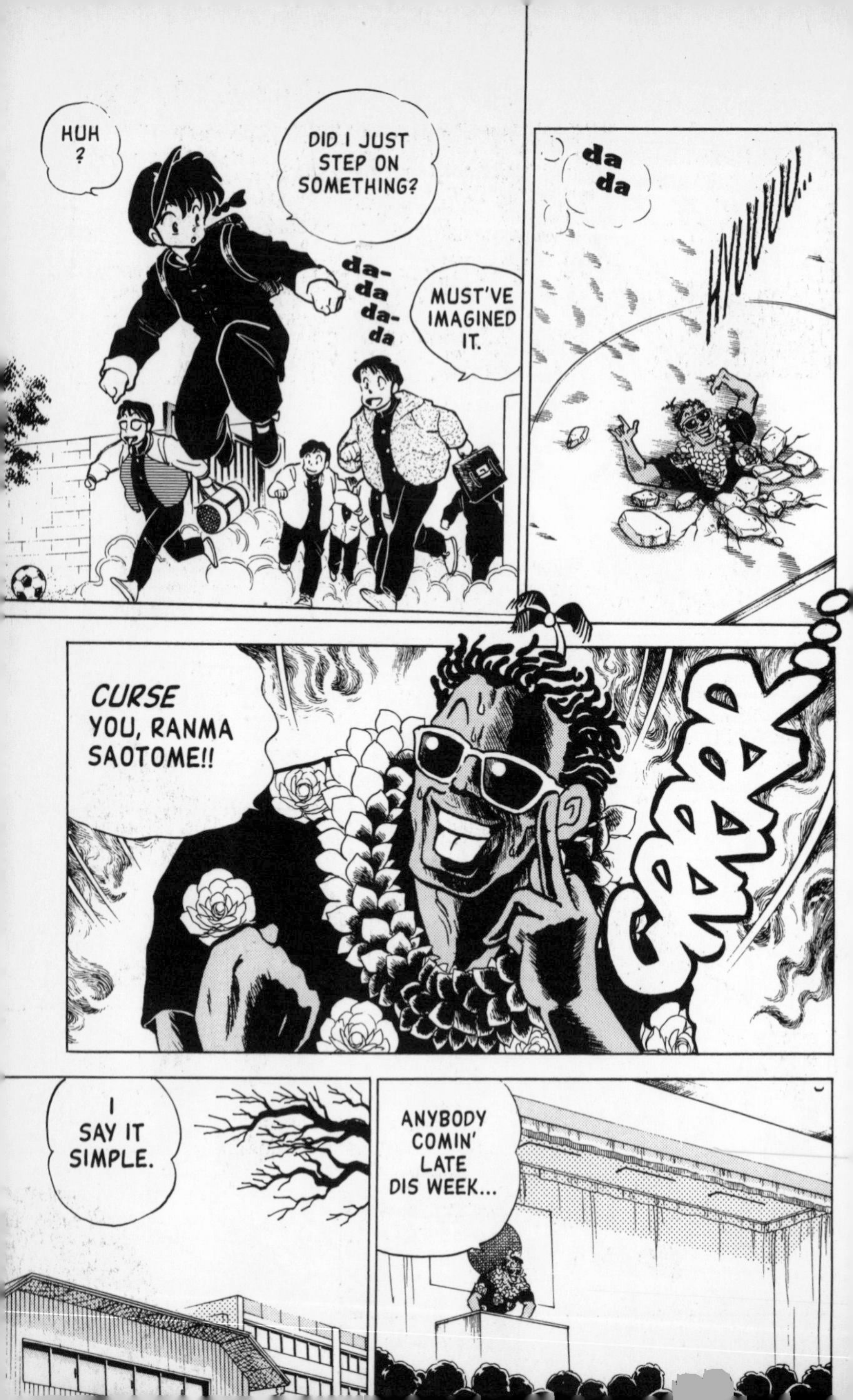
HUH ?
DID I JUST STEP ON SOMETHING?
da-da da-da
MUST'VE IMAGINED IT.
da da
HYUUUU...
CURSE YOU, RANMA SAOTOME!!
GRRRR...
I SAY IT SIMPLE.
ANYBODY COMIN' LATE DIS WEEK...

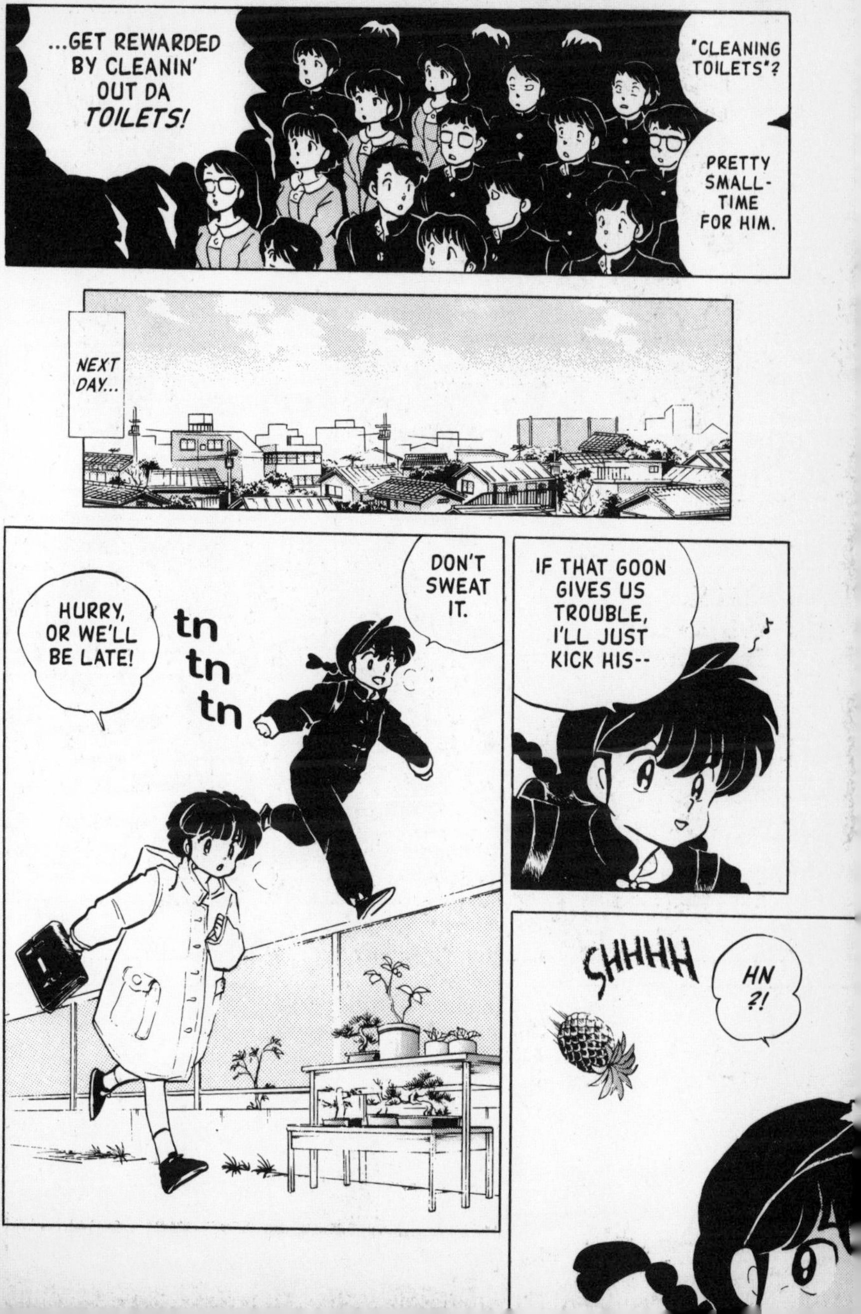
...GET REWARDED BY CLEANIN' OUT DA TOILETS!
"CLEANING TOILETS"?
PRETTY SMALL-TIME FOR HIM.
NEXT DAY...
HURRY, OR WE'LL BE LATE!
tn tn tn
DON'T SWEAT IT.
IF THAT GOON GIVES US TROUBLE, I'LL JUST KICK HIS--
SHHHH
HN ?!

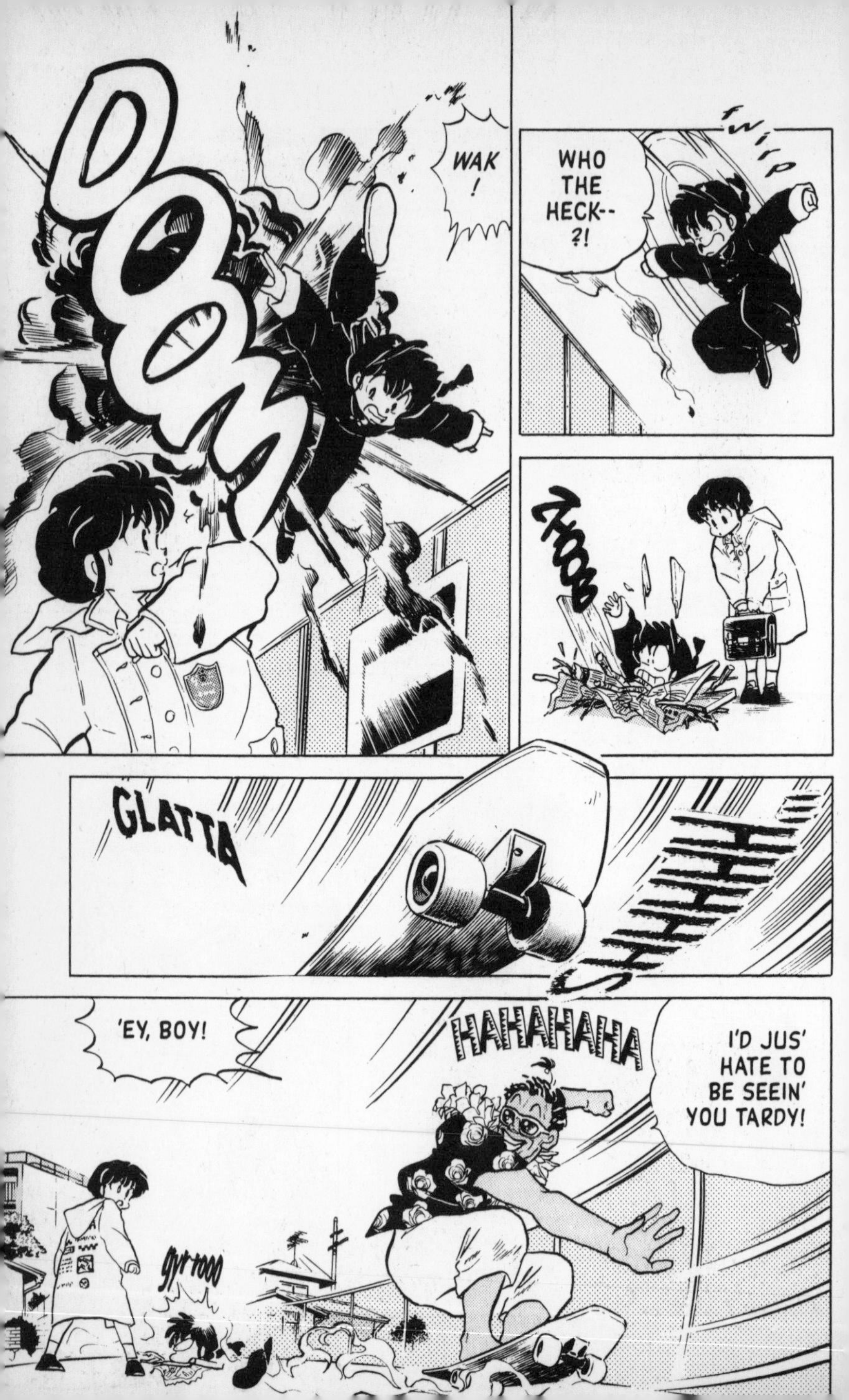
DOOM
WAK!
WHO THE HECK--?!
FWIP
ZOOB
GLATTA
SHHHHH
'EY, BOY!
HAHAHAHA
I'D JUS' HATE TO BE SEEIN' YOU TARDY!
gyr rooo

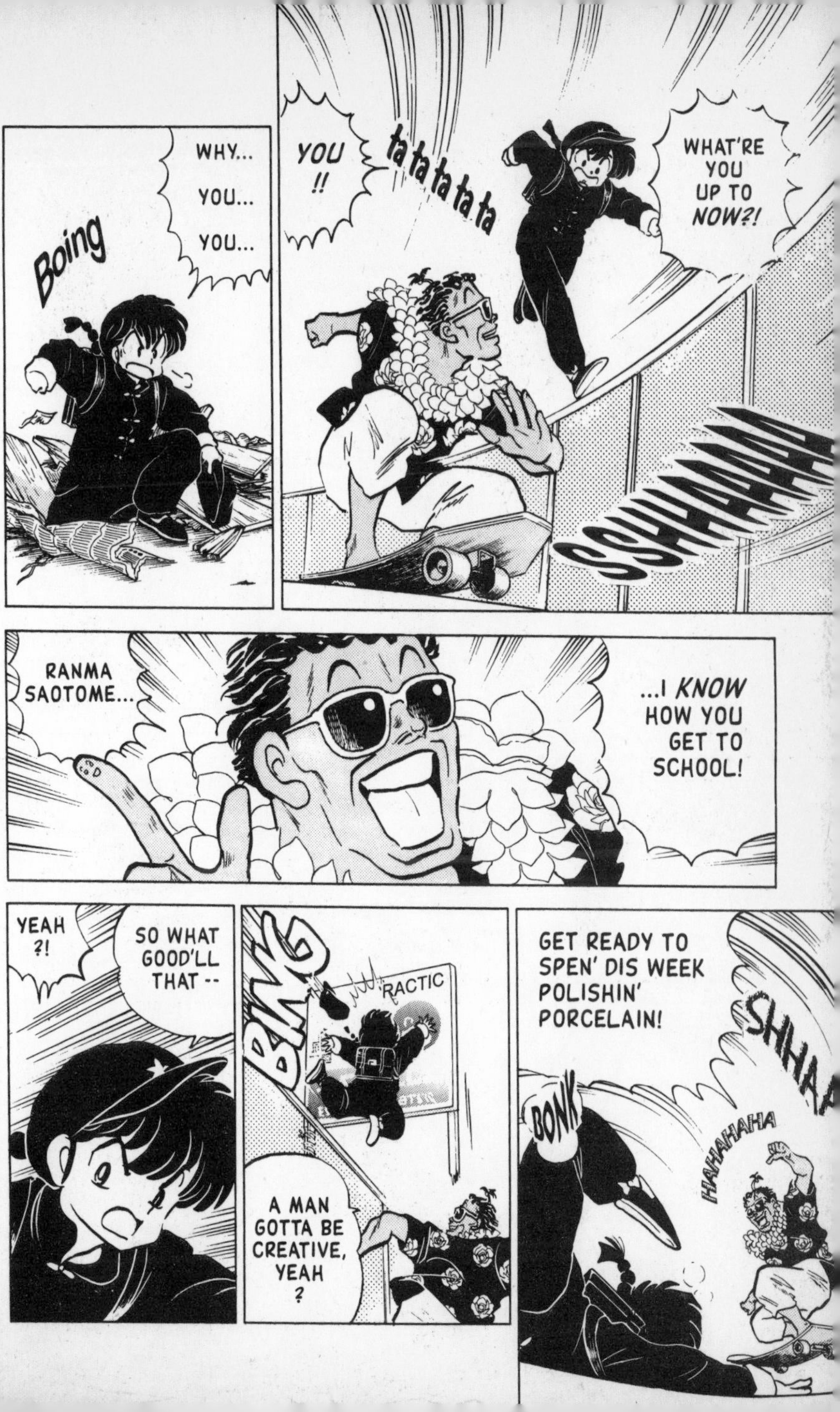
Boing
WHY... YOU... YOU...
YOU !!
ta ta ta ta ta
WHAT'RE YOU UP TO NOW?!
SSHAAAA
RANMA SAOTOME...
...I KNOW HOW YOU GET TO SCHOOL!
YEAH ?!
SO WHAT GOOD'LL THAT --
BING
RACTIC
A MAN GOTTA BE CREATIVE, YEAH ?
GET READY TO SPEN' DIS WEEK POLISHIN' PORCELAIN!
SHHAA
BONK
HAHAHAHA

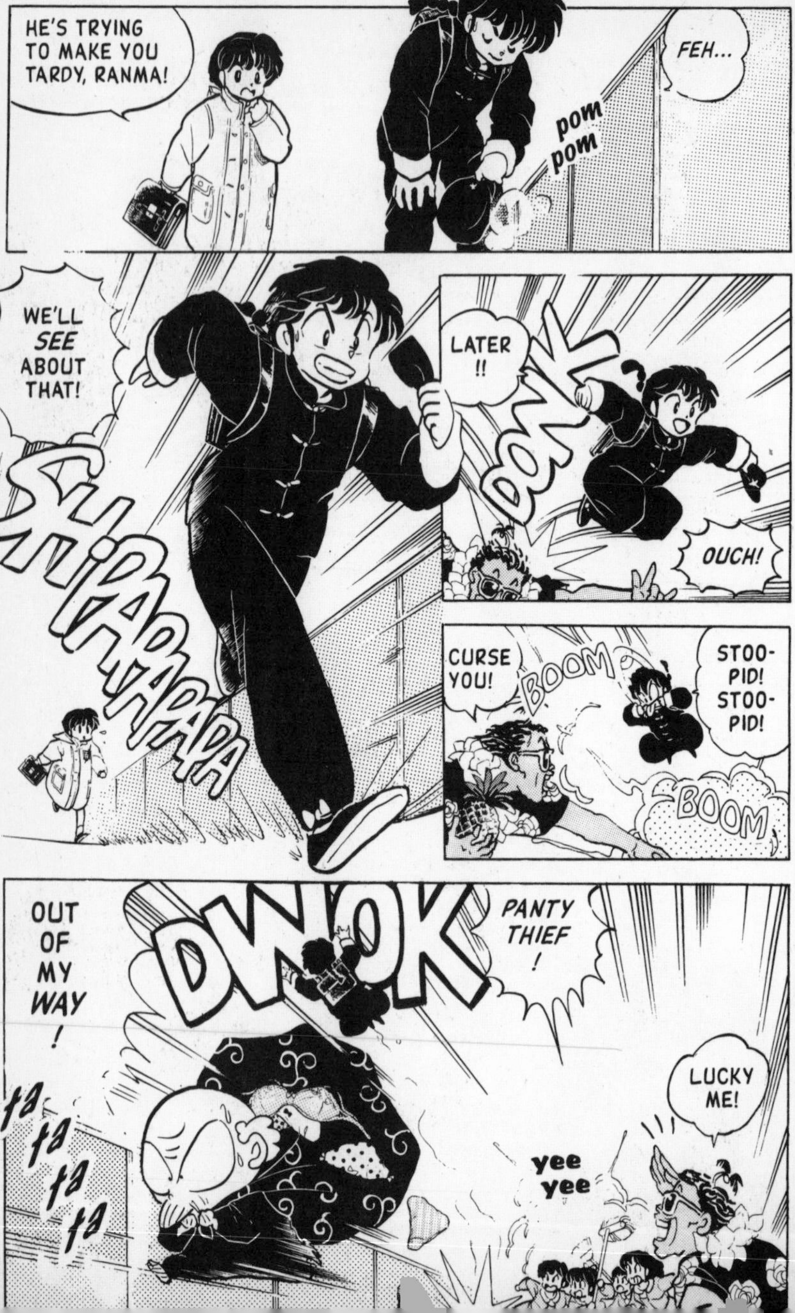
HE'S TRYING TO MAKE YOU TARDY, RANMA!
FEH...
pom pom
WE'LL *SEE* ABOUT THAT!
LATER !!
DONK
OUCH!
CURSE YOU!
BOOM
STOO-PID! STOO-PID!
BOOM
OUT OF MY *WAY* !
DWOK
PANTY THIEF !
ta ta ta ta ta
yee yee
LUCKY ME!

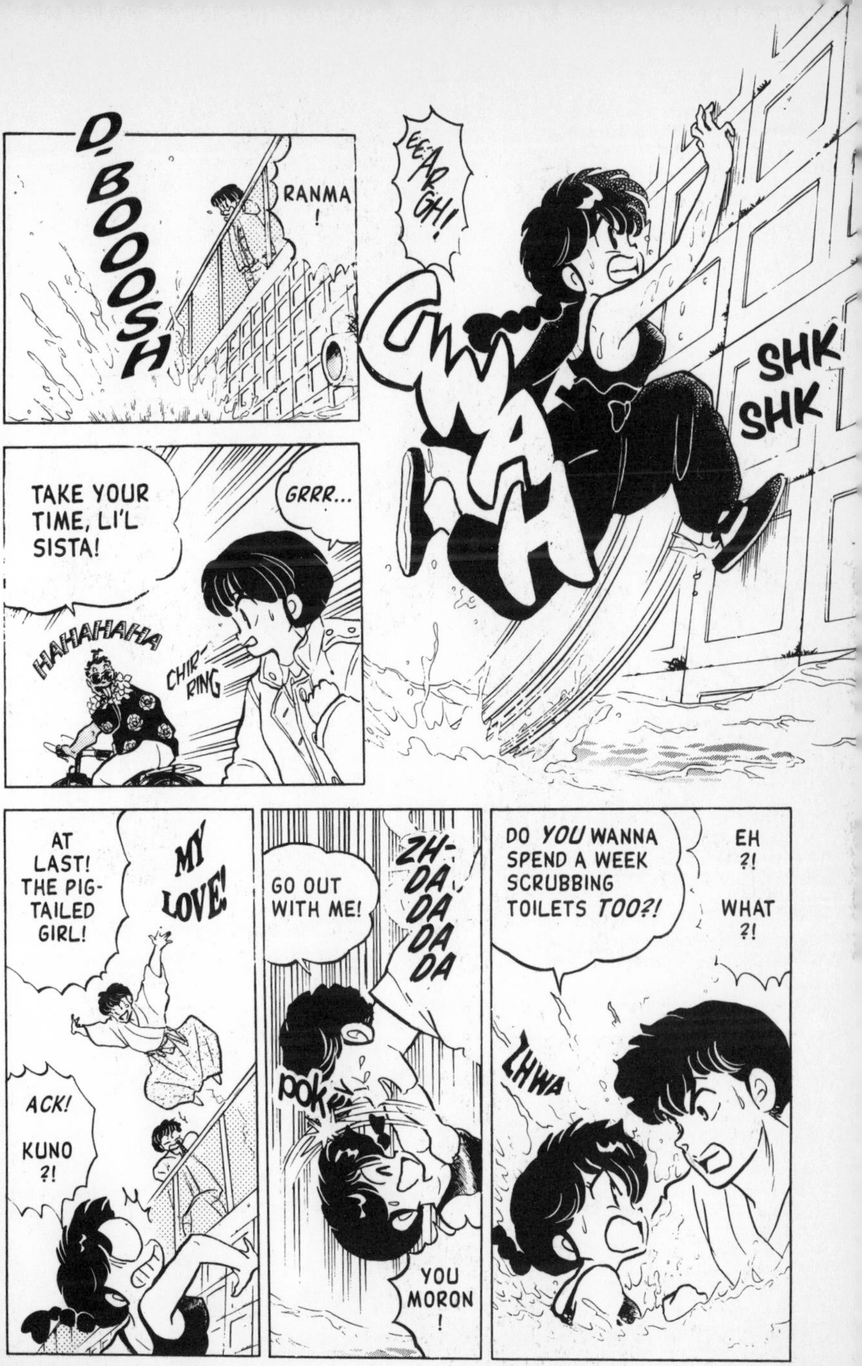
D-BOOOSH
RANMA!
TAKE YOUR TIME, LI'L SISTA!
GRRR...
HAHAHAHA
CHIR-RING
EEEARGH!
SHK SHK
AT LAST! THE PIG-TAILED GIRL!
MY LOVE!
ACK!
KUNO?!
GO OUT WITH ME!
ZH-DA DA DA DA DA
POK
YOU MORON!
DO YOU WANNA SPEND A WEEK SCRUBBING TOILETS TOO?!
EH?!
WHAT?!
ZHWA

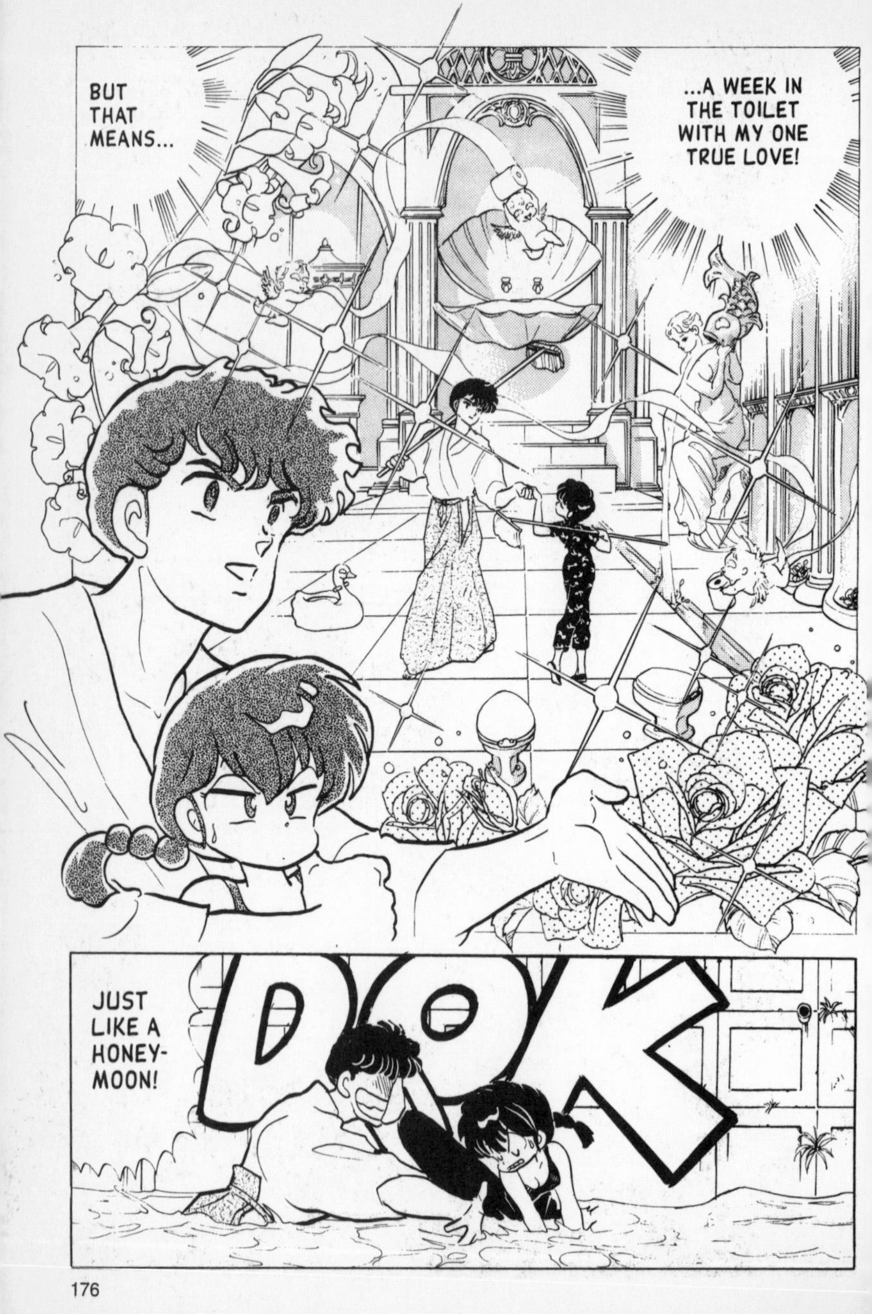
BUT THAT MEANS...
...A WEEK IN THE TOILET WITH MY ONE TRUE LOVE!
JUST LIKE A HONEY-MOON!
DOK

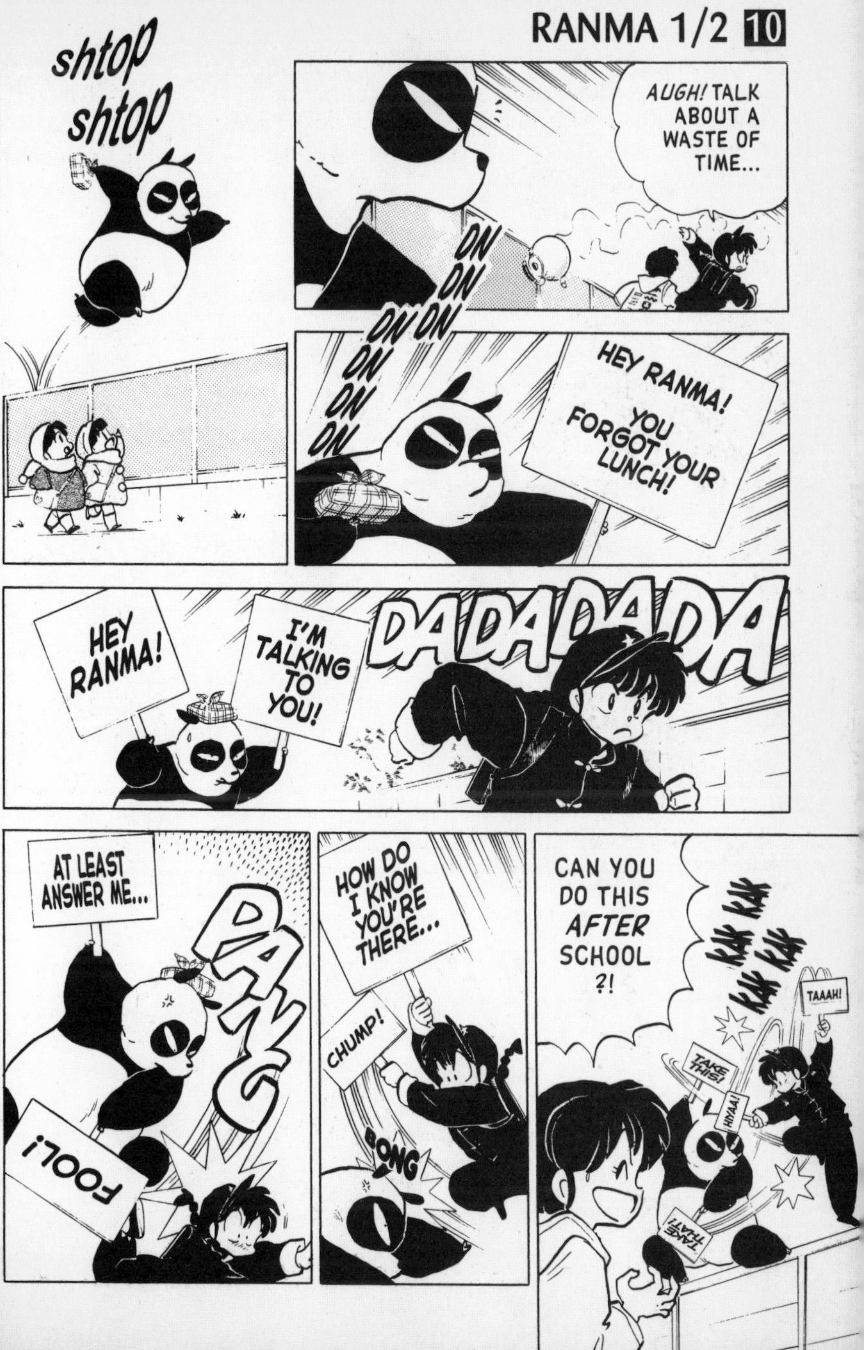
shtop
shtop
AUGH! TALK ABOUT A WASTE OF TIME...
ON ON ON ON
ON ON ON ON ON ON
HEY RANMA!
YOU FORGOT YOUR LUNCH!
HEY RANMA!
I'M TALKING TO YOU!
DADADADA
AT LEAST ANSWER ME...
DANG
FOOL!
HOW DO I KNOW YOU'RE THERE...
CHUMP!
BONG
CAN YOU DO THIS AFTER SCHOOL ?!
KAK KAK
KAK KAK
TAAAH!
TAKE THIS!
HIYAA!
TAKE THAT!

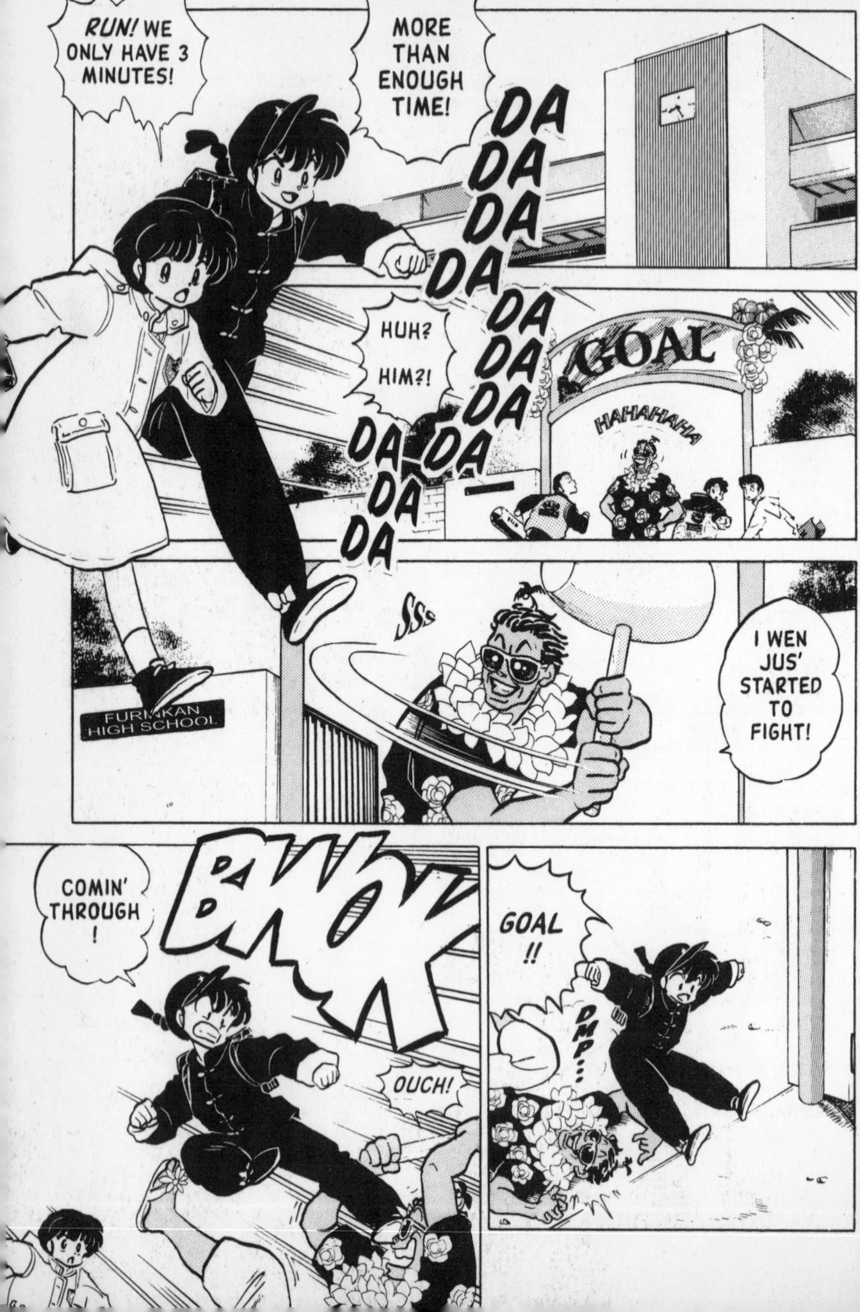
RUN! WE ONLY HAVE 3 MINUTES!
MORE THAN ENOUGH TIME!
DA DA DA DA DA DA DA DA DA DA DA DA
HUH?
HIM?!
GOAL
HAHAHAHA
FURINKAN HIGH SCHOOL
SSS
I WEN JUS' STARTED TO FIGHT!
COMIN' THROUGH!
DA DA
BAK
OUCH!
GOAL!!
DMP...

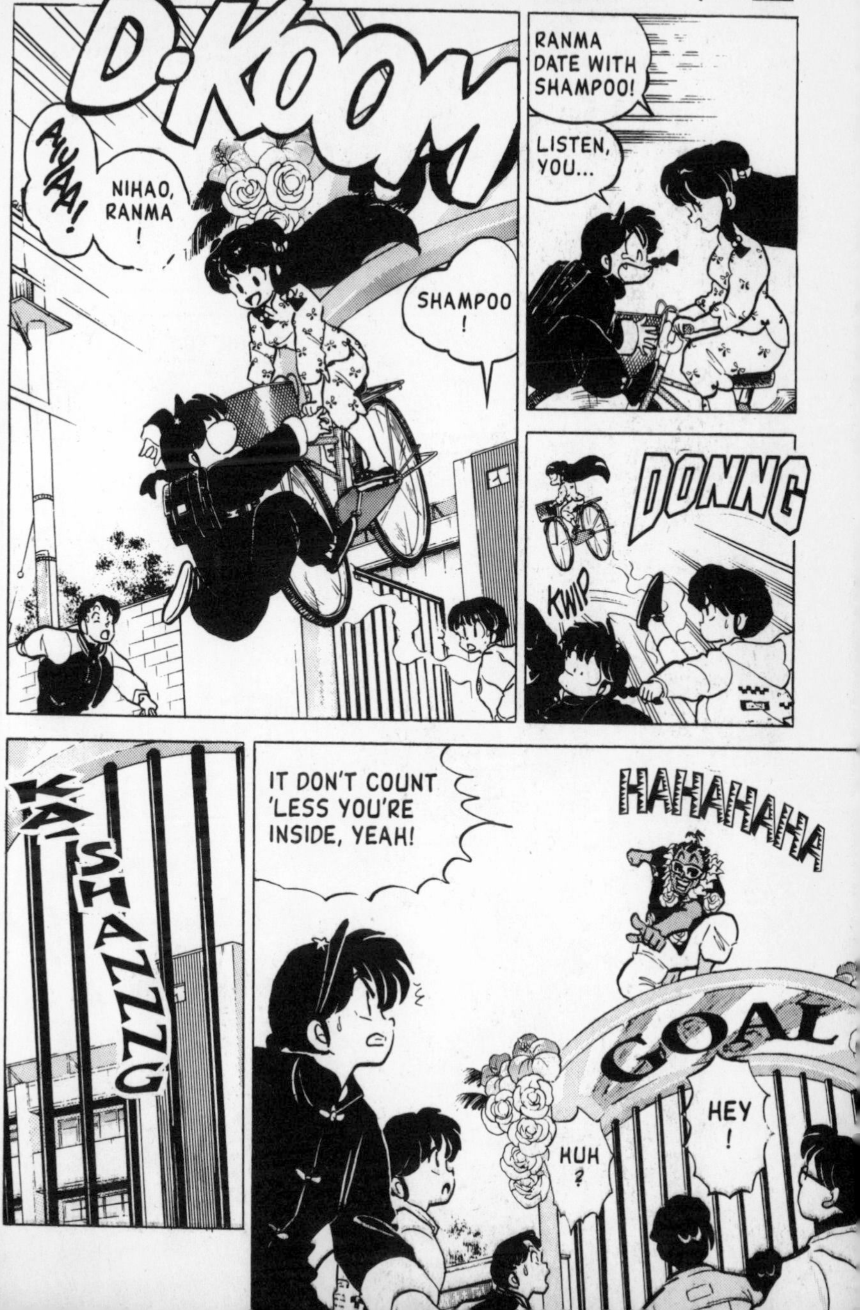
D-KOON
AIYAA!
NIHAO, RANMA !
SHAMPOO !
RANMA DATE WITH SHAMPOO!
LISTEN, YOU...
DONNG
KWIP
KA
SHAZZG
IT DON'T COUNT 'LESS YOU'RE INSIDE, YEAH!
HAHAHAHA
GOAL
HUH ?
HEY !

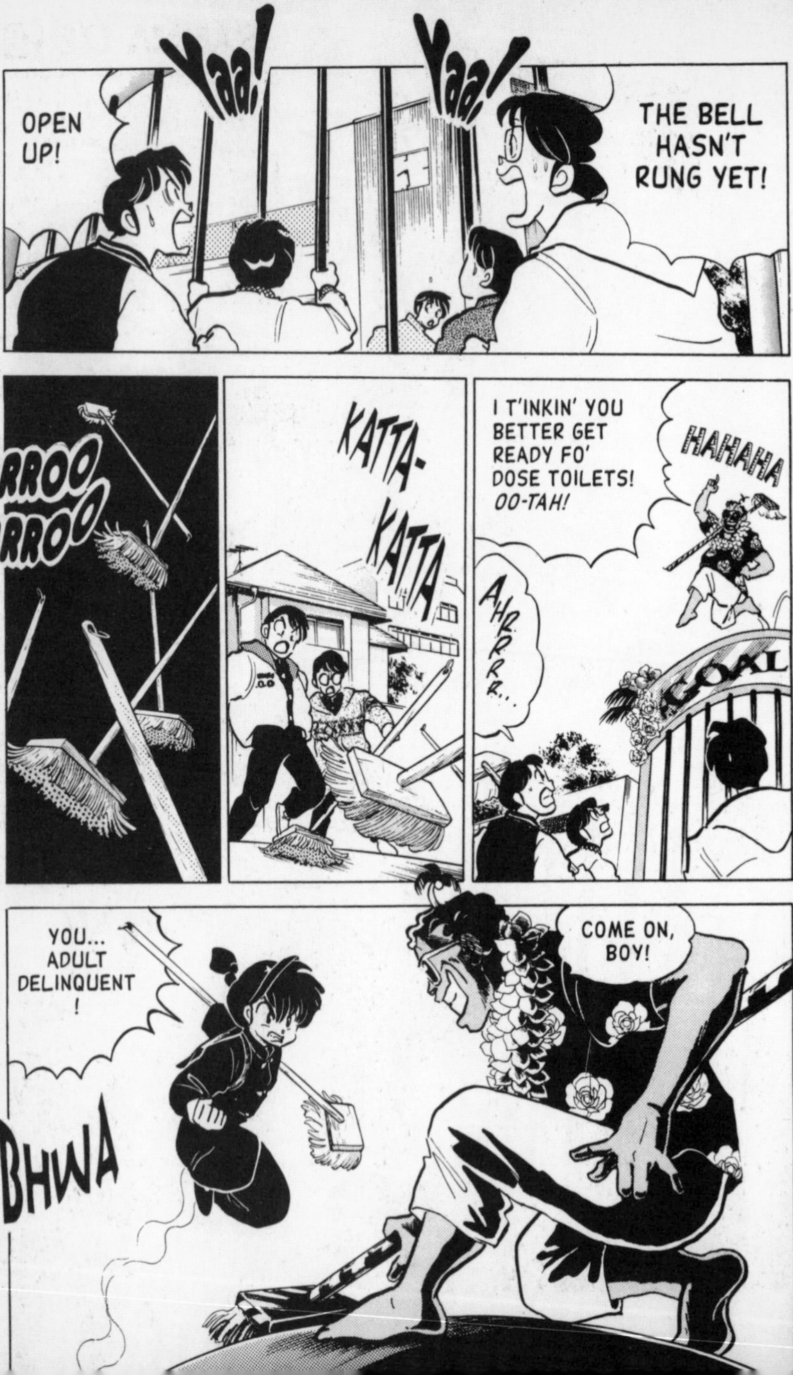
OPEN UP!
Yaa!
Yaa!
THE BELL HASN'T RUNG YET!
BRROO BRROO
KATTA-KATTA
I T'INKIN' YOU BETTER GET READY FO' DOSE TOILETS! OO-TAH!
HAHAHA
AHRRRRR...
GOAL
YOU... ADULT DELINQUENT!
COME ON, BOY!
BHWA

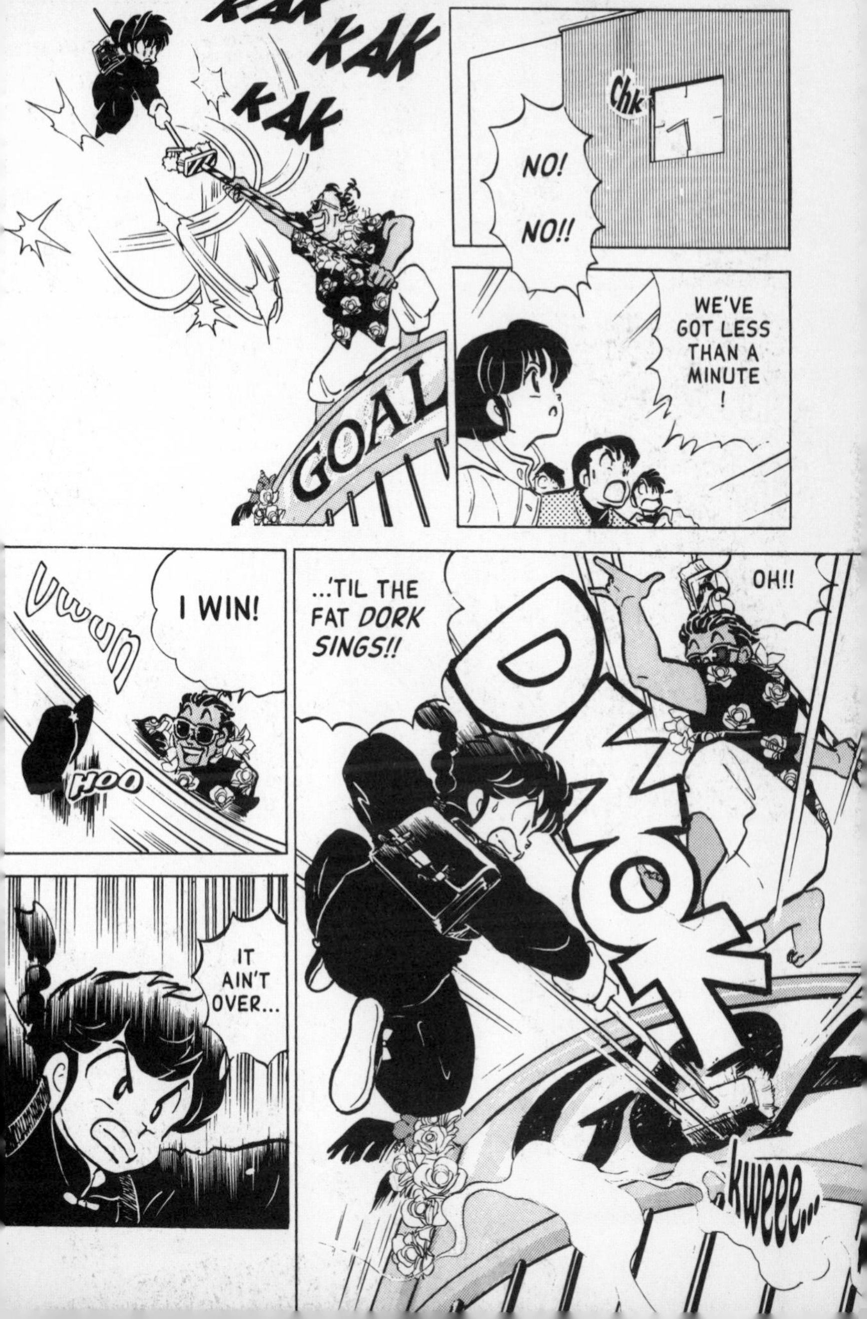
KAK
KAK
KAK
GOAL
Chk
NO!
NO!!
WE'VE GOT LESS THAN A MINUTE !
VWUN
I WIN!
HOO
IT AIN'T OVER...
...'TIL THE FAT DORK SINGS!!
OH!!
kweee...

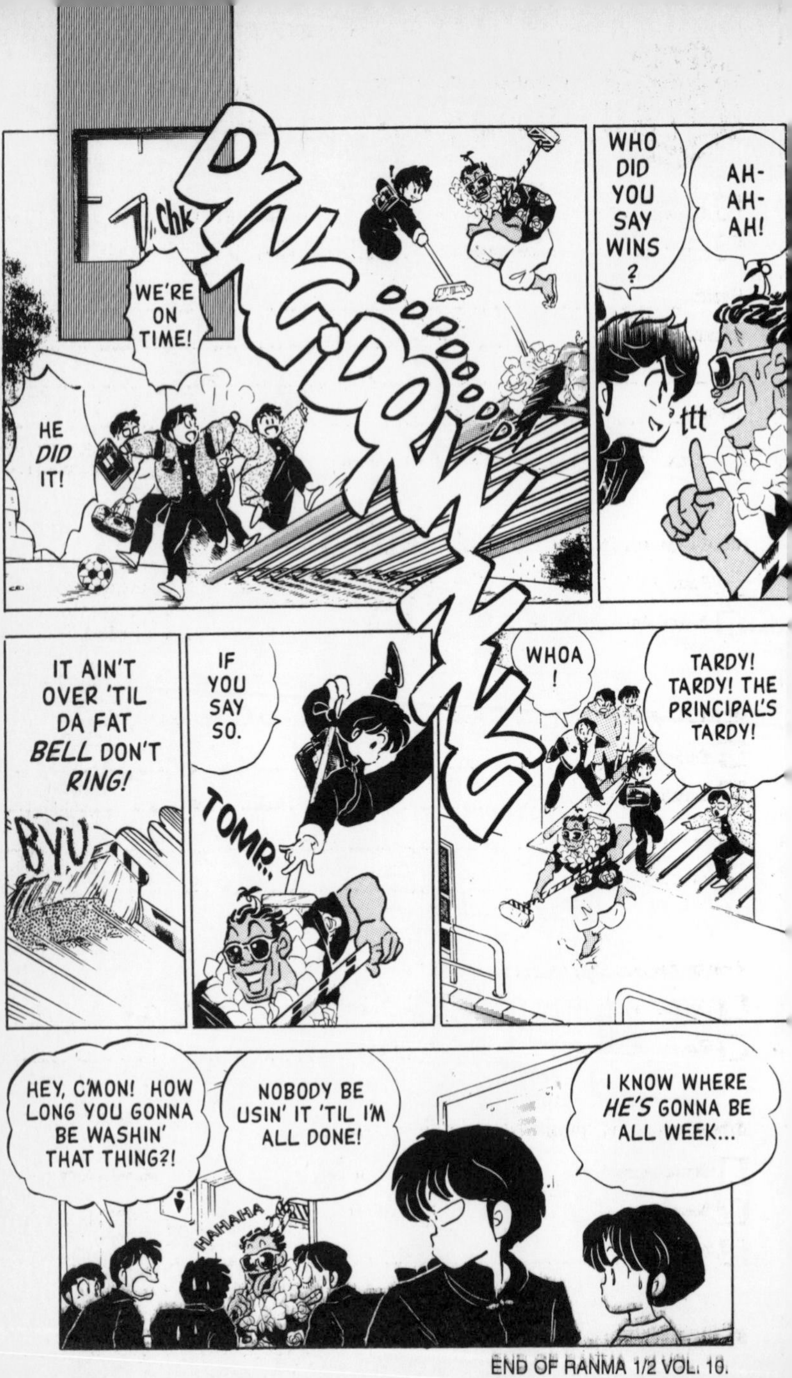
Chk
WE'RE ON TIME!
HE DID IT!
WHO DID YOU SAY WINS?
AH-AH-AH!
ttt
IT AIN'T OVER 'TIL DA FAT BELL DON'T RING!
BYU
IF YOU SAY SO.
TOMP...
WHOA!
TARDY! TARDY! THE PRINCIPAL'S TARDY!
HEY, C'MON! HOW LONG YOU GONNA BE WASHIN' THAT THING?!
NOBODY BE USIN' IT 'TIL I'M ALL DONE!
HAHAHA
I KNOW WHERE HE'S GONNA BE ALL WEEK...

END OF RANMA 1/2 VOL. 10.

COMPLETE OUR SURVEY AND LET
US KNOW WHAT YOU THINK!

☐ Please do NOT send me information about VIZ products, news and events, special offers, or other information.

☐ Please do NOT send me information from VIZ's trusted business partners.

Name: _____

Address: _____

City: _____ **State:** _____ **Zip:** _____

E-mail: _____

☐ **Male** ☐ **Female** **Date of Birth** (mm/dd/yyyy): ___ / ___ / _____ (Under 13? Parental consent required)

What race/ethnicity do you consider yourself? (please check one)

☐ Asian/Pacific Islander ☐ Black/African American ☐ Hispanic/Latino

☐ Native American/Alaskan Native ☐ White/Caucasian ☐ Other: _____

What VIZ product did you purchase? (check all that apply and indicate title purchased)

☐ DVD/VHS _____

☐ Graphic Novel _____

☐ Magazines _____

☐ Merchandise _____

Reason for purchase: (check all that apply)

☐ Special offer ☐ Favorite title ☐ Gift

☐ Recommendation ☐ Other_____

Where did you make your purchase? (please check one)

☐ Comic store ☐ Bookstore ☐ Mass/Grocery Store

☐ Newsstand ☐ Video/Video Game Store ☐ Other:_____

☐ Online (site: _____)

What other VIZ properties have you purchased/own? _____

_____

How many anime and/or manga titles have you purchased in the last year? How many were VIZ titles? (please check one from each column)

ANIME

☐ None
☐ 1-4
☐ 5-10
☐ 11+

MANGA

☐ None
☐ 1-4
☐ 5-10
☐ 11+

VIZ

☐ None
☐ 1-4
☐ 5-10
☐ 11+

I find the pricing of VIZ products to be: (please check one)

☐ Cheap   ☐ Reasonable   ☐ Expensive

What genre of manga and anime would you like to see from VIZ? (please check two)

☐ Adventure   ☐ Comic Strip   ☐ Science Fiction   ☐ Fighting

☐ Horror   ☐ Romance   ☐ Fantasy   ☐ Sports

What do you think of VIZ's new look?

☐ Love It   ☐ It's OK   ☐ Hate It   ☐ Didn't Notice   ☐ No Opinion

Which do you prefer? (please check one)

☐ Reading right-to-left

☐ Reading left-to-right

Which do you prefer? (please check one)

☐ Sound effects in English

☐ Sound effects in Japanese with English captions

☐ Sound effects in Japanese only with a glossary at the back

THANK YOU! Please send the completed form to:

NJW Research
42 Catharine St.
Poughkeepsie, NY 12601

All information provided will be used for internal purposes only. We promise not to sell or otherwise divulge your information.